Rating America's Corporate Conscience

*A Provocative Guide
to the Companies Behind the Products
You Buy Every Day*

Steven D. Lydenberg
Alice Tepper Marlin
Sean O'Brien Strub
and the Council on Economic Priorities

Addison-Wesley Publishing Company, Inc.
Reading, Massachusetts   Menlo Park, California
Don Mills, Ontario   Wokingham, England   Amsterdam   Bonn
Sydney   Singapore   Tokyo   Madrid   Bogotá
Santiago   San Juan

For the second printing of *Rating America's Corporate Conscience*, we have updated information in two areas of particular importance. Company withdrawals from South Africa have been noted in individual profiles and also on the product charts. Major mergers, sales, and acquisitions have been noted in company profiles and in the addendum on page 500. Please check the company profiles and addendum to see if brand-name products in the charts have been affected.

Many of the designations used by manufacturers and sellers to distinguish their products are claimed as trademarks. Where these designations appear in the book and the authors are aware of a trademark claim, the designations have been printed with initial capital letters—for example, Kleenex.

Library of Congress Cataloging-in-Publication Data

Lydenberg, Steven D.
  Rating America's corporate conscience.

  Bibliography: p.
  Includes index.
  1. Industry—Social aspects—United States.
2. Shopping—United States. I. Marlin, Alice Tepper.
II. Strub, Sean O'Brien. III. Title.
HD60.5.U5L918   1986   338.7′4′0973   86-8064
ISBN 0-201-15879-5 (P)
ISBN 0-201-15886-8 (H)

Cover design by Fader, Jones + Zarkades, Inc.
Text design by Kenneth J. Wilson
Set in 10-point Palatino by DEKR Corporation, Woburn, MA

BCDEFGHIJ-DO-8987
Second Printing, April 1987

To Lee B. Thomas, Jr.

Contents

Preface

Each of us, I'm told, has both an implicit "life list" of key goals that reflect our values and philosophies, and a longer day-to-day "shopping list" of chores, errands, and purchases. By evaluating and ranking corporate social performance, *Rating America's Corporate Conscience* enables us to integrate these lists — at the supermarket or drugstore, on the road, at the office, and in investment portfolios. Consumers, investors, and policymakers can now use this guide to make better-informed decisions every day.

The Council on Economic Priorities was founded in 1969, dedicated to the analysis of society's most vital issues. A clear and primary goal of CEP is to enhance corporate performance as it affects society in critically important areas such as military spending, political influence, and fair employment practices. We believe that a well-informed community can express its convictions and play a far more effective and influential role in molding public policy when it is acting upon carefully conducted, documented, and factual research. We hope that the impact of this book will make companies respond by competing to rank number one in good citizenship, charitable contributions, and other areas of social responsibility.

In order to furnish the facts that fuel the corporate conscience, CEP painstakingly gathers and documents data from hundreds of sources: thousand-page reports, obscure federal dockets, arcane technical articles, complex graphs, mountains of computer printouts, annual reports, personal interviews, and more. But CEP does more than just act as a clearinghouse for statistics. In more than a hundred publications, dozens of major studies, and scores of reports and newsletters it informs its members, the general public, and the companies it surveys about the consequences of corporate social behavior.

CEP finds companies that conscientiously comply with regulations and others that flout the law; companies that take the initiative to solve problems and to serve basic human needs; companies that doggedly pursue short-term profits regardless of the broader human consequences. CEP acts as an advocate for social responsibility. Its findings often convince big business that concern for social issues is not only laudable but profitable. In the hands of stockholders, voters, and activist groups, the information CEP provides becomes an effective tool for change. CEP's research and publications present consumers with an alternative to the slick advertising that creates product distinctions that are artificial, trivial, or just plain meaningless.

The Council on Economic Priorities receives its funding from a broad spectrum of individuals, foundations, and other institutions. Royalties earned from this book will go toward research and other relevant activities. (CEP receives less than 2 percent of its funding from major corporations. Only two of the 130 companies profiled in this book — Amoco and Ford Motor Company — are corporate subscribers to CEP's research.)

Many of the crucial problems facing us today — from discrimination in the workplace to nuclear arms proliferation — can be resolved or ameliorated by appropriate and conscientious corporate policies. Buying from companies that create and support such policies can make a real difference. CEP welcomes your comments, data, advice, and support in its campaign to improve the social performance of the giant corporations whose behavior so vitally affects our daily lives. I ardently hope that *Rating America's Corporate Conscience* will be read by everyone who is concerned about the world today — and tomorrow.

Alice Tepper Marlin
New York City
September 1986

Acknowledgments

Only with the help and cooperation of innumerable individuals and organizations, as well as that of many of the 130 corporations included in this book, could we have compiled the broad array of information gathered here.

Among those generous with their time and support, we are particularly grateful to Mary Camper-Titsingh for her help on research and her excellent detailed editing; Jane Gould for her careful research on women's issues as well as her hospitality; Joan Bavaria, Don Falvey, and Franklin Research and Development for their support and encouragement throughout this project; interns Nancy McFadden and Cameron Gordon in New York and Betsy Wright, Jean Breslow, and Judy Knott in Boston who put in many long hours; Andy Kivel and the staff at the Data Center who helped make the search through their files almost painless; and to Clark Moeller for his help in compiling information on military contracting.

Our thanks also to Christine Charlton, Joyce Foster, John Grogan, Jr., Neal Karrer, Angela Lyons, Leslie Mann, Michael Misove, Doris O'Donnell, William Olwell, Susan Rakus, Theodore F. Schneider, Jr., Dorothy Shriver, and Susan Swaney for their thorough and generous assistance in gathering information and for their help in preparing the manuscript.

For their help in reviewing the manuscript and providing substantive and editorial comments, we would like especially to thank Herbert Alexander, Amy Domini, Albert Donnay, Pablo Eisenberg, James Heard, Michael Jacobson, David Johnston, John Lydenberg, Michael McCloskey, Milton Moskowitz, Max Obuszewski, Julia Parzen, Bruce Pottash, Ruth Ruttenberg, Joan Shapiro, Timothy Smith, Tamsin Taylor, as well as CEP board members Robert Cox, Robert Heilbroner, Mary Gardiner Jones, Harry Kahn, Michael Michaelson, John Silberman, Margaret Simms, and Lee B. Thomas, Jr., along with the many others who helped in the review process.

Without the hospitality of many, our job would have been considerably harder. James Biddle and the Andalusia Foundation, along with Marie Cairns and Barbara Farrell, Dwight and Zippie Collins, Todd Collins, Kass Green and Gene Forsberg, and Paul and Barbara Zimmerman all helped in making our tasks much easier.

Special thanks to Robert Lavelle, whose early enthusiasm for the project was an inspiration to us all, and to Cyrisse Jaffee and Lori Snell at Addison-Wesley for their thoroughness and patience as this book entered the editing and production phases. Also our thanks to Willa Seidenberg and Jeannie Smith for being there when needed in the typing of the manuscript.

The cooperation of the companies that responded to our lengthy inquiries was indispensable in compiling information for this project. Likewise, the work of other specialized research and advocacy organizations and their cooperation with us was of great help.

Acknowledgments

PART ONE

Chapter 1

SHOPPING FOR A BETTER WORLD

For years, companies have been evaluated by assessing their financial performance — sales, profits, assets. Their brand-name products have been advertised and promoted using packaging, reliability, price, or a catchy slogan. But it has been virtually impossible to compare companies on their social performance — policies and activities on key issues of social responsibility.

The information in this book will help you cast an economic vote on corporate social responsibility when you shop — whether you're buying toothpaste, a typewriter, or an airline ticket. *Rating America's Corporate Conscience* rates corporate social performance by analyzing comparable data and presenting them in a practical format. For those actively concerned with social issues, *Rating America's Corporate Conscience* provides a new lever for social change. For those in the business community — from chief executive officers to middle managers to analysts and investors — *Rating America's Corporate Conscience* provides a compelling look at an intriguing array of corporate programs and policies. By referring to the product charts and company profiles you can become more fully informed as an effective consumer, investor, worker, or manager.

You'll be able to:

- buy a camera from a company that stopped selling its merchandise in South Africa because it did not want to support apartheid;

- purchase a breakfast cereal made by a company that pledges a generous 2 percent of pre-tax earnings to charity;

- cook your supper on a kitchen range made by a company not involved in the manufacture of nuclear weapons;

- snack on peanut butter made by one of the first major U.S. corporations to institute a comprehensive child-care network for its employees;

- invest in companies that have supported the advancement of women and minorities in management;

- avoid buying from corporations whose policies you feel reflect a disregard for the public good.

We have researched, analyzed, and evaluated the social performance of 130 companies that dominate the market in the food, health and personal care, appliance, home products, oil, airline, hotel, and automobile industries. The large companies, major advertisers, and frequently purchased, nationally distributed brand-name products in this book are familiar to most consumers.

We have presented the data and ratings in two ways. *Product charts*, organized by brand name, highlight and compare corporate performance on selected social issues. These product charts provide a handy checklist on how companies rate on issues of vital concern:

- South Africa

- Nuclear- and conventional-arms contracting

- Charitable contributions

- Representation of women and minorities on boards of directors and in top management

- Disclosure of information on social issues

Each product chart also includes a column headed "Authors' Company of Choice" to further help assess differences among companies.

Company profiles and charts specify and discuss data on each company's social record. These profiles and charts present a more detailed portrait of individual companies and their programs, as well as a look at selected issues and controversies not necessarily covered in the product charts (i.e., labor relations, the environment). Also offered is a description of the company's history and philosophy regarding corporate social responsibility. An overview of the industries listed above offers some general observations on the comparative performance of companies within the same industry.

Assessing a company's overall social record is not the same as determining its profitability; there is no clear-cut bottom line. One cannot successfully average positive performance in one area and negative performance in another. Sometimes the choices may be easy. For instance, few would have trouble distinguishing Polaroid's superior performance from A. H. Robins's, which

Shopping for a Better World

we consider to be dismal. More often, however, a company's performance may be outstanding in one category, unsatisfactory in another, and mixed in yet another. How does one characterize IBM, for example? Here is a company that has taken noteworthy creative steps in job training for disadvantaged youth, provided child-care support for its employees, and exhibited innovative leadership in many other areas. But IBM is also a major military weapons contractor, and by virtue of its sales of computers in South Africa, it could be considered to be a supporter of apartheid.

In assessing a company's record, the issues you feel most strongly about may clearly dictate your choices. For some, the fact that Philip Morris aggressively promotes smoking, despite the well-documented adverse health effects of that habit, may override the company's substantial commitment to minority development or its patronage of the visual arts. We present the facts and indicate our own preferences as an additional guide to evaluating the data. After reviewing the product charts, company charts, and profiles, you will be able to make an overall appraisal. Of course the judgment and final decision is yours — to buy or not to buy.

Interest in the social conduct of U.S. corporations is not a recent phenomenon. In the early 1900s the Progressive political party, along with muckraking journalists, focused the nation's attention on issues such as dangerous working conditions in factories, unsanitary food processing methods, and the exploitation of women and children. Public pressure at that time led to the passage of the Pure Food and Drug Act of 1906 and ultimately to the passage of protective child labor laws.

A second wave of concern about the social role of corporations swept the nation in the late 1960s, spurred on by the civil rights movement and opposition to the Vietnam War. Publication of Rachel Carson's *Silent Spring* and the growing awareness of industry's impact on the environment led to the first "Earth Day" demonstration in 1970; the decade also witnessed a rebirth of the consumer product safety movement, spearheaded by Ralph Nader.

The highly publicized social consciousness of the 1960s and 1970s may appear to have been replaced by the widely proclaimed, self-interested economic consciousness of the 1980s. But a legacy has endured — the expectation that corporations demonstrate a sensitivity and commitment to social issues. This legacy has become institutionalized in government, in the public interest movement, in grass-roots citizen activism, and within the corporate world itself. Over the past decades many companies have taken substantial strides. Amoco, for example, has developed an outstanding program of economic support for community revitalization and minority- and women-owned businesses. Avon's corporate policies have focused on women, minorities, and the poor for almost a decade. The company profiles in this book reveal many other significant corporate initiatives.

But there is a long way to go. Disasters such as Love Canal and other toxic waste disposal controversies demonstrate that issues of arguable corporate irresponsibility and ineptitude are still with us. Less drastic but no less dramatic, many companies in the conduct of their day-to-day business supply oil to the South African government or manufacture nuclear-armed weapons. The implications of corporate behavior can have far-reaching and potentially dangerous repercussions.

Rating America's Corporate Conscience is only a beginning. Since it was necessary to limit the scope of the book, we excluded financial services, retail stores, and supermarket chains due to regional differences and the sheer number of companies. We considered including smaller, "alternative" companies, such as worker-owned cooperatives, organic food producers, or companies owned and run by minorities or women. However, space and time considerations forced us to exclude these as well. We hope a sequel to *Rating America's Corporate Conscience* will permit further explorations of these and other companies not covered here.

Product safety and quality are obviously important issues for consumers. For the most part we've left these assessments to organizations that already provide this information, such as Consumers Union; other resources are listed in Appendix C. However, where a company's record shows a dramatic commitment to public welfare (e.g., Johnson & Johnson's expensive voluntary recall of its drug Zomax), or where a company was involved in a controversy of an exceptionally serious nature (e.g., A. H. Robins's handling of the Dalkon Shield controversy), we have included this information within the company's profile. We have also noted, briefly, debates over the harmfulness of such products as cigarettes, alcoholic beverages, and highly processed foods.

We have reluctantly kept our discussions of environmental issues and labor relations to a minimum, due to a lack of comparable data. However, we have reported major problems in these areas, as well as particularly positive actions taken by companies (respectively, Dow Chemical's battle over the toxic pollutant dioxin and People Express's innovative worker ownership and job rotation programs).

Rating America's Corporate Conscience is a useful tool for the consumer, a resource for the political activist, and a compilation of fascinating information for CEOs, managers, and those who participate in or observe the American business scene. We welcome your comments, data, and advice, and hope to be able to use your feedback in subsequent editions or sequels. Consider this book an invitation to join the Council on Economic Priorities in its campaign to improve the social responsibility of the giant corporations whose actions so profoundly affect our daily lives. By supporting "good" business we can help align private corporate interests with those of the public.

Chapter 2

PROFITS AND
GOOD BUSINESS

This book draws a part of its impetus from the social investing movement, which has grown tremendously since the 1970s. Both individual and large institutional investors have demonstrated since then a strong interest in using social as well as financial criteria in certain investment decisions. This task has been made easier by the availability of "ethical" mutual stock funds, money market funds, and investment advisors.

Much of the current interest in social investing has its roots in the late 1960s, particularly in the "peace portfolios" developed for those seeking to invest in companies free of weapons contracts during the Vietnam War. Two mutual stock funds established then, Pax World and Dreyfus Third Century, are still active today.

Social investing has surfaced again with renewed vigor since 1980. Several of the more recently established socially oriented money market and mutual funds have experienced rapid growth, notably Working Assets and the two Calvert Funds. (See the Quick Guide to Some Socially Responsible Funds and Investment Advisors, pp. 8–9, and Performance of Some Social Investment Funds and Investment Advisors, p. 10.) Investment advisors specializing in social accounts have flourished, too. The Boston-based Franklin Research and Development Corporation, for example, grew from managing $10 million in social accounts in mid-1984 to $50 million by early 1986. Similarly, traditional banking institutions, such as U.S. Trust in Boston, long active in the social investing world, now have thriving special investment units for clients with social concerns. In 1984 a broad coalition of investment firms, non-profit instititutions, and individuals involved in social investing established the Social Investment Forum, which promotes and publicizes ethical investing standards, and disseminates information. Conservatively estimated, $100 billion in U.S. investments were managed under social criteria by late 1985. (Contact the Social Investment Forum or the Council on Economic Priorities for a more

Calvert Social Investment Fund
1700 Pennsylvania Avenue, N.W.
Washington, DC 20006
(800) 368-2748   (301) 951-4800

Calvert operates both a mutual equity fund and a money market fund. The funds avoid companies with military or nuclear power contracts, or those supporting repressive regimes. They seek companies with positive records on product safety, worker relations and safety, pollution control, and minority hiring. Minimum investment in either is $1,000.

Dreyfus Third Century Fund
600 Madison Avenue
New York, NY 10022
(800) 645-6561   (212) 895-1206

This mutual equity fund seeks companies with good pollution control, worker safety, product safety, and minority hiring records. Minimum investment is $2,500.

Joan Bavaria
Franklin Research & Development
711 Atlantic Avenue
Boston, MA 02111
(617) 423-6655

Franklin Research is an investment advisor for socially responsive accounts. Joan Bavaria also heads up the Social Investment Forum, a trade association for institutions and individuals active in social investing.

New Alternatives Fund
295 Northern Boulevard
Great Neck, NY 11021
(516) 466-0808

This mutual equity fund seeks companies that promote solar or alternative energy production, or energy conservation. Minimum investment is $2,500.

Parnassus Fund
1427 Shrader Street
San Francisco, CA 94117
(415) 664-6812

Parnassus is a mutual equity fund founded in January 1985 and not fully operational until July. It is both "contrarian" and socially oriented. (Contrarians take the risky approach of seeking out-of-favor stocks that are undervalued and due to rebound in price.) The fund seeks particular companies that are community and employee oriented. Its return from July 1985 to March 1986 was 27 percent. Minimum investment is $5,000.

(continued)

Pax World Fund
224 State Street
Portsmouth, NH 03801
(603) 431-8022

This mutual "balanced" equity fund (balanced funds invest in both stocks and bonds) avoids tobacco, liquor, and gambling companies or those with military contracts, and seeks firms with positive records in employment and pollution control. Minimum investment is $250.

Robert J. Schwartz
Shearson/American Express
666 Fifth Avenue
New York, NY 10103
(212) 974-3200

Robert Schwartz operates a special unit at Shearson/American Express that specializes in investment advising for socially responsive accounts.

South Shore Bank Money Market Accounts
7054 South Jeffrey Boulevard
Chicago, IL 60649
(312) 288-1000

This bank, operating in a predominantly black neighborhood, is exceptionally committed to community development programs. It solicits below-market-rate deposits, from which it directs proceeds to specific neighborhood development projects. It also offers market-rate money market accounts and certificates of deposit. Deposits are federally insured.

Robert Zevin
U.S. Trust
PO Box 373
Boston, MA 02101
(617) 726-7000

U.S. Trust manages socially responsive accounts for its clients as well as accounts managed under traditional criteria.

Working Assets Money Fund
230 California Street
San Francisco, CA 94111
(800) 543-8800   (415) 989-3200

This money market fund avoids investments with companies that pursue military contracts, generate nuclear power, support repressive regimes, or have poor labor records. It seeks out banks with good records on community development in which to invest. In 1986, Working Assets began offering a "socially responsive" credit card service, with five cents pledged to peace, hunger, and environmental organizations each time their card is used.

**Performance of Some Social Investment Funds
and Investment Advisors
December 31, 1984 to December 31, 1985**

Mutual Fund Total Return Performance

Calvert Social Investment Fund (Managed Growth Portfolio)	26.8%
Dreyfus Third Century Fund	28.6%
New Alternatives Fund	23.4%
Pax World Fund	24.1%
Lipper General Equity Fund Average of 490 Firms	27.2%

Money Market 12-Month Yields

Calvert Social Investment Fund	7.78%
Working Assets	7.54%
Donoghue's Money Market Fund Average	7.71%
South Shore Bank Money Market Account	7.98%
Bank Rate Monitor Average of 50 Top Institutions in Top Five Markets	7.35%

Investment Advisors

Franklin Research & Development	24.9%
Shearson/American Express	25.2%
U.S. Trust	27.6%

complete listing and description of socially managed funds and investment services. Contact CEP for information on its Portfolio Review Service, which analyzes portfolio holdings on social criteria.)

Several circumstances have contributed to this upsurge in social investing:

- An increasingly reliable and sophisticated body of research on corporate social performance has made more information available through private research organizations and public sources.

- Investment advisors and mutual funds using social criteria have established a track record solid enough to demonstrate that investors do not need to sacrifice principles for gains. Nevertheless, some in the investment community continue to debate this claim.

- The socially conscious generation of the 1960s is now making investment decisions, from banking to retirement plans.

- The explosive situation in South Africa has prompted many universities, labor organizations, and state and municipal governments to divest or rule out investing in certain companies that do business in South Africa.

Profits and Good Business

- The Reagan administration's cutbacks in government regulation of the private sector and in funds for social service programs, together with its emphasis on voluntary involvement in social issues by the private sector, have brought an increased public awareness of the need for new and innovative corporate initiatives.

Too often, social investing has been perceived solely in a negative context: portfolios kept free from companies that do business in South Africa, produce nuclear weapons, are major polluters, or have poor labor relations records. But this is only one aspect of ethical investing. Most investment advisors and fund managers stress positive considerations as well. They seek out companies producing high-quality products that contribute positively to immediate social needs, as well as corporations taking creative initiatives in employee relations, community involvement, affirmative action hiring and promotion, and other areas. In fact, most people in the social investment community would argue that these positive elements are often indicative of well-managed companies and should be considered in any investment decision.

At the same time, social responsibility has become an accepted and broadly interpreted concept by many in the corporate community. Some managers of major corporations take the position that financial and social concerns cannot be separated and that a company's sense of social responsibility and its long-term profitability are ultimately linked.

James E. Burke, chairman of Johnson & Johnson, states that "There's an important correlation . . . between a corporation's public responsibility and its ultimate financial performance. Although public service is implied in the charter of all American companies, public responsibility — in reality — is a company's very reason for existing."

This contrasts with the more conventional wisdom that profitability is a company's only rationale for existence. But Johnson & Johnson's ability to survive the Tylenol crises of 1982 and 1986 demonstrated one way in which the reputation of commitment to the public good can become immediately relevant to a company's financial stability. The company's response to the first of these tampering incidents was swift and sure. When cyanide-laced Tylenol capsules resulted in seven deaths in Chicago in 1982, Johnson & Johnson immediately opted for an expensive nationwide recall of the pain reliever, even though the poisonings were in no way Johnson & Johnson's fault and despite the fact that there was no evidence of tampering elsewhere. It then reintroduced Tylenol in tamper-resistant packages, but kept the name — a calculated gamble that proved successful. Again, in the face of renewed tamperings and a second poisoning incident in 1986, the company took the potentially costly step of ceasing to market Tylenol in capsule form as the measure most clearly in the interest of public safety.

Johnson & Johnson was able to weather these crises in the face of intense efforts by the competition to capitalize on them. This was due partly to its solid reputation for commitment to the public good. As Burke put it, "The Tylenol situation dramatically proved that serving the public good is what business is all about."

A business operating with various commitments to social responsibility can do so profitably, as a number of studies have demonstrated. In the area of employee relations, Franklin Research and Devlopment found that the stock of those companies included in the book *The 100 Best Companies to Work for in America* dramatically outperformed the *Standard & Poor's* 500 stock price average over a ten-year period. The stocks rose from a value of just over 100 in 1975 to 700 in 1985, compared with a rise to just over 200 for the *Standard & Poor's* 500. A similar study, reported in Rosabeth Kanter's book, *The Change Masters*, asked human resources experts from the business community to come up with a list of companies most progressive in their relations with employees. The forty-seven companies chosen by these experts were then compared to similar firms of the same size within their industries. It was found that the "progressive" companies were more profitable and fostered greater growth over 20 years than did their counterparts.

Positive performance on environmental issues has also been shown to be beneficial. In 1972 a study by Joseph Bragdon and John A. Marlin that used five different measures of financial performance concluded that the companies within the pulp and paper industry that had the best record on pollution control and the environment were also the most profitable.

Of course, one cannot claim that social responsibility assures profits, or that all profitable companies are socially responsible. Polaroid, a company with one of the best social records, has encountered loss of market share in recent years. American Brands, which in our opinion has a poor social record, has been a consistently profitable company, largely because of its sale of cigarettes. Because numerous factors determine a company's performance, it would be naive to attribute financial success or failure to a single one.

Nevertheless, social considerations are slowly but surely becoming one of the many aspects of running a company well. The role of the chief executive officer in the integration of social accountability issues into the corporate structure cannot be overestimated. A recent study by Michael Useem and Stephen I. Kutner of the Boston University Center for Applied Social Science confirms the conclusion reached by many other studies: the greatest influence on the size and nature of a company's charitable giving program is its CEO. Experts who have studied other social issues, such as employee-involvement and child-care programs, agree that a forceful commitment from top management is essential if meaningful long-term initiatives are to be institutionalized.

The CEO's role is significant because these programs are not always simple to introduce or implement. Projects that are described in a sentence in this book may have taken years of work and a major financial and human commitment. For instance, setting up IBM's information and referral service for child care involved a program that could handle the needs of 240,000 workers in hundreds of cities around the country. It necessitated creating a network of 225 agencies and individuals around the country, at a substantial cost to initiate and a substantial cost to run each year. Similarly, in establishing minority purchasing programs, a company must make a concerted effort to locate minority-owned businesses that can provide quality goods or services. It must also make sure that its buyers change long-established purchasing patterns and continue to search out and support additional minority suppliers year after year. In the best of these programs, the company becomes actively involved in the development of minority-owned businesses, providing technical or financial support that enables these businesses to expand or to upgrade their manufacturing facilities.

Many factors can prompt a corporation to take social initiatives. For pollution control, worker safety, or affirmative action, federal laws and regulations can serve as a powerful incentive. Internal forces, such as a severe financial crisis or a change in the makeup of the work force, can prompt necessary adjustments. Public scandal, or lawsuits alleging hazardous products or improper acts by corporate officers, can also lead to reforms. A stockholder resolution may have similar results.

Whatever the reason, management must be convinced that the initiatives undertaken are in the company's best interests. Eastern Airlines, faced with potential bankruptcy in 1983, agreed to a progressive and precedent-setting employee-involvement program in exchange for union wage concessions. Here the survival of the company was at stake. Less dramatic, but similar in principle, have been the "quality circle" participation programs created by numerous companies in recent years. By increasing employee involvement in production decisions, companies hope to improve productivity and quality control in order to compete with foreign goods and services.

In some cases, changes made are not due to any obvious threat or emergency. Kimberly-Clark invested $2.5 million in the late 1970s in a health and physical fitness center, complete with a counseling program, at its headquarters in Wisconsin. Despite the substantial cost, the company felt its gains in reduced absenteeism, fewer accidents, and a healthier work force justified its investment.

The self-interest served by charitable giving can be broadly or narrowly defined. Certainly, grants by high-technology firms to science education are directly related to the future planning and output of the companies. But insti-

**Profiled Companies Reporting Charitable Contributions
Above 1.5 Percent**

S. C. Johnson & Son	5.0%
Dow Chemical	3.0%
Noxell	2.8%
Pillsbury	2.4%
Polaroid	2.4%
General Mills	2.1%
Anheuser-Busch	1.9%
RCA	1.9%
Pennwalt	1.8%
Atlantic Richfield	1.7%
Beatrice	1.6%
McCormick	1.6%
United Technologies	1.5%

Source: Council on Economic Priorities, based on information
supplied by companies for this book.

tuting programs such as job training and urban revitalization can offer more
general advantages to companies. When a corporation implements minority
banking and purchasing programs, thus changing the way day-to-day business is conducted, the company must be convinced that it will ultimately
benefit because society in general will be positively affected.

If a company's view of its self-interest is limited to compliance with government regulation to avoid federal or state prosecution, its performance on
social issues may fluctuate with shifts in political power and policy. But if a
company's sense of responsibility to society is guided by firm internal principles, then its social performance will be consistent over time and over a range
of issues.

Within the past twenty years the concept of social responsibility has earned
a place in the practice of corporate management. Numerous positive social
programs have been institutionalized in a wide range of companies, as the
examples in this book demonstrate. At the same time there has been a de-
crease in direct federal pressure on corporations. Whether or not this relaxa-
tion of federal pressure will eventually lead to a substantial reduction in corporate social efforts depends on several factors, including the policies of
future administrations and state governments, the attitudes of those rising to
the top of corporate management, and the continuing pressure of public interest organizations and lawyers.

In the meantime, a sharp awareness within the business community of
consumer and investor concern about corporate social behavior can be a com-

Profits and Good Business

pelling factor. Companies fight hard for even a small percentage gain in market share for their products. If and when corporate managers become convinced that their company's social record affects market share, they will be forced to take social initiatives seriously. The resulting changes — large and small — in company policies and practices will have an enormous impact on our daily lives and our future.

Chapter 3

ISSUES

The product charts and company profiles in this book cover a wide range of social issues, allowing readers to decide for themselves which aspects of a company's social performance are most important.

The product charts show how we rated the relative performance of each company on seven issues:

1. Charitable contributions

2. Representation of women on boards of directors and among top corporate officers

3. Representation of minorities on boards of directors and among top corporate officers

4. Disclosure of social information

5. Involvement in South Africa

6. Conventional weapons–related contracting

7. Nuclear weapons–related contracting

While the brand-name product charts give a simple high-middle-low rating for the company's relative record on these issues, the profiles and accompanying company charts provide more detailed facts and figures. Note that the product charts are *not* intended to express any opinions or ratings about the products themselves, but indicate our ratings of the *companies* that make those products.

In addition, we have included specifics on corporate Political Action Committees (PACs) in the charts that follow the company profiles.

We chose these issues both for their current importance and because of the availability of reasonably complete data in comparable formats.

The profiles of the individual companies analyze in greater detail the issues in the charts and describe outstanding positive initiatives a company has taken, as well as highly publicized controversies in which it has been involved. For a complete evaluation, readers should consult both charts and profiles.

Because this book is a tool for decision making and easy reference, we have kept brief our discussions of the issues and the debates surrounding them. However, each of the issues covered in the charts is complicated in its own right and has been the subject of more detailed examination elsewhere. Readers interested in further information on these issues should see Appendix A for a description of our sources of information and research methods, and Appendix C for a listing of related organizations and publications.

PRODUCT CHARTS

Size of Charitable Contributions

The product charts show the relative size of each company's charitable giving program. As important to us as the size, if not more important, is the nature of the giving, which we describe in the profiles. For example, we have emphasized corporate charitable support for new, diverse, and creative nonprofit initiatives that provide and promote food for the hungry, job training for economically disadvantaged youth, child-care support for working parents, minority economic development, and community revitalization — areas of great need that have been recently hurt by the deep federal cuts in social service funding. We have also identified innovative decision making in giving programs, especially those that involve employees at all levels.

Examples of companies covered that have taken a leadership role in innovative and diverse charitable giving include:

- Polaroid, where grants are made by a selection committee of more than 40 employees from all levels. Grants consistently go to a broad range of local community-oriented organizations.

- Amoco, one of the strongest supporters of community-based nonprofit organizations in Chicago. The company is increasingly investing corporate funds, in addition to its foundation grants, in urban revitalization programs.

- General Mills and Pillsbury, both mainstays of the generous spirit in charitable giving that characterizes the Minneapolis business community. General Mills supplemented its giving with a direct corporate investment in a local community revitalization project. Pillsbury's subsidiaries have a free hand in setting their charitable giving goals. Its Burger King division

Distribution of Corporate Contributions

	1983 471 companies		1982 534 companies	
	(millions of dollars)			
Health and human services	$ 367.6	28.7%	$ 397.3	31.0%
Education	498.8	39.0	522.2	40.7
Culture and art	145.2	11.4	145.8	11.4
Civic and community affairs	188.8	14.8	149.3	11.7
Other	78.0	6.1	67.0	5.2
Total	$1,278.4		$1,281.6	

Source: Giving USA, American Association of Fund-Raising Counsel, New York, NY, 1985.

recently developed an unusual incentive-scholarship program for employees who wish to pursue post-high-school education.

- Atlantic Richfield, long a major supporter of community revitalization and minority-oriented projects. This support is supplemented with a strong matching gifts program and additional grants to nonprofit groups for which ARCO employees volunteer.

The more traditional giving programs are mentioned, but only briefly. These programs are directed primarily to post-secondary-school education or channeled through united fund drives such as the United Way or the Community Chest. They are typical of most corporate philanthropic activities. While they represent valuable efforts indeed, we do not feel they necessarily constitute the most direct or innovative response to pressing social needs.

An interesting example of a mixture of both approaches is Standard Oil Company, which has followed the more usual pattern for charitable giving with recent multimillion-dollar grants to academic research closely allied to its business interests (e.g., up to $2 million to Stanford University for computer simulations of petroleum reservoirs). At the same time, it has initiated grants that support Cleveland more directly with substantial funds for energy conservation and urban revitalization.

Until 1935, it was not clear whether companies could legally disburse a portion of their profits for charitable contributions, since shareholders would otherwise be entitled to these diverted funds. In that year the newly created Securities and Exchange Commission ruled that companies could give up to 5 percent of their net earnings before taxes to qualifying nonprofit organizations on a tax-deductible basis. In 1981 this figure was raised to 10 percent.

There are those who still feel that corporate America should concentrate solely on making money, not on giving it away. Economist Milton Friedman, for example, has argued that "Corporations have no money to give to anyone. It belongs to their workers, their employees or their shareholders." The more generally accepted view today is that corporate self-interest should not be narrowly confined to profits. General Mills' chairman, H. Brewster Atwater, has argued that "one of the most important duties of each citizen, whether a corporation or an individual, is to work in a multitude of ways for the betterment of society. In the long run this is a self-interested proposition, in no way inconsistent with a corporation's duties to its shareholders."

Since 1970, corporate philanthropy has grown more than twice as rapidly as that of private foundations. Corporations gave an estimated $3.45 billion in 1984, approaching the $4.36 billion given by foundations. As part of the Reagan administration's effort to increase corporate social giving and "public-private partnerships," its Task Force on Private Sector Initiatives set a goal in 1981 of increasing corporate giving from an average 1 percent of pre-tax net earnings to 2 percent by 1986. Figures reported by the American Association of Fund-Raising Counsel show the corporate average hovering around 1.5 percent from 1982 through 1984. (See Appendix A on the complexities in calculating this figure and why its size is influenced by the method used.)

In certain cities, such as Minneapolis-St. Paul and Baltimore, corporations have banded together to form Five-Percent Clubs. In Kansas City, Seattle, and San Francisco, they have formed Two-Percent Clubs. Members of these clubs publicly commit their companies to these above-average giving levels. The California Chamber of Commerce has been promoting the formation of Two-Percent Clubs around the state since 1983. Minneapolis's Dayton Hudson Corporation has been a particularly strong advocate of "five-percent" giving levels over the years.

The best corporate philanthropy goes beyond larger giving programs to more effective ones. This means:

- professionally managed giving, with charitable grant-making receiving the same care given to other corporate financial decisions;

- effective giving, with more careful screening of grant proposals to determine which will bring the greatest benefit and be most self-sustaining — often accompanied by increased nonfinancial corporate support, such as managerial or technical assistance;

- imaginative giving: higher education and United Way campaigns have long received the majority of charitable contributions in part because they are perceived as noncontroversial.

But, argues James Bere, chairman of Borg-Warner (a prominent proponent of corporate social involvement in Chicago), "Some risk is necessary in philanthropy as well as business. A new approach to a special need may be far

Examples of Two-Percent and Five-Percent Clubs

Minneapolis

Contributors pledge to give 2 percent or 5 percent of domestic pre-tax income to charitable and community projects.

Two-Percent Program: 33 corporate members, including Eaton Corporation, General Mills, Honeywell, International Multifoods, and the St. Paul Companies are pledged to give at least 2 percent.

Five-Percent Program: 71 corporate members, including Dayton Hudson Corporation, H. B. Fuller Company, First Minneapolis Bank, and First St. Paul Bank, are pledged to give at least 5 percent.

Kansas City

Council for Corporate Responsibility (or Two-Percent Club): 107 members pledge to give at least 2 percent of pre-tax income or a minimum of $5,000 (whichever is larger) to local charities. Members include H&R Block, Centerre Bank, and Hallmark Cards, Inc.

Baltimore

Five-Percent Club of Greater Baltimore: 64 corporate members, of whom 53 give at least 5 percent. Members pledge a minimum of $20,000 in annual giving and a goal of 5 percent giving within three years of joining. Members include Black & Decker, Noxell, the Rouse Company, Parks Sausage Company, and Maryland National Bank. Black & Decker and Noxell are the only two companies in this book which to CEP's knowledge have set a giving goal of 5 percent.

San Francisco

San Francisco Chamber of Commerce Two-Percent Club: 50 corporate members, including Bank of America, Kaiser Aluminum, Levi Strauss, I. Magnin, McKesson, Mervyn's (a subsidiary of Dayton Hudson), Saga, Shaklee, and Wells Fargo.

Seattle

Council for Corporate Responsibility: 143 corporate members pledge to contribute 2 percent or more of their pre-tax earnings to educational and social organizations, including Pacific Coca-Cola Bottling, Ranier Bancorporation, Safeway Stores, Seafirst Corporation, The Seattle Times, and Weyerhaeuser Company.

---

better than the established one. . . . Change and innovation are the keys not only of successful business, but also of successful philanthropy." Some community-change activists question what Pablo Eisenberg, president of the Center for Community Change, calls the United Way's right to "monopolize payroll deduction plans on behalf of a minority of charitable groups." A foundation such as Sara Lee's, which has committed 50 percent of its giving to the economically disadvantaged, is still a rare exception.

Issues

Disclosure of charitable giving is an important related issue. (See also p. 27 for how social disclosure in general is evaluated in the product charts.) Many view the publication of comprehensive reports on the distribution of a company's grants as one sign of a well-run and responsive foundation. An absence of well-publicized disclosures may discourage applications from appropriate organizations and increase the likelihood of a narrow, unchanging, and casually conceived pattern of giving. To encourage greater disclosure, the Communications Network, an association of foundation officers, in conjunction with the Council on Foundations, began in 1984 to give annual awards for the best foundation annual reports. In 1985 the Boston Globe and Dayton Hudson foundations were singled out for praise; in 1986 Atlantic Richfield was similarly honored.

Corporations cannot be expected to replace the billions of dollars cut from our federal social-support programs in the 1980s. Nor should they be expected to remedy all of society's ills single-handedly. But professionally organized and managed corporate giving programs can have a sizable and beneficial impact on the communities in which companies operate.

Women and Minority Directors and Officers

The women and minorities columns on the product charts indicate corporate performance in including members of either group on their board of directors or in uppermost levels of management (defined as corporate staff at the vice presidential level or higher). The charts accompanying the company profiles provide the statistics for each company. Where the figures are available, the company profiles also show the percentages of women and minorities among the officials and managers job category, which usually constitutes 10 to 15 percent of a firm's work force.

The fight for equal rights for women and minorities in the United States has been an issue of concern since the early 1960s. The Rev. Martin Luther King, Jr., came to national prominence in that struggle. The passage of the Civil Rights Act of 1964 marked the beginning of our long, slow, and often difficult task of assuring equal and equitable representation for persons of all colors in America. The women's rights movement was born at much the same time and has become the focus of national attention since the 1970s.

While most Americans agree in principle that there should not be discrimination on the basis of sex or color, the implementation of affirmative action programs has often proved difficult.

Representation on a company's board by directors who are not also that company's executives, particularly by women and minorities, was among the first social proposals by shareholders at corporate annual meetings in the early 1970s. Federal regulations have required companies to set and meet

Average Industry Employment of Women and Minorities among Officials and Managers, 1984

	Women	Minorities
Certified air transport	19.4%	10.2%
Drugs	15.7	8.2
Eating and drinking places	29.7	13.8
Food and kindred products	11.4	8.3
Hotels and motels	32.7	15.4
Household appliances	9.6	5.2
Motor vehicles and equipment	6.0	8.7
Office and computing machines	14.0	8.4
Oil and gas field services	6.2	4.9
Soap, cleaners, & toilet goods	27.1	8.3
Tobacco manufacturers	13.4	11.6
Average all industries	23.2%	8.4%

Source: U.S. Equal Opportunity Commission.

their own goals for increasing representation of these two groups in various job categories since the 1960s. These regulations have clearly brought great progress. Unfortunately, the Reagan administration was considering their abolishment in 1985.

There is little question that many companies have offered women and minorities substantial new opportunities in upper management and on boards of directors in the past fifteen years. But the equitable representation by women and minorities is a goal yet to be achieved.

Just over 50 percent of the companies cooperating with this study reported having minorities on their boards, and 37 percent had at least one minority among their top officers. Ninety-two companies provided us with figures for these two categories; it is possible that the percentages for minorities among the nonreporting companies are substantially lower than among those that cooperated.

Of the 92 cooperating companies, 47 had at least one minority on their board. Among these, 39 had one, 7 had two, and only Kimberly-Clark had three. Only 81 companies provided information on minorities in top management. Here, 29 reported at least one minority officer, with 16 having one, 8 with two, 2 with three minority officers, and Coca-Cola, ITT, and Marriott with four each.

Two companies — Anheuser-Busch and Eastern Airlines — had two minority group members both on their boards and among their top officers.

Percentage of Women and Minorities among Officials and Managers
Reported by Profiled Companies

Company	Women	Minorities
Food Industry		
Anheuser-Busch* (1985)	5.8%	9.1%
Beatrice (1984)	16.1	8.6
Coca-Cola* (1985)	?	10.0
Dart & Kraft (1983)	9.6	5.5
General Foods* (1985)	18.0	8.0
McDonald's* (1985)	54.3	22.8
Philip Morris* (1985)	13.8	15.4
R. J. Reynolds* (1985)	19.5	19.2
Sara Lee (1985)	28.3	8.0
Health and Personal Care Industry		
Avon* (1985)	75.0	12.0
Bristol-Myers (1984)	18.5	8.4
Gillette (1984)	19.3	8.3
Johnson & Johnson (1983)	12.8	9.3
Pennwalt (1985)	7.5	5.1
Pfizer (1983)	9.9	6.8
Richardson-Vicks (1985)	18.4	6.7
A. H. Robins (1984)	16.4	10.1
Schering-Plough (1985)	18.0	9.0
SmithKline (1985)	20.5	9.5
Airline Industry		
Eastern (1984)	14.3	11.2
Republic (1984)	26.5	2.4

(Although the black-owned Johnson Products did not answer our inquiries regarding representation of minorities, it clearly surpasses other companies profiled in this book.)

According to Catalyst, a New York–based organization that focuses on career and family issues for women, there were only 46 women serving on boards of directors of the *Fortune* 1350 in 1969 (3 percent). By 1985 the number had grown to 339 serving on 407 boards of the *Fortune* 1000 (41 percent), and in 1986, it rose to 395 women on 439 boards (44 percent). Of these 439 companies, 114 had two or more women directors, with the insurance industry doing particularly well on representation by more than one woman.

Companies profiled in this book have included more women on their boards than the Catalyst figures would lead one to expect. Of the 126 firms for whom we could gather information, 91 companies (73 percent) had at least one woman on their boards. Two-thirds of these (61) had only one

(continued)

Oil Industry		
Amoco (1983)	4.5	6.4
Atlantic Richfield* (1985)	7.5	8.3
Exxon (1984)	8.2	7.8
Mobil (1984)	7.4	7.3
Automobile Industry		
Chrysler* (1985)	5.2	11.4
Ford (1985)	3.7	9.6
GM (1985)	8.9	11.1
Hotel Industry		
Marriott (1985)	29.0	15.0
Ramada (1984)	32.7	14.3
Appliance and Household Products Industries		
Eastman Kodak (1984)	6.7	4.2
GE (1985)	6.3	4.9
IBM (1985)	16.2	10.9
Kimberly-Clark (1985)	11.2	5.2
Scott (1984)	6.6	4.7
Whirlpool (1984)	6.9	3.7
Xerox (1984)	23.0	14.6

* From *Black Enterprise*, February 1986. Copyright February 1986, Earl G. Graves Publishing Co., Inc., 130 Fifth Avenue, New York, NY 10011. All rights reserved.

Source: Council on Economic Priorities, from company responses to CEP questionnaires.

woman, but 27 had two. Anheuser-Busch, Avon, and Philip Morris were the only companies to have three women among their directors.

A substantially lower percentage reported women in top management positions. Only 46 (37 percent) of 128 companies had women at the vice-presidential level on corporate staff. (We did not include women vice presidents of subsidiaries or divisions.) Of these, 30 reported one woman officer, 9 had two, 5 had three, Johnson Products had four, and Pillsbury reported five.

Seven corporations had two or more women both on their boards and in top management — Alberto-Culver, Avon, Campbell, General Mills, General Motors, Johnson Products, and Ogden.

Most major companies now have active affirmative action programs. We did not attempt to evaluate these individually, but described outstanding examples, such as Campbell Soup's commitment to promoting women to upper levels of management. Companies can have active and effective programs for entry and middle management positions without necessarily having these reflected in the number of women or minorities on their boards and in upper

Issues

**Profiled Companies with At Least One Woman Both on
Board of Directors and in Top Management, 1984–1985**

Company	Board	Top Management
Alberto-Culver	2	3
American Home Products	1	1
AMR	1	2
Anheuser-Busch	3	1
Atlantic Richfield	1	1
Avon	3	2
Beatrice	1	3
Black & Decker	1	1
Borden	2	1
Bristol-Myers	1	1
Campbell	2	2
Castle & Cooke	2	1
Coca-Cola	1	1
Dart & Kraft	1	2
Ford	1	1
GE	2	1
General Foods	2	1
General Mills	2	3
Gerber	2	1
Gillette	1	1
GM	2	3
Greyhound	1	1
GTE	1	1
Household International	1	1
IBM	1	1
Johnson Products	2	4
Kellogg	1	1
Marriott	1	3
Mary Kay	1	2
Mobil	2	1
Ogden	2	2
Pillsbury	1	5
Quaker Oats	1	1
3M	1	2
Transamerica	1	1
Trans World Airlines	2	1
UAL	1	2
US Air	1	1
United Technologies	2	1
Warner-Lambert	1	1
Wendy's	1	1
Xerox	1	1

Note: Marriott and Pillsbury gave figures for top management, including 123 and 59 total officers, respectively, a figure higher than for most other companies.

Source: Responses to CEP inquiries and corporate annual reports.

management. Thus, we have noted that IBM has a solid reputation for equal employment opportunities for women and blacks, although it had only one woman and no minorities at the vice-presidential level in 1985.

Overall comparisons of company statistics for women and minorities among their officials and managers should be made only with extreme caution. Because of the nature of their business and their promotion ladders, high-technology industries have a much lower average percentage of women and minorities in officials' jobs. (See Average Industry Employment of Women and Minorities among Officials and Managers, p. 23.) Moreover, companies operating primarily in cities with large minority populations should have substantially higher minority representation in their work force.

It may take as long as twenty years after entering management for an individual to be considered for the topmost decision-making positions. Thus, current figures on top officers may not yet reflect progress made at lower levels. While data gathered for this book identify some companies making progress at the highest levels, it will be another ten years before a more meaningful assessment of long-term progress can be made.

Among the most frequent complaints of women and minorities now working their way up the corporate ladder is that they are being channeled into staff rather than line positions; that is, jobs such as affirmative action or public affairs, which are not on a career track leading to chief executive officer. Unfortunately, a lack of "mentors" at the highest levels can mean that women and minorities climbing the corporate ladder find themselves without natural allies higher up to lend a helping hand. Women and minorities discouraged by an uncertain and at best slow climb to the top at major corporations often break away and start their own firms. This tendency may also slow substantive progress for these two groups among the larger and older companies. The only *Fortune* 500 company now headed by a female CEO is the Washington Post, run by Katharine Graham, who owns a sizable interest in the company.

A further important issue not addressed directly in this book is that of the inequitable salary levels of men and women performing jobs of comparable worth.

Social Disclosure

The social disclosure column in the product charts indicates the company's performance in providing comparable information on social initiatives — through corporate publications and in responses to inquiries by the Council on Economic Priorities or others.

The importance of disclosure of social information is perhaps not as immediately evident as a company's involvement in South Africa or the nuclear

**Profiled Companies Reporting At Least One Minority
on Both Board of Directors
and in Top Management, 1984–1985**

Company	Board	Top Management
Anheuser-Busch	2	2
Avon	1	1
Coca-Cola	1	4
Delta Air Lines	1	1
Eastern Airlines	2	2
Eastman Kodak	1	1
GE	1	1
General Mills	1	2
Johnson & Johnson	1	1
Kellogg	1	1
McDonald's	1	3
Miles Laboratories	1	1
Philip Morris	1	2
Procter & Gamble	1	1
RJR Nabisco	1	1
Scott Paper	1	1
Warner-Lambert	1	2
Xerox	1	1

Note: The black-owned Johnson Products has a predominance of minority group members in both categories, but did not provide us with precise figures.

Source: Company responses to CEP inquiries.

arms race. But a corporation's willingness to provide facts and figures on a range of social endeavors is crucial to investors, consumers, employees, non-profit groups, and anyone who advocates social responsibility.

While outside sources for information on specific issues are vital, the companies themselves remain a primary source for data. Despite the lack of standardized reporting formats in social areas, both from year to year and from company to company, and the absence of outside auditing, we were usually able to glean enough information for overviews and comparisons.

In defining meaningful disclosure we looked for comparable year-to-year figures on the overall size or progress of specific programs, rather than anecdotal accounts. In our opinion it is more important to publish statistics demonstrating increases in the numbers of women and minority group members in the officials and managers job categories than to tell the story of the promotion of isolated individuals or give only the number of women and minorities employed throughout the company.

Companies that regularly publish descriptions of their social activities are particularly helpful. Some of these publications are more useful than others. While many companies now incorporate a page or two on social responsibility in their annual reports, relatively few include meaningful statistics. Ford and Sara Lee, however, are exceptional among companies profiled in this book in regularly publishing complete data on the percentages of women and minorities in all job categories, while Dart & Kraft has been especially diligent in providing hard facts about social programs. (A few years ago, the company was prompted by a church-sponsored shareholder resolution to resume such reporting after it had ceased doing so.) More common are anecdotal accounts of a few specific projects, such as those included in annual reports by American Brands or Tenneco, which we feel give little indication of corporate commitments extending beyond a limited number of traditional projects.

Special reports are a more frequently used format for detailed social reporting, although these reports also tend to vary. ITT's lengthy social responsibility report provides virtually no statistics on the size of its programs, but relies primarily on anecdotes to convey a sense of company commitment. General Motors' voluminous annual "public interest" report includes diverse factual information mixed with lengthy accounts of a more general nature. IBM's yearly summary of social programs is terse but factual and informative.

A similar range exists in corporate charitable giving. Most companies with foundations issue detailed reports. Some, such as those by Atlantic Richfield, General Mills, Pillsbury, and Polaroid, are notable for their thorough detail. But there are also major corporate donors, such as Philip Morris and IBM, that have no formal foundation and issue no regular reports with details of their giving.

The first attempt to require corporations to publicize comparable social statistics came in the early 1970s. With newly passed national legislation on hiring practices and on pollution, it seemed logical that information regarding the companies' compliance with these laws be made public.

In 1971 the Natural Resources Defense Council (NRDC), a Washington-based environmental law center, along with the Nader-affiliated Project on Corporate Responsibility, requested that the Securities and Exchange Commission require publicly held corporations to disclose affirmative action hiring and environmental records, along with financial data, in annual reports or 10-K forms. CEP testified in support of the NRDC's petition. A lengthy battle ensued and the SEC held public hearings on these questions in 1975. Of the 162 corporations commenting on the proposals for increased disclosure at that time, 161 were opposed to the idea. Only Cummins Engine supported the concept. Ultimately the SEC opted for minimal increases in disclosure on environmental issues only, a decision the NRDC appealed without success.

Since that time there have been no further attempts to require corporations to make social disclosures. In 1978, strongly negative initial reactions from the corporate community forced Commerce Secretary Juanita Kreps to drop tentative suggestions that guidelines be formulated for voluntary disclosure of social information. While some companies publish information on social initiatives, many more still do not. Nevertheless, informing shareholders, consumers, employees, and the general public about social activities, and about the social impact of a company's operations, is now recognized as an important aspect of corporate conduct by firms with a commitment to social responsibility.

Of the 130 companies discussed in this book, 57 (44 percent) cooperated by providing detailed factual information on their programs, 57 provided little or no information, and the remaining 16 provided some information, but on a limited basis. (See Appendix A for a description of our long and elaborate efforts to gather as complete information as possible from the companies profiled in this book).

Involvement in South Africa

The South Africa column in the product charts indicates whether or not a company has operations in that country. It also reflects its record on compliance with the Sullivan Principles for fair labor practices there and the strategic importance of its business within the South African economy. (For an explanation of the Sullivan Principles, see below; for an explanation of the Sullivan ratings, see Chapter 4.) The company profiles give details on the nature of the company's business in South Africa, the number of its employees there, and its rating for compliance with the Sullivan Principles. The profiles also point out whether the firm's business is of particular strategic importance to the South African government or military.

The crucial question in the debate over U.S. corporate involvement in South Africa is not whether apartheid should be abolished, but when and how. Apartheid is one of the most bitterly denounced legal systems in the world today. Famed South African novelist Alan Paton, writing in the *New York Times* in 1985, characterized the system this way: "These hated laws are the laws of . . . conquest, the laws made by the conqueror for the conquered. They are the laws made by whites for blacks, and they control movement, work, place of residence, and other innumerable matters." (Mr. Paton was writing to urge Americans and American businesses not to use economic means to pressure the South African government for change, but instead to use their "moral power.")

U.S. Corporations with Over 1,000 Employees in South Africa as of 1986

Allegheny International	2,025
American Brands	1,044
American Cyanamid	1,167
Caltex Petroleum[1]	2,186
Coca-Cola[2]	4,288
Colgate-Palmolive	1,234
CPC International	1,108
Emhart[2]	1,159
GM[2]	4,307
Goodyear Tire & Rubber	2,471
IBM[2]	1,485
Johnson & Johnson	1,389
Mobil	3,182
Norton[2]	1,228
RJR Nabisco	2,772
Sohio	1,503
3M	1,174
UAL[2]	1,035
Union Carbide	1,299
USG Corp	2,631
United Technologies	1,261

1. Caltex is jointly owned by the Chevron and Texaco oil companies.
2. Has subsequently withdrawn or announced plans to sell operations.

Note: Ford, although now a minority owner in the South African Motor Corporation, still employs 7,174 persons.

Source: U.S. and Canadian Investment in South Africa, Investor Responsibility Research Center, Washington, D.C., 1986. The information in this table is used by permission of the Investor Responsibility Research Center Inc. Copyright 1986, Investor Responsibility Research Center Inc.

For the most part, U.S. companies operating in South Africa have spoken out against apartheid. But until recently nearly all argued that, by maintaining their presence in that country and applying pressure for orderly change from within, they could be more effective in dismantling apartheid. Their basic framework for doing so is the Sullivan Principles. Many critics argue that the very presence of major U.S. corporations gives moral and economic support to the Pretoria government, which has demonstrated little intention of offering meaningful change. These critics attack the Sullivan Principles as an inadequate response to an intolerable status quo.

The Sullivan Principles were established in the mid-1970s by Rev. Leon Sullivan, a black minister from Philadelphia and member of the board of directors of General Motors since 1971. Their purpose was to encourage U.S. companies to implement nondiscriminatory labor practices in workplaces in South Africa and to support progressive projects for blacks in the communities in which the companies operate. Each year the Arthur D. Little consulting firm independently evaluates those companies that are signatories of the Principles and rates their actual compliance. Between October 1984 and October 1985 the number of signatories increased from 128 to 178. According to the Investor Responsibility Research Center (IRRC), there are approximately 280 U.S. companies in South Africa.

In late 1984, Sullivan proposed for the first time that signatories should work politically to oppose apartheid. In May 1985, he further declared that if apartheid is not abolished by 1987, all U.S. companies should withdraw from South Africa. Thus, although compliance with the original Sullivan Principles is still an important indication of a company's efforts to work for fair treatment of all races within South Africa, the pressure to discontinue any involvement is mounting.

Church leaders associated with the Interfaith Center on Corporate Responsibility, arguing for withdrawal in 1984, stated: "We do not believe that being a responsible employer or active philanthropist in South Africa offsets the many ways in which U.S. companies give the South Africa government support and sustenance." Those advocating that American companies remain argue that withdrawal would be little more than a symbolic gesture. Its practical effect would be to deny work to blacks and "colored" persons who have well-paid jobs in integrated workplaces. Further, they assert that withdrawal would remove a beneficial model for employment practices and a positive force that works to support black schools, health care, legal assistance, and low-interest loan funds.

With an increasingly volatile situation within South Africa since late 1984 and with the international community applying more pressure on the Pretoria government, the previous benchmark for measuring the progressiveness of individual U.S. corporations in their operations — their Sullivan rating — has diminished somewhat.

Among the companies we studied, Polaroid is exceptional. In 1977 it chose to cease sales entirely in South Africa because of concern that its products were being used by the government there to enforce apartheid regulations. More recently, an increasing number of companies have withdrawn from South Africa, although without making specific reference to apartheid. According to the IRRC, 28 U.S. companies left South Africa in 1985, up from 7 the year before. PepsiCo, for example, sold its bottling operations there, and in 1985 Coca-Cola announced it would turn over majority ownership of its business to a South African firm within two years. Chrysler sold its minority ownership in the Sigma auto manufacturing company, and Ford, through a merger with a South African car company, is now a minority partner in the new firm.

United States oil companies are heavily involved in South Africa. According to the IRRC, over 90 percent of the international oil companies on the *Standard & Poor's* top 500 list have South African operations. Their presence is considered of particular strategic importance because of the country's dependence on imported oil. Computer firms doing business in South Africa arouse controversy as well because of the role computers play in enforcing the elaborate apartheid regulations throughout the country. In contrast, other heavily involved industries, such as major U.S. drug companies (almost 90 percent of which have operations there), are not considered essential to the current Pretoria government's strength or enforcement of apartheid.

South African involvement has become one of the most controversial issues within the social investment community. Numerous state and municipal governments and universities have decided since 1980 to divest their pension fund portfolios of all holdings in companies in South Africa or in those companies with poor records of compliance with the Sullivan Principles. According to the IRRC, 1985 saw 46 colleges and universities vote to divest part or all of their South Africa–related holdings, while only 39 had done so from 1977 through 1984. Similarly, 10 states and 45 city and county legislatures passed restrictions on South Africa–related investments in 1985. Through 1984 only 7 states had taken such steps. Debates have raged over the legal, ethical, and financial aspects of these decisions to divest.

To help consumers especially concerned with the South African issue, we have indicated in our charts whether a company has operations in South Africa, and if it does, how it rates in its compliance with the Sullivan Principles; and whether the company conducts strategically important business with the South African government.

Of the 130 companies profiled in this book, 55 (42 percent) had operations in South Africa as of early 1986.

Conventional and Nuclear Weapons–Related Contracts

The nuclear- and conventional-arms contracting columns in the product charts indicate our rating of a company's involvement in weapons-related contracting. The company profiles and the accompanying charts provide details on the size and nature of this work. Also noted in the profile are work on the Strategic Defense Initiatives ("Star Wars") missile defense system, and improper billing controversies.

Among the companies in this book, the appliance industry had the heaviest concentration of weapons-related contractors. Major players here included General Electric, Raytheon (which manufactures Amana, Caloric, and Speed

Top 30 Department of Defense Prime Contractors
Fiscal Year 1985

Company	Millions of Dollars
McDonnell Douglas	$8,857
General Dynamics	7,440
Rockwell International	6,264
GE	5,891
Boeing	5,458
Lockheed	5,082
United Technologies	3,906
Hughes	3,551
Raytheon	2,999
Grumman	2,733
Martin Marietta	2,717
Westinghouse	1,941
Textron	1,920
Honeywell	1,908
IBM	1,783
Sperry	1,628
GM	1,614
LTV	1,585
Litton	1,528
ITT	1,503
Texas Instruments	1,426
Allied Signal	1,348
RCA	1,315
Tenneco	1,250
Northrop	1,195
Ogden	1,156
TRW	1,079
Ford	1,019
Eaton	923
Royal Dutch Shell	893

Source: Department of Defense.

Queen appliances), United Technologies (owner of the Carrier air conditioner company), and the Litton conglomerate. RCA, with its home entertainment businesses, and IBM, a giant in the typewriter and personal computer marketplaces, have major roles in arms contracting as well. However, some appliance companies, such as Maytag and Whirlpool, manufacture only consumer product lines.

By adding to its previously substantial military business, General Motors' 1985 acquisition of Hughes Aircraft places it among the top U.S. military contractors. Ford's Aerospace division has long made defense a part of that company's overall production.

It may surprise readers to find food producers involved in weapons work, but Tenneco is a major shipbuilder as well as agricultural grower. Another conglomerate, IC Industries, producer of Old El Paso Mexican foods, has divisions substantially involved in weapons-related work.

Most of those concerned about the nuclear and conventional arms races, CEP included, favor negotiations of mutual, verifiable reductions in the superpowers' arsenals. But protests and international treaties have come and gone over the past 30 years with little discernible effect. While there is virtually unanimous agreement that the nuclear arms race must be halted and nuclear arsenals reduced, opinions on how reductions can be accomplished differ sharply.

Protests against nuclear weapons date back to the 1950s, when early antinuclear activists sailed boats into atmospheric-testing sites in the South Pacific. In the 1960s, the "Ban the Bomb" movement lost momentum once a joint U.S.-USSR treaty banned the atmospheric testing of nuclear and thermonuclear weapons. But the 1980s brought a resurgence in awareness of the full implications of a possible nuclear holocaust. A worldwide educational effort by physicians and scientists, as well as activists urging a freeze or reduction of the superpowers' nuclear arsenals, resulted in the formation of many organizations in the United States and abroad dedicated to the prevention of nuclear war.

Numerous cities and towns around the United States (including Chicago in March 1986) have designated themselves nuclear-free zones, declaring their intention not to have nuclear arms–related research or work within their confines. Takoma Park, Maryland, has gone a step further in deciding it would not even do business with companies having nuclear contracts. Such moves have been encouraged by the Baltimore-based Nuclear Free America. This organization urges consumers to boycott nuclear arms contractors in protest against the U.S. government's massive spending, and against corporations that profit from the nuclear arms race.

The huge and rapidly growing U.S. military budget has also aroused fears about the possible harmful effects of an exacerbated conventional arms race on the U.S. economy. Like many analysts, CEP has linked the enormous U.S. federal budget deficits since 1980 largely to bloated Department of Defense spending. In addition, studies by CEP and others demonstrate the detrimental consequences of military spending on an economy. Military procurement is an inefficient way of creating employment because civilian spending creates more jobs per dollar spent. Excessive military spending has also been shown to be harmful to U.S. commercial competitiveness. One reason is that civilian technological development is impeded by the diversion of scientists and engi-

Public Corporations with the Greatest Prime Contract Funding for Primary Nuclear Warfare Systems, Fiscal Year 1983[1]

Company	DoD Contract Awards	DoE Contract Funding	Total
		(millions of dollars)	
Rockwell International	$3,521	$634	$4,155
Boeing	2,474	—	2,474
GE	878	134	1,012
Lockheed	942	—	942
General Dynamics	900	—	900
Martin Marietta[2]	883	—	883
Du Pont	—	700[4]	700
AT&T	31	650[4]	681
Allied	14	490	504
EG&G	—	470	470
Union Carbide[2]	—	385[4]	385
Eaton	355	—	355
ITT	250	—	250
Northrop[3]	242	—	242
Tenneco	241	—	241
Westinghouse	233	—[5]	233
GenCorp	233	—	233
TRW	214	—	214
GTE	203	—	203
UNC Resources	—	178	178
Avco	177	—	177

neers to military projects. Another contributing factor is the relatively lower rates of investments in new plants and equipment by countries with proportionately higher military spending.

Since 1980, some church groups have called on corporations to develop ethical guidelines in deciding whether or not to bid for military contracts. But companies almost invariably argue that it is not their prerogative to determine how much of what kind of military production the federal government requires. These decisions are questions of national security, they assert, and should be the responsibility of democratically elected officials.

In response, church groups and various other critics argue that some weapons, such as antipersonnel, chemical, and nuclear weapons, are qualitatively different from others. Companies would be exercising commonly accepted moral principles when considering the implications of producing these weapons.

(continued)

Morton Thiokol	145	—	145
McDonnell Douglas	145	—	145
Honeywell	144	—	144
Monsanto	—	143	143
E-Systems	142	—	142
Raytheon	122	—	122
Sperry	105	—	105
Hercules	94	—	94
RCA	88	—	88

1. The 30 investor-owned companies that received the largest total prime contract awards from the Departments of Defense and Energy in FY 1983 for nuclear warfare systems designated primary by IRRC. Private contractors that would appear on a comprehensive list include the University of California and Mason & Hangar-Silas Mason.
2. In 1984, Martin Marietta replaced Union Carbide as contractor for management of DoE's Oak Ridge complex, including the Y-12 nuclear weapons components plant.
3. Contract awards for what may be Northrop's largest defense program, the Advanced Technology (Stealth) Bomber, are classified. If FY 1983 awards for the Stealth, still in the early stages of R&D in that year, were included, it is likely that Northrop would be ranked three to four places higher.
4. IRRC estimates of primary portion.
5. A small portion of DoE contract awards to the Westinghouse-managed Bettis Laboratory support the Trident submarine program. Because the actual total could not be reliably estimated, these awards are not included here.

Source: Stocking the Arsenal, Investor Responsibility Research Center, Washington, D.C., 1985, from Defense and Energy Departments' unclassified contract award listings. The information in this table is used by permission of the Investor Responsibility Research Center Inc. Copyright 1985, Investor Responsibility Research Center Inc.

Other critics of excessive military spending point out that companies actively pursue military contracts, lobby hard for funding weapons systems that they are developing or already have under contract, and contribute campaign funds through their political action committees (as well as donations by individual executives) to members of Congress in key positions to influence arms legislation. Through such actions these companies take an active advocacy role in military decision making.

Political Action Committee Contributions

Concern about excessive corporate influence on the democratic process prompted our inclusion of PAC information in this book. The Political Action Committee column accompanying the company profiles gives figures of contributions to federal congressional campaigns in the 1983–1984 election cycle and shows how these contributions were divided between Republicans and

Democrats. In a few profiles we have gone into further detail on company PAC activities.

Corporations have many avenues with which to influence the political process. But because of the recent dramatic growth in corporate PACs, the mounting controversy about their roles, and the availability of comparable figures on their contributions, we chose PACs as one measure of a company's political activism.

An active PAC is often only a part of a company's overall political efforts, which may also include lobbying or opposing referenda and initiatives at the state or municipal level. Philip Morris, for example, has been one of the largest PAC contributors to federal candidates in recent years; it has also aggressively lobbied in opposition to state laws restricting smoking in public places and contributed heavily in opposition to similar initiatives and referendum campaigns. Oil company PACs also tend to be huge; their influence is of particular concern to environmentalists. Amoco's well-funded PAC, Sun's activism in soliciting PAC contributions from shareholders, and Mobil's more general public political stances are discussed in the profiles. Among the largest PAC contributors are major defense contractors, many of which have recently been accused of illegal billing procedures and cost overruns on military contracts, which we have noted in their profiles.

Opponents of the present PAC system, such as Common Cause, argue that special interests — corporate and otherwise — have gained excessive influence over members of Congress, which leads to an increasingly factionalized political process, where the voices of these special interests drown out those advocating the public interest. PAC advocates, in contrast, assert that their activities enhance the ability of ordinary citizens to gain influence by uniting with like-minded others, and that PACs broaden debates in a democratic fashion.

Corporations were first allowed to create PACs in 1974, through campaign finance reform legislation that followed the disclosure of numerous illegal corporate contributions to President Nixon's 1972 reelection campaign. The number of business and special-interest PACs has grown dramatically since then, up to over 1,600 for businesses and just under 700 for trade associations as of 1985. Labor PACs, totaling just under 400, are also large spenders. Labor PACs spent a total of $47.4 million in 1983 and 1984; corporate PACs, $59.1 million; and trade associations, $53.9 million. (For PAC contributions to candidates, see PACs by Type and Contributions on page 41.)

As the number of PACs has grown, so have concerns over their influence, particularly their tendency to favor incumbents. By giving primarily to incumbents, sponsors of PACs appear to be most concerned with simply currying favor with those already in power. According to the Federal Election Commission, incumbents received approximately 72 percent of all PAC contributions

Top 30 Corporate Contributors to Federal Candidates
1983–1984*

Lockheed PAC	$420,441
Tenneco Employees Good Government Fund	366,700
Philip Morris PAC	356,875
Rockwell International Good Govt. Committee	342,140
Amoco PAC	307,499
United Technologies PAC	285,280
American Family PAC	278,350
Sunbelt Good Govt. Comm. of Winn-Dixie Stores	261,825
Harris Corp. Federal PAC	261,550
General Dynamics Voluntary Political Contribution Plan	256,031
Northrop Employees PAC	231,630
Litton Industries Employees Political Action Assistance Committee	228,000
American Security Council PAC FKA: National Security PAC	226,888
E. F. Hutton Group PAC	226,488
Merrill Lynch PAC	224,350
Civic Involvement Program/General Motors	223,867
Grumman PAC	223,410
FMC Good Government Program	220,650
Fluor Public Affairs Committee	212,800
Union Pacific Fund for Effective Government	207,115
Non-Partisan Political Support Committee for General Electric Employees	204,125
Union Oil Political Awareness Fund	201,300
Avco PAC	194,650
Exxon PAC	193,350
Westinghouse Electric Employees Political Participation Program	188,285
UPS PAC	186,528
TRW Good Govt. Fund	183,595
Sun PAC	182,650
Hughes Aircraft Active Citizenship Fund	182,645
Continental Telecom PAC	182,150

* See also the table on page 42.
Source: Federal Election Commission.

to federal candidates in the 1983–1984 election cycle, while only 16 percent went to challengers. Of the total $38.9 million in *corporate* PAC contributions to federal candidates in 1983 and 1984, $30.5 million (77 percent) went to incumbents and only $4.3 million (11 percent) went to challengers. Another $4.1 million was spent in campaigns in which there was no incumbent and all candidates were running for the first time.

Top 20 PAC Contributors to Federal Candidates
1983–1984

Realtors PAC	$2,429,552
American Medical Association PAC	1,839,464
Build PAC of the National Association of Home Builders	1,625,539
National Education Association PAC	1,574,003
UAW–V–CAP	1,405,107
Seafarers Political Activity Donation	1,322,410
Machinists Non-Partisan Political League	1,306,497
Active Ballot Club (United Food & Commercial Workers Int'l Union)	1,271,974
Committee on Letter Carriers Political Education	1,234,603
National Association of Retired Federal Employees PAC	1,099,243
Committee for Thorough Agricultural Political Education of Associated Milk Producers	1,087,658
Automobile and Truck Dealers Election Action Committee	1,057,165
American Federation of State, County, and Municipal Employees—P.E.O.P.L.E. Qualified	905,806
National Association of Life Underwriters PAC	900,200
American Bankers Association Bankpac	882,850
National Committee for an Effective Congress	796,522
Engineers Political Education Committee/ Int'l Union of Operating Engineers	775,722
Citizens for the Republic	762,320
National PAC	749,500
Marine Engineers' Beneficial Association PAC	735,642

Source: Federal Election Commission.

In preparing this book, we analyzed the distribution of PAC contributions among incumbents and challengers for a sampling of the companies included. It appeared that these corporate PACs gave a consistent 90 percent or more of their funds to incumbents.

There is widespread concern in Congress about the influence of PACs. As Massachusetts congressman Barney Frank put it when speaking of a candidate's dilemma in accepting PAC contributions: "We [members of Congress] are the only human beings in the world who are expected to take thousands of dollars from perfect strangers on important matters and not be affected by it."

PACs by Type and Contributions to Candidates, 1983–1984

Committee Type	Number of Committees	Total Contributions
Corporations	1,508	$38,808,700
Labor organizations	285	26,205,562
Non-connected organizations	508	15,270,401
Trade/member/health organizations	564	28,195,995
Cooperative	49	2,621,313
Corporations without stock	92	1,499,762
Total	3,006	$112,601,733

Source: Federal Election Commission.

Critics are especially concerned that PACs have indirectly opened flood-gates channeling corporate funds to national candidates. In 1975 the Sun Company won a Federal Election Commission ruling allowing businesses to spend corporate funds to establish and run their PACs and *to solicit funds* for these PACs. Corporations can thus spend a dollar (or more) to raise a dollar. In addition, although it is illegal to do so, employees are sometimes pressured to contribute to the company PACs. For example, in 1985, Mutual Bank in Boston pleaded guilty to violations of federal law as a result of a strongly worded letter from its president, Keith G. Willoughby, to its officers. According to the *Boston Globe*, Willoughby noted that only 19 bank officers had contributed to the company PAC: "This is unacceptable. . . . Every single officer of this institution should — must — consider it a part of his or her position to contribute. I hope none of you is so naive as to think that political contributions — even those from PACs despite all the pious rhetoric — do not play a vital part [in the passage of legislation]." (At the time of the guilty plea, Willoughby wrote employees that he did not know "that [he] was required to include a disclaimer emphasizing under federal law everyone has a right to refuse to make contributions.")

PACs are not the only form of political spending by corporations. Immense amounts are spent on lobbying. Corporate contributions to ballot question campaigns (initiatives and referenda) have been upheld by the U.S. Supreme Court. In certain states direct business contributions to local candidates are still permissible. Personal contributions from management can also be a form of corporate influence.

Public financing of congressional campaigns is advocated by Common Cause and by many organizations, office holders, and individuals who wish to see the influence of PACs reduced. They point to the relatively smaller role PACs play in the now publicly financed presidential campaigns. While public

Profiled Companies with PAC Expenditures over $100,000, 1983–1984

Company	Dollars	% Dem.	% Rep.
Philip Morris	$374,172	58%	42%
Tenneco	366,700	17	83
Amoco	307,499	16	84
United Technologies	285,280	36	64
Dow Chemical	284,700	8	92
GTE	228,790	50	50
GM	228,017	23	77
Litton Industries	227,500	22	78
GE	226,550	53	47
Exxon	193,350	15	85
Sun	183,150	9	91
RJR Nabisco	176,180	57	43
Shell Oil	174,220	19	81
McDonald's	173,275	20	80
PepsiCo	165,524	15	85
Pillsbury	161,107	14	86
ITT	161,075	35	65
Holiday Inns	152,870	21	79
Greyhound	146,250	37	63
Chevron	145,020	29	71
Raytheon	138,125	50	50
Mobil	138,019	17	83
Pfizer	134,450	45	55
Coca-Cola	129,270	56	44
Abbott Laboratories	126,875	21	79
Texaco	125,410	20	80
Kellogg	120,499	47	53
General Mills	109,405	33	67
Household International	107,700	38	62
IC Industries	104,302	48	52

Note: The totals here include PAC expenditures by subsidiaries of companies as well as parent companies. The Federal Election Commission's list of top corporate spenders lists only spending by single PACs. Thus, for example, Dow—with eight separate PACs—shows up high on CEP's list, but not on the FEC's.

Source: Federal Election Commission.

financing would not eliminate PACs entirely, it would certainly restrain the powerful influence they exert on national politics.

We did not include a PAC column in the product charts because, while this is an important and controversial issue, we felt it was both more complex and of less general concern than the other issues. However, this information does appear on the charts accompanying the company profiles.

Of the 130 companies in this book, 86, or two-thirds, had PACs. Of these 86, the PACs of 30 companies gave over $100,000 to congressional candidates, while another 35 gave under $50,000. Of the 30 that gave over $100,000, 15 gave more than 75 percent of their contributions to Republican candidates, led by Dow Chemical and Sun with 92 percent and 91 percent, respectively. Six of these 30 companies gave 50 percent or more to Democratic candidates, the two largest donors being Philip Morris and RJR Nabisco, with 58 percent and 57 percent, respectively. Of Ogden's $41,000 in PAC giving, 85 percent went to Democratic candidates, the highest percentage for any company profiled in this book.

COMPANY CHARTS

For information about the company charts accompanying the profiles, see Chapter 4.

PROFILES

The profiles highlight exceptional social initiatives or controversies in which individual companies have been recently involved. They also provide additional pertinent information to explain and supplement our ratings of the companies covered in the product charts.

Wherever possible, we have attempted to give an overall feeling for the character of a company concerning social issues, along with a brief explanation of what is involved in initiating model programs to tackle social problems. Just as companies vary widely in the extent of their programs, so the profiles vary in what we have chosen to highlight; the differing lengths of the profiles also reflect the broad range of information we were able to find. But we have made every effort to include figures and facts on programs in a format that facilitates comparisons among companies.

We have paid particular attention to several issues that do not show up in the charts, notably minority economic development programs.

Where possible, we have given figures on the size and scope of minority banking or minority purchasing programs. Under these programs, corporations commit themselves to subcontracting a certain dollar value of work with minority-owned businesses, or to conduct a set amount of their banking with minority-owned financial institutions. Some companies have similar programs for placing subcontracts with women-owned companies or with businesses owned or operated by the handicapped. We have reported these figures as well, when available.

In the area of employee relations, we have mentioned major difficulties or long-term union-management accords in cases where they have played a prominent role in the companies' recent history. We have highlighted companies that appear to treat their employees particularly well, either through comprehensive and imaginative benefits packages or through worker participation and involvement programs. Many of the other firms profiled in this book also reported various benefit or employee-involvement programs. But in the absence of evidence of an outstanding program, we chose to provide details in exceptional cases only. In particular, we have confined mention of employee-involvement programs to the airline and automobile industries, where they have been especially controversial since 1980. This is a rapidly changing and expanding field, with a variety of programs and related debates over their merits that were beyond the scope of this book.

The most lengthy profiles are, for the most part, those of companies with both extensive initiatives and controversies — General Motors, for example. We found few companies that had extensive social programs without some negatives as well.

For certain companies, specific controversies have dominated their recent history — A. H. Robins and Dow Chemical, for example. Yet even here the overall record is often mixed. Dow, for example, had the most generous charitable giving program among companies profiled in this book.

In other cases we have documented one particular program on which a company has made an exceptional effort, such as Kellogg's minority banking program or Ralston Purina's participation in a neighborhood revitalization project, but these companies did not cooperate in providing details on other programs.

For various companies, primarily those that did not cooperate in providing CEP with information for this book, the profiles are brief. We cannot be certain that this reflects an absence of initiatives, but our attempts to locate evidence of notable social efforts, both from the companies and from outside sources, have yielded little of substance.

Many of the profiles contain examples of exceptional pioneering efforts in areas now being addressed by many other companies. Some of these include:

- 3M's early commitment to pollution prevention in its manufacturing operations;

- Kimberly-Clark's decision to spend heavily on physical fitness facilities and counseling services for its employees;

- Beatrice's prominent role in aiding food banks to feed the hungry around the country;

- General Electric's leadership role in promoting educational opportunities in engineering for women and minorities;

- Clorox's support for youth programs in its economically depressed head-quarters city of Oakland, California.

Our belief is that as you read the profiles and compare our ratings and the information in the accompanying charts, an overall view will emerge of the nature and extent of a company's commitment to the public good.

Chapter 4

HOW TO USE THIS BOOK

When using this book, be sure to consult both the product charts and the company charts and profiles. The product charts permit a quick comparative overview of how we rated different manufacturers on specific social issues. But for a fuller picture of a company's particular strengths or weaknesses when it comes to addressing social problems, you will need to read the profiles.

Note that the product charts do not comment on or recommend the products themselves. For many products, ranging from vitamins to automobiles, you will want to give careful consideration to issues of safety, reliability, and appropriateness to your needs.

PRODUCT CHARTS

By glancing across the columns in the product charts, you can obtain an approximate idea of the degree to which we believe a company is committed to charitable contributions, women and minorities among directors and top officers, disclosure of social information, involvement in South Africa, and conventional- or nuclear-arms contracting.

The significance of the symbols used for each issue is described below. See also Appendix A for a more complete discussion of how CEP determined these figures and their significance.

Size of Charitable Contributions

$$$. The company contributed what CEP views as an *above-average*, over 1.0 percent of net pre-tax earnings to charitable causes.

$$. The company contributed what CEP views as an *average*, over 0.6 percent to 1.0 percent of net pre-tax earnings to charitable causes.

$. The company contributed what CEP views as a *below-average* 0.6 percent or less of net pre-tax earnings to charitable causes.

Of the companies for which it was possible to calculate pre-tax earnings, approximately equal numbers fell into each of the above three categories.

See profile. For a number of companies for which we obtained a dollar figure on charitable giving it was nevertheless not possible to calculate this figure as a percentage of pre-tax earnings. This problem usually arose when companies had losses in previous years, but also occurred if they were privately held and did not release earnings figures. For these categories, "See profile" appears in their charitable contributions column, and the dollar figure on their giving is listed in the profile.

?. For these companies we were unable to ascertain the size or nature of giving programs. They apparently have no foundation. They may or may not give directly to charitable organizations, but provided no information to CEP in this area.

Women and Minority Directors and Officers

♀♀♀. The company had at least two women or at least two minorities *both* on its board of directors and among its top officers.

♀♀. The company had at least one woman or at least one minority *both* on its board of directors and among its top officers.

♀. The company had at least one woman or at least one minority in *one* of these two categories.

No. This means that the company had *no* women and *no* minorities on either its board of directors or among its top officers. (See also the *Note* below.)

?. For those companies that refused to provide CEP with information on minorities among their boards of directors and top officers, we have listed a question mark.

Note: For a limited number of companies, information on minorities was available only for the board of directors. If there was a minority on the board, we gave the company a **♀**. If there were no minorities on the board, we gave the company a **No**. In both cases it is possible the company has minorities among its top officers and would have received a higher rating if more information had been supplied.

For the representation of women on boards of directors and among top officers our information is complete.

Social Disclosure

✍✍✍. The company responded to CEP's questionnaires or otherwise publishes factual information on several social programs.

📖📖. The company did not respond to CEP's questionnaires, but provided what we consider limited cooperation with CEP on a single issue, or publishes factual information on a single issue (usually charitable contributions).

No. The company did not respond to CEP's questionnaires and does not publish information on its socially related programs in its annual report or in other special reports that we could locate.

Approximately equal numbers of companies fell into the 📖📖📖 and **No** categories, with a substantially smaller number receiving the 📖📖 rating.

Involvement in South Africa

No. The company had no operations in South Africa as of early 1987. It may also endorse the Sullivan Principles but has no employees or equity interest in South Africa (rating IV). (For a complete explanation of the Sullivan Principles, refer to Chapter 3; see page 53 for an explanation of the ratings.)

Yes A. As of 1985 the company received the highest "making good progress" rating (I) for compliance with the Sullivan Principles, and has not been identified by a coalition of 50 Protestant and Roman Catholic church groups as serving a particularly strategic role by supplying goods that help the South African government and its apartheid laws.

Yes B. As of 1985 the company's South African operations have received the second-highest "making progress" rating (II) for compliance with the Sullivan Principles, or despite a higher Sullivan rating, the company was considered by a coalition of 50 Protestant and Roman Catholic church groups as serving a particularly strategic role by supplying goods that help the South African government and its apartheid laws.

Yes C. The company has operations in South Africa and is not a signatory of the Sullivan Principles, or it received a low rating for compliance with the Sullivan Principles (rating IIIA or IIIB), or that it was a new signatory in 1985 (rating V) and therefore had not been independently evaluated. Companies might be recent signatories because they only recently acquired South African subsidiaries. Companies with operations in South Africa may also comply in practice with the Sullivan Principles, although they are not signatories.

Yes A/B or **Yes B/C**. If a company has several subsidiaries in South Africa, their compliance with the Sullivan Principles is evaluated separately, and these ratings occasionally vary for the different subsidiaries. Where subsidiaries with more than two-thirds of a company's total number of workers in South Africa received one rating, we have classed that company as totally in that category. But in those few cases where the number of its workers in its subsidiaries was more or less evenly divided into two categories, we have given the company a split rating.

Size of Charitable Contributions	Women Directors and Officers	Minority Directors and Officers	Social Disclosure	Brand Name	Company (Profile Page)	Involvement in South Africa	Conv. Weapons–Related Contracts	Nuclear Weapons–Related Contracts	Authors' Company of Choice
$ $ $	🚶 🚶 🚶	🚶 🚶	✍ ✍ ✍	Yoplait yogurts	General Mills (p. 135)	No	No	No	✔
③	④	⑤	⑥	①	②	⑦	⑧	⑨	⑩

Explanation

1. Brand-name product
2. Manufacturer (company profile appears on p. 135)
3. Contributed over 1.0% of net pre-tax earnings to charitable causes
4. Has at least two women on both its board of directors and among its top officers
5. Has at least one minority on both its board of directors and among its top officers
6. Cooperated in providing information on its social programs
7. No operations in South Africa
8. No conventional weapons–related contracts
9. No nuclear arms–related contracts
10. The company is preferred by the authors

Yes/?. Unilever is a signatory of the European Economic Community's code for companies in member countries with South African operations. There is no outside evaluation of compliance with this code. Swiss-based Nestlé has operations in South Africa, although Switzerland is not a member of the European Economic Community. We found no evaluation of its operations there.

Conventional Weapons–Related Contracts

No. We were unable to locate more than $10 million in weapons-related contracts for this company with the Department of Defense in 1984. The vast majority of the companies in this category had no weapons-related contracts. We did not feel that contracts of less than $10 million were sufficient to rank

How to Use This Book

Size of Charitable Contributions	Women Directors and Officers	Minority Directors and Officers	Social Disclosure	Brand Name	Company (Profile Page)	Involvement in South Africa	Conv. Weapons–Related Contracts	Nuclear Weapons–Related Contracts	Authors' Company of Choice
$ $	No	?	No	Amana Caloric Glenwood Modern Maid	Raytheon (p. 367)	Yes B/C	✈ ✈ ✈	Yes	
③	④	⑤	⑥	①	②	⑦	⑧	⑨	⑩

Explanation

1. Brand-name products
2. Manufacturer (company profile appears on p. 367)
3. Contributed between 0.6% and 1.0% of net pre-tax earnings to charitable causes
4. Has no women on its board of directors or among its top officers
5. Refused to disclose if minorities are on its board of directors or among its top officers
6. Did not cooperate in providing information on its social programs
7. Has subsidiaries in South Africa that received average and poor ratings for compliance with the Sullivan Principles
8. Arms contracts total more than 3% of sales
9. Involved in nuclear weapons–related work
10. The company is not preferred by the authors

a company as a substantial arms contractor. When a company had arms-related contracts of between $1 million and $10 million, we have noted the size of the contracts in its profile. (See Appendix A for details on which contracts were considered arms-related.)

✈✈. Weapons-related contracts with the Department of Defense were under 3 percent of the company's sales for 1984.

✈✈✈. Weapons-related contracts with the Department of Defense totaled more than 3 percent of the company's sales for 1984.

Of the companies profiled in this book, 99 had no substanitial weapons-related contracts, 20 had military contracts equaling 3 percent or less of total sales, and 11 had military business accounts equaling over 3 percent of total sales.

Nuclear Weapons–Related Contracts

Yes. The company is involved in nuclear-related arms work. See the profiles for details on its size and nature.

No. The company is not involved in nuclear-related arms work.

Authors' Company of Choice

A ✔ in this column indicates that this company is one that the authors of this book have selected as their personal preference after considering information in the company profiles and the data reflected by the product chart ratings. *No preference or opinion is expressed about the products themselves.* Readers may agree or disagree with our company preferences, depending on how strongly they feel about particular issues. Our preferences are not "recommendations" by CEP in any sense, but are personal choices given the particular priorities of the three authors. Our choices are included to illustrate one way in which this book might be used. You can use this column to note your own choices.

CHARTS WITH THE COMPANY PROFILES

The charts accompanying the company profiles are similar to the product charts but are more detailed. They also include data on Political Action Committee contributions to federal candidates.

% to Charity

The figure in this box is the actual percentage of net pre-tax earnings that the company gave to charitable organizations. The greater the percentage, the more of its profits a company donated to philanthropic causes. Generally, a 1 percent giving level is considered average. (See Appendix A for a discussion of the difficulties and intricacies involved in these calculations.)

If calculations of this percentage were not possible due to losses in previous years or to an absence of earnings figures (in the case of privately held corporations), **See profile** indicates that details on the dollar value of the company's giving are included in the profile. A **?** means we could find no information on a company's giving program.

Women Directors and Officers

The number in the left-hand side of this box is the number of women on the company's board of directors. The number in the right-hand side is the number of women in the company's top management, defined as vice presidential level among corporate staff or heads of divisions or subsidiaries.

Minority Directors and Officers

The same as above, except that a **?** means that the company failed or refused to supply this information for publication in this book.

Social Disclosure

The same rating system and criteria are used for the letter grades in this box as were used for the symbols in the product charts for this column. Here **A** means best disclosure; **C**, average disclosure; and **F**, poor disclosure. These are the only three grades given here.

Sullivan Rating (South Africa)

In this box we have provided the actual rating for compliance with the Sullivan Principles as listed in the independent evaluation conducted by the Arthur D. Little consulting firm for 1985. The ratings are given in roman numerals as follows:

I   Making good progress
IIA   Making progress, based on full reporting
IIB   Making progress, based on short-form reporting
IIIA Needs to become more active; passed all basic requirements but received low point rating
IIIB Needs to become more active; did not pass basic requirements
IV   Endorser with no employees and no equity
V   New signatory (not rated)

Companies with fewer than 25 employees or less than 50 percent equity in their operations were allowed to complete a short, rather than a long, form in reporting on their employment practices (see rating II above). However, a company can only receive a I rating if it has completed the long-form report.

Non-signatory means that a company was not considered a signatory of the Sullivan Principles as of 1985, although it has operations in that country.

% Military Contracts

The figure in this box gives the company's arms-related Department of Defense contracts as a percentage of its sales for 1984. (See Appendix A for research methods used in calculating this figure.)

Negligible in this box means that the company had between $1 million and $10 million in arms-related prime contracts in 1984. These are noted briefly in the company profile, but we did not class these companies as major military contractors in the product chart listings.

GENERAL MILLS, INC.											
	Women		Minorities				Contracts		PAC Contributions		
% to Charity	Directors	Officers	Directors	Officers	Social Disclosure	Sullivan Rating	% Military	Nuclear Weapons–Related	Dollar Amount	% to Republicans	% to Democrats
2.1%	2	3	1	2	A	None	None	None	$109,405	67%	33%
①	②		③	④	⑤	⑥		⑦	⑧		

Explanation

1. Gave 2.1% of net pre-tax earnings to charities
2. Has two women on its board of directors and three women among its top officers
3. Has one minority on its board of directors and two minorities among its top officers
4. Best disclosure of social information for this book
5. Not involved in South Africa
6. No conventional weapons–related contracts
7. No nuclear weapons–related contracts
8. Its PACs gave $109,405 to federal candidates in 1983 and 1984; 67% went to Republican candidates, 33% to Democratic candidates

Nuclear Weapons–Related Contracts

This box indicates whether or not a company is involved in nuclear weapons–related work.

PAC (Political Action Committee) Contributions

The dollar figure in the first box is the total given by the company's Political Action Committees to federal candidates in the 1983–1984 election cycle.

The percentage figures represent the proportion of these funds contributed to Republican and Democratic candidates. No funds were given to candidates of any other party.

A Note on Mergers, Acquisitions, and Divestitures

Hardly a week went by, as we were preparing this book, that one or another of the companies we were covering was not in the financial news be-

How to Use This Book

RAYTHEON COMPANY											
	Women		Minorities				Contracts		PAC Contributions		
% to Charity	Directors	Officers	Directors	Officers	Social Disclosure	Sullivan Rating	% Military	Nuclear Weapons– Related	Dollar Amount	% to Republicans	% to Democrats
0.8%	0	0	?	?	F	IIB/ IIIA	51.6%	Yes	$138,125	50%	50%
①	②		③	④	⑤		⑥	⑦	⑧		

Explanation

1. Gave 0.8% of net pre-tax earnings to charities
2. Has no women on its board of directors and no women among its top officers
3. Would not disclose if there are minorities on its board of directors or among its top officers
4. Did not provide social information for this book
5. Operations in South Africa received second and third ratings for compliance with the Sullivan Principles
6. Department of Defense contracts represented 51.6% of the company's total sales for 1984
7. Involved in nuclear arms–related work
8. Its PACs gave $138,125 to federal candidates in 1983 and 1984; 50% went to Republican candidates, 50% to Democratic candidates

cause of acquisitions, major divestitures or restructuring, friendly takeovers, or all-out battles for ownership.

These restless stirrings in the business community caused a number of problems for us in the final stages of preparing the manuscript. For example, General Foods, for which we had written a complete profile, was taken over by Philip Morris; Richardson-Vicks was acquired by Procter & Gamble; Hoover was taken over by the Chicago Pacific Corporation, for which we had not gathered information. Revlon was acquired by Pantry Pride, which in turn immediately sold several of Revlon's major divisions. General Electric and RCA merged. Dart & Kraft announced it would be splitting into two separate companies. At the same time, other companies, particularly in the food and oil industries, were busy selling off subsidiaries not directly related to their primary line of business. For example, General Mills spun off its toy and fashion subsidiaries, PepsiCo sold its sporting goods and trucking businesses, and Atlantic Richfield disposed of all its non-oil concerns.

Because of complications in making major changes in the format of this book in the late stages, we opted to note major acquisitions after November 1985 in the profiles of the companies, but did not attempt to integrate the changes into the product charts or to add profiles of the new corporate players in these consumer markets. (See also the addendum on page 500.)

While the relative merits of conglomerates versus single-industry companies and the problems caused by mergers and acquisitions are beyond the scope of this book, we should note nevertheless that many people in the business press have been critical of most acquisitions and mergers as disruptive to management, workers, and the conduct of their business. (Beatrice's history over the past decade is one frequently cited example here.) Furthermore, the more wide-flung a company's interests are the more likely it seems to be involved in areas of major controversy. For instance, both General Foods and Nabisco are now owned by tobacco manufacturers.

PART TWO

Chapter 5

IN THE SUPERMARKET
Food Product Companies

CHARITABLE CONTRIBUTIONS AND COMMUNITY INVOLVEMENT

Of the companies profiled in this chapter, Anheuser-Busch, Beatrice, General Mills, McCormick, and Pillsbury have given over 1.5 percent of pre-tax earnings to charity. General Mills stands out for its particularly strong charitable giving program. Pillsbury also provides well-rounded support for community projects. Its Burger King subsidiary has recently established an innovative scholarship program to encourage post-secondary-school education among its employees. Sara Lee's charitable giving, which devotes 50 percent to the economically disadvantaged, accompanied by an unusual awards program, is also noteworthy. Individual social programs at Kellogg (minority banking) and Quaker Oats (charitable contributions) can be singled out for praise, but, unfortunately, neither company provided complete information for this book.

Beatrice, along with other major food companies, supports the Second Harvest National Food Bank Network and similar organizations devoted to feeding the hungry. Since 1980 many food companies, including General Mills, Sara Lee, and Kraft, have been providing both surplus food products and technical and financial assistance, supplementing federal programs that support the food banks.

REPRESENTATION OF WOMEN AND MINORITIES IN MANAGEMENT

Four food companies had at least one minority and one woman both in their top management and on their board of directors: Anheuser-Busch, Coca-Cola, General Mills, and Kellogg. Anheuser-Busch was the only food company with two minority group members in both categories. Three companies — Campbell, General Mills, and Ogden — had at least two women in both categories.

INVOLVEMENT IN SOUTH AFRICA

Almost three-quarters of the food companies profiled in this chapter have no involvement in South Africa. General Foods and PepsiCo sold their interests there in 1985. Of those with operations in that country, Borden and Kellogg had the best records for compliance with the Sullivan Principles. Sara Lee and Coca-Cola announced sales of their operations in South Africa in 1986.

CONVENTIONAL- OR NUCLEAR-ARMS CONTRACTS

The Tenneco conglomerate is by far the largest military contractor within the food industry. Another conglomerate, IC Industries, makers of Old El Paso Mexican foods, is a military contractor as well.

POLITICAL ACTION COMMITTEE CONTRIBUTIONS

The most active PACs in the food industry belong to Philip Morris, Tenneco, and RJR Nabisco, followed by McDonald's, PepsiCo, Pillsbury, Coca-Cola, Kellogg, General Mills, and IC Industries.

OTHER CONTROVERSIES

For numerous food industry companies, records of social initiatives are offset somewhat by controversies. Campbell's strong community support for its headquarters city of Camden, New Jersey, and its commitment to the hiring and promotion of women were tempered by a lengthy and bitter confrontation with farm workers (now resolved) over working conditions in Ohio. Coca-Cola, which has undertaken moderate social efforts, grappled with a dispute from 1978 to 1985 over the alleged brutal suppression of unions at an independent Guatemalan bottling plant, which eventually aroused international protest. Beatrice, with its moderately well-rounded social programs, is an archetypical example of a conglomerate built on numerous acquisitions and sales of subsidiaries, which has reportedly led to discontent among some of its employees. Although the Swiss-owned Nestlé was subject to a long boycott because of its refusal to alter its marketing of infant formula in developing nations, it is now praised for its improved marketing practices by those who formerly led the boycott.

American Brands, Philip Morris, and RJR Nabisco (formerly R. J. Reynolds Industries) face increasing litigation related to consumers' claims that tobacco companies knowingly produce, advertise, and sell a product — cigarettes — that is a serious and potentially fatal health hazard. (In initial trials, however, these companies have been found not liable.) In 1985 the U.S. Office of Technology Assessment estimated that $12 billion to $35 billion would be spent

In the Supermarket

**Minority Purchasing Programs
Reported by Profiled Food Product Companies**

	Purchases from Minority Vendors	Total Sales
	(millions of dollars)	
Anheuser-Busch (1985)	$ 30.0	$ 7,000
Beatrice (1983)	38.1	9,327
Borden (1984)	31.0	4,568
Campbell (1985)	45.0	4,185
Coca-Cola (1985)	51.0	7,904
Dart & Kraft (1984)	19.8	9,759
General Foods (1984)	22.0	8,600
General Mills (1984)	3.7	5,600
International Multifoods (1985)	2.6	1,314
PepsiCo (1984)	20.0	7,699
Philip Morris (1984)	150.0	13,813
Pillsbury (1984)	4.6	4,172
RJR Nabisco (1984)	70.0	12,312

Source: Company responses to CEP inquiries.

that year to treat smoking-related diseases and that there were 314,000 smoking-related deaths.

Among cigarette companies, CEP credits Philip Morris for its particularly aggressive support of minority economic development and its patronage of the arts.

Along with other major advertisers for wine and beer, Anheuser-Busch, which has taken some strong social steps, has been occasionally attacked by some people concerned with alcoholism and drunk driving.

The nutritional quality of processed foods served by the fast-food chains is a matter of heated debate. There were apparently few major differences among the menus offered by the companies we profiled.

Among fast-food chains, Burger King and its parent company, Pillsbury, appear to have a good record for charitable giving programs and community involvement. McDonald's widely publicizes its donations and support to traditional causes such as youth athletics, muscular dystrophy, and the handicapped. However, since it did not provide overall information about charitable giving and other programs to CEP, a comparison with other companies was difficult to make.

A further issue raised in connection with the fast-food industry (and with the consumption of beef in general) is the destruction of forests in Central American countries due to expanding cattle ranching there. Douglas Shane's *Hoofprints on the Forest*, published in 1980 by the U.S. Department of State's Office of Environmental Affairs, is one of the more complete studies of this problem, which has evoked some heated controversy. But the issue is a complicated one and the role of fast-food companies is not clear. For these reasons we have not attempted to explore this issue in detail.

We have not attempted an overall assessment of the nutritional quality or other health-related aspects of food company products, nor have we included comparisons with the rapidly growing network of "health food" firms. But we have noted particular health-related controversies.

Consumers should be aware of health issues in making their purchasing decisions for food products. The Center for Science in the Public Interest is a strong advocate of improved nutritional policies from many major United States food companies. Foods high in fat, sugar, and salt can contribute to high blood pressure, heart disease, cancer, tooth decay, or obesity.

BEVERAGES

COCOA MIXES

Size of Charitable Contributions	Women Directors and Officers	Minority Directors and Officers	Social Disclosure	Brand Name	Company (Profile Page)	Involvement in South Africa	Conv. Weapons–Related Contracts	Nuclear Weapons–Related Contracts	Authors' Company of Choice
$ $ $	🏃🚶	🚶	✍ ✍ ✍	Swiss Miss	Beatrice (p. 118)	No	No	No	
$ $	🏃	?	No	Hershey	Hershey (p. 140)	No	No	No	✔
✳	No	?	No	Carnation Quik	Nestlé (p. 150)	Yes ?	No	No	

✳ = See company profile
? = No information available
Single figure ($, 🚶) = Minimal
Double figure ($$, 🚶🚶, ✍✍, 🚶🚶) = Moderate
Triple figure ($$$, 🚶🚶🚶, ✍✍✍, 🚶🚶🚶) = Substantial

No = No involvement or participation
Yes = Involvement or participation. A, B, C in the South African column reflect the degree of compliance with Sullivan Principles and/or involvement in strategic industries.

See Chapter 4 for a detailed discussion of chart symbols.

BEVERAGES

FRUIT AND VEGETABLE JUICES, DRINKS, AND MIXES

Size of Charitable Contributions	Women Directors and Officers	Minority Directors and Officers	Social Disclosure	Brand Name	Company (Profile Page)	Involvement in South Africa	Conv. Weapons–Related Contracts	Nuclear Weapons–Related Contracts	Authors' Company of Choice
$ $ $	🧍🧍	🧍	✍️ ✍️ ✍️	Hunt's Tropicana	Beatrice (p. 118)	No	No	No	
$	🧍🧍	🧍	✍️ ✍️ ✍️	Bama Sippin Pack Wylers	Borden (p. 120)	Yes A	No	No	
$ $	🧍🧍🧍	🧍	✍️ ✍️ ✍️	Juice Works Pepperidge Farm V-8	Campbell Soup (p. 122)	No	No	No	✔
*	🧍🧍	?	No	Dole	Castle & Cooke (p. 125)	No	No	No	
$	🧍🧍	🧍🧍	✍️ ✍️ ✍️	Five Alive Hi-C Minute Maid	Coca-Cola (p. 126)	No	No	No	

FRUIT AND VEGETABLE JUICES, DRINKS, AND MIXES *(cont'd.)*

Size of Charitable Contributions	Women Directors and Officers	Minority Directors and Officers	Social Disclosure	Brand Name	Company (Profile Page)	Involvement in South Africa	Conv. Weapons-Related Contracts	Nuclear Weapons-Related Contracts	Authors' Company of Choice
$ $ $	✦ ✦	✦	✍ ✍ ✍	Country Time Crystal Light Kool Aid Tang	General Foods (p. 132)	No	No	No	
✱	No	?	No	Juicy Juice Libby's	Nestlé (p. 150)	Yes ?	No	No	
$ $ $	✦	✦ ✦	✍ ✍ ✍	Citrus Hill	Procter & Gamble (p. 226)	No	No	No	✔
$ $ $	✦	✦ ✦	✍ ✍ ✍	Del Monte Hawaiian Punch	RJR Nabisco (p. 164)	Yes A/B	No	No	
$ $ $	✦	✦	✍ ✍ ✍	Capri Sun	Sara Lee (p. 167)	No	No	No	

✱ = See company profile
? = No information available
Single figure ($, ✦) = Minimal
Double figure ($$, ✦✦, ✍✍, ✦✦) = Moderate
Triple figure ($$$, ✦✦✦, ✍✍✍, ✦✦✦) = Substantial

No = No involvement or participation
Yes = Involvement or participation. A, B, C in the South African column reflect the degree of compliance with Sullivan Principles and/or involvement in strategic industries.

See Chapter 4 for a detailed discussion of chart symbols.

BEVERAGES

GROUND AND INSTANT COFFEES

Size of Charitable Contributions	Women Directors and Officers	Minority Directors and Officers	Social Disclosure	Brand Name	Company (Profile Page)	Involvement in South Africa	Conv. Weapons-Related Contracts	Nuclear Weapons-Related Contracts	Authors' Company of Choice
$	✦✦	✦	✍✍✍	Kava	Borden (p. 120)	Yes A	No	No	
$	✦✦	✦✦	✍✍✍	Butternut Maryland Club	Coca-Cola (p. 126)	No	No	No	
$ $ $	✦✦	✦	✍✍	Yuban Brim Maxim Maxwell House Mellow Roast Sanka	General Foods (p. 132)	No	No	No	
✱	No	?	No	Chase & Sanborn Hills Bros. MJB Nescafé Taster's Choice	Nestlé (p. 150)	Yes ?	No	No	
$ $ $	✦	✦✦	✍✍✍	Folgers High Point	Procter & Gamble (p. 226)	No	No	No	✔

✱ = See company profile
? = No information available
Single figure ($, ✦) = Minimal
Double figure ($$, ✦✦, ✍✍, ✦✦) = Moderate
Triple figure ($$$, ✦✦✦, ✍✍✍, ✦✦✦) = Substantial

No = No involvement or participation
Yes = Involvement or participation. A, B, C in the South African column reflect the degree of compliance with Sullivan Principles and/or involvement in strategic industries.

See Chapter 4 for a detailed discussion of chart symbols.

BEVERAGES

SOFT DRINKS

Size of Charitable Contributions	Women Directors and Officers	Minority Directors and Officers	Social Disclosure	Brand Name	Company (Profile Page)	Involvement in South Africa	Conv. Weapons–Related Contracts	Nuclear Weapons–Related Contracts	Authors' Company of Choice
$	👤 👤	👤 👤	✍ ✍ ✍	Coca-Cola Fanta Fresca Mello Yello Ramblin' Root Beer Sprite Tab	Coca-Cola (p. 126)	No	No	No	
$ $	No	👤	✍ ✍ ✍	Mountain Dew Pepsi Slice	PepsiCo (p. 153)	Yes C	No	No	
$ $	👤 👤	👤 👤	✍ ✍ ✍	7-Up	Philip Morris (p. 155)	No	No	No	
$ $ $	👤	👤 👤	✍ ✍ ✍	Crush Hires Root Beer	Procter & Gamble (p. 226)	No	No	No	✔
$ $	👤 👤	👤	✍ ✍	Gatorade	Quaker Oats (p. 160)	No	No	No	

* = See company profile
? = No information available
Single figure ($, 👤) = Minimal
Double figure ($$, 👤👤, ✍✍, 👤👤) = Moderate
Triple figure ($$$, 👤👤👤, ✍✍✍, 👤👤👤) = Substantial

No = No involvement or participation
Yes = Involvement or participation. A, B, C in the South African column reflect the degree of compliance with Sullivan Principles and/or involvement in strategic industries.

See Chapter 4 for a detailed discussion of chart symbols.

BEVERAGES

TEAS AND TEA MIXES

Size of Charitable Contributions	Women Directors and Officers	Minority Directors and Officers	Social Disclosure	Brand Name	Company (Profile Page)	Involvement in South Africa	Conv. Weapons–Related Contracts	Nuclear Weapons–Related Contracts	Authors' Company of Choice
$ $	♀ ♀	♀	✍ ✍ ✍	Celestial Seasonings	Dart & Kraft (p. 130)	No	No	No	
?	♀ ♀	♀ ♀	✍ ✍	Salada	Kellogg (p. 143)	Yes A	No	No	
*	No	?	No	Nestea	Nestlé (p. 150)	Yes ?	No	No	
$ $ $	♀	♀ ♀	✍ ✍ ✍	Tender Leaf	Procter & Gamble (p. 226)	No	No	No	✔
$	No	No	No	Lipton	Unilever (p. 171)	Yes ?	No	No	

* = See company profile
? = No information available
Single figure ($, ♀) = Minimal
Double figure ($$, ♀♀, ✍✍, ♀♀) = Moderate
Triple figure ($$$, ♀♀♀, ✍✍✍, ♀♀♀) = Substantial

No = No involvement or participation
Yes = Involvement or participation. A, B, C in the South African column reflect the degree of compliance with Sullivan Principles and/or involvement in strategic industries.

See Chapter 4 for a detailed discussion of chart symbols.

BREADS AND BAKED GOODS

BREADS AND BAKED GOODS

Size of Charitable Contributions	Women Directors and Officers	Minority Directors and Officers	Social Disclosure	Brand Name	Company (Profile Page)	Involvement in South Africa	Conv. Weapons–Related Contracts	Nuclear Weapons–Related Contracts	Authors' Company of Choice
$ $ $	⋀ ⋀	⋀ ⋀ ⋀	📢 📢	*Campbell Taggart brands:* Colonial Earth Grains Grant's Farms Kilpatricks Rainbo	Anheuser-Busch (p. 115)	No	No	No	✔
$ $	⋀ ⋀ ⋀	⋀	📢 📢 📢	Pepperidge Farm brand	Campbell Soup (p. 122)	No	No	No	✔
$	⋀	⋀	No	Thomas' Muffins	CPC Int'l. (p. 129)	Yes B	No	No	
$ $ $	⋀ ⋀	⋀	📢 📢 📢	Entenmann's baked goods Oroweat breads	General Foods (p. 132)	No	No	No	
$ $	⋀	?	No	Aunt Fanny's baked goods	IC Industries (p. 141)	No	✈ ✈	No	
$ $	⋀	?	📢 📢	Drake's baked goods *Continental bakery brands:* Beefsteak Breads Ding Dongs, Sno Balls, etc. Hostess Twinkies Home Pride Wonder Bread	Ralston Purina (p. 162)	No	No	No	

BREADS AND BAKED GOODS

CAKE AND PANCAKE MIXES

Size of Charitable Contributions	Women Directors and Officers	Minority Directors and Officers	Social Disclosure	Brand Name	Company (Profile Page)	Involvement in South Africa	Conv. Weapons–Related Contracts	Nuclear Weapons–Related Contracts	Authors' Company of Choice
$$$	🧍🧍	🧍	✍✍✍	Swan's Down	General Foods (p. 132)	No	No	No	
$$$	🧍🧍🧍	🧍🧍	✍✍✍	Betty Crocker Bisquick	General Mills (p. 135)	No	No	No	✔
$$$	🧍🧍	No	✍✍✍	Hungry Jack Pillsbury	Pillsbury (p. 158)	No	No	No	✔
$$$	🧍	🧍🧍	✍✍✍	Duncan Hines	Procter & Gamble (p. 226)	No	No	No	✔
$$	🧍🧍	🧍	✍✍	Aunt Jemima	Quaker Oats (p. 160)	No	No	No	

* = See company profile
? = No information available
Single figure ($, 🧍) = Minimal
Double figure ($$, 🧍🧍, ✍✍, 🧍🧍) = Moderate
Triple figure ($$$, 🧍🧍🧍, ✍✍✍, 🧍🧍🧍) = Substantial

No = No involvement or participation
Yes = Involvement or participation. A, B, C in the South African column reflect the degree of compliance with Sullivan Principles and/or involvement in strategic industries.

See Chapter 4 for a detailed discussion of chart symbols.

CANNED AND PREPARED FOODS

BAKED BEANS

Size of Charitable Contributions	Women Directors and Officers	Minority Directors and Officers	Social Disclosure	Brand Name	Company (Profile Page)	Involvement in South Africa	Conv. Weapons–Related Contracts	Nuclear Weapons–Related Contracts	Authors' Company of Choice
$ $	♠ ♠ ♠	♠ ♠ ♠	✍ ✍ ✍	Campbell's	Campbell Soup (p. 122)	No	No	No	✔
$ $ $	♠	No	✍ ✍	Heinz	Heinz (p. 138)	No	No	No	✔
$ $	♠	?	No	B & M Friends	IC Industries (p. 141)	No	✈ ✈	No	
$ $	♠ ♠	♠	✍ ✍	Van Camp's	Quaker Oats (p. 160)	No	No	No	✔

✳ = See company profile
? = No information available
Single figure ($, ♠) = Minimal
Double figure ($$, ♠♠, ✍✍, ✈✈) = Moderate
Triple figure ($$$, ♠♠♠, ✍✍✍, ✈✈✈) = Substantial

See Chapter 4 for a detailed discussion of chart symbols.

No = No involvement or participation
Yes = Involvement or participation. A, B, C in the South African column reflect the degree of compliance with Sullivan Principles and/or involvement in strategic industries.

CANNED AND PREPARED FOODS

CHINESE FOOD

Size of Charitable Contributions	Women Directors and Officers	Minority Directors and Officers	Social Disclosure	Brand Name	Company (Profile Page)	Involvement in South Africa	Conv. Weapons–Related Contracts	Nuclear Weapons–Related Contracts	Authors' Company of Choice
$ $ $	♀♀	♀	✍✍✍	La Choy	Beatrice (p. 118)	No	No	No	✔
$ $	No	No	✍✍	Chun King (frozen)	ConAgra (p. 128)	No	No	No	
$ $ $	♀	♀♀	✍✍✍	Chun King (canned)	RJR Nabisco (p. 164)	Yes A/B	No	No	

* = See company profile
? = No information available
Single figure ($, ♀) = Minimal
Double figure ($$, ♀♀, ✍✍, ♀♀) = Moderate
Triple figure ($$$, ♀♀♀, ✍✍✍, ♀♀♀) = Substantial

No = No involvement or participation
Yes = Involvement or participation. A, B, C in the South African column reflect the degree of compliance with Sullivan Principles and/or involvement in strategic industries.

See Chapter 4 for a detailed discussion of chart symbols.

In the Supermarket

CANNED AND PREPARED FOODS

FRUITS AND VEGETABLES

Size of Charitable Contributions	Women Directors and Officers	Minority Directors and Officers	Social Disclosure	Brand Name	Company (Profile Page)	Involvement in South Africa	Conv. Weapons–Related Contracts	Nuclear Weapons–Related Contracts	Authors' Company of Choice
*	🚶🚶	No	✍✍✍	Ranch Style	American Home Products (p. 406)	Yes A/B	No	No	
$ $ $	🚶🚶	🚶	✍✍✍	Hunt's	Beatrice (p. 118)	No	No	No	✔
*	🚶🚶	?	No	Dole	Castle & Cooke (p. 125)	No	No	No	
*	No	?	No	Contadina Libby's	Nestlé (p. 150)	Yes ?	No	No	
?	🚶🚶🚶	?	No	Progresso	Ogden (p. 152)	No	✈✈✈	No	
$ $ $	🚶🚶	No	✍✍✍	Green Giant Le Sueur	Pillsbury (p. 158)	No	No	No	✔
$ $ $	🚶	🚶🚶	✍✍✍	Del Monte	RJR Nabisco (p. 164)	Yes A/B	No	No	

CANNED AND PREPARED FOODS

MEXICAN FOOD

Size of Charitable Contributions	Women Directors and Officers	Minority Directors and Officers	Social Disclosure	Brand Name	Company (Profile Page)	Involvement in South Africa	Conv. Weapons–Related Contracts	Nuclear Weapons–Related Contracts	Authors' Company of Choice
$ $ $	♦ ♦	♦	✍ ✍ ✍	Gebhardt Rosarita	Beatrice (p. 118)	No	No	No	✔
$ $	No	No	✍ ✍	Patio	ConAgra (p. 128)	No	No	No	
$ $	♦	?	No	Old El Paso	IC Industries (p. 141)	No	✈ ✈	No	
$ $ $	No	?	No	Tio Sancho	McCormick (p. 146)	No	No	No	
?	♦ ♦ ♦	?	No	Las Palmas	Ogden (p. 152)	No	✈ ✈ ✈	No	
$ $ $	♦	♦ ♦	✍ ✍ ✍	Ortega	RJR Nabisco (p. 164)	Yes A/B	No	No	

* = See company profile
? = No information available
Single figure ($, ♦) = Minimal
Double figure ($$, ♦♦, ✍✍, ✈✈) = Moderate
Triple figure ($$$, ♦♦♦, ✍✍✍, ✈✈✈) = Substantial

No = No involvement or participation
Yes = Involvement or participation. A, B, C in the South African column reflect the degree of compliance with Sullivan Principles and/or involvement in strategic industries.

See Chapter 4 for a detailed discussion of chart symbols.

CANNED AND PREPARED FOODS

PASTA

Size of Charitable Contributions	Women Directors and Officers	Minority Directors and Officers	Social Disclosure	Brand Name	Company (Profile Page)	Involvement in South Africa	Conv. Weapons–Related Contracts	Nuclear Weapons–Related Contracts	Authors' Company of Choice
✱	⚊ ⚊	No	✍ ✍ ✍	Chef Boy-ar-dee	American Home Products (p. 406)	Yes A/B	No	No	
$ $	⚊ ⚊ ⚊	⚊	✍ ✍ ✍	Franco American	Campbell Soup (p. 122)	No	No	No	✔

✱ = See company profile
? = No information available
Single figure ($, ⚊) = Minimal
Double figure ($$, ⚊⚊, ✍✍, ⚊⚊) = Moderate
Triple figure ($$$, ⚊⚊⚊, ✍✍✍, ⚊⚊⚊) = Substantial

No = No involvement or participation
Yes = Involvement or participation. A, B, C in the South African column reflect the degree of compliance with Sullivan Principles and/or involvement in strategic industries.

See Chapter 4 for a detailed discussion of chart symbols.

CANNED AND PREPARED FOODS

SOUPS, BROTHS, AND SOUP MIXES

Size of Charitable Contributions	Women Directors and Officers	Minority Directors and Officers	Social Disclosure	Brand Name	Company (Profile Page)	Involvement in South Africa	Conv. Weapons–Related Contracts	Nuclear Weapons–Related Contracts	Authors' Company of Choice
$	♂♂ ♂	♂	✍✍✍	Snow's chowders	Borden (p. 120)	Yes A	No	No	
$ $	♂♂♂	♂	✍✍✍	Campbell Swanson	Campbell Soup (p. 122)	No	No	No	✔
$	♂	♂	No	Knorr	CPC Int'l. (p. 129)	Yes B	No	No	
*	No	?	No	Crosse & Blackwell	Nestlé (p. 150)	Yes ?	No	No	
?	♂♂♂	?	No	Progresso	Ogden (p. 152)	No	✈✈✈	No	
$ $ $	♂♂	♂♂	✍✍	College Inn	RJR Nabisco (p. 164)	Yes A/B	No	No	
$	No	No	No	Lipton	Unilever (p. 171)	Yes ?	No	No	

* = See company profile
? = No information available
Single figure ($, ♂) = Minimal
Double figure ($$, ♂♂, ✍✍, ✈✈) = Moderate
Triple figure ($$$, ♂♂♂, ✍✍✍, ✈✈✈) = Substantial

No = No involvement or participation
Yes = Involvement or participation. A, B, C in the South African column reflect the degree of compliance with Sullivan Principles and/or involvement in strategic industries.

See Chapter 4 for a detailed discussion of chart symbols.

CANNED AND PREPARED FOODS

SPAGHETTI SAUCES

Size of Charitable Contributions	Women Directors and Officers	Minority Directors and Officers	Social Disclosure	Brand Name	Company (Profile Page)	Involvement in South Africa	Conv. Weapons–Related Contracts	Nuclear Weapons–Related Contracts	Authors' Company of Choice
$ $ $	♦ ♦	♦	✍ ✍ ✍	Aunt Nellie's	Beatrice (p. 118)	No	No	No	
$ $	♦ ♦ ♦	♦	✍ ✍ ✍	Prego	Campbell Soup (p. 122)	No	No	No	✔
?	♦	?	No	Ragu	Chesebrough-Pond's (p. 210)	Yes C	No	No	
?	♦ ♦ ♦	?	No	Progresso	Ogden (p. 152)	No	✈ ✈ ✈	No	

* = See company profile
? = No information available
Single figure ($, ♦) = Minimal
Double figure ($$, ♦♦, ✍✍, ✈✈) = Moderate
Triple figure ($$$, ♦♦♦, ✍✍✍, ✈✈✈) = Substantial

No = No involvement or participation
Yes = Involvement or participation. A, B, C in the South African column reflect the degree of compliance with Sullivan Principles and/or involvement in strategic industries.

See Chapter 4 for a detailed discussion of chart symbols.

CANNED AND PREPARED FOODS

TUNA

Size of Charitable Contributions	Women Directors and Officers	Minority Directors and Officers	Social Disclosure	Brand Name	Company (Profile Page)	Involvement in South Africa	Conv. Weapons–Related Contracts	Nuclear Weapons–Related Contracts	Authors' Company of Choice
$ $ $	⋀	No	✍ ✍	Star-Kist	Heinz (p. 138)	No	No	No	✔
$ $	⋀	?	✍ ✍	Chicken of the Sea	Ralston Purina (p. 162)	No	No	No	

* = See company profile
? = No information available
Single figure ($, ⋀) = Minimal
Double figure ($$, ⋀⋀, ✍✍, ⋀⋀) = Moderate
Triple figure ($$$, ⋀⋀⋀, ✍✍✍, ⋀⋀⋀) = Substantial

No = No involvement or participation
Yes = Involvement or participation. A, B, C in the South African column reflect the degree of compliance with Sullivan Principles and/or involvement in strategic industries.

See Chapter 4 for a detailed discussion of chart symbols.

CEREALS, HOT AND COLD

HOT AND COLD CEREALS

Size of Charitable Contributions	Women Directors and Officers	Minority Directors and Officers	Social Disclosure	Brand Name	Company (Profile Page)	Involvement in South Africa	Conv. Weapons–Related Contracts	Nuclear Weapons–Related Contracts	Authors' Company of Choice
$ $ $	🚶🚶🚶	🚶	✍✍✍	*Post brands:* Fruit Pebbles Post Toasties Raisin Bran, etc.	General Foods (p. 132)	No	No	No	
$ $ $	🚶🚶🚶	🚶🚶	✍✍✍	*General Mills brands:* Cheerios Cocoa Puffs Total Wheaties, etc.	General Mills (p. 135)	No	No	No	✔
$	🚶🚶	🚶🚶	✍✍	*Kellogg Brands:* Corn Flakes Fruit Loops Rice Krispies Special K, etc.	Kellogg (p. 143)	Yes A	No	No	
$ $ $	🚶🚶	No	✍✍✍	Farina	Pillsbury (p. 158)	No	No	No	✔
$ $	🚶🚶	🚶	✍✍	*Quaker brands:* Cap'n Crunch Life Quaker Oats, etc.	Quaker Oats (p. 160)	No	No	No	
$ $	🚶	?	✍✍	*Ralston brands:* Cabbage Patch Kids Chex, etc.	Ralston Purina (p. 162)	No	No	No	
$ $ $	🚶	🚶🚶	✍✍✍	*Nabisco brands:* Cream of Wheat Shredded Wheat, etc.	RJR Nabisco (p. 164)	Yes A/B	No	No	

CONDIMENTS AND STAPLES

CATSUP, MUSTARD, AND MEAT SAUCES

Size of Charitable Contributions	Women Directors and Officers	Minority Directors and Officers	Social Disclosure	Brand Name	Company (Profile Page)	Involvement in South Africa	Conv. Weapons–Related Contracts	Nuclear Weapons–Related Contracts	Authors' Company of Choice
*	🕴🕴	No	👍👍👍	Gulden's	American Home Products (p. 406)	Yes A/B	No	No	
$ $ $	🕴🕴	🕴	👍👍👍	Hunt's	Beatrice (p. 118)	No	No	No	✔
$ $ $	🕴	No	👍👍	Heinz	Heinz (p. 138)	No	No	No	✔
$ $ $	🕴	🕴🕴	👍👍👍	A-1 Del Monte Grey Poupon	RJR Nabisco (p. 164)	Yes A/B	No	No	

* = See company profile
? = No information available
Single figure ($, 🕴) = Minimal
Double figure ($$, 🕴🕴, 👍👍, 🕴🕴) = Moderate
Triple figure ($$$, 🕴🕴🕴, 👍👍👍, 🕴🕴🕴) = Substantial

No = No involvement or participation
Yes = Involvement or participation. A, B, C in the South African column reflect the degree of compliance with Sullivan Principles and/or involvement in strategic industries.

See Chapter 4 for a detailed discussion of chart symbols.

In the Supermarket

CONDIMENTS AND STAPLES
COOKING OILS, SHORTENING, AND SPRAY-ON OILS

Size of Charitable Contributions	Women Directors and Officers	Minority Directors and Officers	Social Disclosure	Brand Name	Company (Profile Page)	Involvement in South Africa	Conv. Weapons–Related Contracts	Nuclear Weapons–Related Contracts	Authors' Company of Choice
*	♦ ♦	No	✍ ✍ ✍	Pam	American Home Products (p. 406)	Yes A/B	No	No	
$ $ $	♦ ♦	♦	✍ ✍ ✍	Sunlite Wesson	Beatrice (p. 118)	No	No	No	
$	♦	♦	No	Mazola	CPC Int'l. (p. 129)	Yes B	No	No	
?	♦ ♦ ♦	?	No	Hain Hollywood	Ogden (p. 152)	No	✈ ✈ ✈	No	
$ $ $	♦ ♦	♦	✍ ✍ ✍	Crisco Puritan	Procter & Gamble (p. 226)	No	No	No	✔
$ $ $	♦ ♦	♦	✍ ✍ ✍	Fleishmann's Planters	RJR Nabisco (p. 164)	Yes A/B	No	No	
$	No	No	No	Spry	Unilever (p. 171)	Yes ?	No	No	

* = See company profile
? = No information available
Single figure ($, ♦) = Minimal
Double figure ($$, ♦♦, ✍✍, ✈✈) = Moderate
Triple figure ($$$, ♦♦♦, ✍✍✍, ✈✈✈) = Substantial

No = No involvement or participation
Yes = Involvement or participation. A, B, C in the South African column reflect the degree of compliance with Sullivan Principles and/or involvement in strategic industries.

See Chapter 4 for a detailed discussion of chart symbols.

CONDIMENTS AND STAPLES

FLOURS AND WHEAT GERM

Size of Charitable Contributions	Women Directors and Officers	Minority Directors and Officers	Social Disclosure	Brand Name	Company (Profile Page)	Involvement in South Africa	Conv. Weapons–Related Contracts	Nuclear Weapons–Related Contracts	Authors' Company of Choice
$ $ $	♀ ♀	♀	✍ ✍ ✍	Martha White	Beatrice (p. 118)	No	No	No	
$ $ $	♀ ♀ ♀	♀ ♀	✍ ✍ ✍	Gold Medal La Piña Red Band	General Mills (p. 135)	No	No	No	✔
$ $ $	♀	No	✍ ✍ ✍	Kretschmer Robin Hood	International Multifoods (p. 142)	No	No	No	
$ $ $	♀ ♀	No	✍ ✍ ✍	Pillsbury's Best	Pillsbury (p. 158)	No	No	No	✔

* = See company profile
? = No information available
Single figure ($, ♀) = Minimal
Double figure ($$, ♀♀, ✍✍, ♀♀) = Moderate
Triple figure ($$$, ♀♀♀, ✍✍✍, ♀♀♀) = Substantial

No = No involvement or participation
Yes = Involvement or participation. A, B, C in the South African column reflect the degree of compliance with Sullivan Principles and/or involvement in strategic industries.

See Chapter 4 for a detailed discussion of chart symbols.

CONDIMENTS AND STAPLES

JAMS AND JELLIES

Size of Charitable Contributions	Women Directors and Officers	Minority Directors and Officers	Social Disclosure	Brand Name	Company (Profile Page)	Involvement in South Africa	Conv. Weapons–Related Contracts	Nuclear Weapons–Related Contracts	Authors' Company of Choice
$	⚘ ⚘	⚘	✍ ✍ ✍	Bama	Borden (p. 120)	Yes A	No	No	
$ $	⚘ ⚘	⚘	✍ ✍ ✍	Kraft	Dart & Kraft (p. 130)	No	No	No	
$ $ $	No	No	No	Smucker's	Smucker (p. 170)	No	No	No	

* = See company profile
? = No information available
Single figure ($, ⚘) = Minimal
Double figure ($$, ⚘⚘, ✍✍, ⚘⚘) = Moderate
Triple figure ($$$, ⚘⚘⚘, ✍✍✍, ⚘⚘⚘) = Substantial

No = No involvement or participation
Yes = Involvement or participation. A, B, C in the South African column reflect the degree of compliance with Sullivan Principles and/or involvement in strategic industries.

See Chapter 4 for a detailed discussion of chart symbols.

CONDIMENTS AND STAPLES

MAYONNAISE AND SALAD DRESSINGS

Size of Charitable Contributions	Women Directors and Officers	Minority Directors and Officers	Social Disclosure	Brand Name	Company (Profile Page)	Involvement in South Africa	Conv. Weapons–Related Contracts	Nuclear Weapons–Related Contracts	Authors' Company of Choice
?	No	🧍	No	Seven Seas	Anderson Clayton (p. 114)	No	No	No	
$ $ $	🧍	🧍	🥤🥤🥤	Hidden Valley Ranch	Clorox (p. 409)	No	No	No	✔
$	🧍	🧍	No	Hellmann's Best Foods	CPC Int'l. (p. 129)	Yes B	No	No	
$ $	🧍🧍	🧍	🥤🥤🥤	Kraft Miracle Whip Philadelphia Brand	Dart & Kraft (p. 130)	No	No	No	
$ $ $	🧍🧍	🧍	🥤🥤🥤	Good Seasons	General Foods (p. 132)	No	No	No	
?	🧍🧍🧍	?	No	Hain	Ogden (p. 152)	No	✈✈✈	No	
$	No	No	No	Wishbone	Unilever (p. 171)	Yes ?	No	No	

CONDIMENTS AND STAPLES

PASTA

Size of Charitable Contributions	Women Directors and Officers	Minority Directors and Officers	Social Disclosure	Brand Name	Company (Profile Page)	Involvement in South Africa	Conv. Weapons–Related Contracts	Nuclear Weapons–Related Contracts	Authors' Company of Choice
$	✦✦	✦	✍ ✍ ✍	Cremettes Ronco	Borden (p. 120)	Yes A	No	No	
$	✦	✦	No	Muellers	CPC Int'l. (p. 129)	Yes B	No	No	
$ $ $	✦✦ ✦	✦	✍ ✍ ✍	Ronzoni	General Foods (p. 132)	No	No	No	
$ $	✦	?	No	American Beauty Delmonico Light 'N Fluffy P & R San Giorgio Skinner	Hershey (p. 140)	No	No	No	✔

◑ = See company profile
? = No information available
Single figure ($, ✦) = Minimal
Double figure ($$, ✦✦, ✍✍, ✦✦) = Moderate
Triple figure ($$$, ✦✦✦, ✍✍✍, ✦✦✦) = Substantial

No – No involvement or participation
Yes = Involvement or participation. A, B, C in the South African column reflect the degree of compliance with Sullivan Principles and/or involvement in strategic industries.

See Chapter 4 for a detailed discussion of chart symbols.

CONDIMENTS AND STAPLES

PEANUT BUTTER

Size of Charitable Contributions	Women Directors and Officers	Minority Directors and Officers	Social Disclosure	Brand Name	Company (Profile Page)	Involvement in South Africa	Conv. Weapons—Related Contracts	Nuclear Weapons—Related Contracts	Authors' Company of Choice
$ $ $	♀ ♀	♀	✍ ✍ ✍	Peter Pan	Beatrice (p. 118)	No	No	No	
$	♀	♀	No	Skippy	CPC Int'l. (p. 129)	Yes B	No	No	
$ $ $	♀	♀ ♀	✍ ✍ ✍	Jif	Procter & Gamble (p. 226)	No	No	No	✔
$ $ $	No	No	No	Smucker's	Smucker (p. 170)	No	No	No	

* = See company profile
? = No information available
Single figure ($, ♀) = Minimal
Double figure ($$, ♀♀, ✍✍, ♀♀) = Moderate
Triple figure ($$$, ♀♀♀, ✍✍✍, ♀♀♀) = Substantial

No = No involvement or participation
Yes = Involvement or participation. A, B, C in the South African column reflect the degree of compliance with Sullivan Principles and/or involvement in strategic industries.

See Chapter 4 for a detailed discussion of chart symbols.

In the Supermarket

CONDIMENTS AND STAPLES

SPICES

Size of Charitable Contributions	Women Directors and Officers	Minority Directors and Officers	Social Disclosure	Brand Name	Company (Profile Page)	Involvement in South Africa	Conv. Weapons–Related Contracts	Nuclear Weapons–Related Contracts	Authors' Company of Choice
?	人	?	No	Adolph's	Chesebrough-Pond's (p. 210)	Yes C	No	No	
$ $	人	?	No	Ac'cent	IC Industries (p. 141)	No	✈ ✈	No	
$ $ $	No	?	No	McCormick Schilling	McCormick (p. 146)	No	No	No	✔
$ $ $	No	?	No	Durkee's	SCM (p. 371)	No	No	No	

* = See company profile
? = No information available
Single figure ($, 人) = Minimal
Double figure ($$, 人人, ✈✈) = Moderate
Triple figure ($$$, 人人人, ✈✈✈) = Substantial

No = No involvement or participation
Yes = Involvement or participation. A, B, C in the South African column reflect the degree of compliance with Sullivan Principles and/or involvement in strategic industries.

See Chapter 4 for a detailed discussion of chart symbols.

CONDIMENTS AND STAPLES

SYRUPS AND MOLASSES

Size of Charitable Contributions	Women Directors and Officers	Minority Directors and Officers	Social Disclosure	Brand Name	Company (Profile Page)	Involvement in South Africa	Conv. Weapons-Related Contracts	Nuclear Weapons-Related Contracts	Authors' Company of Choice
$	🧍	🧍	No	Golden Griddle Karo	CPC Int'l. (p. 129)	Yes B	No	No	
$ $ $	🧍 🧍	🧍	✍ ✍ ✍	Log Cabin	General Foods (p. 132)	No	No	No	
$ $	🧍 🧍	🧍	✍ ✍	Aunt Jemima	Quaker Oats (p. 160)	No	No	No	✔
$ $ $	🧍	🧍 🧍	✍ ✍ ✍	Brer Rabbit Vermont Maid	RJR Nabisco (p. 164)	Yes A/B	No	No	
$	No	No	No	Mrs. Butterworth's	Unilever (p. 171)	Yes ?	No	No	

* = See company profile
? = No information available
Single figure ($, 🧍) = Minimal
Double figure ($$, 🧍🧍, ✍✍, 🧍🧍) = Moderate
Triple figure ($$$, 🧍🧍🧍, ✍✍✍, 🧍🧍🧍) = Substantial

No = No involvement or participation
Yes = Involvement or participation. A, B, C in the South African column reflect the degree of compliance with Sullivan Principles and/or involvement in strategic industries.

See Chapter 4 for a detailed discussion of chart symbols.

CONDIMENTS AND STAPLES

VINEGARS

Size of Charitable Contributions	Women Directors and Officers	Minority Directors and Officers	Social Disclosure	Brand Name	Company (Profile Page)	Involvement in South Africa	Conv. Weapons–Related Contracts	Nuclear Weapons–Related Contracts	Authors' Company of Choice
$ $ $	𝚨	No	✍✍	Heinz	Heinz (p. 138)	No	No	No	✔
?	𝚨 𝚨 𝚨	?	No	Progresso	Ogden (p. 152)	No	✈ ✈ ✈	No	
$ $ $	𝚨	𝚨 𝚨	✍ ✍ ✍	Regina	RJR Nabisco (p. 164)	Yes A/B	No	No	

* = See company profile
? = No information available
Single figure ($, 𝚨) = Minimal
Double figure ($$, 𝚨𝚨, ✍✍, ✈✈) = Moderate
Triple figure ($$$, 𝚨𝚨𝚨, ✍✍✍, ✈✈✈) = Substantial

No = No involvement or participation
Yes = Involvement or participation. A, B, C in the South African column reflect the degree of compliance with Sullivan Principles and/or involvement in strategic industries.

See Chapter 4 for a detailed discussion of chart symbols.

DAIRY AND NON-DAIRY PRODUCTS

BUTTER AND MARGARINE

Size of Charitable Contributions	Women Directors and Officers	Minority Directors and Officers	Social Disclosure	Brand Name	Company (Profile Page)	Involvement in South Africa	Conv. Weapons–Related Contracts	Nuclear Weapons–Related Contracts	Authors' Company of Choice
?	No	♠	No	Chiffon	Anderson Clayton (p. 114)	No	No	No	
$ $ $	♠ ♠	♠	✍ ✍ ✍	Hotel Bar	Beatrice (p. 118)	No	No	No	
$	♠	♠	No	Mazola Nucoa	CPC Int'l. (p. 129)	Yes B	No	No	
$ $	♠ ♠	♠	✍ ✍ ✍	Breakstone's Parkay	Dart & Kraft (p. 130)	No	No	No	
$ $ $	♠	♠ ♠	✍ ✍ ✍	Blue Bonnet Fleishmann's	RJR Nabisco (p. 164)	Yes A/B	No	No	
$	No	No	No	Imperial Promise Shedd's	Unilever (p. 171)	Yes ?	No	No	

✱ = See company profile
? = No information available
Single figure ($, ♠) = Minimal
Double figure ($$, ♠♠, ✍✍, ♠♠) = Moderate
Triple figure ($$$, ♠♠♠, ✍✍✍, ♠♠♠) = Substantial

No = No involvement or participation
Yes = Involvement or participation. A, B, C in the South African column reflect the degree of compliance with Sullivan Principles and/or involvement in strategic industries.

See Chapter 4 for a detailed discussion of chart symbols.

In the Supermarket

DAIRY AND NON-DAIRY PRODUCTS

CHEESE AND YOGURT

Size of Charitable Contributions	Women Directors and Officers	Minority Directors and Officers	Social Disclosure	Brand Name	Company (Profile Page)	Involvement in South Africa	Conv. Weapons–Related Contracts	Nuclear Weapons–Related Contracts	Authors' Company of Choice
$ $ $	⋀ ⋀	⋀	✍ ✍ ✍	Country Line cheeses Meadow Gold and Viva brands Mountain High yogurts	Beatrice (p. 118)	No	No	No	
$	⋀ ⋀	⋀	✍ ✍ ✍	Borden brand	Borden (p. 120)	Yes A	No	No	
$ $	⋀ ⋀	⋀	✍ ✍ ✍	Breakstone Breyers Kraft Light 'n Lovely Philadelphia Sealtest	Dart & Kraft (p. 130)	No	No	No	
$ $ $	⋀ ⋀ ⋀	⋀ ⋀	✍ ✍ ✍	Yoplait yogurts	General Mills (p. 135)	No	No	No	✔
$ $ $	⋀	No	✍ ✍ ✍	Kaukauna Cheese	International Multifoods (p. 142)	No	No	No	
?	⋀ ⋀	⋀ ⋀	✍ ✍	Whitney's yogurts	Kellogg (p. 143)	Yes A	No	No	
*	No	?	No	Wispride cheese	Nestlé (p. 150)	Yes ?	No	No	

DAIRY AND NON-DAIRY PRODUCTS
CONDENSED MILK

Size of Charitable Contributions	Women Directors and Officers	Minority Directors and Officers	Social Disclosure	Brand Name	Company (Profile Page)	Involvement in South Africa	Conv. Weapons–Related Contracts	Nuclear Weapons–Related Contracts	Authors' Company of Choice
$	♀♀	♀	✍✍✍	Eagle	Borden (p. 120)	Yes A	No	No	✔
$$	♀	?	No	Pet	IC Industries (p. 141)	No	✈✈	No	
✳	No	?	No	Carnation	Nestlé (p. 150)	Yes ?	No	No	

DAIRY AND NON-DAIRY PRODUCTS
NON-DAIRY CREAMER

Size of Charitable Contributions	Women Directors and Officers	Minority Directors and Officers	Social Disclosure	Brand Name	Company (Profile Page)	Involvement in South Africa	Conv. Weapons–Related Contracts	Nuclear Weapons–Related Contracts	Authors' Company of Choice
$	♀♀	♀	✍✍✍	Cremora	Borden (p. 120)	Yes A	No	No	✔
✳	No	?	No	Coffee Mate	Nestlé (p. 150)	Yes ?	No	No	

DAIRY AND NON-DAIRY PRODUCTS

NON-DAIRY DESSERT WHIP

Size of Charitable Contributions	Women Directors and Officers	Minority Directors and Officers	Social Disclosure	Brand Name	Company (Profile Page)	Involvement in South Africa	Conv. Weapons–Related Contracts	Nuclear Weapons–Related Contracts	Authors' Company of Choice
\$ \$ \$	♀ ♀	♀	✍ ✍ ✍	Reddi-wipp	Beatrice (p. 118)	No	No	No	✔
\$ \$ \$	♀ ♀	♀	✍ ✍ ✍	Cool Whip	General Foods (p. 132)	No	No	No	
\$	No	No	No	Lucky Whip	Unilever (p. 171)	Yes ?	No	No	

* = See company profile
? = No information available
Single figure (\$, ♀) = Minimal
Double figure (\$\$, ♀♀, ✍✍, ♀♀) = Moderate
Triple figure (\$\$\$, ♀♀♀, ✍✍✍, ♀♀♀) = Substantial

No = No involvement or participation
Yes = Involvement or participation. A, B, C in the South African column reflect the degree of compliance with Sullivan Principles and/or involvement in strategic industries.

See Chapter 4 for a detailed discussion of chart symbols.

DESSERTS AND SNACKS

CANDY

Size of Charitable Contributions	Women Directors and Officers	Minority Directors and Officers	Social Disclosure	Brand Name	Company (Profile Page)	Involvement in South Africa	Conv. Weapons-Related Contracts	Nuclear Weapons-Related Contracts	Authors' Company of Choice
*	↑↑	No	✍✍✍	Brach's	American Home Products (p. 406)	Yes A/B	No	No	
$	↑↑	↑	✍✍✍	Haviland brand	Borden (p. 120)	Yes A	No	No	
$$	↑↑↑	↑	✍✍✍	Godiva	Campbell Soup (p. 122)	No	No	No	✔
$$	↑	?	No	*Hershey brands:* Kit-Kat Mr. Goodbar Reeses, etc.	Hershey (p. 140)	No	No	No	✔
$$	↑	?	No	Whitman's	IC Industries (p. 141)	No	✈✈	No	
*	?	?	No	*Mars brands:* M & M's Milky Way Snickers, etc.	Mars (p. 149)	No	No	No	
*	No	?	No	*Nestlé brands:* Crunch, etc.	Nestlé (p. 150)	Yes ?	No	No	
$$$	↑↑	↑↑	✍✍✍	*Nabisco brands:* Baby Ruth Butterfinger Chuckles Junior Mints Life Savers, etc.	RJR Nabisco (p. 164)	Yes A/B	No	No	

DESSERTS AND SNACKS

CHIPS AND SNACK FOODS

Size of Charitable Contributions	Women Directors and Officers	Minority Directors and Officers	Social Disclosure	Brand Name	Company (Profile Page)	Involvement in South Africa	Conv. Weapons–Related Contracts	Nuclear Weapons–Related Contracts	Authors' Company of Choice
$	🧍	?	No	Blue Bell	American Brands (p. 113)	Yes C	No	No	
$ $ $	🧍 🧍	🧍 🧍 🧍	✍ ✍	Eagle brand	Anheuser-Busch (p. 115)	No	No	No	
$	🧍 🧍	🧍	✍ ✍ ✍	Cracker Jacks Wise brand	Borden (p. 120)	Yes A	No	No	
$ $ $	🧍 🧍 🧍	🧍 🧍	✍ ✍ ✍	Bugles	General Mills (p. 135)	No	No	No	✔
$ $	No	🧍	✍ ✍ ✍	*Lay brands:* Doritos Fritos, etc.	PepsiCo (p. 153)	Yes C	No	No	
$ $ $	🧍	🧍 🧍	✍ ✍ ✍	Pringles	Procter & Gamble (p. 226)	No	No	No	✔
$ $ $	🧍	🧍 🧍	✍ ✍ ✍	Planters brand	RJR Nabisco (p. 164)	Yes A/B	No	No	
$ $ $	No	?	No	Durkee's brand	SCM (p. 371)	No	No	No	

DESSERTS AND SNACKS

COOKIES AND CRACKERS

Size of Charitable Contributions	Women Directors and Officers	Minority Directors and Officers	Social Disclosure	Brand Name	Company (Profile Page)	Involvement in South Africa	Conv. Weapons–Related Contracts	Nuclear Weapons–Related Contracts	Authors' Company of Choice
$	⚲	?	No	*Sunshine Cookies:* Chiparoos Hydrox Vienna Fingers, etc.	American Brands (p. 113)	Yes C	No	No	
$	⚲	?	No	*Sunshine Crackers:* Cheez-it Hi Ho Krispy, etc.	American Brands (p. 113)	Yes C	No	No	
$ $	⚲ ⚲ ⚲	⚲	✍ ✍ ✍	Pepperidge Farm brand	Campbell Soup (p. 122)	No	No	No	✔
*	?	?	No	Twix	Mars (p. 149)	No	No	No	
?	⚲ ⚲ ⚲	?	No	Hain brand	Ogden (p. 152)	No	✈ ✈ ✈	No	
$ $ $	⚲	⚲ ⚲	✍ ✍ ✍	*Nabisco Cookies:* Chips Ahoy Fig Newtons Lorna Doones Oreo, etc.	RJR Nabisco (p. 164)	Yes A/B	No	No	
$ $ $	⚲	⚲ ⚲	✍ ✍ ✍	*Nabisco Crackers:* Ritz Saltines Triscuits, etc.	RJR Nabisco (p. 164)	Yes A/B	No	No	

DESSERTS AND SNACKS

GRANOLA BARS

Size of Charitable Contributions	Women Directors and Officers	Minority Directors and Officers	Social Disclosure	Brand Name	Company (Profile Page)	Involvement in South Africa	Conv. Weapons–Related Contracts	Nuclear Weapons–Related Contracts	Authors' Company of Choice
$ $ $	♀ ♀ ♀	♀ ♀	☜ ☜ ☜	Nature Valley	General Mills (p. 135)	No	No	No	✔
$ $	♀	?	No	New Trail	Hershey (p. 140)	No	No	No	✔
?	♀ ♀	♀ ♀	☜ ☜	Rice Krispies Bars	Kellogg (p. 143)	Yes A	No	No	
$ $ $	♀ ♀	No	☜ ☜ ☜	Milk Break Milk Bars	Pillsbury (p. 158)	No	No	No	✔
$ $	♀ ♀	♀	☜ ☜	Granola Dipps	Quaker Oats (p. 160)	No	No	No	
$ $	♀	?	☜ ☜	S'mores	Ralston Purina (p. 162)	No	No	No	

* = See company profile
? = No information available
Single figure ($, ♀) = Minimal
Double figure ($$, ♀♀, ☜☜, ♀♀) = Moderate
Triple figure ($$$, ♀♀♀, ☜☜☜, ♀♀♀) = Substantial

See Chapter 4 for a detailed discussion of chart symbols.

No = No involvement or participation
Yes — Involvement or participation. A, B, C in the South African column reflect the degree of compliance with Sullivan Principles and/or involvement in strategic industries.

DESSERTS AND SNACKS

GUM

Size of Charitable Contributions	Women Directors and Officers	Minority Directors and Officers	Social Disclosure	Brand Name	Company (Profile Page)	Involvement in South Africa	Conv. Weapons– Related Contracts	Nuclear Weapons– Related Contracts	Authors' Company of Choice
$ $ $	🖐	🖐 🖐	✍ ✍ ✍	Bubble Yum Care*Free Lifesaver	RJR Nabisco (p. 164)	Yes A/B	No	No	
$ $ $	🖐 🖐	🖐 🖐	✍ ✍ ✍	Certs Chicklets Dentyne Trident, etc.	Warner-Lambert (p. 243)	Yes B	No	No	
$	🖐	No	No	*Wrigley brands:* Double Mint Freedent Juicy Fruit, etc.	Wrigley (p. 173)	No	No	No	

* = See company profile
? = No information available
Single figure ($, 🖐) = Minimal
Double figure ($$, 🖐🖐, ✍✍, 🖐🖐) = Moderate
Triple figure ($$$, 🖐🖐🖐, ✍✍✍, 🖐🖐🖐) = Substantial

No = No involvement or participation
Yes = Involvement or participation. A, B, C in the South African column reflect the degree of compliance with Sullivan Principles and/or involvement in strategic industries.

See Chapter 4 for a detailed discussion of chart symbols.

In the Supermarket

DESSERTS AND SNACKS

NUTS

Size of Charitable Contributions	Women Directors and Officers	Minority Directors and Officers	Social Disclosure	Brand Name	Company (Profile Page)	Involvement in South Africa	Conv. Weapons–Related Contracts	Nuclear Weapons–Related Contracts	Authors' Company of Choice
$ $ $	♁ ♁	♁	✍ ✍ ✍	Fisher	Beatrice (p. 118)	No	No	No	✔
$ $ $	♁	♁ ♁	✍ ✍ ✍	Planters	RJR Nabisco (p. 164)	Yes A/B	No	No	
$	No	?	No	Sun Giant	Tenneco (p. 332)	Yes C	✈ ✈ ✈	Yes	

✳ = See company profile
? = No information available
Single figure ($, ♁) = Minimal
Double figure ($$, ♁♁, ✍✍, ✈✈) = Moderate
Triple figure ($$$, ♁♁♁, ✍✍✍, ✈✈✈) = Substantial

No = No involvement or participation
Yes = Involvement or participation. A, B, C in the South African column reflect the degree of compliance with Sullivan Principles and/or involvement in strategic industries.

See Chapter 4 for a detailed discussion of chart symbols.

DESSERTS AND SNACKS

PUDDINGS

Size of Charitable Contributions	Women Directors and Officers	Minority Directors and Officers	Social Disclosure	Brand Name	Company (Profile Page)	Involvement in South Africa	Conv. Weapons–Related Contracts	Nuclear Weapons–Related Contracts	Authors' Company of Choice
$ $ $	🧍 🧍	🧍	✍ ✍ ✍	Jell-O Minute Tapioca	General Foods (p. 132)	No	No	No	✔
$ $ $	🧍	🧍 🧍	✍ ✍ ✍	My*T*Fine Royal	RJR Nabisco (p. 164)	Yes A/B	No	No	

FAST FOODS

FAST-FOOD RESTAURANTS

Size of Charitable Contributions	Women Directors and Officers	Minority Directors and Officers	Social Disclosure	Brand Name	Company (Profile Page)	Involvement in South Africa	Conv. Weapons–Related Contracts	Nuclear Weapons–Related Contracts	Authors' Company of Choice
$ $	No	No	✍ ✍	Taco Plaza	ConAgra (p. 128)	No	No	No	
$ $	🧍	?	No	Friendly's	Hershey (p. 140)	No	No	No	✔
$ $ $	🧍	No	✍ ✍ ✍	Mister Donut	International Multifoods (p. 142)	No	No	No	

FAST FOODS

FAST-FOOD RESTAURANTS *(cont'd.)*

Size of Charitable Contributions	Women Directors and Officers	Minority Directors and Officers	Social Disclosure	Brand Name	Company (Profile Page)	Involvement in South Africa	Conv. Weapons–Related Contracts	Nuclear Weapons–Related Contracts	Authors' Company of Choice
$ $	♀♀	♀	✍✍✍	Howard Johnson's Roy Rogers Bob's Big Boy	Marriott (p. 298)	No	No	No	
$	♀♀	♀♀	✍✍	McDonald's	McDonald's (p. 147)	No	No	No	
$ $	No	♀♀	✍✍✍	Pizza Hut Taco Bell La Petite Boulangerie	PepsiCo (p. 153)	Yes C	No	No	
$ $ $	♀♀	No	✍✍✍	Burger King	Pillsbury (p. 158)	No	No	No	✔
$ $ $	♀♀	♀♀	✍✍✍	Kentucky Fried Chicken†	RJR Nabisco (p. 164)	Yes A/B	No	No	
✳	♀♀♀	♀	✍✍✍	Wendy's	Wendy's International (p. 172)	No	No	No	

✳ – See company profile
? = No information available
Single figure ($, ♀) = Minimal
Double figure ($$, ♀♀, ✍✍, ♀♀) = Moderate
Triple figure ($$$, ♀♀♀, ✍✍✍, ♀♀♀) = Substantial

No = No involvement or participation
Yes = Involvement or participation. A, B, C in the South African column reflect the degree of compliance with Sullivan Principles and/or involvement in strategic industries.

See Chapter 4 for a detailed discussion of chart symbols.

† Sale to PepsiCo was announced in July 1986.

FROZEN FOODS

CAKES AND PIES

Size of Charitable Contributions	Women Directors and Officers	Minority Directors and Officers	Social Disclosure	Brand Name	Company (Profile Page)	Involvement in South Africa	Conv. Weapons–Related Contracts	Nuclear Weapons–Related Contracts	Authors' Company of Choice
$ $	🯅 🯅 🯅	🯅	✍ ✍ ✍	Pepperidge Farm	Campbell Soup (p. 122)	No	No	No	✔
$ $ $	🯅	No	✍ ✍	Weight Watchers	Heinz (p. 138)	No	No	No	✔
?	🯅 🯅	🯅 🯅	✍ ✍	Mrs. Smith's Pies	Kellogg (p. 143)	Yes A	No	No	
$ $ $	🯅	🯅	✍ ✍ ✍	Sara Lee	Sara Lee (p. 167)	No	No	No	

* = See company profile
? = No information available
Single figure ($, 🯅) = Minimal
Double figure ($$, 🯅🯅, ✍✍, 🯅🯅) = Moderate
Triple figure ($$$, 🯅🯅🯅, ✍✍✍, 🯅🯅🯅) = Substantial

No = No involvement or participation
Yes = Involvement or participation. A, B, C in the South African column reflect the degree of compliance with Sullivan Principles and/or involvement in strategic industries.

See Chapter 4 for a detailed discussion of chart symbols.

FROZEN FOODS

FROZEN DESSERTS

Size of Charitable Contributions	Women Directors and Officers	Minority Directors and Officers	Social Disclosure	Brand Name	Company (Profile Page)	Involvement in South Africa	Conv. Weapons–Related Contracts	Nuclear Weapons–Related Contracts	Authors' Company of Choice
*	⚤⚤	?	No	Dole Fruit 'N' Juice Frozen Bars	Castle & Cooke (p. 125)	No	No	No	
$ $	⚤⚤	⚤	✍✍✍	Polar Bars	Dart & Kraft (p. 130)	No	No	No	
$ $ $	⚤⚤	⚤	✍✍✍	Jello-O Pops	General Foods (p. 132)	No	No	No	
*	No	No	✍✍✍	Eskimo Pie	Reynolds Metals (p. 428)	No	No	No	

* = See company profile
? = No information available
Single figure ($, ⚤) = Minimal
Double figure ($$, ⚤⚤, ✍✍, ⚤⚤) = Moderate
Triple figure ($$$, ⚤⚤⚤, ✍✍✍, ⚤⚤⚤) = Substantial

No = No involvement or participation
Yes = Involvement or participation. A, B, C in the South African column reflect the degree of compliance with Sullivan Principles and/or involvement in strategic industries.

See Chapter 4 for a detailed discussion of chart symbols.

FROZEN FOODS

ICE CREAM

Size of Charitable Contributions	Women Directors and Officers	Minority Directors and Officers	Social Disclosure	Brand Name	Company (Profile Page)	Involvement in South Africa	Conv. Weapons–Related Contracts	Nuclear Weapons–Related Contracts	Authors' Company of Choice
$$$	🯅🯅	🯅	✍✍✍	Louis Sherry	Beatrice (p. 118)	No	No	No	
$	🯅🯅	🯅	✍✍✍	Gelare Lady Borden	Borden (p. 120)	Yes A	No	No	
*	🯅🯅	?	No	Dole Sorbets	Castle & Cooke (p. 125)	No	No	No	
$$	🯅🯅	🯅	✍✍✍	Breyers Früsen Gladjé Sealtest	Dart & Kraft (p. 130)	No	No	No	
$$	🯅	?	No	Friendly's	Hershey (p. 140)	No	No	No	✔
$$$	🯅🯅	No	✍✍✍	Häagen-Dazs Seduto	Pillsbury (p. 158)	No	No	No	✔

* = See company profile
? = No information available
Single figure ($, 🯅) = Minimal
Double figure ($$, 🯅🯅, ✍✍, 🯅🯅) = Moderate
Triple figure ($$$, 🯅🯅🯅, ✍✍✍, 🯅🯅🯅) = Substantial

No = No involvement or participation
Yes = Involvement or participation. A, B, C in the South African column reflect the degree of compliance with Sullivan Principles and/or involvement in strategic industries.

See Chapter 4 for a detailed discussion of chart symbols.

FROZEN FOODS

MAIN COURSES AND MEALS

Size of Charitable Contributions	Women Directors and Officers	Minority Directors and Officers	Social Disclosure	Brand Name	Company (Profile Page)	Involvement in South Africa	Conv. Weapons–Related Contracts	Nuclear Weapons–Related Contracts	Authors' Company of Choice
$ $	♀♀♀	♀	(disclosure)(disclosure)(disclosure)	Le Menu Mrs. Pauls Swanson	Campbell Soup (p. 122)	No	No	No	✔
$ $	No	No	(disclosure)(disclosure)	Banquet Classic Lite Dinner Classics Morton Singleton (fish)	ConAgra (p. 128)	No	No	No	
$ $ $	♀♀♀	♀♀	(disclosure)(disclosure)(disclosure)	Gorton's	General Mills (p. 135)	No	No	No	✔
$ $ $	♀	No	(disclosure)(disclosure)	Weight Watchers	Heinz (p. 138)	No	No	No	
*	No	?	No	Lean Cuisine Stouffer's	Nestlé (p. 150)	Yes ?	No	No	
$ $ $	♀♀	No	(disclosure)(disclosure)(disclosure)	Green Giant Van de Kamp's Stir Fry Entrees	Pillsbury (p. 158)	No	No	No	✔

* = See company profile
? = No information available
Single figure ($, ♀) = Minimal
Double figure ($$, ♀♀, (disclosure)(disclosure), ♀♀) = Moderate
Triple figure ($$$, ♀♀♀, (disclosure)(disclosure)(disclosure), ♀♀♀) = Substantial

No = No involvement or participation
Yes = Involvement or participation. A, B, C in the South African column reflect the degree of compliance with Sullivan Principles and/or involvement in strategic industries.

See Chapter 4 for a detailed discussion of chart symbols.

FROZEN FOODS

PANCAKES AND WAFFLES

Size of Charitable Contributions	Women Directors and Officers	Minority Directors and Officers	Social Disclosure	Brand Name	Company (Profile Page)	Involvement in South Africa	Conv. Weapons–Related Contracts	Nuclear Weapons–Related Contracts	Authors' Company of Choice
$ $	⋏	?	No	Downy Flake	IC Industries (p. 141)	No	✈ ✈	No	
?	⋏ ⋏	⋏ ⋏	✍ ✍	Eggo	Kellogg (p. 143)	Yes A	No	No	
$ $	⋏ ⋏	⋏	✍ ✍	Aunt Jemima	Quaker Oats (p. 160)	No	No	No	✔

* = See company profile
? = No information available
Single figure ($, ⋏) = Minimal
Double figure ($$, ⋏⋏, ✍✍, ⋏⋏) = Moderate
Triple figure ($$$, ⋏⋏⋏, ✍✍✍, ⋏⋏⋏) = Substantial

No = No involvement or participation
Yes = Involvement or participation. A, B, C in the South African column reflect the degree of compliance with Sullivan Principles and/or involvement in strategic industries.

See Chapter 4 for a detailed discussion of chart symbols.

In the Supermarket

FROZEN FOODS

PIZZA

Size of Charitable Contributions	Women Directors and Officers	Minority Directors and Officers	Social Disclosure	Brand Name	Company (Profile Page)	Involvement in South Africa	Conv. Weapons–Related Contracts	Nuclear Weapons–Related Contracts	Authors' Company of Choice
?	↑↑ ↑	↑	No	Ellio's	Greyhound (p. 416)	No	No	No	
*	No	?	No	Stouffer's	Nestlé (p. 150)	Yes ?	No	No	
$ $ $	↑ ↑	No	✍ ✍ ✍	Totino	Pillsbury (p. 158)	No	No	No	✔
$ $	↑ ↑	↑	✍ ✍	Celeste	Quaker Oats (p. 160)	No	No	No	

* = See company profile
? = No information available
Single figure ($, ↑) = Minimal
Double figure ($$, ↑↑, ✍✍, ↑↑) = Moderate
Triple figure ($$$, ↑↑↑, ✍✍✍, ↑↑↑) = Substantial

No = No involvement or participation
Yes = Involvement or participation. A, B, C in the South African column reflect the degree of compliance with Sullivan Principles and/or involvement in strategic industries.

See Chapter 4 for a detailed discussion of chart symbols.

FROZEN FOODS

VEGETABLES

Size of Charitable Contributions	Women Directors and Officers	Minority Directors and Officers	Social Disclosure	Brand Name	Company (Profile Page)	Involvement in South Africa	Conv. Weapons–Related Contracts	Nuclear Weapons–Related Contracts	Authors' Company of Choice
$ $ $	⚊⚊	⚊	✍️ ✍️ ✍️	Bird's Eye	General Foods (p. 132)	No	No	No	
$ $ $	⚊	No	✍️ ✍️	Ore-Ida	Heinz (p. 138)	No	No	No	
$ $ $	⚊⚊	No	✍️ ✍️ ✍️	Green Giant	Pillsbury (p. 158)	No	No	No	✔

* = See company profile
? = No information available
Single figure ($, ⚊) = Minimal
Double figure ($$, ⚊⚊, ✍️✍️, ⚊⚊) = Moderate
Triple figure ($$$, ⚊⚊⚊, ✍️✍️✍️, ⚊⚊⚊) = Substantial

No = No involvement or participation
Yes = Involvement or participation. A, B, C in the South African column reflect the degree of compliance with Sullivan Principles and/or involvement in strategic industries.

See Chapter 4 for a detailed discussion of chart symbols.

INFANT AND BABY FOOD

BABY FOOD

Size of Charitable Contributions	Women Directors and Officers	Minority Directors and Officers	Social Disclosure	Brand Name	Company (Profile Page)	Involvement in South Africa	Conv. Weapons–Related Contracts	Nuclear Weapons–Related Contracts	Authors' Company of Choice
$ $ $	👤 👤	👤	No	Gerber	Gerber (p. 137)	No	No	No	
$ $ $	👤	No	✍ ✍	Heinz	Heinz (p. 138)	No	No	No	
*	No	?	No	Beech-Nut	Nestlé (p. 150)	Yes ?	No	No	

* = See company profile
? = No information available
Single figure ($, 👤) = Minimal
Double figure ($$, 👤👤, ✍✍, 👤👤) = Moderate
Triple figure ($$$, 👤👤👤, ✍✍✍, 👤👤👤) = Substantial

No = No involvement or participation
Yes = Involvement or participation. A, B, C in the South African column reflect the degree of compliance with Sullivan Principles and/or involvement in strategic industries.

See Chapter 4 for a detailed discussion of chart symbols.

INFANT AND BABY FOOD

INFANT FORMULA

Size of Charitable Contributions	Women Directors and Officers	Minority Directors and Officers	Social Disclosure	Brand Name	Company (Profile Page)	Involvement in South Africa	Conv. Weapons–Related Contracts	Nuclear Weapons–Related Contracts	Authors' Company of Choice
$	🚶	No	No	Similac Isomil	Abbott Labs (p. 202)	Yes B	No	No	
✳	🚶 🚶	No	📢 📢 📢	S-26 SMA Nursoy Promil	American Home Products (p. 406)	Yes A/B	No	No	
$ $ $	🚶 🚶	?	📢 📢 📢	Enfamil ProSobec	Bristol-Myers (p. 208)	Yes B	No	No	✔

✳ = See company profile
? = No information available
Single figure ($, 🚶) = Minimal
Double figure ($$, 🚶🚶, 📢📢, 🚶🚶) = Moderate
Triple figure ($$$, 🚶🚶🚶, 📢📢📢, 🚶🚶🚶) = Substantial

No = No involvement or participation
Yes = Involvement or participation. A, B, C in the South African column reflect the degree of compliance with Sullivan Principles and/or involvement in strategic industries.

See Chapter 4 for a detailed discussion of chart symbols.

PET FOOD

CAT FOOD

Size of Charitable Contributions	Women Directors and Officers	Minority Directors and Officers	Social Disclosure	Brand Name	Company (Profile Page)	Involvement in South Africa	Conv. Weapons–Related Contracts	Nuclear Weapons–Related Contracts	Authors' Company of Choice
$$$	웃웃	웃	✍✍✍	Bonkers	Beatrice (p. 118)	No	No	No	
*	웃웃	?	No	Figaro	Castle & Cooke (p. 125)	No	No	No	
$$$	웃	No	✍✍	9 Lives	Heinz (p. 138)	No	No	No	✔
*	?	?	No	Kal Kan	Mars (p. 149)	No	No	No	
*	No	?	No	Bright Eyes Fancy Feast Friskies	Nestlé (p. 150)	Yes ?	No	No	
$$	웃웃	웃	✍✍	Moist Meals Puss 'n Boots	Quaker Oats (p. 160)	No	No	No	✔
$$	웃	?	✍✍	*Purina brands:* Cat Chow Meow Mix Tender Vittles Thrive	Ralston Purina (p. 162)	No	No	No	

* = See company profile
? = No information available
Single figure ($, 웃) = Minimal
Double figure ($$, 웃웃, ✍✍, 웃웃) = Moderate
Triple figure ($$$, 웃웃웃, ✍✍✍, 웃웃웃) = Substantial

No = No involvement or participation
Yes = Involvement or participation. A, B, C in the South African column reflect the degree of compliance with Sullivan Principles and/or involvement in strategic industries.

See Chapter 4 for a detailed discussion of chart symbols.

PET FOOD

DOG FOOD

Size of Charitable Contributions	Women Directors and Officers	Minority Directors and Officers	Social Disclosure	Brand Name	Company (Profile Page)	Involvement in South Africa	Conv. Weapons–Related Contracts	Nuclear Weapons–Related Contracts	Authors' Company of Choice
?	No	(person)	No	Gaines brands	Anderson Clayton (p. 114)	No	No	No	
$ $	(person)(person)(person)	(person)	(hand)(hand)(hand)	Recipe	Campbell Soup (p. 122)	No	No	No	✔
$ $ $	(person)	No	(hand)(hand)	Meaty Bone	Heinz (p. 138)	No	No	No	✔
✱	?	?	No	Kal Kan brand	Mars (p. 149)	No	No	No	
✱	No	?	No	New Breed Come 'N Get It Mighty Dog	Nestlé (p. 150)	Yes ?	No	No	
$ $	(person)(person)	(person)	(hand)(hand)	Ken-L-Ration Kibble	Quaker Oats (p. 160)	No	No	No	✔
$ $	(person)	?	(hand)(hand)	*Purina brands:* Bonz Dog Chow Hi Pro	Ralston Purina (p. 162)	No	No	No	
$ $ $	(person)	(person)(person)	(hand)(hand)(hand)	Milk Bones	RJR Nabisco (p. 164)	Yes A/B	No	No	

AMERICAN BRANDS, INC.

Headquartered in New York City, this company is the direct descendant of the mammoth American Tobacco Company, which was broken up by the U.S. government in a 1911 antitrust suit. Its Lucky Strike, Carlton, and Pall Mall brands now command less than 10 percent of the U.S. cigarette market.

Like other U.S. tobacco companies, it has diversified in the past 20 years. It now sells liquors, office supplies, crackers, soap, and life insurance; it also operates the Pinkerton detective agency.

Unlike the case for Philip Morris and RJR Nabisco, CEP could locate little evidence that American Brands has made a concerted effort in minority economic development, social disclosure, or charitable giving. The company did not respond to CEP's questionnaires.

It gave $1.7 million in 1981, according to the Taft *Corporate Giving Directory*, but this represented a small 0.3 percent of the company's pre-tax earnings. Its giving concentrated on education (50 percent) and health and welfare (30 percent), with a heavy emphasis on united fund campaigns and hospitals.

In 1985 the company became a signatory of the Sullivan Principles. Its various subsidiaries have over 1,000 employees in South Africa.

AMERICAN BRANDS, INC.											
	Women		Minorities				Contracts		PAC Contributions		
% to Charity	Directors	Officers	Directors	Officers	Social Disclosure	Sullivan Rating	% Military	Nuclear Weapons—Related	Dollar Amount	% to Republicans	% to Democrats
0.3%	1	0	?	?	F	V	None	None	None		

? = No information available
See also Appendix D for a listing of this company's products and services.

ANDERSON CLAYTON & CO.

Once king of the international cotton traders, Anderson Clayton is now widely diversified and firmly involved in foods. Since 1985, it has undergone a major restructuring, selling off its substantial Mexican and Brazilian food businesses to Unilever. In late 1986, Anderson Clayton was acquired by Quaker Oats. (See addendum on page 500.)

The company did not respond to CEP's questionnaires. We could locate no information on its social initiatives.

	Women		Minorities				Contracts		PAC Contributions		
% to Charity	Directors	Officers	Directors	Officers	Social Disclosure	Sullivan Rating	% Military	Nuclear Weapons–Related	Dollar Amount	% to Republicans	% to Democrats
?	0	0	0	1	F	None	None	None	None		

ANDERSON CLAYTON & CO.

? = No information available
See also Appendix D for a listing of this company's products and services.

ANHEUSER-BUSCH COMPANIES, INC.

This number-one brewer in the United States, with well over one-third of the beer market as of 1985, is known as an aggressive marketer and advertiser. Apparently it has implemented strong minority economic development and charitable giving programs (a strong 1.9 percent of pre-tax earnings in 1984), but the company did not provide information for this book.

Anheuser-Busch adopted a fighting stance in 1982 when Rev. Jesse Jackson requested that it improve its minority programs. The company asserted that its efforts at the time were excellent and that it saw no need for additional initiatives. Jackson's civil rights organization, Operation PUSH, then called for a boycott. For a year, the two engaged in public debate. The company cited 1982 figures showing that it purchased $18 million annually from minority-owned suppliers; that its minority banking program had placed $2 million in deposits in minority-owned institutions and held a $5 million credit line; and that 9.6 percent of its officers and managers were minorities. (In 1986, *Black Enterprise* magazine reported that minorities made up 9.1 percent of Anheuser-Busch's officials and managers, and women, 5.8 percent. It also reported that the company maintains a minority purchasing program of approximately $30 million and $14.5 million in deposits, lines of credit, and payroll accounts with minority-owned banks.)

Jackson pointed out that only four of the company's nearly 950 distributorships were then minority owned — only one of these by a black — and called for across-the-board improvement in the company's efforts. The company cited its plans for a $5 million loan fund for minorities wishing to purchase distributorships. After a year of the boycott, Jackson and Anheuser-Busch reached an agreement resulting in some improvements in the firm's minority programs.

Anheuser-Busch has among the best records in this book on inclusion of women and minorities on its board of directors and among its highest level officers.

Claims of aggressive marketing practices by the company have occasionally provoked controversy. In 1984 it settled a monopolistic practices suit with the federal government for $2 million. It had been accused of requiring beer vendors at various major league baseball parks and other stadiums to sell only Anheuser-Busch products. In 1978 it paid $750,000 to settle an earlier federal suit alleging that the company had paid retailers cash rebates to stock its products. According to the *New York Times*, the company had reported $500,000 in cash rebates and other payments between 1971 and 1975.

Anheuser-Busch is among the largest advertisers in the country, with a reported $364 million advertising budget in 1985. Beer and wine commercials on radio and television came under attack in 1985 from a coalition of organizations headed by the Center for Science in the Public Interest (CSPI). The coalition proposed a ban on such ads or equal time to point out the dangers of alcohol abuse. (Manufacturers of distilled spirits do not now advertise on the airwaves.) Of particular concern to this coalition were industry ads aimed at young adults, that, it felt, encouraged heavy drinking or glamorized alcohol through testimonials by sports and entertainment figures. The beer and wine companies argued that they were only trying to increase their shares of the market, not encourage excessive drinking. Broadcasters strongly opposed the proposals as well. In April 1985, the Federal Trade Commission denied the coalition's request for a ban on these commercials.

Beer company practices that promote drinking on college campuses are also under increasing scrutiny, as more states raise their drinking age to 21 in an effort to reduce drunk driving accidents.

Like other companies in the industry, Anheuser-Busch asserts that the last thing it wants is drunk drivers. Its charitable foundation supports such organizations as Students Against Drunken Driving (SADD) and Mothers Against Drunk Driving (MADD). It gives an annual $600,000 contribution to the Alcoholic Beverage Medical Research Foundation at Johns Hopkins University, and has initiated a "Know When to Say When" campaign to combat alcohol abuse in bars. CSPI criticizes this and similar industry campaigns as inadequate and aimed almost solely at drunk driving.

The company's charitable contributions for 1983 totaled $8 million, an excellent 2.3 percent of its pre-tax earnings. In 1984, its giving rose to $9 million, but fell as a percentage of earnings because of sharply higher 1983 profits. These gifts appear to go to largely traditional recipients. According to the Taft *Corporate Giving Directory,* 30 percent of the company's 1982 giving went to education, and 12 percent to hospitals. Welfare received 50 percent, including such organizations as the United Way and the St. Louis Soccer Park Fund, to which Anheuser-Busch has given $400,000. It was cited in *The 100*

ANHEUSER-BUSCH COMPANIES, INC.											
	Women		Minorities				Contracts		PAC Contributions		
% to Charity	Directors	Officers	Directors	Officers	Social Disclosure	Sullivan Rating	% Military	Nuclear Weapons–Related	Dollar Amount	% to Republicans	% to Democrats
1.9%	3	1	2	2	C	None	None	None	$37,948	40%	60%

See also Appendix D for a listing of this company's products and services.

Best Companies to Work for in America (Levering et al.) as a tough company that instills intense loyalty in its workers. Since 1974 it has had "Quality of Work Life" programs encouraging worker participation in production decisions. The company efforts to facilitate communications between management and employees include a counseling service and suggestion plan. It recently stopped providing free beer for workers on breaks, although it still supplies them with two free cases per month.

BEATRICE COMPANIES, INC.

Beatrice's public record is somewhat inconsistent concerning social initiatives. Media-oriented events, such as multimillion-dollar sponsorship of car races and the Chicago Marathon, overshadow some moderately innovative efforts in charitable giving. Beatrice's support of food banks and nonprofit hunger relief organizations is impressive. The company's commitment to minority development is well-rounded.

In the past four decades, this Chicago-based conglomerate has acquired over 400 companies, many of which it has subsequently sold off. The company itself was taken private in 1985 and is reportedly planning to sell off many of its major divisions, including Tropicana orange juice. These numerous acquisitions and divestitures have reportedly caused disruption and dissatisfaction among its employees.

In 1983 Beatrice contributed 3.5 million pounds of food, valued at $1.5 million, to Second Harvest. Beatrice was among the first companies to provide financial as well as technical and administrative assistance to this exemplary hunger relief organization.

Second Harvest is part of an extensive network of food banks that has sprung up in the United States since the early 1980s. It was created with federal assistance in 1979 to distribute to the needy food that might otherwise go to waste. Six major food companies contributed a total of 2.5 million pounds of food that year. By 1984 Second Harvest coordinated food distribution through a network of 74 local food banks around the country, receiving 60 million pounds of food from 225 companies since 1979. Nineteen eighty-three was the final year for federal funding for Second Harvest, which now receives one-third of its $900,000 budget from private-sector contributions, including General Mills, Kraft, RJR Nabisco, and Sara Lee. Companies receive a tax credit on products, including food donated to charities.

BEATRICE COMPANIES, INC.											
	Women		Minorities				Contracts		PAC Contributions		
% to Charity	Directors	Officers	Directors	Officers	Social Disclosure	Sullivan Rating	% Military	Nuclear Weapons–Related	Dollar Amount	% to Republicans	% to Democrats
1.6%	1	3	1	0	A	V	None	None	$8,900	64%	36%

See also Appendix D for a listing of this company's products and services.

In addition to its in-kind food giving, Beatrice has a strong record on cash contributions, having disbursed $9.1 million in 1984. Its foundation proclaims commitment to "high-quality, innovative" giving, and concentrates in several areas, including hunger, child care, the family, literacy, and technical assistance. In an innovative program, it makes three $15,000 awards yearly (up from $10,000 in 1983) to nonprofit groups that have found creative solutions to management problems. Award recipients in 1983 and 1984 included an emergency shelter for teenage girls, a training center for the hearing impaired, and a home care program for the elderly. These awards were developed by Esmark, a company acquired by Beatrice in 1984.

Beatrice's matching gift program has an unusual new component. In addition to matching dollar for dollar employee contributions of up to $3,000 to most nonprofit groups, the company selects thematically related organizations to which, during a three- to four-year cycle, it doubles every employee gift of up to $250. At present, under the theme "the family," selected organizations include the National Coalition Against Domestic Violence, the National Committee for the Prevention of Child Abuse, Second Harvest, and the Child Fund.

Its minority purchasing totaled a substantial $38 million in 1983. Minority banking activities included a $9.2 million credit line with minority-owned banks; $755,000 in certificates of deposit; $77 million in annual tax payments channeled through minority institutions; and two operating accounts with an average daily balance of $100,000 each. Some $49,000 in company insurance premiums went to minority firms as well.

The percentage of women and minorities among Beatrice's officers and managers was 16.1 percent and 8.6 percent, respectively, as of 1984.

Only in 1985 did Beatrice become a signatory of the Sullivan Principles for its Playtex International subsidiary, which employs approximately 500 persons in South Africa. In August 1986, Beatrice announced plans to sell its Playtex subsidiary. (See addendum on page 500.)

An environmental lawsuit against John J. Rily Tannery, a division of Beatrice from 1978 to 1983, gained national attention as it came to trial in 1986. Along with W. R. Grace and Company, Rily is accused of contaminating the water supply in one neighborhood of Woburn, Massachusetts, and thereby causing increased leukemia deaths among children there. This has become a test case for litigation over corporate liabilities in damages from improper disposal of hazardous and toxic wastes. In August 1986, Beatrice was acquitted of all charges, while court cases involving W. R. Grace continued.

The company responded to CEP's questionnaires.

BORDEN, INC.

Borden, under the leadership of former chairman Augustine Marusi, took a commendable leadership role in the promotion of minority purchasing programs in the 1970s. With headquarters in Columbus, Ohio, and New York City, the company is a major chemical producer as well as food processor, manufacturing plastic coatings and wrappings, formaldehyde, and various adhesives. Its social initiatives now appear moderate.

Marusi chaired the National Minority Supplier Development Council (NMSDC), from 1976 to 1980, during which period the Council conducted a major membership drive to boost the number of its corporate participants. Companies working with NMSDC agree to develop a written policy for promoting their purchases from minority-owned vendors, to incorporate this policy into their management structure, and to report total minority purchases to NMSDC on a confidential basis.

Borden purchased a substantial $23.7 million from minority suppliers in 1983 (up from $18 million in 1982), and an impressive $31 million in 1984. Its minority banking program relies solely on tax payments ($46 million in 1983), which are not the most useful form of deposits for small banks.

As a major chemical company, Borden must cope with environmental concerns. A 1985 study by the INFORM research organization, *Cutting Chemical Wastes,* profiled a Borden plant in Fremont, California, which had eliminated most of its hazardous wastes in water discharges since 1981. The study provided interesting insights on the difficulties of instituting this exemplary program at the plant and of replicating it at other Borden plants.

Borden's charitable giving program is below average, with its $1.1 million given in 1984 representing less than 0.4 percent of pre-tax earnings. According to *Corporate Foundation Profiles,* one-third of the company's 1983 giving went to united fund drives and one-quarter to education. In 1984, the firm

BORDEN, INC.											
	Women		Minorities				Contracts		PAC Contributions		
% to Charity	Directors	Officers	Directors	Officers	Social Disclosure	Sullivan Rating	% Military	Nuclear Weapons–Related	Dollar Amount	% to Republicans	% to Democrats
0.4%	2	1	1	0	A	I	None	None	$16,000	64%	36%

See also Appendix D for a listing of this company's products and services.

expanded its matching gifts program to include hospitals, cultural organizations, and higher education, but matched only $33,000 that year.

Borden's work force is approximately 60 percent unionized.

In South Africa, Borden produces food and packaging products. It employs somewhat more than 300 persons in operations that have consistently received the top rating for compliance with the Sullivan Principles.

The company responded to CEP's questionnaires.

CAMPBELL SOUP COMPANY

With over 1,000 products, Campbell is a major and powerful presence throughout the processed foods industry.

Campbell has strongly supported revitalization efforts in Camden, New Jersey, its headquarters since the firm was founded in 1869; promoted women to high levels of management; and instituted comprehensive minority economic development programs. At the same time, it has resolved a long controversy over unionizing efforts and the living conditions of migrant farm workers in Ohio. Its health claims for some of its products have occasionally been attacked.

Rather than leave for the suburbs as Camden deteriorated in the 1950s and 1960s, Campbell elected to stay, building its new headquarters and two other facilities. In addition, it contributed to a revolving loan fund for low-income housing renovation and to a loan fund for minority-owned businesses, helped organize a development corporation for major economic revitalization projects, improved the city's network of day-care facilities, and supported youth job training and recreation programs. In 1984, Campbell CEO Gordon McGovern headed the Cooper's Ferry Development Association, which is working toward the revitalization of a 75-acre site on Camden's downtown waterfront, where the company will build its new world headquarters. The firm gave $118,000 to Camden in 1984 for a wide variety of summer recreational and youth job programs, which it has supported for the past 10 years, and has completed a three-year grant to Jaycee Housing Counselling, a service organization that created low-income apartments and a community center in one badly deteriorated downtown block.

The company has an impressive minority purchasing program, with $45 million purchased in 1985. The program reports special emphasis on purchases of agricultural products. Campbell has placed $1 million in certificates of deposit with minority-owned banks, some of these at below-market rates. It reinsures about 5 percent of its life insurance through minority-owned brokers as well.

Campbell has a reputation for fair treatment toward women; in 1984 it had two women vice presidents, and CEO McGovern is committed to promoting women to middle- and top-management positions. According to Donna Ecton, Campbell's vice president for administration, the company's decentralization and new "independent business unit" concept have allowed many women to rise to plant manager and assistant plant manager positions. Ms. Ecton serves on Campbell's Operations Committee, which consists of six top company officers.

Campbell offers on-site day care, and reportedly spends $175,000 annually to subsidize tuition there for its employees' children. Other worker benefits include an in-house dental clinic, a new health and fitness program (which cost the company $700,000), flextime, and a discount store selling Campbell products.

Its charitable contributions for 1985 were a fairly strong $3.1 million, or just over 1 percent of pre-tax earnings. Of this, 27 percent went to educational institutions. The company matches employee gifts of up to $2,000 to higher education.

According to the Taft *Corporate Giving Directory,* another 25 percent of the company's contributions goes to hospitals, 25 percent to child welfare and youth organizations, and the remainder to civic and public affairs groups. One such group is the Black People's Unity Movement of Camden, an economic development corporation focusing on job creation for minorities, which has received over $500,000 since it was founded in the late 1960s.

Less praiseworthy, in our opinion, is Campbell's practice of giving equipment to secondary schools in return for Campbell product labels brought to school by students. (It gives away about $2 million annually under this program.) Such promotional ploys by Campbell and other food companies have been occasionally criticized by parents, educators, and consumer advocates concerned with the use of public schools for commercial ends. For a more thorough description of this issue, see Sheila Harty's book *Hucksters in the Classroom.*

The company has also been involved in a major controversy over living and working conditions of migrant farm workers who harvest the tomatoes that go into Campbell's products. The controversy arose in Ohio, where, according to a 1981 report by the Subcommittee on Migrants of the Ohio Senate Education and Labor Committee, migrant workers were living in substandard and unsanitary housing, working 10 to 12 hours a day, receiving low wages, violating child labor laws, and being exposed to hazardous chemicals. The migrants, however, were not directly employed by Campbell, but by the

CAMPBELL SOUP COMPANY											
	Women		Minorities				Contracts		PAC Contributions		
% to Charity	Directors	Officers	Directors	Officers	Social Disclosure	Sullivan Rating	% Military	Nuclear Weapons—Related	Dollar Amount	% to Republicans	% to Democrats
1.0%	2	2	1	0	A	None	None	None	None		

See also Appendix D for a listing of this company's products and services.

farmers who have tomato and cucumber contracts with the company and other food processors. The Farm Labor Organizing Committee (FLOC), which had been trying to organize Ohio migrant laborers since 1967, argued that Campbell and other food processors could influence working conditions on the farms. In their turn, the farmers argued that they were bound by pre-harvest fixed-price contracts to the food processing companies and could not increase wages or improve working conditions without losing their profits.

After some insubstantial unionizing successes in the early 1970s, FLOC tried in 1978 to set up three-party negotiations that would include the processors. When these companies refused, FLOC called a strike and then a boycott.

Campbell responded to this controversy by setting up a number of programs for migrant workers. Its contracts with growers stipulated that above-standard housing must be provided for migrant laborers. If the housing had to be built, the company subsidized 50 percent of the cost. It also provided health-care insurance and day-care facilities. But unions termed these steps insignificant in the face of the underlying work conditions. As one church sponsor of a shareholder resolution put it at Campbell's 1984 annual meeting, "Why should we give charity to workers when just wages would allow them to help themselves?"

In 1985, after seven years, negotiations took a step forward when the National Council of Churches helped establish a committee to oversee a series of union elections. The committee, headed by former Secretary of Labor John Dunlop and made up of four members nominated by FLOC and four by Campbell and the growers, supervised an initial round of elections in the summer of 1985. But amid numerous union charges of unfair voting procedures, the committee at first withheld validation of some of the elections.

Finally, in February 1986, a joint agreement among Campbell, the growers, and FLOC was signed and the boycott was suspended. FLOC won new contracts for 600 workers, including wage guarantees of $4.50 per hour, one paid holiday, medical insurance, union recognition, and the establishment of committees to study improvements in pesticide control, housing, and day care.

The company has faced other problems as well. Advertising its soup as "good food" landed Campbell in hot water in the early 1980s, when it claimed its product was "health insurance" and contained more vitamins than certain vegetables. The Center for Science in the Public Interest filed complaints with the Federal Trade Commission concerning these ads, arguing that the health claims were unjustified in light of the high salt content of most Campbell soups. (A 10-ounce serving may contain up to 1,600 milligrams of sodium, while total recommended daily intake is 1,100 to 3,300 milligrams for a healthy adult.) In response to pressure from the New York attorney general, Campbell agreed to withdraw these ads.

The company responded to CEP's questionnaires.

CASTLE & COOKE, INC.

A dispute with some church groups over its labor practices abroad and in the United States during the late 1970s led Castle & Cooke to adopt a basic set of human rights principles to guide its operations.

The dispute surrounding this Hawaiian-based fruit and vegetable company, with an extensive network of farming operations and produce suppliers throughout the Pacific basin, was a bitter one. Castle & Cooke was accused by some church groups of questionable labor practices in the Philippines, Honduras, and the United States, charges which the company denied.

Castle & Cooke's president, D. J. Kirchhoff, attacked church groups at that time as "enemies of the free enterprise system" and criticized their use of corporate annual meetings as a battleground for "divisive and abrasive" political issues.

Despite the charges and countercharges, however, dialogue was kept open and the company eventually agreed to establish new guidelines based on human rights principles.

In early 1985, the firm sold its Bumble Bee tuna unit to private investors. Later that year, under severe financial pressures and facing a hostile takeover bid, Castle & Cooke agreed to merge with Flexi-Van, a transportation equipment leasing company.

The Castle & Cooke foundation gave no charitable contributions in 1983, a year in which the company suffered a loss.

The company did not respond to CEP's questionnaires.

CASTLE & COOKE, INC.											
	Women		Minorities				Contracts		PAC Contributions		
% to Charity	Directors	Officers	Directors	Officers	Social Disclosure	Sullivan Rating	% Military	Nuclear Weapons–Related	Dollar Amount	% to Republicans	% to Democrats
*	2	1	?	?	F	None	None	None	$14,500	52%	48%

* = See profile   ? = No information available
See also Appendix D for a listing of this company's products and services.

COCA-COLA COMPANY

Coca-Cola has a substantial record for support of minority economic development, but has encountered some controversy abroad, where more than half of its tremendous profits — over $670 million in 1985 — are earned.

In the early 1980s, Coca-Cola began a substantial effort to upgrade its minority economic development programs. After a brief boycott, called by Rev. Jesse Jackson in 1981, the company entered into a "covenant" with Operation PUSH. It agreed to increase its black-owned distributorships from 2 to 32 of 4,000 total; to increase its business with black-owned banks (it now has a $10 million credit line with a consortium of minority banks); to add a black member to its board of directors; and to establish a $1.8 million venture capital fund for black-owned businesses. Its Minority Capital Fund had made $2 million in loans to minority businesses by 1984.

Coca-Cola purchased $5 million in goods from Hispanic businesses in 1984 as part of its overall $50 million minority purchasing program. (Its 1985 purchasing from minority businesses totaled $51 million in 1985.) On a recent $100 million expansion of its Atlanta headquarters, a minority-owned construction firm received 35 percent of the general contracts.

The company is perhaps unique among major U.S. firms in having three Hispanic-Americans in the highest levels of its senior management — chief executive officer, president, and senior vice president for marketing. Coca-Cola would not provide fair hiring statistics for this book. It reported to *Black Enterprise* magazine in 1986 that minorities constituted 10 percent of its officers and managers, but did not provide figures for women.

In 1985 the firm gave just over $5 million in charitable contributions, a moderate 0.5 percent of pre-tax earnings, and budgeted $6 million for 1986.

For seven years the company was under intense scrutiny by some church groups and others because of a bitter, brutal, and highly publicized labor

COCA-COLA COMPANY											
	Women		Minorities				Contracts		PAC Contributions		
% to Charity	Directors	Officers	Directors	Officers	Social Disclosure	Sullivan Rating	% Military	Nuclear Weapons–Related	Dollar Amount	% to Republicans	% to Democrats
0.5%	1	1	1	4	A	IIA	None	None	$129,270	44%	56%

See also Appendix D for a listing of this company's products and services.

dispute at an independent Guatemalan bottling franchise. The conflict began in 1978 when unions appeared to have successfully organized the bottling plant. Within two years, two of the union's officers were murdered and 27 top members of Guatemala's union movement were kidnapped at a public meeting. Initially Coca-Cola refused to become involved, since it was not the owner of the plant. Church groups protested at Coca-Cola's annual meeting, and the International Union of Food and Allied Workers called for a worldwide boycott of Coca-Cola products. In 1980, the company agreed to arrange the sale of the bottling franchise to another operator but to retain "management control" until 1985, in order to assure trade union rights.

In February 1984, the new operators declared bankruptcy. The workers, charging the operators with union-busting and siphoning off assets, occupied the plant. After considerable international pressure, Coca-Cola again arranged with the union to find new owners who would allow union organizing. In March 1985, after prolonged negotiations, new owners reopened the plant, formally recognized the union, and signed a two-year contract.

Coca-Cola was the second-largest U.S. employer in South Africa in 1986 (behind GM), with approximately 4,300 workers. It received the second-highest rating for its compliance with the Sullivan Principles in 1985. Also in 1985, the company announced plans to hand over majority interest in South African bottling operations to a local company "within two years," according to the *Wall Street Journal*. In late 1986, Coca-Cola announced plans to withdraw entirely.

In an innovative move in 1986, Coca-Cola pledged $10 million toward the establishment of a foundation in South Africa set up to support black housing, business and education. This Equal Opportunity Fund will be administered by a committee of black South Africans, including Bishop Desmond Tutu.

The company responded to CEP's questionnaires.

CONAGRA, INC.

Once primarily a grain firm, this Nebraska-based company has now also emerged as an important food products company. It acquired Banquet frozen foods from RCA in 1980, Singleton and Sea-Alaska frozen fish foods in 1982, and Armour Foods (now Armour Processed Meats) from Greyhound in 1983. It also produces Country Pride poultry.

When ConAgra bought Armour, it severely antagonized unions there. Greyhound had been negotiating with Armour unions in early 1983 for substantial wage benefit reductions, from approximately $10 per hour to $8. When the unions refused to comply, Greyhound sold the company, in effect canceling the union contracts at its plants. When ConAgra reopened the 13 meat processing plants, it hired non-union workers at wages averaging $6 per hour, according to the United Food and Commercial Workers International Union (UFCW). Average wage rates for many major meat processing companies were $8 and up as of 1985, UFCW reports, with the industry leaders — Oscar Mayer (owned by General Foods, now a part of Philip Morris) and Hormel — averaging $9 to $10 per hour. (Hormel has subsequently had major union problems at one plant.)

In May 1985, the UFCW called for a boycott on Armour processed meat products (not to be confused with Armour-Dial's personal care products, which are still owned by Greyhound and not being boycotted). ConAgra informed CEP that 55 percent of its work force is unionized and that it has "good relationships" with its unions.

The company reports that its charitable giving in 1984 was slightly above 1 percent of pre-tax earnings. That year its foundation gave $423,000 primarily to traditional causes such as education, federated fund drives, and the arts in Nebraska.

The company responded in a limited way to CEP's questionnaires.

CONAGRA, INC.											
	Women		Minorities				Contracts		PAC Contributions		
% to Charity	Directors	Officers	Directors	Officers	Social Disclosure	Sullivan Rating	% Military	Nuclear Weapons–Related	Dollar Amount	% to Republicans	% to Democrats
1.0%	0	0	0	0	C	None	None	None	$41,700	84%	16%

See also Appendix D for a listing of this company's products and services.

CPC INTERNATIONAL INC.

New Jersey–based CPC is a highly decentralized corn milling and food processing company conducting approximately two-thirds of its business overseas.

In South Africa its operations employ over 1,000 persons. From 1981 through 1985 it received the second-highest "making progress" rating for compliance with the Sullivan Principles for fair labor practices in that country.

The Investor Responsibility Research Center reports CPC charitable cash gifts of $1.5 million worldwide in 1984.

The company did not respond to CEP's questionnaires.

CPC INTERNATIONAL INC.											
	Women		Minorities				Contracts		PAC Contributions		
% to Charity	Directors	Officers	Directors	Officers	Social Disclosure	Sullivan Rating	% Military	Nuclear Weapons–Related	Dollar Amount	% to Republicans	% to Democrats
0.5%	2	0	1	0	F	IIA	None	None	None		

See also Appendix D for a listing of this company's products and services.

DART & KRAFT, INC.

This Chicago-based company was the product of an unlikely marriage that lasted only six years. The Dart Industries conglomerate was headed by well-known Justin Dart, described by the authors of *Everybody's Business* as "a stalwart of the Republican right wing," when it merged in 1980 with the huge food manufacturer, Kraft, with a record of social initiatives. The new company appeared to be continuing Kraft's efforts; however, it provided no information for this book, so details on its programs were scanty. In 1986 it announced that the two companies would split, with Kraft keeping the Duracell battery line.

One of the company's strongest efforts is Kraft's minority banking program. As of 1984, it had a $10 million credit line with minority-owned financial institutions, $3.3 million in term deposits, and $125 million in annual tax payments. The company purchased a fairly substantial $19.8 million in goods from minority suppliers in 1984, up from $15.5 million in 1983.

In Chicago, it provided a $50,000 grant to a low-interest revolving loan fund for minority businesses administered by the Chicago Economic Development Corporation (CEDCO). More recently, along with several other companies, Kraft has bought and is renovating a building that will be turned over to CEDCO for use as an "incubator" for new minority-owned businesses. In 1985, the company purchased a $500,000 share in the newly formed Chicago Equity Fund, which will serve as a source of corporate funds for low-income housing renovations. In the early 1980s, Kraft's president, Arthur W. Woelfle, served as chief corporate fund-raiser for the NAACP.

In its 1983 annual report, the company announced a long-term charitable giving goal of 2 percent of its pre-tax net earnings, a level substantially above that for most companies covered in this book. Its $6.7 million given in 1984

DART & KRAFT, INC.											
	Women		Minorities				Contracts		PAC Contributions		
% to Charity	Directors	Officers	Directors	Officers	Social Disclosure	Sullivan Rating	% Military	Nuclear Weapons–Related	Dollar Amount	% to Republicans	% to Democrats
1.0%	1	2	1	?	A	IIA	Negligible	None	$66,434	96%	4%

? = No information available
See also Appendix D for a listing of this company's products and services.

was just under 1 percent of the previous years' pre-tax earnings by CEP's calculations.

The company has been a strong supporter of the Second Harvest network of food banks, which distribute food to the hungry. The 5.1 million pounds of food Dart & Kraft has contributed to Second Harvest are almost one-tenth of the 60 million pounds this organization has received from all companies since 1979. (For further details on Second Harvest, see page 118.)

In 1983 the representation of minority group members and women among top management was 5.5 percent and 9.6 percent, respectively, up slightly from the previous year but substantially lower than two other Chicago-based food companies, Beatrice and Sara Lee.

In South Africa, its manufacturing operations, which employ 200 persons, received the second-highest "making progress" rating for compliance with the Sullivan Principles in 1985, upgraded from the previous year when it failed to report on its labor practices. In 1986 Kraft sold its operations in South Africa.

CEP located $8.2 million in arms-related prime contracts received by its Duracell battery subsidiary in 1984, although the company is not rated here as a major military contractor.

The company did not respond to CEP's questionnaires but regularly includes substantial specific data on its social programs in its annual report.

GENERAL FOODS CORPORATION

This major force in the U.S. markets for coffee, processed meats, and breakfast cereals has what we consider to be a moderate record when it comes to social initiatives. Its minority-oriented venture capital subsidiary is an unusual effort for a food company. Its charitable giving and summer jobs programs are both strong. But it has been sued for its practices in marketing highly sugared cereals to children. In September 1985, Philip Morris acquired General Foods in a $5.8 billion merger. (See the Philip Morris profile.)

General Foods is the only food company profiled in this book to fund its own Minority Enterprise Small Business Investment Corporation (MESBIC). MESBICS are venture capital companies set up to help minority-owned businesses get off the ground or expand their operations. MESBICS can be run by banks, by individuals, or by corporations. But there are only a dozen or so industrial companies in the United States that operate their own MESBICS. (See also the profiles of Amoco, Ford, General Motors, and Sun in this book.)

The company founded the North Street Capital Corporation in 1970; in 1984 it had a moderate capitalization of $1.7 million. (Equitable Life Assurance operates the largest MESBIC in the country, Equico, capitalized at over $10 million.) In its early years, North Street funded primarily start-ups of small "mom-and-pop" businesses — a highly risky approach and one that proved financially unsuccessful.

In recent years, North Street has moved toward larger investments in firms with proven track records. Expansion or buy-outs (by minority owners) are North Street's preferred approaches today, although they still are involved in start-ups when a unique product is involved.

General Foods' summer jobs program for financially needy high school students is an interesting one. The company contributes to an escrow account an amount equivalent to the students' salaries for their nine-weeks' work, to be used for post-high-school education. Of the 80 teenagers employed each summer, about 85 percent are minority group members. Students may participate for more than one summer. In its first 14 years, the program was allocated $1.4 million by General Foods.

In 1986 *Black Enterprise* magazine reported that minority group members held 8 percent of the officers' and managers' jobs and women, 18 percent. The magazine particularly praised the company's "mentoring" program which matches nonwhite male middle managers singled out for potential promotion with senior executives who then act as career "godparents." The company purchased $22 million from minority vendors in 1984.

Charitable contributions totaled $6.9 million in 1984, or a quite strong 1.4 percent of pre-tax earnings. Of this, 35 percent went for "socioeconomic" development (approximately half of this to the United Way); 26 percent to higher education, with the company matching $670,000 in employee gifts; 23 percent to research in nutrition and food sciences, primarily to universities; and 9 percent to food industry and public policy issues, including $50,000 for a study of child-care needs in Westchester County and $150,000 in support of National Public Radio's "All Things Considered."

The firm's products have been occasionally attacked by nutrition advocates. In the opinion of Michael Jacobson of the Center for Science in the Public Interest, "What with products like Kool-Aid, coffee, sugared cereals, hot dogs, and Jell-O, General Foods is probably the nation's, if not the world's, largest producer of junk foods."

General Foods' advertising of highly sugared cereals is the target of a lawsuit first filed in 1977, when the Federal Trade Commission was considering imposing a ban on such ads, aimed primarily at children. (General Foods, along with other cereal, candy, and broadcasting companies, successfully opposed the FTC proposal.) Filing the suit was the San Francisco-based Committee on Children's Television (CCT). It argued that though promoted and labeled as cereals, Alpha Bits, Honeycomb, Fruity Pebbles, Sugar Crisp, and Cocoa Pebbles are "in fact more accurately described as sugar products or candies." They contain 38 to 50 percent sugar. CCT was particularly concerned that the ads gave children the impression that they would have "magical powers" or become particularly popular as a result of eating these cereals.

The lawsuit was originally filed in 1977, but was dismissed before trial by a Los Angeles county judge in 1979. Then, after a lengthy appeal in 1983, the California Supreme Court unanimously ruled that the dismissal was in error and the suit could be brought to trial. As of early 1986 negotiations were proceeding between General Foods and the plaintiffs on a possible settlement of the suit.

GENERAL FOODS CORPORATION											
	Women		Minorities				Contracts		PAC Contributions		
% to Charity	Directors	Officers	Directors	Officers	Social Disclosure	Sullivan Rating	% Military	Nuclear Weapons–Related	Dollar Amount	% to Republicans	% to Democrats
1.4%	2	1	0	1	A	None	None	None	None		

See also Appendix D for a listing of this company's products and services.

In mid-1985 General Foods sold a minority interest in the Cerebos Food Corporation in South Africa because of a disagreement with the majority shareholders over "product strategy." The company no longer has any equity interests in that country.

The company responded in a limited fashion to CEP's questionnaires.

GENERAL MILLS, INC.

Like many companies headquartered in Minneapolis, this large food-products firm has taken substantial social initiatives. Its commitment to generous and innovative charitable giving, and its direct corporate investments in community revitalization, have been particularly impressive.

Most ambitious was its involvement in rehabilitation of the Stevens Square neighborhood of Minneapolis during the 1970s. General Mills ultimately committed $9 million in renovating one-third, or 750, of the units in this deteriorating neighborhood with a large elderly population. The company's seven-year involvement led to the general revitalization of the whole neighborhood, although it sustained losses of nearly $850,000 as developer.

As an outgrowth of this project, the firm has now entered into a joint venture, called ALTCARE, with the Wilder Foundation. Their goal is to develop and finance cost-effective long-term home care programs for the elderly to delay their placement in nursing homes. Over a five-year period, General Mills anticipates investing $5.3 million in this project.

More generally, the company is a strong supporter of minority-owned businesses through the Metropolitan Economic Development Association (MEDA) in Minneapolis. Founded in 1971, MEDA had helped start 72 minority-owned businesses through 1984, with a remarkable success rate for keeping them in business. The association provides crucial technical assistance as well as financing in the difficult task of getting small businesses off the ground. Along with other Minneapolis companies such as Pillsbury and 3M, General Mills has given both financial and staff support to MEDA. Because MEDA's experience, expertise, and pooled resources can provide a solid basis for launching successful enterprises, corporations can minimize their risks by channeling funds through it.

Along with Honeywell, International Multifoods, the St. Paul Companies, and others, General Mills is a member of the Minneapolis Two-Percent Club, whose members pledge to keep yearly charitable giving to at least 2 percent of average pre-tax earnings. General Mills' $8.2 million given in 1984 emphasized community-oriented projects. Of the company foundation's $975,000 earmarked for civic groups, $200,000 supported job training programs. Twenty thousand dollars each went to the Twin Cities Opportunities Industrialization Center and to MEDA; $30,000 supported H.I.R.E.D., which assists in the employment of the handicapped; $71,000 went to housing programs; and $124,000 funded community improvement projects, including $20,000 for emergency services for Southeast Asian refugees. The foundation's $1.9 million in gifts to education (31 percent of its total giving) went primarily in small grants, including $600,000 matching employee gifts; $135,000 for liberal arts colleges; $380,000 for various scholarship funds (including $228,000 for the children of company employees); and $18,000 for vocational education. General Mills' cash giving totaled $7.1 million in 1985, although this was a financially difficult year for the company.

In 1982 a Community Action Team was organized at General Mills. Through 1984, it matched 500 of its employees with community groups for volunteer work. A Retirement PLUS program, which began in 1984, pairs company retirees with local service organizations.

Like other major food companies, General Mills supports the Second Harvest network of food banks for the hungry. More than 2.3 million pounds of General Mills' surplus food went to Second Harvest in 1985. One company executive, on seven months' loan, helped this nonprofit group set up a nationwide system for sanitation inspection in its food-bank warehouses.

The company has been criticized by some health and nutrition activists for marketing highly sugared and refined foods, as have other large food producers. Along with some broadcasting, cereal, and candy companies, General Mills successfully opposed restrictions on televised advertising of highly sugared foods to children under twelve in the late 1970s. (See the General Foods profile.)

Savvy magazine in 1982 singled it out as one of the best companies for women workers. There were 13 women and 10 minority members among its top 167 officers in 1984. The company would not release the percentage of women and minorities among its officials and managers for publication in this book. But it is among the best companies profiled in this book on inclusion of women and minority group members on its board of directors and highest level officers. Approximately 10 percent of its work force is unionized.

The company's minority purchasing program was a modest $3.7 million in 1984. (This contrasts with the more substantial programs of other food companies, such as Campbell's $44 million or Beatrice's $38 million.)

The company responded to CEP's questionnaires.

GENERAL MILLS, INC.											
	Women		Minorities				Contracts		PAC Contributions		
% to Charity	Directors	Officers	Directors	Officers	Social Disclosure	Sullivan Rating	% Military	Nuclear Weapons–Related	Dollar Amount	% to Republicans	% to Democrats
2.1%	2	3	1	2	A	None	None	None	$109,405	67%	33%

See also Appendix D for a listing of this company's products and services.

GERBER PRODUCTS COMPANY

With over two-thirds of the market share, this giant of the baby-food industry has a reputation for supporting its hometown community. According to the authors of *Everybody's Business*, "the whole town of Fremont," site of Gerber's headquarters in Michigan, rose up in its defense when the Texas-based Anderson Clayton company attempted a takeover in 1977.

In the 1970s, in response to protests from nutritionists, Gerber, along with other baby-food manufacturers, stopped adding salt to most of their products.

In early 1986 Gerber faced a highly publicized series of complaints that glass shards were being found in its baby foods. In a similar crisis in 1984, Gerber promptly recalled two lots of baby food which federal authorities found had been contaminated with glass. But with the over 200 complaints in early 1986 unsubstantiated by the company or federal regulatory agencies, Gerber chose not to issue a recall.

Gerber has a well-endowed charitable foundation, which disbursed $800,000 in contributions in 1985. According to the Taft *Corporate Giving Directory*, approximately 20 percent of this amount went to scholarships for employees' children, and an equal amount to educational institutions. Another 20 percent went to hospitals and nutritional foundations and 15 percent supported united fund drives. The company also gave $300,000 directly, for a total of $1.1 million, or a quite strong 1.4 percent of pre-tax earnings.

The company operates a chain of 57 for-profit child-care centers.

Gerber did not respond to CEP's questionnaires.

GERBER PRODUCTS COMPANY											
	Women		Minorities				Contracts		PAC Contributions		
% to Charity	Directors	Officers	Directors	Officers	Social Disclosure	Sullivan Rating	% Military	Nuclear Weapons–Related	Dollar Amount	% to Republicans	% to Democrats
1.4%	2	1	1	0	F	None	None	None	None		

See also Appendix D for a listing of this company's products and services.

H. J. HEINZ COMPANY

The H. J. Heinz Company appears to continue to produce quality products, care for its employees, and provide the kind of substantial philanthropy for which its founder was originally known.

At the turn of the century, Henry J. Heinz ran model factories in Pittsburgh and was among the few members of the food industry to support passage of the Pure Food Act in 1906. The company's progressive orientation was praised by the authors of *The 100 Best Companies to Work for in America* in 1984.

Heinz's fairly substantial charitable giving program totaled $4.4 million in 1985, up from $3.8 million in 1984. Support went primarily to health (29 percent), education (24 percent), and cultural organizations (17 percent). Its Weight Watchers Foundation is particularly supportive of nutritional issues. The company is one of the few profiled in this book that has demonstrated particular concern for developing nations, in the form of an unusual $500,000 grant in 1983 to the University of Pittsburgh for training of Third World leaders. Heinz matched over $592,000 in employee gifts to nonprofit organizations in 1985, $2 for each $1 given by employees.

In 1982, with a host of multinational corporations disinvesting from the recently independent African nation of Zimbabwe, Heinz bought a major soap, vegetable oil, and margarine company there. This is a joint venture with the Zimbabwe government, which owns 49 percent of the company and has four seats on its nine-member board. Heinz's was reportedly the first major new foreign investment in Zimbabwe in that country's first two years of independence.

While Heinz's annual report discloses little social information aside from a brief account of charitable giving, it is unusually appealing aesthetically. The

H. J. HEINZ COMPANY											
	Women		Minorities				Contracts		PAC Contributions		
% to Charity	Directors	Officers	Directors	Officers	Social Disclosure	Sullivan Rating	% Military	Nuclear Weapons-Related	Dollar Amount	% to Republicans	% to Democrats
1.2%	1	0	0	0	C	None	None	None	None		

See also Appendix D for a listing of this company's products and services.

In the Supermarket

96-page 1984 report had a 46-page center section dedicated to the tomato, with full-color reproductions of specially commissioned works by major artists. In previous years the company has paid tribute to great chefs of the world and to poets among its employees. In 1979 it celebrated "the bicentennial anniversary of the first recorded mention of ketchup in America."

The company did not respond to CEP's questionnaires.

HERSHEY FOODS CORPORATION

This candy, restaurant (Friendly's), and food products company has a reputation for maintaining the moral values and social commitment of its founder, Milton Hershey.

More than 50 percent of the company's stock is owned by a unique, philanthropically oriented school. Milton Hershey established this school in 1909 and left the majority of the company's stock to it when he died. Originally for fatherless boys, in 1976 the school changed its charter to admit girls and include children whose parents, though living, were not able to care for them. Its 1,200 students range from kindergarten to 12th grade, and live with house parents in groups of 12 to 14 in 87 houses on the school's 10,000 acres. Full scholarships, clothing, medical, and dental care are provided.

Half of the company's traditional charitable giving program goes to education. One-third matches employees' gifts, according to the Taft *Corporate Giving Directory.* Another third went to Lehigh University in 1983. According to the Public Management Institute (PMI), the Pennsylvania-based company gives mostly in the Hershey, Harrisburg, and Lebanon region of the state, making a few large grants rather than more numerous small ones. PMI cites a $539,000 gift to the Hershey National Track and Field Youth Program, an athletic program for children nine to fourteen years of age. The company's 1981 contributions totaled $1.5 million, a quite substantial 1.4 percent of pre-tax earnings. Its foundation gave $1.7 million in 1984 (1.0 percent of pre-tax earnings), but no figures were available for additional direct giving.

The company had a policy of not advertising its products at all until 1969. At that time the rapid gains in market share by Mars forced it to reevaluate this policy, and it is now among major advertisers.

The company did not respond to CEP's questionnaires.

HERSHEY FOODS CORPORATION												
	Women		Minorities				Contracts		PAC Contributions		
% to Charity	Directors	Officers	Directors	Officers	Social Disclosure	Sullivan Rating	% Military	Nuclear Weapons–Related	Dollar Amount	% to Republicans	% to Democrats
1.0%	2	0	?	?	F	None	None	None	None		

? = No information available
See also Appendix D for a listing of this company's products and services.

IC INDUSTRIES, INC.

From mufflers (Midas) to Mexican food (Old El Paso), this Chicago-based conglomerate is well represented in the consumer marketplace. But that is not all. It also runs a railroad, produces refrigeration and hydraulic pump systems, and contracts with the military.

IC industries is one of the few major food producers with military contracts, and its involvement is increasing. By CEP's calculations, its Abex division received $29.9 million in 1984 in prime contracts from the Department of Defense. It provides the military with pumps, hydraulic systems, and generators. In 1984 IC acquired Pneumo Corporation which makes engine casings and hydraulic components for the M-1 tank, nuclear submarines, and howitzers. Its prime contracts totaled $32.5 million in 1984, but its total military business, including subcontracted work, reportedly reached $400 million that year.

The Investor Responsibility Research Center reports $1.5 million in 1983 charitable giving by IC Industries.

In late 1986, IC Industries purchased Ogden's food lines. (See addendum on page 500.)

The company did not respond to CEP's questionnaires.

IC INDUSTRIES, INC.											
	Women		Minorities				Contracts		PAC Contributions		
% to Charity	Directors	Officers	Directors	Officers	Social Disclosure	Sullivan Rating	% Military	Nuclear Weapons– Related	Dollar Amount	% to Republicans	% to Democrats
0.8%	1	0	?	?	F	None	1.5%	None	$104,302	52%	48%

? = No information available
See also Appendix D for a listing of this company's products and services.

INTERNATIONAL MULTIFOODS CORPORATION

This medium-sized food company has, like many other Minneapolis companies, made a commitment to responsible corporate citizenship.

International Multifoods has a $440,000 minority banking program, as well as a minority purchasing program, which increased from $1.1 million in 1984 to $2.6 million in 1985.

It has a fairly generous charitable giving program: $733,000 in 1985, or 1.3 percent of its pre-tax earnings. Approximately 18 percent of its giving went to Canada and Latin America, where the company has substantial interests.

In the United States, $74,000 went to the United Way and other federated drives; $268,000 went to education, and $56,000 to civic projects. The company also gave $24,000 to food banks for the hungry. Release time is available to its employees for volunteer services, and the company reports that workers put in 10 hours of additional volunteer time on the average for each hour given off from work.

In late 1986, International Multifoods announced plans to sell off its consumer product lines. (See addendum on page 500.)

The company responded to CEP's questionnaires.

INTERNATIONAL MULTIFOODS CORPORATION											
	Women		Minorities				Contracts		PAC Contributions		
% to Charity	Directors	Officers	Directors	Officers	Social Disclosure	Sullivan Rating	% Military	Nuclear Weapons–Related	Dollar Amount	% to Republicans	% to Democrats
1.3%	1	0	0	?	A	None	None	None	$4,641	100%	0%

? = No information available
See also Appendix D for a listing of this company's products and services.

KELLOGG COMPANY

Number one in the breakfast cereals industry, Kellogg has at least one outstanding social program: its support for minority banking. It has received limited praise for its recent emphasis on nutritional issues in advertising and is the only major cereal company carrying a union label on its packages.

Kellogg has one of the best minority banking programs among the firms profiled in this book. The company uses below-market-rate certificates of deposit and operating accounts, the most profitable forms of patronage for these institutions. In addition, it hires an outside consultant to determine which minority-owned banks are most active in promoting development in economically depressed neighborhoods.

There are three types of operating accounts in the Kellogg program: freight, workers' compensation, and disbursement accounts. In Memphis, Tennessee; Omaha, Nebraska; and San Leandro, California; its plant disbursement accounts are kept with minority banks, which handle the daily expenses of operating the plants exclusive of payroll. These accounts bring substantial business to the banks. Kellogg's freight payment accounts, for example, approximate $80 million annually. Kellogg also takes the unusual step of placing certificates of deposit (CDs) in minority banks at below-market rates. (Most companies use CDs at market rates in their programs.) The $2.5 to $3 million in Kellogg's CD program is larger than deposits by most companies covered in this book.

Because corporate accounts are potentially so large, they can be tremendously helpful in providing financial stability to minority banks, which often do not have large patrons in the neighborhoods where they operate. For 15 years, the National Bankers Association — the Washington-based trade association of minority- and women-owned banks — has been urging the corporate community to make greater use of such banks as a simple and direct means of helping economically depressed communities attain a measure of financial stability.

Many corporate minority banking programs rely primarily on Treasure Tax and Loan (TT&L) accounts. This means that they channel payroll, excise, and income tax payments, due to the federal government on a periodic basis throughout the year, through minority-owned banks. TT&L payments must be passed through any federally approved bank on their way to the IRS; thus, companies may easily choose one that is minority owned. The payments stay there only overnight, however, before being passed on, so the potential for generating income from these funds is fairly limited. For these reasons Kellogg, unlike most other corporations, has chosen to discontinue its TT&L accounts and concentrate on the more meaningful operating accounts.

In the late 1970s Kellogg, along with other major cereal, candy, and broadcasting companies, successfully fought proposed restrictions on advertising highly sugared products to children under twelve. More recently the company has won guarded praise from Action for Children's Television (ACT) for its ads, aimed at both children and adults, stressing the importance of balanced breakfasts and the health benefits of good nutrition in general. ACT has given Kellogg, along with McDonald's, awards for sponsorship of high-quality children's television programming over the years.

Kellogg's use of nutritional concerns in its advertising is not free of controversy. In 1984, in advertisements for its All-Bran cereal, the company cited statistics linking high-fiber diets to low cancer rates. These advertisements became the focus of a debate among nutrition activists, food manufacturers, and others over to what extent food manufacturers should be permitted to make health claims in advertisements for their products, an issue which must ultimately be decided by the U.S. Food and Drug Administration.

As a large company in a small town, Kellogg is crucial to the economy of Battle Creek, Michigan. While the firm can be said to generally support the city, its methods have not always won approval. In 1982 its heavy-handed advocacy of a merger of the city of Battle Creek with the outlying township caused an outcry. The company threatened to build its proposed world headquarters elsewhere if the merger didn't go through, on the grounds that such a merger would help revitalize this small, declining city. Kellogg's threats raised hackles among politicians, especially in the outlying township, who were not sure they wanted the merger.

Kellogg tempered the offer by promising to set aside $1.6 million — money it stood to gain in reduced property taxes under the merger — for an economic revitalization fund. It reportedly also extracted similar promises from other businesses. After a heated campaign that drew nationwide attention,

KELLOGG COMPANY											
	Women		Minorities				Contracts		PAC Contributions		
% to Charity	Directors	Officers	Directors	Officers	Social Disclosure	Sullivan Rating	% Military	Nuclear Weapons–Related	Dollar Amount	% to Republicans	% to Democrats
?	1	1	1	1	C	I	None	None	$120,499	53%	47%

? = No information available
See also Appendix D for a listing of this company's products and services.

In the Supermarket

the merger was overwhelmingly approved by both the city and township in a November 1982 referendum.

The William K. Kellogg Foundation, a private foundation established by the company's founder, is among the 10 largest in the country. In his book *The Golden Donors,* Waldemar Nielsen praises the Kellogg Foundation's work in support of rural and agricultural projects, child welfare, and public education. Although the foundation shies away from social activism, it is, in Nielsen's view, "very high among the genuinely creative and productive major American foundations." We could find no record of charitable giving by the company itself.

The company has a South African manufacturing facility employing over 300 workers. Its rating for compliance with the Sullivan Principles was the highest in 1985, up from second highest in 1983 and 1984.

The company did not respond to CEP's questionnaires.

MCCORMICK & COMPANY, INC.

Actively utilizing a participatory management style, McCormick's "Multiple Management Committees" involve workers in a broad range of business decisions. These committees are not a recent innovation; they were established during the 1930s, and are an integral part of this Baltimore-based spice company's corporate culture.

McCormick was among the first corporations in America to establish a profit-sharing plan, in 1943. As of 1985, the plan included about 4,000 of the company's workers. The firm matches, on a 20 percent basis, employee contributions to a retirement fund; workers may contribute up to 10 percent of their salaries. McCormick set up a PAYSOP plan in 1984, under which employees get company stock equivalent to ½–¾ percent of their annual salary.

Its charitable foundation matches employee gifts to educational and cultural organizations. The *National Directory of Corporate Charity* lists McCormick's 1981 contributions at $437,000. No more current data was available.

The company did not respond to CEP's questionnaires.

McCORMICK & COMPANY, INC.											
	Women		Minorities				Contracts		PAC Contributions		
% to Charity	Directors	Officers	Directors	Officers	Social Disclosure	Sullivan Rating	% Military	Nuclear Weapons–Related	Dollar Amount	% to Republicans	% to Democrats
1.6%	0	0	?	?	F	None	None	None	$3,500	77%	23%

? = No information available
See also Appendix D for a listing of this company's products and services.

MCDONALD'S CORPORATION

The story of this Chicago-based company is well known: golden arches, billions of burgers sold, the largest restaurant chain in the world — the legacy of a fast-food outlet founded by a milkshake equipment salesman in 1955. When it comes to community projects, McDonald's is often a prominent presence as well. But details on its overall programs proved hard to come by because the company did not respond to CEP's questionnaires, and the extent of its commitment is difficult to determine.

As of 1984, McDonald's reportedly had the best record among fast-food companies for franchising to blacks, with 138 owners. A spokesperson for the National Black McDonald's Operators Association told CEP in early 1986 that there were approximately 175 black owners operating approximately 250 restaurants. It has two women and three minorities among its top officers. Robert Beavers, the first black appointed to the company's board of directors in 1984, worked his way up through the organization. According to a 1986 *Black Enterprise* article, women hold a most impressive 54.3 percent of its officers' and managers' positions and minorities an equally impressive 22.8 percent.

Staff benefits at the company are substantial. These include a profit-sharing plan that typically augments salaries by 10 percent a year, a three-month sabbatical after ten years' service, and a President's Awards program that carries a cash bonus equal to one-third of an employee's salary.

As the nation's largest employer of youth, McDonald's has been both praised and criticized. Its training programs for teenagers, many of them from inner-city ghettos, are reputed to be excellent. But the jobs themselves provide low pay, low prestige, and routine work.

According to the Taft *Corporate Giving Directory*, company giving "exceeded" $1 million in 1983, a meager 0.2 percent of its pre-tax earnings. But CEP could locate no more precise figures and the company provided none.

McDONALD'S CORPORATION											
	Women		Minorities				Contracts		PAC Contributions		
% to Charity	Directors	Officers	Directors	Officers	Social Disclosure	Sullivan Rating	% Military	Nuclear Weapons–Related	Dollar Amount	% to Republicans	% to Democrats
0.2%	0	2	1	3	C	None	None	None	$173,275	80%	20%

See also Appendix D for a listing of this company's products and services.

Over the years, substantial McDonald grants have gone to the Olympics, the Special Olympics, muscular dystrophy (over $15 million), and the Ronald McDonald houses, which were started in Philadelphia in 1974 by a local franchisee and later adopted by the parent company as a nationwide undertaking. A network of 60 Ronald McDonald houses near children's hospitals nationwide provides accommodations for the parents of critically ill children.

After a lone gunman killed 21 people in a California McDonald's in 1984, the company donated $1 million to a fund for the victims' families and turned the store site over to the community for a memorial park. Action for Children's Television, an advocacy group often critical of corporate advertising and programming, has given McDonald's awards for its long-standing sponsorship of ABC Afterschool Specials and for public service announcements alerting children to the dangers of drugs.

Its giving program reportedly has four areas of primary commitment: youth and family issues, urban development projects, educational and business opportunities for minorities, and support for Chicago-based nonprofit organizations.

According to *The National Directory of Corporate Charity*, McDonald's franchises, which make up 70 percent of its outlets, give approximately three times the amount given by the parent company. Community involvement is among their requirements. Free products, special promotions for community projects and charities, loaned employees, "McJobs" for disabled youth, and direct contributions are all part of the McDonald's formula. The McJobs program was set up in 1982, and in its first two years provided 300 jobs for disabled youths in four cities.

Nutrition activists such as the Center for Science in the Public Interest have faulted fast-food restaurant chains for preparing and selling food high in fat and salt and have called for ingredient labeling on their foods. CSPI was particularly concerned that McDonald's and most other major fast-food chains were frying their food largely in beef tallow, making for particularly high levels of saturated fat. Burger King and McDonald's responded to the criticism by announcing in the spring of 1986 that they would not fry most of their foods, with the exception of french fries, in beef tallow.

MARS, INCORPORATED

Mars is a huge, privately held, family-run company so secretive that the *Washington Post* once claimed that before 1981 "no Mars executive had talked to anyone outside the trade press for forty years."

It dominates the U.S. candy market and is a major presence in the pet food and candy business in Europe and elsewhere around the world. It reportedly pays its factory employees well (it is non-union), promotes worker involvement, and is attuned to community issues near its plant sites.

It lobbied hard against proposed limitations on advertising heavily sugared products to children in the late 1970s, not surprising for an aggressive marketer and the 54th largest advertiser in the country in 1985. (See the General Foods profile.)

The Mars Foundation's 1984 charitable contributions were $744,000; these went primarily to education and to the National Symphony Orchestra in Washington, D.C. Since Mars is a private company, no comparison with profits is possible.

The company did not respond to CEP's questionnaires.

MARS, INCORPORATED											
	Women		Minorities				Contracts		PAC Contributions		
% to Charity	Directors	Officers	Directors	Officers	Social Disclosure	Sullivan Rating	% Military	Nuclear Weapons–Related	Dollar Amount	% to Republicans	% to Democrats
*	?	?	?	?	F	None	None	None	None		

* = See profile   ? = No information available
See also Appendix D for a listing of this company's products and services.

NESTLÉ S. A.

We could locate little information on social initiatives by Nestlé's U.S. operations or by the Nestlé-owned Carnation company. A single social issue dominates Nestlé's recent past: its marketing practices for infant formula in developing nations and a seven-year international boycott over these activities. This boycott was ended in 1984 and Nestlé has since received praise for its current marketing policies.

Several factors contributed to the boycott. First, Nestlé controlled an estimated 30 to 50 percent of the infant formula market. Second, protesters could not use the shareholder resolution process to enter into a dialogue with this Swiss company, as they could with U.S. infant formula manufacturers Abbott Labs, American Home Products and Bristol-Myers. Third, Nestlé was particularly outspoken in its opposition to marketing changes.

Many church groups were among the first to call for an end to the aggressive marketing of infant formula in the poorer countries of the world. They argued that contaminated water, improper labeling and misunderstanding of instructions in regions of high illiteracy were leading to infant malnutrition and deaths. They objected particularly to the use of company-paid "milk nurses" in maternity wards, to the distribution of free formula samples by hospitals, and to advertising that suggested to some the superiority of infant formula to mother's milk.

Nestlé did not differ from other companies in initially refusing to change these practices. But the debate rapidly became highly charged. A Swiss activist group printed a pamphlet called "Nestlé Kills Babies." The company sued for libel — and won. In the United States, church groups accused the firm of making contributions to a politically conservative policy center that was in turn circulating a *Fortune* article calling pro-boycott religious organizations

NESTLÉ S. A.											
	Women		Minorities				Contracts		PAC Contributions		
% to Charity	Directors	Officers	Directors	Officers	Social Disclosure	Sullivan Rating	% Military	Nuclear Weapons–Related	Dollar Amount	% to Republicans	% to Democrats
*	0	0	?	?	F	?	None	None	$27,550	95%	5%

* = See profile   ? = No information available
See also Appendix D for a listing of this company's products and services.

"Marxists marching under the banner of Christ." According to the *Washington Post*, Nestlé asserted that its contributions were not connected with the policy center's circulation of the article.

After the World Health Organization's adoption in 1981 of a formal code for marketing infant formula in developing nations, Nestlé began a slow series of concessions in its practices. However, led by a nationwide coalition called INFACT, the boycott continued. It wasn't until 1984 that company representatives and INFACT sat down together for the negotiations that finally ended this long controversy. INFACT termed this settlement a major victory, praised Nestlé for its cooperation, and urged consumers to again purchase the company's products. Churches now credit Nestlé with being the industry leader on this issue.

Both Nestlé and Carnation, which Nestlé acquired in 1984, have foundations in the United States. But information obtained by CEP on their giving suggests relatively small programs: $160,000 by Nestlé in 1981 and $275,000 by Carnation in 1984.

Carnation had a large work force in South Africa — over 1,000 in 1984. From 1981 through 1984 it consistently received the lowest rating — "did not pass basic requirements" — for compliance with the Sullivan Principles. Only two other U.S. firms (the Interpublic Group and the Masonite Corporation) were ranked in this category in 1984. In 1985 Carnation sold its South African subsidiary. Nestlé's Swiss parent company has 10 factories in South Africa. (Switzerland is not a member of the European Economic Community [EEC] and hence Nestlé would not be required to sign the EEC code of conduct for companies with operations in South Africa.)

The company did not respond to CEP's questionnaires.

OGDEN CORPORATION

Not many U.S. corporations boast a chief executive officer who quotes Shakespeare and is described by *Financial World* magazine as "the philosopher CEO." But Ogden does with its long-time chairman, Ralph Ablon.

Built from a bankrupt utility holding company in the 1950s, New York–based Ogden is now an odd smorgasbord of businesses, including Progresso and Hain food products; security guards; management of racetrack, entertainment, and sports complexes; office and industrial plant maintenance; scrap metal recycling; and hydroelectric and solid-waste power plant construction. In late 1986, Ogden sold its food lines to IC Industries. (See addendum on page 500.)

Ogden's Political Action Committee gave to a higher percentage of Democratic candidates than any other company PAC covered in this book. Very often, corporate contributions are weighted heavily to Republican candidates; Ogden's substantial Democratic PAC contributions are exceptional.

Until 1985 the company owned the Avondale Shipyard, the fourth largest shipbuilding outfit in the country. Among other projects, Avondale had contracted with the Department of Defense to construct auxiliary oilers, convert various vessels for rapid-deployment military shipping in crisis situations, produce dock-landing ships to carry amphibious military vehicles, and refurbish the nuclear-capable battleship *Iowa*. Its military contracts totaled $1.2 billion in 1985, up from $587 million in 1984.

In 1985 Ogden sold Avondale to the shipyard's non-union workers, who purchased the company through an Employee Stock Ownership Plan. Although it is unlikely that Ogden will be a major Department of Defense contractor in the future, it retained a 30 percent share of stock in the new company, which will continue its defense-related work.

The company did not respond to CEP's questionnaires.

OGDEN CORPORATION											
	Women		Minorities				Contracts		PAC Contributions		
% to Charity	Directors	Officers	Directors	Officers	Social Disclosure	Sullivan Rating	% Military	Nuclear Weapons–Related	Dollar Amount	% to Republicans	% to Democrats
?	2	2	?	?	F	None	27.5%	None	$41,424	15%	85%

? = No information available
See also Appendix D for a listing of this company's products and services.

PEPSICO, INC.

Sodas, snack foods, and fast-food restaurants make up the majority of PepsiCo's business. (The company recently sold off its North American Van Lines and Wilson sporting goods concerns.)

PepsiCo appears to have a rapidly growing minority purchasing program, sizable deposits with minority banks, and substantial, if traditional, social initiatives by its Frito-Lay subsidiary. But the company states that its subsidiaries operate with considerable autonomy and that headquarters does not "devote time and resources to developing standard formats by which our divisions can report their respective social responsibility programs or to prepare reports of 'grand totals' of a particular activity." So an overall assessment of the company's record is difficult to make.

PepsiCo's president, Roger Enrico, has spoken out strongly in support of minority purchasing programs. In 1984 the company doubled purchases from minority-owned suppliers to $20 million. Frito-Lay started its own minority purchasing program in 1983; by 1984 its purchases totaled $4.5 million. Plans were to quadruple this figure to $19 million in 1985. Together, the company and its subsidiaries project that minority purchasing will average $50 million annually over the next five years. PepsiCo also has a minority banking program with a substantial $6 million in short-term deposits.

It would not disclose figures on women and minorities in upper management to CEP.

PepsiCo's foundation reports $4 million given in 1984 (0.9 percent of pre-tax earnings), but the company estimates that a "tally [of] the funding by each of our operations of socially responsible activities" might total as much as $10 million. Contributions included $1.4 million to health and human services, $1.2 million to education, $1 million to the arts, and $0.4 million to community organizations. Recent major grants have included $1.8 million for

PEPSICO, INC.											
	Women		Minorities				Contracts		PAC Contributions		
% to Charity	Directors	Officers	Directors	Officers	Social Disclosure	Sullivan Rating	% Military	Nuclear Weapons–Related	Dollar Amount	% to Republicans	% to Democrats
0.9%	0	0	1	0	A	IV	None	None	$165,524	85%	15%

See also Appendix D for a listing of this company's products and services.

a summer performing arts festival at the State University of New York at Purchase; $600,000 for health and fitness research (the company is known for its emphasis on fitness and exercise among employees); and $1 million to the United Negro College Fund, plus smaller grants to other minority education programs.

The foundation encourages staff volunteerism with an interesting twist on its matching grants program. The company will double its usual dollar-for-dollar match of employees' gifts to nonprofit organizations if they do volunteer work with the group as well. Additionally, in 1983 the company began making 10 yearly $1,000 grants to support organizations with which workers volunteer. To encourage giving by its 400 franchised bottling plants, PepsiCo recently established the John Reese Awards, which match grants up to $1,000 to nonprofit groups. A total of $350,000 had been committed to this program through 1985.

Frito-Lay dominates the snack-food business in the United States, reportedly due in part to its superior commitment to sales and service for even the smallest stores. Frito-Lay's social commitments in Dallas, its headquarters city, are well documented: a yearly carnival to benefit the handicapped and disadvantaged, a learning center opened in a hospital in 1984, volunteering by employees, and a largely traditional charitable giving program (55 percent to United Way and other social service organizations, 8 percent to civic organizations, and 10 percent to 15 percent each to health, education, and the arts).

In 1984 the company sold its bottling plant in South Africa, which at the time employed over 500 persons. PepsiCo had become a signatory of the Sullivan Principles the previous year. It remains in the "endorser" category in 1985, supporting the principles and their goals, although the company no longer has operations there. In 1986 PepsiCo acquired Kentucky Fried Chicken, which has operations in South Africa. In 1987 PepsiCo announced plans to sell these South African operations by year's end.

The company responded to CEP's questionnaires.

PHILIP MORRIS COMPANIES, INC.

Philip Morris's sales of cigarettes have earned the company sizable profits but provoked criticism from those in the health community concerned with the possible health risks linked to tobacco consumption. The company has vigorously pursued positive social initiatives in several areas, particularly minority economic development. In 1985 it acquired General Foods. (See the General Foods profile.)

Philip Morris's minority banking program is especially noteworthy. Throughout the 1970s and early 1980s its treasurer, Harrison Poole, was among the strongest advocates of minority banking within the corporate community. The company's program not only established credit lines with minority- and women-owned banks but also borrowed on these lines, a step rarely undertaken by large corporations. (As of 1983 the firm had borrowed over $17 million under this program.) Its minority purchasing program is also very strong, with $150 million in 1984 purchases.

Further strengthening these commitments have been the "covenants" reached with Rev. Jesse Jackson's Operation PUSH by the Seven-Up and Miller Brewing subsidiaries in 1982 and 1984, respectively. An impressive 15 percent of Seven-Up's bank deposits were pledged to minority institutions, as were payroll accounts amounting to $3 million yearly. Under its Foodservice National Account Program, inaugurated in 1982, Seven-Up will guarantee up to 30 percent of bank loans to minority group members wishing to purchase fountain wholesalerships. Similarly, Miller set up a $30 million loan fund for minorities wishing to purchase distributorships, and pledged to buy 20 percent of subcontracted goods from minority vendors where such services were available.

The percentage of minorities among Philip Morris's officials and managers has risen from 5.7 percent in 1972 to 15.4 percent in 1985. For women the figures have grown from 5.8 percent in 1972 to 13.8 percent 13 years later. The company's Upward Mobility program mandates a corporation-wide search for promotions to top positions. Approximately 42 percent of its promotions to the professional and managerial levels from 1982 to 1985 were minority group members. Two of its top 12 officers are minorities.

Philip Morris is very aggressive in the political arena. In his book on politics and the tobacco industry, *The Smoke Ring*, Peter Taylor characterizes Philip Morris as "the company which is perhaps the most critical of the medical evidence against the product to which it owes [its] success." The company confronts the health issue directly in its annual reports. In 1983 it stated: "Philip Morris continues to challenge the assertion that there is conclusive proof of a cause-and-effect relationship between cigarette smoking and chronic diseases." The annual report also spoke out against the nearly 400 pieces of "restrictive" anti-smoking legislation introduced around the country that year, but asserted that "most were defeated when logic prevailed."

In 1985 the American Cancer Society cited Philip Morris's sponsorship of the Virginia Slims women's pro-tennis tour as the kind of cigarette promotion that glamorizes smoking by women. Lung cancer was, for the first time in 1985, the leading cause of cancer deaths among women, and for many years has been the primary cause of such fatalities among men.

Recently, cigarette companies have been criticized for the increasing promotion of smoking in developing countries. Cigarette consumption is on the decline in the United States and Europe, so the poorer developing nations are viewed by tobacco companies as a potential growth market. Critics are concerned not only about health problems caused by cigarette smoking in these countries, but also by the possibility that these campaigns will induce people to buy tobacco with money otherwise needed for food and other basics.

Along with other tobacco companies, Philip Morris faces numerous product liability suits because of the alleged harmfulness of its products. In the first of these suits coming to trial in late 1985 and early 1986, tobacco companies were found not liable.

In 1978 and 1980, Philip Morris contributed heavily in opposition to initiatives that would have limited smoking in public places in Florida and California. These opposition campaigns — extremely expensive, hard-hitting, and controversial — were successful in defeating the initiatives. But a similar measure passed despite an equally intense campaign in San Francisco in 1982. In addition, through its Miller and Seven-Up subsidiaries, the company has financed opposition to bottle deposit initiatives aimed at promoting recycling around the country over the years. (Beer and soda companies have proposed "litter taxes" as an alternative to deposits.)

The company reports that over 2,000 shareholders and employees contributed to its Political Action Committee in 1983. PAC contributions to congres-

PHILIP MORRIS COMPANIES, INC.												
	Women		Minorities				Contracts		PAC Contributions			
% to Charity	Directors	Officers	Directors	Officers	Social Disclosure	Sullivan Rating	% Military	Nuclear Weapons—Related	Dollar Amount	% to Republicans	% to Democrats	
0.9%	3	0	1	2	A	None	None	None	$374,172	42%	58%	

See also Appendix D for a listing of this company's products and services.

sional candidates by the company and its subsidiaries totaled $374,000 during the 1983–1984 election cycle, greater than those of any other company PACs listed in this book. (Tenneco's PAC gave out $367,000.)

Most highly publicized of its philanthropic activities has been Philip Morris's patronage of the arts. Philip Morris has sponsored museum exhibits of the works of Jasper Johns, Edward Hopper, Wassily Kandinsky, pop and op artists, as well as masterpieces from the Vatican collection. It incorporated a branch of the Whitney Museum of American Art into its world headquarters building, which opened in 1982. Philip Morris also supports the Alvin Ailey American Dance Theater and the Joffrey Ballet, as well as the Marlboro School of Music in Vermont.

The company's direct corporate giving for 1984 was $11.7 million, almost 1 percent of its pre-tax earnings. Slightly over one-third of its contributions go to education, and an additional third reportedly goes to the arts. The company will put in two dollars for every employee dollar contributed to most nonprofit groups (up to $1,000), and then match dollar for dollar up to $25,000. The company matched $955,000 in such contributions in 1984.

In 1983 Philip Morris headed up the New York City Partnerships/Summer Jobs Program, which found approximately 19,000 jobs for disadvantaged youth in the city. (Metropolitan Life and Coopers & Lybrand led this effort in 1985 and 1986, respectively.) The company also participated in similar summer jobs programs in Louisville, Kentucky, and Richmond, Virginia, where it operates tobacco processing plants.

Working for Philip Morris brings a number of unusual benefits, most notably a profit-sharing plan under which 3 percent of the company's pre-tax profits are set aside and distributed to most employees in a percentage proportional to wages. In addition, an employee stock ownership program provides salaried employees with company stock worth 0.5 to 0.75 percent of their annual compensation, for which the company gets an equivalent tax write-off. Most educational expenses for employees are reimbursed. In New York City, workers have access to a 24-hour-a-day child care information and referral service.

The company responded to CEP's questionnaires.

PILLSBURY COMPANY

Pillsbury funds a diverse mix of economic development, arts, and traditional organizations in its headquarters city of Minneapolis. In 1985, its Burger King subsidiary initiated an incentive-scholarship program for employees who enroll in post-secondary-school courses.

Pillsbury operates a dual-tier charitable giving system, with subsidiaries and plant communities setting up and administering their own contribution programs. As the parent company, Pillsbury accounted for approximately two-thirds of the total $4.2 million given in 1984, concentrating on the Minneapolis region. Community and civic projects received 15 percent of these gifts, with an emphasis on urban revitalization, minority economic development, and provision of food for the hungry. Support for the arts received a strong 26 percent. Traditional charities, such as the United Way, the YMCA, and higher education, found substantial support as well. Its 1985 giving rose sharply to $6 million, or a strong 2.4 percent of pre-tax earnings.

Although its Burger King subsidiary made only a modest $440,000 in contributions in 1984, it plans a rapid rise to $2.5 million in 1986. The vast majority of these funds are going to its innovative Crew Education Assistance Program. Burger King employees, 75 percent of whom are under 21 years old and 41 percent of whom are minority group members, will be able to accumulate $2,000 in a scholarship fund for post-secondary-school education, including vocational training as well as college. Accumulating in increments of $200 and $400 every three months, the scholarship fund reaches $2,000 after two years and can be used by individuals after they have left the company.

This Miami-based fast-food chain's recent interest in education found expression as well in a $200,000 grant toward improving the career counseling curriculum in the Washington, D.C., school system (a project co-funded with the Ford and Clark foundations); in a minority scholarship program at the

PILLSBURY COMPANY											
	Women		Minorities				Contracts		PAC Contributions		
% to Charity	Directors	Officers	Directors	Officers	Social Disclosure	Sullivan Rating	% Military	Nuclear Weapons–Related	Dollar Amount	% to Republicans	% to Democrats
2.4%	1	5	0	0	A	None	None	None	$161,107	86%	14%

See also Appendix D for a listing of this company's products and services.

University of Miami's School of Business Administration; and in a five-day symposium for outstanding teachers and principals from around the country.

Pillsbury's Steak & Ale (S&A) restaurant division allocated $50,000 of its total $139,000 in 1984 to the Family Place, a program for battered wives and children in S&A's headquarters city of Dallas.

In 1984 the company initiated several programs aimed at increasing the promotion of minorities and women. Burger King, in accordance with Rev. Jesse Jackson's Operation PUSH, stepped up its minority franchising, hiring, recruiting, and promotions. Its goal is to have blacks own 15 percent of its franchises by 1988. In 1984 only 40 of its 2,400 franchised outlets (under 2 percent) were owned by blacks.

In 1984 Pillsbury inaugurated its Motivation and Performance Seminars, aimed specifically at improving upward mobility for blacks within the company. (As of 1985, the company had five women and no minorities among its top 59 officers, although this is a larger number of total top officers than for most companies in this book.) In addition, its restaurant group has three women and four minorities among its 69 officers at a vice presidential level or higher. The company has a minority purchasing program ($4.6 million in 1984) and a modest minority banking program, with a $1 million credit line and at least one operating account.

Pillsbury's Häagen-Dazs subsidiary was sued by a socially progressive Vermont-based ice cream manufacturer, Ben & Jerry's, for unfair marketing practices. Ben & Jerry's protested Häagen-Dazs's policy of requiring its distributors to carry no other "gourmet" ice creams, using the slogan "What's the dough boy afraid of?" Ben & Jerry's campaign attracted national attention and the lawsuit was settled out of court in 1985. Häagen-Dazs, although admitting no wrongdoing at that time, agreed to allow its distributors to carry Ben & Jerry's ice cream as well.

The company responded to CEP's questionnaires.

QUAKER OATS COMPANY

A generous matching-fund contributions program and some moderate commitments to community development projects characterize this Chicago-based food company's social commitment. But without cooperation from Quaker Oats in providing information for this book, it was difficult to determine how far-reaching its overall initiatives have been.

The Quaker Oats 1985 annual report puts charitable cash giving from its foundation at $2.3 million, or 1.0 percent of pre-tax earnings. (This figure almost certainly understates the company's total cash giving. Its annual report indicates an additional $4 million in product and cash giving by the company itself. But it provides no breakdown on what percentage was in fact cash. Quaker Oats did not respond to CEP's questionnaires.)

Quaker Oats' diverse grants support a wide variety of civic and urban affairs groups and programs oriented toward women, minorities, and youth. "Social justice and solution of major public concerns" is one of the company's primary giving goals. A $50,000 gift helped start the Chicago Economic Development Corporation's revolving loan fund for minority-owned businesses. In 1985, the company purchased a $250,000 share in the Chicago Equity Fund, a multimillion-dollar pool of corporate funds devoted to lower- and moderate-income housing renovations. (Sara Lee and Dart & Kraft each purchased $500,000 shares at that time.)

Quaker's matching gift program is strong, putting in three dollars for each dollar employees contribute, up to $300. Retirees as well as present employees qualify. Quaker then matches dollar for dollar up to $6,000. More than $1 million, or almost 45 percent of its foundation's 1985 grants was made in matching gifts. In 1984 the company established a "Dollars for Doers" program, providing grants of up to $500 to qualified service organizations in

QUAKER OATS COMPANY												
	Women		Minorities					Contracts		PAC Contributions		
% to Charity	Directors	Officers	Directors	Officers	Social Disclosure	Sullivan Rating	% Military	Nuclear Weapons–Related	Dollar Amount	% to Republicans	% to Democrats
1.0%	1	1	1	?	C	None	None	None	$28,953	85%	15%

? = No information available
See also Appendix D for a listing of this company's products and services.

In the Supermarket

which Quaker employees are active volunteers. In its first year, $42,000 in grants were awarded. In 1985 this figure jumped to $71,460.

The company's Fisher-Price Toys division enjoys a particularly good reputation for the high quality of its products, its responsible policies on advertising to children, and its emphasis on safety.

As of 1985, three of Fisher-Price's ten vice presidents were women. In 1982, *Savvy* magazine had high praise for Quaker Oats for its "long history of recruiting women for professional and executive positions." Quaker has had a profit-sharing plan for its employees since 1967.

In late 1986, Quaker Oats acquired Anderson Clayton. (See addendum on page 500.)

RALSTON PURINA COMPANY

This St. Louis–based food and grain company did not respond to CEP's questionnaires, and we could locate little information on its social initiatives. However, during the 1970s it spearheaded the redevelopment of a 140-acre tract in a deteriorating downtown St. Louis neighborhood. This project is now completed.

It is unusual for nonfinancial businesses to become directly involved in neighborhood development projects — banks and insurance companies have on the whole taken more adventurous steps in this area. (General Mills and Amoco are two other companies profiled in this book that have committed corporate funds to revitalization programs.) The more usual approach — Dayton Hudson's in Minneapolis, for example — is to channel grants through a corporate foundation in support of inner-city renewal activities. With direct corporate investment, however, the commitment to revitalization programs becomes part of a company's day-to-day business, rather than a strictly charitable activity. Although both Ralston Purina and General Mills lost some of their investment on their ventures (Amoco cleared a profit in Chicago), the cost to the corporation was still minimal when compared with the scope of the projects.

Ralston Purina made a dual decision in the late 1960s: to keep and expand its corporate headquarters in downtown St. Louis, and to help upgrade the economically depressed La Salle Park neighborhood in the vicinity. The city, in financial straits at that time, was also anxious to see renewal in the neighborhood. Ralston formed the La Salle Park Redevelopment Corporation, and agreed to put up the $1.2 million required to obtain matching federal grants. The first phase, construction of 140 new units of low- and moderate-income housing, was completed in 1975. The second and third phases consisted of

RALSTON PURINA COMPANY												
	Women		Minorities				Contracts		PAC Contributions			
% to Charity	Directors	Officers	Directors	Officers	Social Disclosure	Sullivan Rating	% Military	Nuclear Weapons-Related	Dollar Amount	% to Republicans	% to Democrats	
0.8%	1	0	?	?	C	None	None	None	$10,650	96%	4%	

? = No information available
See also Appendix D for a listing of this company's products and services.

rehabilitating the 120 or so buildings in the neighborhood. Ralston itself renovated 12; others were rehabilitated by "homesteaders" who purchased buildings at low prices from the city and rehabilitated these themselves. As the project got off the ground, an increasing number of commercial developers took part. The rehabilitated housing was sold primarily to moderate- and upper-middle-income families; commercial space was also developed. By 1984 the project was 95 percent complete.

Ralston committed some $3 million as principal developer in La Salle Park. It recovered all but $300,000 of this amount, but footed the bill for considerable overhead expenses as well, such as the salary for a full-time project coordinator.

Ralston's role in this redevelopment was the subject of controversy. The *St. Louis Post-Dispatch* ran a series of articles criticizing the project in 1980, citing problems with relocation of the former residents of the area, along with tax breaks and low land prices for the company. The city and the St. Louis business community in turn defended Purina.

Along with other major cereal companies, Ralston Purina has been criticized by nutrition and children's television activists for its marketing of highly sugared cereals to children. In 1984 Ralston Purina acquired Continental Bakery from ITT. Continental is best known for such baked goods as Wonder Bread and Hostess snacks, including Twinkies. In 1986 it purchased the Drake's baked goods and snacks from Borden.

The company's founder, William Danforth, was "an indefatigable do-gooder," according to Waldemar Nielsen in *The Big Foundations*. In 1927 he created the Danforth Foundation, which is not officially connected to the company. In its early history it concentrated on education, often with a religious overtone. In the 1960s, according to Nielsen, the foundation developed "creative, socially pertinent and professionally competent programs," many of which addressed urban, racial, and black-education problems.

The *National Directory of Corporate Charity* puts the combined giving of Ralston and its foundation at $3 million in 1981, a fairly strong 1.1 percent of earnings before taxes. (The foundation alone gave $1.7 million in 1982, $2.1 million in 1983, and $2.6 million in 1984. These figures may understate the company's full program because they do not include direct corporate giving.)

The company did not answer CEP's questionnaires.

RJR NABISCO

Aggressive diversification has made R. J. Reynolds, a name once nearly synonymous with tobacco, a major player in the fast-food, liquor, canned fruit, and baked goods industries as well. After acquiring Nabisco in 1985 and changing its name to RJR Nabisco, it has become one of the largest food and consumer products companies in the United States.

Over the years, RJR has been at the center of many controversies over smoking and health. It has substantial operations in South Africa and has had major labor relations problems in the United States. But the company has also taken notable social initiatives, particularly in minority economic development.

In 1982 the Heublein liquor company, owners of the Kentucky Fried Chicken (KFC) fast-food restaurants (acquired soon after by Reynolds), agreed to increase its programs in support of black-owned businesses. At the prompting of Rev. Jesse Jackson's Operation PUSH, the company established a Capital Formation Fund of $10 million, which had guaranteed $13.1 million in loans to blacks for the acquisition and building of KFC franchises by March 1985. This fund, managed by a black-owned Chicago bank, financed a total of 24 franchises.

As of 1984, RJR had a strong minority purchasing program of $70 million, although its competitor Philip Morris had a purchasing program of $150 million that year. In addition, the company subcontracted about $30 million in business to women-owned firms. Its minority banking program was a substantial one, with $24 million in credit lines with minority-owned banks (including the $10 million KFC fund) as well as operating accounts with annual deposits of $28 million. Over 20 percent of its group life insurance was placed with black-owned companies. RJR would not release statistics to CEP for its hiring record by job category, but it reported to *Black Enterprise* magazine for a 1986 article that women and minorities both held just over 19 percent of its managerial positions.

The company's charitable giving program totaled $21.4 million in 1984, or a fairly strong 1.4 percent of pre-tax earnings, and was particularly supportive of minority education programs. RJR was the largest corporate contributor to the United Negro College Fund in both 1983 and 1984. Of the company's $21.4 million given in 1984, $8.4 million (39 percent) went to education, especially business- and agriculture-related programs; $5.5 million (26 percent) supported medical research, particularly on the causes of chronic degenerative diseases; $1.1 million (5 percent) went to United Way drives; and $1.6 million (8 percent) went to the arts.

The company pays its employees' tuition for college-level courses and provides a counseling service at its headquarters in Winston-Salem, North Carolina. It matches employee gifts to the arts and provides two dollars for every employee dollar contributed to higher education, up to $10,000. It disbursed $1.4 million under this program in 1984.

One of the company's longest controversies has been with its tobacco workers. R. J. Reynolds tobacco products have been on the AFL-CIO's "do not patronize" list since 1955. The Bakery, Confectionery and Tobacco Workers Union called for a boycott of the company's tobacco products in protest of its "virulent anti-unionism." In contrast, some of Reynolds's other subsidiaries enjoy comfortable relations with their unionized work force.

Antismoking activists have criticized RJR, along with other tobacco companies, for increasingly strong marketing of cigarettes in poor, developing nations. Additionally, these companies have been subject to recent product liability litigation claiming health damage to consumers from cigarette smoking. In the first of these cases coming to trial in late 1985 and early 1986, tobacco companies were acquitted of liability claims.

The firm has joined the fight to keep the image of smoking clean. (See the Philip Morris profile for a fuller discussion.) In 1985 it sponsored an advertisement that raised questions about the reported links between smoking and heart disease. In April 1985, the Coalition on Smoking or Health (which includes the American Heart Association, the American Lung Association, and the American Cancer Society) filed an unfair-advertising complaint with the Federal Trade Commission (FTC). The Coalition asserted that this ad misrepresented current scientific thinking on the health risks associated with smoking. The company disputed this contention. In June 1986, the FTC charged RJR with making false statements in this advertisement. RJR challenged the FTC charges. In August 1986, the FTC charges were overturned by an administrative law judge, a ruling the FTC staff was expected to appeal.

The company was the largest contributor to well-funded campaigns opposing ballot proposals in California and in Dade County, Florida, in 1978, 1979,

RJR NABISCO											
	Women		Minorities				Contracts		PAC Contributions		
% to Charity	Directors	Officers	Directors	Officers	Social Disclosure	Sullivan Rating	% Military	Nuclear Weapons–Related	Dollar Amount	% to Republicans	% to Democrats
1.4%	2	0	1	1	A	I/IIA	None	None	$176,180	43%	57%

See also Appendix D for a listing of this company's products and services.

and 1980, seeking to limit smoking in public places. Philip Morris was the second-largest contributor. These ballot proposals were defeated; the Dade County margin was especially close. A similar proposal in San Francisco passed in 1982, despite massive opposition spending by the tobacco industry.

RJR's Political Action Committee has been an active one, providing $176,000 in contributions to selected congressional candidates in the 1983–1984 election cycle (some $200,000 less than Philip Morris's PAC disbursement for the same period).

The Defense Department listed $243 million in prime contracts with RJR during 1984, mostly for transport by its Sea-Land subsidiary. These contracts placed RJR seventy-first among the Pentagon's top prime contractors, but they were not arms-related as far as CEP could determine. Since this subsidiary was spun off in 1984, RJR was not listed among the top one hundred military contractors in 1985.

RJR is a major employer in South Africa, and received the highest Sullivan rating for its Del Monte food canning operations in 1985, but the second-highest for its Kentucky Fried Chicken subsidiary, which employs approximately 1,200 of RJR's total 2,800 workers there. (PepsiCo agreed to purchase Kentucky Fried Chicken from RJR in mid-1986.)

RJR bought Nabisco in 1985 for $4.9 billion. Nabisco is a strong supporter of Second Harvest and its food bank network. Nabisco's corporate foundation reportedly contributed $550,000 in 1982. Nabisco employed just under 1,000 workers and received the second-highest "making progress" rating for compliance with the Sullivan Principles in 1985.

The company responded to CEP's questionnaires.

SARA LEE CORPORATION

This large, diverse, Chicago-based company is best known for its foods, but also produces Hanes clothing, Electrolux vacuum cleaners, Fuller brushes, and Kiwi waxes and polishes. Its charitable contribution program is dedicated almost entirely to the economically disadvantaged and to the arts, with a substantial and innovative award component. Its support for minority economic development and community revitalization has been moderate in the past, but is now expanding. The company was the target of highly publicized complaints over working conditions at its Hanes textile plants in the early 1980s.

Established in 1981, the Sara Lee Foundation has taken the notable step of dedicating 50 percent of its giving to "programs that assist the economically disadvantaged" and an additional 40 percent to arts and cultural organizations. No other company profiled in this book has devoted such high percentages to either cause.

Sara Lee's grants to groups supporting the disadvantaged cover a wide range of organizations and issues, including traditional charitable recipients such as the United Negro College Fund and the United Way. For example, in 1984 Sara Lee began a three-year, $33,000 grant to the Girl Scouts of Chicago for two neighborhood activity centers in minority neighborhoods. Numerous other small Sara Lee grants go to support groups working on hunger, health care, job placement, and youth education. Its largest arts grants were $220,000 to the Art Institute of Chicago, $100,000 to the Goodman Theater, and $220,000 to the League of Chicago Theaters to launch a discount-ticket outlet.

In addition, the firm has created innovative and substantial awards to programs promoting self-sufficiency for the poor. In 1984 its $100,000 Leadership Award went to the People Working Cooperative, a home repair service that will initiate a pilot project of home modification for the disabled, the elderly, and low-income families in Cincinnati. An Arizona job-training center for women on welfare received the 1985 award. It will use the $100,000 to set up a low-interest revolving loan fund available to its clients in their first six months of work. The center helped 325 women in 1984.

The company's two $50,000 Chicago Spirit awards went in 1985 to the Center for New Horizons — a community renewal organization in one of Chicago's poorest neighborhoods — for a revolving loan fund for housing rehabilitation, and to Housing Opportunities and Maintenance for the Elderly, to increase public awareness of the housing difficulties encountered by the elderly in Chicago, 40 percent of whom live below the poverty level.

Sara Lee has pledged to maintain its contributions at 2 percent of pre-tax *domestic* earnings. Its $3.9 million given in 1985 was 1.3 percent of *total* pre-tax earnings.

In-kind donations stood at $6.5 million in 1984, including food to the Second Harvest National Food Bank Network (see pp. 118–119 for details), and 30,000 vacuum cleaners from its Electrolux division to Gifts in Kind, a nonprofit organization devoted to the redistribution of nonfood goods to health and human care agencies throughout the country.

A new program, begun in 1985, matched some thirty Sara Lee executives with community service organizations needing corporate representatives on their boards. (Two serve with Second Harvest and one with Gifts in Kind.)

Sara Lee's minority economic development efforts have not been as extensive as those of other Chicago companies such as Amoco or Dart & Kraft, but are being upgraded. Its minority banking program jumped from $1 million in certificates of deposit in 1984 to $2.6 million as of 1985. Its minority purchasing program, which was operating at a low level, was being revised as well.

Also in 1985, the Sara Lee Neighborhood Redevelopment Corporation was formed; it purchased a $500,000 share in the Chicago Equity Fund, which has raised $6 million in corporate funds for local rehabilitation of low- and medium-income housing. Previously, along with Quaker Oats and Dart & Kraft, Sara Lee had contributed $50,000 toward the Chicago Economic Development Corporation's Corporate Loan Fund, which promotes minority-owned businesses.

Women among the company's officers and managers totaled a substantial 28.3 percent in 1985 (up slightly from 1984), and minorities totaled 8.0 percent (down from 10.8 percent the previous year). Of the companies profiled in this book, only Sara Lee and Ford published their complete equal employment opportunity hiring statistics by job category in their annual reports.

SARA LEE CORPORATION											
	Women		Minorities				Contracts		PAC Contributions		
% to Charity	Directors	Officers	Directors	Officers	Social Disclosure	Sullivan Rating	% Military	Nuclear Weapons–Related	Dollar Amount	% to Republicans	% to Democrats
1.3%	2	0	1	0	A	V	None	None	None		

See also Appendix D for a listing of this company's products and services.

In the Supermarket

In the early 1980s the company faced a highly publicized confrontation over working conditions at its Hanes textile factories, which it had acquired in 1979. In 1980 the Occupational Safety and Health Agency (OSHA) cited Hanes for workplace violations allegedly causing tendonitis and other physical disabilities among employees. In 1981 the company reached an agreement with OSHA for improving work conditions and implemented a pilot ergonomics project designed to improve physical working conditions. But complaints continued on into 1983, with workers claiming inadequate improvements. Church groups and others filed a shareholder resolution on the issue at the company's annual meeting. The company asserted that problems were not as widespread as claimed, and linked the discontent to a then unsuccessful unionizing effort by the Amalgamated Clothing and Textile Workers Union. It nevertheless established a Medical Task Force and implemented a full-scale ergonomics program to improve working conditions.

In 1985 the company told CEP that "the Hanes Group has heard and responded to the concerns of its employees voiced in recent years." But in 1985 the South Carolina–based, church-affiliated Connective Ministry Across the South published a highly critical assessment of the programs implemented by Hanes the previous year, terming them "primarily window dressing." In a survey of 927 Hanes employees by the Ministry, 89 percent responded negatively to the question, "Do you think Hanes is a better place or a worse place to work than it was a year ago?" Again, 89 percent of the workers responding to the survey suggested that production requirements be lowered in order to reduce job-related physical disabilities.

In late 1984 Sara Lee acquired a worldwide network of consumer-product lines from Australian Nicholas Kiwi, Ltd., best known in the United States for its shoe polishes. Kiwi's operations in South Africa employ approximately 200 persons. Sara Lee became a signatory of the Sullivan Principles in 1985. In late 1986, Sara Lee announced plans to sell these operations.

The company responded to CEP's questionnaires.

J. M. SMUCKER COMPANY

Jams, jellies, and preserves have been the business of this Ohio firm for 90 years. The Smucker family still runs the company and reportedly owns 30 percent of its stock.

According to the Taft *Corporate Giving Directory*, Smucker's gave $250,000 in 1984, half of which went to education and 30 percent to the arts. The company's stated giving goal is 2 percent of pre-tax earnings.

The company did not respond to CEP's questionnaires.

J. M. SMUCKER COMPANY											
	Women		Minorities				Contracts		PAC Contributions		
% to Charity	Directors	Officers	Directors	Officers	Social Disclosure	Sullivan Rating	% Military	Nuclear Weapons–Related	Dollar Amount	% to Republicans	% to Democrats
1.1%	0	0	0	0	F	None	None	None	None		

See also Appendix D for a listing of this company's products and services.

UNILEVER N. V.

Best known in the United States as the owner of Lever Brothers and Thomas J. Lipton companies, this Anglo-Dutch giant is one of the world's largest consumer products company. We could locate little information on the social activities of this huge conglomerate or its U.S. subsidiaries.

Barron's described Unilever in 1983 as "employing more people throughout the world than some nations have soldiers in their armies." It is thus not surprising to find that the company has extensive operations in South Africa. It employs 6,800 persons there, more than are employed by any U.S. company in that country. Unilever is a signatory of the ten-nation European Economic Community's code of conduct for firms in South Africa. Adopted in 1977, this code pledges signatories support for black unions, desegregated workplaces, job training for blacks, and wage levels above the minimum for poverty subsistence. Compliance with the code is voluntary and not monitored by outside agencies.

According to the Ethical Investment Research and Information Service in London, Unilever's charitable contributions totaled £1 million in 1983, or 0.1 percent of its profits before taxes. In the United States, the Taft *Corporate Giving Directory* reports 1984 giving by the Lipton Foundation at $600,000.

In late 1986, Unilever acquired Chesebrough-Pond's. (See addendum on page 500.)

The company did not respond to CEP's questionnaires.

UNILEVER N. V.											
	Women		Minorities				Contracts		PAC Contributions		
% to Charity	Directors	Officers	Directors	Officers	Social Disclosure	Sullivan Rating	% Military	Nuclear Weapons–Related	Dollar Amount	% to Republicans	% to Democrats
0.1%	0	0	0	0	F	?	None	None	None		

See also Appendix D for a listing of this company's products and services.

WENDY'S INTERNATIONAL, INC.

The "baby" of the big three burger chains, Wendy's was founded in 1969. Its social initiatives appear at this time to be minimal.

As of 1985, Wendy's had no minority purchasing program, but was in the process of establishing one. The company reports that it does not record fair hiring statistics by job category. (Companies with government contracts are required to file these with federal authorities; Wendy's has no government contracts.) At the end of 1984, 68 of Wendy's 1,935 franchised restaurants (3.5 percent) were operated by minority group members.

According to the Investor Responsibility Research Center, Wendy's entered into an agreement in 1984 with WENBUR, a South African affiliate, to open ten restaurants in that country within three years. In mid-1985 a company spokesperson confirmed that negotiations on opening South African outlets had taken place, but told us that as of that time there were no Wendy's outlets in that country and that he "could not predict the future."

Wendy's has been characterized by CSPI as "a company with a split personality when it comes to nutrition," winning praise for its light menus and salad bars, but losing points for the high fat content of such items as its Triple Cheeseburger.

The company responded to CEP's questionnaires.

WENDY'S INTERNATIONAL, INC.											
	Women		Minorities				Contracts		PAC Contributions		
% to Charity	Directors	Officers	Directors	Officers	Social Disclosure	Sullivan Rating	% Military	Nuclear Weapons–Related	Dollar Amount	% to Republicans	% to Democrats
*	1	1	0	2	A	None	None	None	None		

* = See profile
See also Appendix D for a listing of this company's products and services.

In the Supermarket

WM. WRIGLEY JR. COMPANY

Wrigley is an anomaly in this day of huge conglomerates and multi-product companies: a major company relying on a single product — gum.

Wrigley has had a Group Achievement Fund since 1949 to reward increased worker productivity. From 1979 through 1983 it paid out $19 million, equivalent to over 7 percent of the earned wages of those eligible. Employees may set aside on a pre-tax basis up to 10 percent of their salaries in a special retirement account, with the company contributing an additional six dollars for every ten dollars employees put in.

The *National Directory of Corporate Charities* lists $293,000 in charitable contributions by Wrigley in 1983, a moderate 0.5 percent of pre-tax earnings.

The company did not respond to CEP's questionnaires.

WM. WRIGLEY JR. COMPANY											
	Women		Minorities				Contracts		PAC Contributions		
% to Charity	Directors	Officers	Directors	Officers	Social Disclosure	Sullivan Rating	% Military	Nuclear Weapons–Related	Dollar Amount	% to Republicans	% to Democrats
0.5%	1	0	0	0	F	None	None	None	None		

See also Appendix D for a listing of this company's products and services.

Chapter 6

IN THE DRUGSTORE
Health and Personal Care
Product Companies

CHARITABLE CONTRIBUTIONS AND COMMUNITY INVOLVEMENT

Noxell and Pennwalt are the two companies profiled in this chapter that gave more than 1.5 percent of pre-tax earnings to charities.

Outstanding among the companies listed in this chapter for their community involvement are Johnson & Johnson (J&J) and Procter & Gamble (P&G). Both are traditional companies with a long record of commitment to quality, accompanied by thorough and comprehensive efforts in community and employee relations.

Much praise has also been accorded J&J's handling of the Tylenol and Zomax crises, in which the company chose expensive voluntary recalls to assure maximum public well-being. J&J's commitments to the revitalization of its headquarters city of New Brunswick, New Jersey, are impressive as well. P&G, with a solid reputation as a good corporate citizen in its headquarters city of Cincinnati, has been especially thorough in developing a family-oriented benefits program for employees.

Avon is notable for its foundation's commitments to community, women's, and minority projects, and for its substantial minority purchasing and banking programs. Among pharmaceutical and personal care companies mentioned in this book, J&J, Avon, and Abbott reported the largest minority purchasing programs with $21 million, $15 million, and $14.8 million, respectively.

REPRESENTATION OF WOMEN AND MINORITIES IN MANAGEMENT

Avon, Johnson Products, and Warner-Lambert had at least one woman and one minority both in top management and on their board of directors. Alberto-Culver, Avon, and Johnson Products had at least two women both in top management and on their board of directors. Only the black-owned Johnson Products had two or more minorities in both categories.

INVOLVEMENT IN SOUTH AFRICA

Approximately two-thirds of the companies in this chapter have operations in South Africa, with four receiving our highest rating for their compliance with the Sullivan Principles (American Cyanamid, Gillette, J&J, and Pfizer); three classed as unrated recent signatories (Chesebrough-Pond's, S. C. Johnson & Son, and Revlon); and the rest falling in between. Those not involved in South Africa are Alberto-Culver, Avon, Johnson Products, Mary Kay, Noxell, and Rapid-American, with A. H. Robins and Pennwalt recently having withdrawn. Revlon and Richardson-Vicks announced plans to withdraw in 1986.

CONVENTIONAL- AND/OR NUCLEAR-ARMS CONTRACTS

Conventional or nuclear arms contracting are not major issues for any of the companies profiled in this chapter.

POLITICAL ACTION COMMITTEE CONTRIBUTIONS

Pharmaceutical companies with the most active PACs were Pfizer and Abbott Labs, followed at some distance by J&J and Bristol-Myers.

OTHER CONTROVERSIES

The safety, efficacy, and marketing of drugs are significant issues for many of the companies profiled in this chapter. An independent comparison of the overall record of drug companies in these areas was beyond our scope, but we have noted some major controversies. Among the groups following these issues most closely is the Nader-affiliated Health Research Group.

Thousands of lawsuits over A. H. Robins's manufacture and sale of the contraceptive device known as the Dalkon Shield have forced this company to seek the protection of bankruptcy courts, an unprecedented occurrence within the industry. SmithKline Beckman pleaded guilty in 1984 to withholding reports of adverse and potentially fatal side effects from its newly marketed antihypertensive drug Selacryn.

Mixed records characterize many in the pharmaceutical industry. Warner-Lambert was involved in several major controversies during the late 1970s, but has recently made a strong effort in several social areas. The extremely secretive American Home Products, criticized by some church groups for its infant formula marketing practices at home and abroad, enjoys a cordial relationship with its unions, and asserts that it is now more open with the public and attuned to social issues.

**Minority Purchasing Programs
Reported by Profiled Health and Personal Care Product Companies**

	Purchases from Minority Vendors	Total Sales
	(millions of dollars)	
Abbott (1983)	$14.8	$2,927
Avon (1984)	15.0	3,127
Gillette (1985)	5.4	2,400
Johnson & Johnson (1983)	21.0	5,972
Noxell (1984)	1.0	350
Pennwalt (1984)	1.1	1,047
Pfizer (1983)	8.0	3,750
Richardson-Vicks (1984)	4.3	1,280
A. H. Robins (1984)	0.02	632
Schering-Plough (1985)	1.2	1,927
Warner-Lambert (1984)	6.0	3,167

Source: Company responses to CEP inquiries.

In contrast, American Cyanamid, which was involved in a controversy over its requirement that certain female workers be sterilized in order to work in a paint pigment plant during the 1970s, provided CEP with no information on social initiatives. Similarly American Brands, a marketer of cigarettes and liquor, has no apparent record of substantial social involvement that CEP could locate.

Consumers purchasing over-the-counter drugs such as cold or cough remedies, antihistamines, or pain relievers should be aware of the safety and effectiveness of these products before making a purchase. The Health Research Group in its book *Over-the-Counter Pills That Don't Work* asserts, for example, that many best-selling items on drugstore shelves are ineffective for recommended uses, have safety problems, or are unnecessarily costly.

COSMETICS

Size of Charitable Contributions	Women Directors and Officers	Minority Directors and Officers	Social Disclosure	Brand Name	Company (Profile Page)	Involvement in South Africa	Conv. Weapons–Related Contracts	Nuclear Weapons–Related Contracts	Authors' Company of Choice
$ $	�566 �566 �566	�566 �566	✍ ✍ ✍	Avon	Avon (p. 206)	No	No	No	✔
$ $ $	�566 �566	�566	✍ ✍ ✍	Almay Max Factor	Beatrice (p. 118)	No	No	No	
?	�566	?	No	Cutex	Chesebrough-Pond's (p. 210)	Yes C	No	No	
?	�566 �566	?	No	Mary Kay	Mary Kay (p. 219)	No	No	No	
$ $ $	�566	No	✍ ✍ ✍	Cover Girl	Noxell (p. 221)	No	No	No	

COSMETICS *(cont'd.)*

Size of Charitable Contributions	Women Directors and Officers	Minority Directors and Officers	Social Disclosure	Brand Name	Company (Profile Page)	Involvement in South Africa	Conv. Weapons–Related Contracts	Nuclear Weapons–Related Contracts	Authors' Company of Choice
$ $	↑	↑	✍ ✍ ✍	Coty	Pfizer (p. 224)	Yes A	No	No	
$	↑	?	No	Revlon Natural Wonder	Revlon (p. 230)	Yes C	No	No	
$ $	↑	No	✍ ✍ ✍	Maybelline	Schering-Plough (p. 237)	Yes B	No	No	
?	↑	?	No	Alexandra de Markoff Charles of the Ritz Yves St. Laurent	Squibb (p. 241)	Yes B	No	No	

* = See company profile
? = No information available
Single figure ($, ↑) = Minimal
Double figure ($$, ↑↑, ✍✍, ↑↑) = Moderate
Triple figure ($$$, ↑↑↑, ✍✍✍, ↑↑↑) = Substantial

No = No involvement or participation
Yes = Involvement or participation. A, B, C in the South African column reflect the degree of compliance with Sullivan Principles and/or involvement in strategic industries.

See Chapter 4 for a detailed discussion of chart symbols.

COSMETICS

PERFUMES AND FRAGRANCES

Size of Charitable Contributions	Women Directors and Officers	Minority Directors and Officers	Social Disclosure	Brand Name	Company (Profile Page)	Involvement in South Africa	Conv. Weapons–Related Contracts	Nuclear Weapons–Related Contracts	Authors' Company of Choice

$ $ $	No	No	No	CIE
				Geoffrey Beene
				L'Air du Temps
				Niki de St.
				   Phalle
				Parfums Pierre
				   Cardin
					American Cyanamid (p. 205)	Yes A	No	No	

$ $	♀♀♀	♀♀	✍✍✍	Fantasque Louis Feraud Parri Elle	Avon (p. 206)	No	No	No	✔
?	♀	?	No	*Prince Matchabelli:* Aviance Aziza Chimere Wind Song, etc.	Chesebrough-Pond's (p. 210)	Yes C	No	No	
∗	No	?	No	Gloria Vanderbilt Paloma Picasso Polo Ralph Lauren	Nestlé (p. 150)	Yes ?	No	No	

PERFUMES AND FRAGRANCES *(cont'd.)*

Size of Charitable Contributions	Women Directors and Officers	Minority Directors and Officers	Social Disclosure	Brand Name	Company (Profile Page)	Involvement in South Africa	Conv. Weapons-Related Contracts	Nuclear Weapons-Related Contracts	Authors' Company of Choice
$ $	⋀	⋀	✍ ✍ ✍	Coty Stetson	Pfizer (p. 224)	Yes A	No	No	
$	⋀	?	No	Charlie Ciara Jontue Scoundrel	Revlon (p. 230)	Yes C	No	No	
?	⋀	?	No	*Charles of the Ritz:* Enjoli Gianni Versace Yves St. Laurent	Squibb (p. 241)	Yes B	No	No	

* = See company profile
? = No information available
Single figure ($, ⋀) = Minimal
Double figure ($$, ⋀⋀, ✍✍, ⋀⋀) = Moderate
Triple figure ($$$, ⋀⋀⋀, ✍✍✍, ⋀⋀⋀) = Substantial

No = No involvement or participation
Yes = Involvement or participation. A, B, C in the South African column reflect the degree of compliance with Sullivan Principles and/or involvement in strategic industries.

See Chapter 4 for a detailed discussion of chart symbols.

DIAPERS

DISPOSABLE DIAPERS

Size of Charitable Contributions	Women Directors and Officers	Minority Directors and Officers	Social Disclosure	Brand Name	Company (Profile Page)	Involvement in South Africa	Conv. Weapons–Related Contracts	Nuclear Weapons–Related Contracts	Authors' Company of Choice
$$	♀	♀	✍🏻 ✍🏻 ✍🏻	Huggies	Kimberly-Clark (p. 422)	Yes C	No	No	
$$$	♀ ♀	♀ ♀	✍🏻 ✍🏻 ✍🏻	Luvs Pampers	Procter & Gamble (p. 226)	No	No	No	✔

* = See company profile
? = No information available
Single figure ($, ♀) = Minimal
Double figure ($$, ♀♀, ✍🏻✍🏻, ♀♀) = Moderate
Triple figure ($$$, ♀♀♀, ✍🏻✍🏻✍🏻, ♀♀♀) = Substantial

No = No involvement or participation
Yes = Involvement or participation. A, B, C in the South African column reflect the degree of compliance with Sullivan Principles and/or involvement in strategic industries.

See Chapter 4 for a detailed discussion of chart symbols.

PERSONAL HYGIENE

DEODORANTS

Size of Charitable Contributions	Women Directors and Officers	Minority Directors and Officers	Social Disclosure	Brand Name	Company (Profile Page)	Involvement in South Africa	Conv. Weapons-Related Contracts	Nuclear Weapons-Related Contracts	Authors' Company of Choice
$ $ $	No	No	No	Lady's Choice Old Spice	American Cyanamid (p. 205)	Yes A	No	No	
$ $ $	☆ ☆	☆	✍ ✍ ✍	Almay	Beatrice (p. 118)	No	No	No	
$ $ $	☆ ☆	?	✍ ✍ ✍	Ban Mum Tickle Ultra Ban	Bristol-Myers (p. 208)	Yes B	No	No	
$ $	☆ ☆	No	✍ ✍ ✍	Dry Idea Right Guard Soft 'n Dry	Gillette (p. 212)	Yes A	No	No	
?	☆ ☆	☆	No	Dial	Greyhound (p. 416)	No	No	No	
$ $ $	☆	No	✍ ✍ ✍	Fresh	Pennwalt (p. 222)	No	No	No	
$ $	☆	☆	✍ ✍ ✍	Musk for Men Stetson	Pfizer (p. 224)	Yes A	No	No	

(Continued on next page)

DEODORANTS *(cont'd.)*

Size of Charitable Contributions	Women Directors and Officers	Minority Directors and Officers	Social Disclosure	Brand Name	Company (Profile Page)	Involvement in South Africa	Conv. Weapons–Related Contracts	Nuclear Weapons–Related Contracts	Authors' Company of Choice
$ $ $	↟	↟ ↟	🖐 🖐 🖐	Secret Sure	Procter & Gamble (p. 226)	No	No	No	✔
*	?	?	No	Brut 33 Fabergé brand	Rapid American (p. 229)	No	No	No	
$	↟	?	No	Hi & Dri Mitchum	Revlon (p. 230)	Yes C	No	No	
?	↟	?	No	Jean Naté	Squibb (p. 241)	Yes B	No	No	
$	↟	No	No	Tussy	Sterling Drug (p. 242)	Yes B	No	No	

* = See company profile
? = No information available
Single figure ($, ↟) = Minimal
Double figure ($$, ↟↟, 🖐🖐, ↟↟) = Moderate
Triple figure ($$$, ↟↟↟, 🖐🖐🖐, ↟↟↟) = Substantial

No = No involvement or participation
Yes = Involvement or participation. A, B, C in the South African column reflect the degree of compliance with Sullivan Principles and/or involvement in strategic industries.

See Chapter 4 for a detailed discussion of chart symbols.

In the Drugstore

PERSONAL HYGIENE

RAZOR BLADES

Size of Charitable Contributions	Women Directors and Officers	Minority Directors and Officers	Social Disclosure	Brand Name	Company (Profile Page)	Involvement in South Africa	Conv. Weapons–Related Contracts	Nuclear Weapons–Related Contracts	Authors' Company of Choice
$ $	No	No	No	Wilkinson brand	Allegheny International (p. 348)	Yes C	No	No	
$ $	人 人	No	✍ ✍ ✍	*Gillette brands:* Atra Trak II	Gillette (p. 212)	Yes A	No	No	✔
$ $ $	人 人	人 人	✍ ✍ ✍	Schick brand	Warner-Lambert (p. 243)	Yes B	No	No	

* = See company profile
? = No information available
Single figure ($, 人) = Minimal
Double figure ($$, 人人, ✍✍, 人人) = Moderate
Triple figure ($$$, 人人人, ✍✍✍, 人人人) = Substantial

No = No involvement or participation
Yes = Involvement or participation. A, B, C in the South African column reflect the degree of compliance with Sullivan Principles and/or involvement in strategic industries.

See Chapter 4 for a detailed discussion of chart symbols.

PERSONAL HYGIENE

SANITARY NAPKINS AND TAMPONS

Size of Charitable Contributions	Women Directors and Officers	Minority Directors and Officers	Social Disclosure	Brand Name	Company (Profile Page)	Involvement in South Africa	Conv. Weapons–Related Contracts	Nuclear Weapons–Related Contracts	Authors' Company of Choice
$ $ $	↑ ↑	↑	🖐 🖐 🖐	Playtex	Beatrice (p. 118)	No	No	No	
$ $	↑	↑ ↑	🖐 🖐 🖐	Assure Carefree Silhouettes Sure & Natural	Johnson & Johnson (p. 214)	Yes A	No	No	✔
$ $	↑	↑	🖐 🖐 🖐	Kotex Light Days New Freedom	Kimberly-Clark (p. 422)	Yes C	No	No	
$ $ $	↑	↑ ↑	🖐 🖐 🖐	Always	Procter & Gamble (p. 226)	No	No	No	✔

* = See company profile
? = No information available
Single figure ($, ↑) = Minimal
Double figure ($$, ↑↑, 🖐🖐, ↑↑) = Moderate
Triple figure ($$$, ↑↑↑, 🖐🖐🖐, ↑↑↑) = Substantial

No = No involvement or participation
Yes = Involvement or participation. A, B, C in the South African column reflect the degree of compliance with Sullivan Principles and/or involvement in strategic industries.

See Chapter 4 for a detailed discussion of chart symbols.

PERSONAL HYGIENE

SHAMPOOS

Size of Charitable Contributions	Women Directors and Officers	Minority Directors and Officers	Social Disclosure	Brand Name	Company (Profile Page)	Involvement in South Africa	Conv. Weapons–Related Contracts	Nuclear Weapons–Related Contracts	Authors' Company of Choice
$	🚶	No	No	Selsun Blue	Abbott Labs (p. 202)	Yes B	No	No	
?	🚶🚶🚶	No	No	Alberto-VO5	Alberto-Culver (p. 204)	No	No	No	
$ $ $	No	No	No	Breck	American Cyanamid (p. 205)	Yes A	No	No	
$ $ $	🚶🚶	🚶	✍️✍️✍️	Jhirmack	Beatrice (p. 118)	No	No	No	
$ $ $	🚶🚶	?	✍️✍️✍️	Clairol	Bristol-Myers (p. 208)	Yes B	No	No	
$ $	🚶🚶	No	✍️✍️✍️	Mink Difference Silkience White Rain	Gillette (p. 212)	Yes A	No	No	
$ $ $	🚶	🚶	✍️✍️✍️	Agree Enhance Hälsa	S. C. Johnson & Son (p. 420)	Yes C	No	No	

(Continued on next page)

SHAMPOOS (cont'd.)

Size of Charitable Contributions	Women Directors and Officers	Minority Directors and Officers	Social Disclosure	Brand Name	Company (Profile Page)	Involvement in South Africa	Conv. Weapons–Related Contracts	Nuclear Weapons–Related Contracts	Authors' Company of Choice
$ $	🖎	🖎 🖎	✍ ✍ ✍	Affinity Baby Shampoo	Johnson & Johnson (p. 214)	Yes A	No	No	✔
?	🖎 🖎 🖎	🖎 🖎 🖎	No	Afro Sheen Ultra Sheen Ultra Wave	Johnson Products (p. 218)	No	No	No	
$ $ $	🖎	🖎 🖎	✍ ✍ ✍	Head & Shoulders Lilt Pert Prell	Procter & Gamble (p. 226)	No	No	No	✔
*	?	?	No	Fabergé	Rapid American (p. 229)	No	No	No	
$	🖎	?	No	Aquamarine Flex Milk Plus 6	Revlon (p. 230)	Yes C	No	No	
?	🖎	No	✍ ✍ ✍	Mill Creek Pantene Vidal Sassoon	Richardson-Vicks (p. 232)	No	No	No	
$	No	No	No	Dimension	Unilever (p. 171)	Yes ?	No	No	

✱ = See company profile
? = No information available
Single figure ($, 🖎) = Minimal
Double figure ($$, 🖎🖎, ✍✍, 🖎🖎) = Moderate
Triple figure ($$$, 🖎🖎🖎, ✍✍✍, 🖎🖎🖎) = Substantial

No = No involvement or participation
Yes = Involvement or participation. A, B, C in the South African column reflect the degree of compliance with Sullivan Principles and/or involvement in strategic industries.

See Chapter 4 for a detailed discussion of chart symbols.

In the Drugstore

PERSONAL HYGIENE

SHAVING CREAMS

Size of Charitable Contributions	Women Directors and Officers	Minority Directors and Officers	Social Disclosure	Brand Name	Company (Profile Page)	Involvement in South Africa	Conv. Weapons-Related Contracts	Nuclear Weapons-Related Contracts	Authors' Company of Choice
$ $ $	No	No	No	Old Spice	American Cyanamid (p. 205)	Yes A	No	No	
$	♀	?	No	Colgate	Colgate-Palmolive (p. 211)	Yes A/B	No	No	
$ $	♀ ♀	No	✍ ✍ ✍	Foamy Trak II	Gillette (p. 212)	Yes A	No	No	✔
$ $ $	♀	♀	✍ ✍ ✍	Edge	S. C. Johnson & Son (p. 420)	Yes C	No	No	✔
$ $ $	♀	No	✍ ✍ ✍	Noxema	Noxell (p. 221)	No	No	No	✔
$ $	♀	♀	✍ ✍ ✍	Barbasol	Pfizer (p. 224)	Yes A	No	No	

* = See company profile
? = No information available
Single figure ($, ♀) = Minimal
Double figure ($$, ♀♀, ✍✍, ♀♀) = Moderate
Triple figure ($$$, ♀♀♀, ✍✍✍, ♀♀♀) = Substantial

See Chapter 4 for a detailed discussion of chart symbols.

No = No involvement or participation
Yes = Involvement or participation. A, B, C in the South African column reflect the degree of compliance with Sullivan Principles and/or involvement in strategic industries.

PERSONAL HYGIENE

SKIN CARE PRODUCTS

Size of Charitable Contributions	Women Directors and Officers	Minority Directors and Officers	Social Disclosure	Brand Name	Company (Profile Page)	Involvement in South Africa	Conv. Weapons–Related Contracts	Nuclear Weapons–Related Contracts	Authors' Company of Choice
$	⚲	?	No	Jergens	American Brands (p. 113)	Yes C	No	No	
$ $ $	No	No	No	La Prairie	American Cyanamid (p. 205)	Yes A	No	No	
$ $ $	⚲ ⚲	?	✍ ✍ ✍	Keri Lotion Sea Breeze	Bristol-Myers (p. 208)	Yes B	No	No	
?	⚲	?	No	Pond's Vaseline Intensive Care	Chesebrough-Pond's (p. 210)	Yes C	No	No	
$ $	⚲ ⚲	No	✍ ✍ ✍	Aapri Deep Magic	Gillette (p. 212)	Yes A	No	No	
$ $	⚲	⚲ ⚲	✍ ✍ ✍	Purpose	Johnson & Johnson (p. 214)	Yes A	No	No	✔
$ $ $	⚲	⚲	✍ ✍ ✍	Curel Soft Sense	S. C. Johnson & Son (p. 420)	Yes C	No	No	

SKIN CARE PRODUCTS *(cont'd.)*

Size of Charitable Contributions	Women Directors and Officers	Minority Directors and Officers	Social Disclosure	Brand Name	Company (Profile Page)	Involvement in South Africa	Conv. Weapons–Related Contracts	Nuclear Weapons–Related Contracts	Authors' Company of Choice
$ $ $	♀	No	✍ ✍ ✍	Noxema Raintree	Noxell (p. 221)	No	No	No	✔
$ $	♀	♀	✍ ✍ ✍	Pacquin	Pfizer (p. 224)	Yes A	No	No	
$ $ $	♀	♀ ♀	✍ ✍ ✍	Wondra	Procter & Gamble (p. 226)	No	No	No	✔
$	♀	?	No	Milk Plus 6	Revlon (p. 230)	Yes C	No	No	
?	♀	No	✍ ✍ ✍	Oil of Olay	Richardson-Vicks (p. 232)	No	No	No	
$ $ $	♀ ♀	♀ ♀	✍ ✍ ✍	Lubriderm	Warner-Lambert (p. 243)	Yes B	No	No	

* = See company profile
? = No information available
Single figure ($, ♀) = Minimal
Double figure ($$, ♀♀, ✍✍, ♀♀) = Moderate
Triple figure ($$$, ♀♀♀, ✍✍✍, ♀♀♀) = Substantial

No = No involvement or participation
Yes = Involvement or participation. A, B, C in the South African column reflect the degree of compliance with Sullivan Principles and/or involvement in strategic industries.

See Chapter 4 for a detailed discussion of chart symbols.

PERSONAL HYGIENE

SOAPS

Size of Charitable Contributions	Women Directors and Officers	Minority Directors and Officers	Social Disclosure	Brand Name	Company (Profile Page)	Involvement in South Africa	Conv. Weapons–Related Contracts	Nuclear Weapons–Related Contracts	Authors' Company of Choice
$	⋏	?	No	Aloe & Lanolin Fiesta Jergens	American Brands (p. 113)	Yes C	No	No	
$	⋏	?	No	Cashmere Bouquet Irish Spring Palmolive Gold	Colgate-Palmolive (p. 211)	Yes A/B	No	No	
?	⋏ ⋏	⋏	No	Dial Tone	Greyhound (p. 416)	No	No	No	
$ $ $	⋏	⋏ ⋏	✍ ✍ ✍	Camay Coast Ivory Safeguard Zest	Procter & Gamble (p. 226)	No	No	No	✔
$	No	No	No	Caress Dove Lifebuoy Lux Shield	Unilever (p. 171)	Yes ?	No	No	

* = See company profile
? = No information available
Single figure ($, ⋏) = Minimal
Double figure ($$, ⋏⋏, ✍✍, ⋏⋏) = Moderate
Triple figure ($$$, ⋏⋏⋏, ✍✍✍, ⋏⋏⋏) = Substantial

No = No involvement or participation
Yes = Involvement or participation. A, B, C in the South African column reflect the degree of compliance with Sullivan Principles and/or involvement in strategic industries.

See Chapter 4 for a detailed discussion of chart symbols.

PERSONAL HYGIENE

SUNTAN LOTIONS

Size of Charitable Contributions	Women Directors and Officers	Minority Directors and Officers	Social Disclosure	Brand Name	Company (Profile Page)	Involvement in South Africa	Conv. Weapons–Related Contracts	Nuclear Weapons–Related Contracts	Authors' Company of Choice
\$ \$ \$	⚇ ⚇	?	☝ ☝ ☝	PreSun	Bristol-Myers (p. 208)	Yes B	No	No	
\$ \$	⚇	⚇ ⚇	☝ ☝ ☝	Sundown	Johnson & Johnson (p. 214)	Yes A	No	No	✔
?	⚇	No	☝ ☝ ☝	Mill Creek	Richardson-Vicks (p. 232)	No	No	No	
\$ \$	No	No	☝ ☝ ☝	Sun Block 15	A. H. Robins (p. 234)	No	No	No	
\$ \$	⚇	No	☝ ☝ ☝	Coppertone Solarcaine Sudden Tan	Schering-Plough (p. 237)	Yes B	No	No	
?	⚇	?	No	Bain de Soleil	Squibb (p. 241)	Yes B	No	No	

* = See company profile
? = No information available
Single figure (\$, ⚇) = Minimal
Double figure (\$\$, ⚇⚇, ☝☝, ⚇⚇) = Moderate
Triple figure (\$\$\$, ⚇⚇⚇, ☝☝☝, ⚇⚇⚇) = Substantial

No = No involvement or participation
Yes = Involvement or participation. A, B, C in the South African column reflect the degree of compliance with Sullivan Principles and/or involvement in strategic industries.

See Chapter 4 for a detailed discussion of chart symbols.

PERSONAL HYGIENE

TOOTHPASTES

Size of Charitable Contributions	Women Directors and Officers	Minority Directors and Officers	Social Disclosure	Brand Name	Company (Profile Page)	Involvement in South Africa	Conv. Weapons–Related Contracts	Nuclear Weapons–Related Contracts	Authors' Company of Choice
$	♀	?	No	Colgate Ultra-brite	Colgate-Palmolive (p. 211)	Yes A/B	No	No	
$ $ $	♀ ♀	♀	✍ ✍ ✍	Crest Gleem	Procter & Gamble (p. 226)	No	No	No	✔
$	No	No	No	Aim Close-up Pepsodent	Unilever (p. 171)	Yes ?	No	No	

* = See company profile
? = No information available
Single figure ($, ♀) = Minimal
Double figure ($$, ♀♀, ✍✍, ♀♀) = Moderate
Triple figure ($$$, ♀♀♀, ✍✍✍, ♀♀♀) = Substantial

No = No involvement or participation
Yes = Involvement or participation. A, B, C in the South African column reflect the degree of compliance with Sullivan Principles and/or involvement in strategic industries.

See Chapter 4 for a detailed discussion of chart symbols.

REMEDIES

BANDAGES

Size of Charitable Contributions	Women Directors and Officers	Minority Directors and Officers	Social Disclosure	Brand Name	Company (Profile Page)	Involvement in South Africa	Conv. Weapons–Related Contracts	Nuclear Weapons–Related Contracts	Authors' Company of Choice
$	★	?	No	Curad Curity	Colgate- Palmolive (p. 211)	Yes A/B	No	No	
$ $	★	★ ★	☝ ☝ ☝	Band-Aid	Johnson & Johnson (p. 214)	Yes A	No	No	✔

* = See company profile
? = No information available
Single figure ($, ★) = Minimal
Double figure ($$, ★★, ☝☝, ★★) = Moderate
Triple figure ($$$, ★★★, ☝☝☝, ★★★) = Substantial

No = No involvement or participation
Yes = Involvement or participation. A, B, C in the South African column reflect the degree of compliance with Sullivan Principles and/or involvement in strategic industries.

See Chapter 4 for a detailed discussion of chart symbols.

REMEDIES

COLD AND HAY FEVER REMEDIES

Size of Charitable Contributions	Women Directors and Officers	Minority Directors and Officers	Social Disclosure	Brand Name	Company (Profile Page)	Involvement in South Africa	Conv. Weapons– Related Contracts	Nuclear Weapons– Related Contracts	Authors' Company of Choice
∗	⚤ ⚤	No	✋ ✋ ✋	Dristan Primatene	American Home Products (p. 406)	Yes A/B	No	No	
$ $ $	⚤ ⚤	?	✋ ✋ ✋	Comtrex 4-Way	Bristol-Myers (p. 208)	Yes B	No	No	
∗	⚤	⚤ ⚤	No	Alka-Seltzer	Miles Labs (p. 220)	No	No	No	
$ $ $	⚤	No	✋ ✋ ✋	Allerest Sinarest	Pennwalt (p. 222)	No	No	No	
?	⚤	No	✋ ✋ ✋	Formula 44 Nyquil Sinex Vicks	Richardson-Vicks (p. 232)	No	No	No	

COLD AND HAY FEVER REMEDIES *(cont'd.)*

Size of Charitable Contributions	Women Directors and Officers	Minority Directors and Officers	Social Disclosure	Brand Name	Company (Profile Page)	Involvement in South Africa	Conv. Weapons– Related Contracts	Nuclear Weapons– Related Contracts	Authors' Company of Choice
$ $	No	No	🤏 🤏 🤏	Chapstick Dimetapp	A. H. Robins (p. 234)	No	No	No	
$ $	🚶	No	🤏 🤏	Afrin Chlor-Trimeton Coricidin Drixoral	Schering-Plough (p. 237)	Yes B	No	No	
$ $	🚶	🚶	🤏 🤏 🤏	Contac A.R.M. Sine-Off	SmithKline Beckman (p. 239)	Yes B	No	No	
$	🚶	No	No	Neo-Synephrine	Sterling Drug (p. 242)	Yes B	No	No	
$ $ $	🚶 🚶	🚶 🚶	🤏 🤏 🤏	Sinutab	Warner-Lambert (p. 243)	Yes B	No	No	

* = See company profile
? = No information available
Single figure ($, 🚶) = Minimal
Double figure ($$, 🚶🚶, 🤏🤏, 🚶🚶) = Moderate
Triple figure ($$$, 🚶🚶🚶, 🤏🤏🤏, 🚶🚶🚶) = Substantial

No = No involvement or participation
Yes = Involvement or participation. A, B, C in the South African column reflect the degree of compliance with Sullivan Principles and/or involvement in strategic industries.

See Chapter 4 for a detailed discussion of chart symbols.

REMEDIES

COUGH AND SORE THROAT REMEDIES

Size of Charitable Contributions	Women Directors and Officers	Minority Directors and Officers	Social Disclosure	Brand Name	Company (Profile Page)	Involvement in South Africa	Conv. Weapons–Related Contracts	Nuclear Weapons–Related Contracts	Authors' Company of Choice
?	☀	?	No	Pertussin	Chesebrough-Pond's (p. 210)	Yes C	No	No	
$ $ $	☀	?	✍ ✍ ✍	Cēpacol Novahistine	Dow Chemical (p. 411)	Yes B	No	No	
$ $ $	☀	☀ ☀	✍ ✍ ✍	Chloraseptic	Procter & Gamble (p. 226)	No	No	No	✔
?	☀	No	✍ ✍ ✍	Creama Coat Vicks Vaporizer	Richardson-Vicks (p. 232)	No	No	No	
$ $	No	No	✍ ✍ ✍	Extend 12 Robitussin	A. H. Robins (p. 234)	No	No	No	
?	☀	?	No	Spec T	Squibb (p. 241)	Yes B	No	No	
$ $ $	☀ ☀	☀ ☀	✍ ✍ ✍	Benylin Halls	Warner-Lambert (p. 243)	Yes B	No	No	

* = See company profile
? = No information available
Single figure ($, ☀) = Minimal
Double figure ($$, ☀☀, ✍✍, ☀☀) = Moderate
Triple figure ($$$, ☀☀☀, ✍✍✍, ☀☀☀) = Substantial

No = No involvement or participation
Yes = Involvement or participation. A, B, C in the South African column reflect the degree of compliance with Sullivan Principles and/or involvement in strategic industries.

See Chapter 4 for a detailed discussion of chart symbols.

REMEDIES

DIGESTION AIDS

Size of Charitable Contributions	Women Directors and Officers	Minority Directors and Officers	Social Disclosure	Brand Name	Company (Profile Page)	Involvement in South Africa	Conv. Weapons–Related Contracts	Nuclear Weapons–Related Contracts	Authors' Company of Choice
*	‡‡ (2 figures)	No	3 icons	Riopan	American Home Products (p. 406)	Yes A/B	No	No	
?	‡ (1 figure)	No	No	Arm & Hammer baking soda	Church & Dwight (p. 408)	No	No	No	
*	‡ (1 figure)	‡‡ (2 figures)	No	Alka-Seltzer	Miles Labs (p. 220)	No	No	No	
$$$	‡ (1 figure)	‡‡ (2 figures)	3 icons	Pepto-Bismol	Procter & Gamble (p. 226)	No	No	No	
$	‡ (1 figure)	?	No	Tums	Revlon (p. 230)	Yes C	No	No	
?	‡ (1 figure)	No	3 icons	Tempo	Richardson-Vicks (p. 232)	No	No	No	
$$	‡ (1 figure)	No	3 icons	Di-Gel	Schering-Plough (p. 237)	Yes B	No	No	
$$$	‡‡ (2 figures)	‡‡ (2 figures)	3 icons	Bromo Seltzer Gelusil Rolaids	Warner-Lambert (p. 243)	Yes B	No	No	

REMEDIES

PAIN RELIEVERS

Size of Charitable Contributions	Women Directors and Officers	Minority Directors and Officers	Social Disclosure	Brand Name	Company (Profile Page)	Involvement in South Africa	Conv. Weapons–Related Contracts	Nuclear Weapons–Related Contracts	Authors' Company of Choice
✳	🧍🧍	No	✍✍✍	Advil Anacin Arthritis Pain Formula	American Home Products (p. 406)	Yes A/B	No	No	
$ $ $	🧍🧍	?	✍✍✍	Bufferin Datril Excedrin	Bristol-Myers (p. 208)	Yes B	No	No	
$ $	🧍	🧍🧍	✍✍✍	Tylenol	Johnson & Johnson (p. 214)	Yes A	No	No	✔
$ $ $	🧍	🧍🧍	✍✍✍	Encaprin Norwich	Procter & Gamble (p. 226)	No	No	No	✔
$ $	🧍	No	✍✍✍	St. Joseph's	Schering-Plough (p. 237)	Yes B	No	No	
$ $	🧍	🧍	✍✍✍	Ecotrin	SmithKline Beckman (p. 239)	Yes B	No	No	
$	🧍	No	No	Bayer Panadol Midol	Sterling Drug (p. 242)	Yes B	No	No	

REMEDIES

VITAMINS

Size of Charitable Contributions	Women Directors and Officers	Minority Directors and Officers	Social Disclosure	Brand Name	Company (Profile Page)	Involvement in South Africa	Conv. Weapons–Related Contracts	Nuclear Weapons–Related Contracts	Authors' Company of Choice
$ $ $	No	No	No	Centrum Stresstabs	American Cyanamid (p. 205)	Yes A	No	No	
*	♀	♀ ♀	No	Bugs Bunny Flintstones One-A-Day	Miles Labs (p. 220)	No	No	No	
?	♀	No	✍ ✍ ✍	Life Stage Plus	Richardson-Vicks (p. 232)	No	No	No	
$ $	No	No	✍ ✍ ✍	Allbee Z-Bec	A. H. Robins (p. 234)	No	No	No	
$ $ $	♀ ♀	♀ ♀	✍ ✍ ✍	Myadec	Warner-Lambert (p. 243)	Yes B	No	No	✔

* = See company profile
? = No information available
Single figure ($, ♀) = Minimal
Double figure ($$, ♀♀, ✍✍, ♀♀) = Moderate
Triple figure ($$$, ♀♀♀, ✍✍✍, ♀♀♀) = Substantial

No = No involvement or participation
Yes = Involvement or participation. A, B, C in the South African column reflect the degree of compliance with Sullivan Principles and/or involvement in strategic industries.

See Chapter 4 for a detailed discussion of chart symbols.

ABBOTT LABORATORIES

This Chicago-based drug company has been involved in a number of controversies over the years, particularly over the sale of its cyclamate artificial sweetener in the United States and the marketing of infant formula abroad. Its minority purchasing program is a sizable one, but we could locate little information on other social initiatives.

When the Food and Drug Administration (FDA) banned cyclamates as a possible cancer hazard in 1970, Abbott began a long and persistent campaign to overturn this decision. Its first petition to the FDA in 1973 was denied in 1976. The company then asked for a hearing on the issue before an FDA administrative law judge, who ruled against the company in 1978. The company again petitioned the FDA for a re-review in 1982. In mid-1985 the National Academy of Sciences announced that new studies carried out at the FDA's request had found that cyclamates were carcinogenic only when used in conjunction with other substances, such as saccharin. The FDA said it would need an additional year to decide whether to lift the ban on cyclamates. According to *Business Week*, Abbott continued to market cyclamates in Canada and Europe after their use was disallowed in the United States.

Along with American Home Products and Bristol-Myers, Abbott opposed proposed restrictions on the marketing of infant formula in developing nations in the late 1970s. However, along with these three companies it has agreed to comply with the 1981 World Health Organization Code for regulating these practices.

The company's 1983 annual report listed charitable contributions of $4.5 million, including in-kind gifts. Cash disbursements apparently totaled $2.4 million, a moderate 0.6 percent of pre-tax earnings. The largest single donation went to the United Way. About 60 percent of the contributions went to

ABBOT LABORATORIES											
	Women		Minorities				Contracts		PAC Contributions		
% to Charity	Directors	Officers	Directors	Officers	Social Disclosure	Sullivan Rating	% Military	Nuclear Weapons–Related	Dollar Amount	% to Republicans	% to Democrats
0.6%	1	0	0	?	F	IIA	None	None	$126,875	79%	21%

? = No information available
See also Appendix D for a listing of this company's products and services.

education. The company matched $175,000 in employee gifts to hospitals and education.

The company has a strong minority purchasing program ($14.8 million in 1983) that began in 1975.

Its South African plant employs approximately 140 persons, half of whom are white, and received the second-highest "making progress" rating from 1981 through 1985 for compliance with the Sullivan Principles for fair labor practices in that country.

The company did not respond to CEP's questionnaires.

ALBERTO-CULVER COMPANY

This diverse Chicago-based consumer products company (Milani foods, professional cleaning chemicals and equipment, and a well-known line of personal care items) did not disclose information on its social initiatives for this book.

In declining to answer CEP's questionnaire, Alberto-Culver stated that it has a charitable giving program but does not release details on its size or nature. It also stated that it uses "several" minority-owned suppliers, but again gave no statistics.

ALBERTO-CULVER COMPANY											
	Women		Minorities					Contracts		PAC Contributions	
% to Charity	Directors	Officers	Directors	Officers	Social Disclosure	Sullivan Rating	% Military	Nuclear Weapons–Related	Dollar Amount	% to Republicans	% to Democrats
?	2	3	0	0	F	None	None	None	None		

? = No information available
See also Appendix D for a listing of this company's products and services.

AMERICAN CYANAMID COMPANY

This pharmaceutical, chemical, and consumer products company headquartered in Wayne, New Jersey, was involved in the 1970s in a series of public controversies. The authors of *Everybody's Business* described its reputation at that time as slipping "from bad to worse." The company did not respond to CEP's questionnaires, and we located few positive social initiatives.

Most dramatic of these controversies in the 1970s was an incident at its Willow Island, West Virginia, chemical plant, where the company required female workers in its pigments division to be sterilized in order to retain their jobs. (In the event of pregnancy, exposure to lead was potentially harmful to the fetus — hence the policy.) Rather than lose their jobs or be demoted, five female workers chose to be sterilized. These women later sued the company, charging sex discrimination in the sterilization regulation. An out-of-court settlement was eventually reached. At the same time, the women asked the Occupational Safety and Health Administration (OSHA) to ban such sterilization policies as hazardous to workers' health. (An initial OSHA ruling against Cyanamid, which carried a $10,000 fine, was overturned by two administrative law judges.) In response to a union- and church-sponsored resolution on this issue in 1980, Cyanamid set up a board-level Public Responsibility Committee to oversee and review health, safety, and environmental policies.

Cyanamid's wholly owned South African operations employ approximately 700 persons and have consistently received top ratings for compliance with the Sullivan Principles from 1981 through 1985. A South African plywood company employing 480 workers, of which Cyanamid owns 30 percent, received the second-highest compliance rating in 1985.

According to the Taft *Corporate Giving Directory,* the company made a fairly substantial $2.8 million in charitable contributions in 1984 (1.2 percent of pre-tax earnings), which went primarily to higher education.

AMERICAN CYANAMID COMPANY											
	Women		Minorities				Contracts		PAC Contributions		
% to Charity	Directors	Officers	Directors	Officers	Social Disclosure	Sullivan Rating	% Military	Nuclear Weapons– Related	Dollar Amount	% to Republicans	% to Democrats
1.2%	0	0	0	0	F	I/IIB	None	None	$57,200	71%	29%

See also Appendix D for a listing of this company's products and services.

AVON PRODUCTS, INC.

Avon has become a giant within the cosmetics industry through door-to-door sales by its representatives. Since the mid-1970s it has taken a notable public stand supporting women and minorities.

In 1985, for example, Avon expanded its credit line with minority-owned banks to $34 million, the largest line reported by any company profiled in this book, and a major increase from $9 million the previous year. The remainder of Avon's minority banking program is substantial, but less exceptional: tax payments in 1984 totaling $102 million, and $1.5 million in certificates of deposit.

The company's former chief executive officer, William Chaney, headed the National Minority Supplier Development Council in the early 1980s, and strongly advocated greater corporate patronage of minority- and women-owned businesses. The company's own purchases from minority vendors totaled $15 million in 1984, unchanged from the previous year; the goal for 1985 was $16.5 million. This record is second only to Johnson & Johnson's among the health and personal care product companies profiled in this chapter. Avon also uses minority-owned insurance companies, and urges its pension trust to invest through minority brokers.

The company's total 1984 charitable giving came to $2.6 million, $1.8 million of this through its foundation. Since 1977 Avon's foundation has been headed by Glenn Clarke, developer of the company's minority purchasing program. Its stated concerns are now "particularly women, minorities, and the disadvantaged." Approximately 40 percent given in 1984 went toward civic and community programs (including 13 percent to united fund drives), and 42 percent to education. Its education grants are "primarily earmarked for scholarships for women and minorities," along with scholarships for employees' children. Its arts grants are also directed to minority groups. In addition

AVON PRODUCTS, INC.											
	Women		Minorities				Contracts		PAC Contributions		
% to Charity	Directors	Officers	Directors	Officers	Social Disclosure	Sullivan Rating	% Military	Nuclear Weapons–Related	Dollar Amount	% to Republicans	% to Democrats
0.7%	3	2	1	1	A	None	None	None	$50,320	61%	39%

See also Appendix D for a listing of this company's products and services.

to these gifts, Avon provides technical advice and assistance to nonprofit groups, awards grants to organizations with which employees volunteer, and hosts an unusual series of lunches, at which representatives from low-profile community organizations are given an opportunity to publicize their work before a select audience from the corporate community.

Following Revlon's lead in 1981, Avon became the second cosmetics company to make a major ($750,000) contribution toward research on alternatives to the use of live animals in product development and testing.

Within the corporation, Avon reformed its Corporate Responsibility Committee as the Minority and Women's Participation Council in 1984, including on it an outside member of its board of directors. It has created the position of Vice President for Affirmative Action, and recently conducted a company-wide survey and re-evaluation of its promotions practices for minorities and women.

It has a strong representation of women and minorities in management — three women and one minority on its board of directors, two women and one minority among its top corporate staff, and six more women at the vice presidential level in its divisions. Although the company would not make its equal employment opportunity statistics available in this book, it reported to *Black Enterprise* magazine in 1986 that 75 percent of its officials' and managers' positions were held by women — a remarkably high figure — and 12 percent by minorities.

Having sold Tiffany's jewelry store and its Mallinckrodt health care division, Avon will again concentrate on its beauty care lines. But its sales have been suffering (Avon's 1985 sales were $2.5 billion, down from $2.6 billion in 1984, and it lost $60 million that year) as more and more women work regular jobs, making it more difficult to recruit a commission-paid sales force to sell its products door-to-door.

The company responded to CEP's questionnaires.

BRISTOL-MYERS COMPANY

This pharmaceutical company is headquartered in New York City. Its social initiatives appear moderate and varied.

In its diverse efforts to aid minorities and women, Bristol-Myers helped found the Newark, New Jersey–based Technical Training Project (TTP) in 1969. A job-training and placement service for minority youth, TTP places about 30 graduates each year. Starting in the late 1970s, Bristol-Myers has provided 140 after-school intern positions for minority high school students at its headquarters over a seven-year period. In Stamford, Connecticut, and Syracuse, New York, its divisions participate in summer youth job programs. For over 10 years it has awarded $50,000 annually (raised to $75,000 in 1984) in scholarships to women over 30 starting or resuming career training.

The company reports a well-rounded effort in fair hiring and promotion within its ranks. As of 1984, 18.5 percent of its officials and managers were women and 8.4 percent were minority members, a moderate showing compared with other pharmaceutical companies profiled in this book.

Its charitable giving program is fairly strong: $8.2 million in 1985, 1.2 percent of pre-tax earnings, with an emphasis on unrestricted funding to health research as well as support for health and community organizations — 55 percent of total giving. A relatively small 25 percent of its giving goes to education. It matches employee gifts of up to $5,000.

The company's minority banking program made $67 million in tax payments during 1984; there is also a minority purchasing program for which no overall figures were available. In Stamford, Connecticut, the firm took the unusual step of making an interest-free $100,000 loan through New Neighborhoods, Inc., to help finance the construction of moderately priced condominiums for purchase by its black and Hispanic Clairol employees there.

BRISTOL-MYERS COMPANY											
	Women		Minorities				Contracts		PAC Contributions		
% to Charity	Directors	Officers	Directors	Officers	Social Disclosure	Sullivan Rating	% Military	Nuclear Weapons–Related	Dollar Amount	% to Republicans	% to Democrats
1.2%	1	1	?	?	A	IIA	None	None	$85,570	74%	26%

? = No information available
See also Appendix D for a listing of this company's products and services.

Faced with the threat of an animal-rights group campaign directed at the company's research and product development tests, Bristol-Myers responded with $500,000 contribution toward the establishment of the Center for Alternatives to Animal Testing at Johns Hopkins University, and later committed an additional $200,000. It gave $100,000 to the Fund for the Replacement of Animals in Medical Experiments in the United Kingdom as well. The company is among the most prominent in the pharmaceutical industry making financial and policy commitments on the animal-rights issue. (See also the Procter & Gamble and Revlon profiles.)

Along with other manufacturers of infant formula, Bristol-Myers opposed proposals to sharply restrict marketing practices in the Third World in the late 1970s. But the company has voluntarily complied with the World Health Organization's 1981 worldwide code for marketing infant formula in developing nations. Church groups report that Bristol-Myers has been the most conscientious of the U.S. infant formula manufacturers in keeping an open dialogue on their plans for implementing the code.

Along with American Home Products and Sterling Drug, Bristol-Myers was charged by the Federal Trade Commission in the early 1970s with making misleading claims for some of its pain relievers, charges that were ultimately upheld in the courts.

In June 1986, the company recalled all Excedrin in capsule form after two deaths in Seattle were tied to cyanide-contaminated capsules, and shortly thereafter Bristol-Myers announced that it would cease using the capsule form for its over-the-counter medicines.

Bristol-Myers is a signatory of the Sullivan Principles for nondiscriminatory labor practices in South Africa, where it employs about 350 workers. It has consistently received the second-highest "making progress" rating.

The company did not respond to CEP's questionnaires. However, it publishes a yearly detailed analysis of its social initiatives in equal opportunity hiring and community involvement.

CHESEBROUGH-POND'S INC.

This diverse consumer products company makes little information public on its social programs in the United States. Chesebrough-Pond's discloses no dollar figures for its charitable giving, but reports support of several scholarship programs for blacks and Hispanics. It has a minority purchasing program, but again gives no indication of its size.

Chesebrough-Pond's became a signatory of the Sullivan Principles in October 1985, after a shareholder resolution urging endorsement of the Principles earlier that year had received an exceptionally strong 23 percent vote of support, despite management opposition. According to the company, it previously had voluntarily complied with the basic requirements of the Sullivan Principles in its South African cosmetics operations, which employ over 500 persons. These included an integrated workplace, wages above poverty level, equal pay for equal work, an extensive loan program for black employees, a concerted effort to train and promote its black workers (49 percent of Chesebrough's managerial and sales jobs were held by blacks in 1984, up from 23 percent in 1979), and black union representation. The company had not signed the Sullivan Principles prior to 1985 out of concern about "the possibility of ill-advised future changes and additions to the Principles."

In 1985 the company acquired Stauffer Chemical, which also has operations in South Africa and had not been a signatory to the Sullivan Principles prior to 1985. Stauffer has a public record of substantial charitable contributions, with $2.5 million disbursed in 1983.

In late 1986, Chesebrough-Pond's was acquired by Unilever. (See addendum on page 500.)

The company responded in a limited way to CEP's questionnaires.

CHESEBROUGH-POND'S INC.											
	Women		Minorities					Contracts		PAC Contributions	
% to Charity	Directors	Officers	Directors	Officers	Social Disclosure	Sullivan Rating	% Military	Nuclear Weapons–Related	Dollar Amount	% to Republicans	% to Democrats
?	1	0	?	?	F	V	None	None	None		

? = No information available
See also Appendix D for a listing of this company's products and services.

In the Drugstore

COLGATE-PALMOLIVE COMPANY

CEP could locate little information on social programs of note by this large consumer products company, headquartered in New York. Since 1974 the company has sponsored the annual Colgate Women's Games, a track and field event for 20,000 young women, most of them minority-group members in the Greater New York region. The firm had donated $350,000 in scholarships to participants through 1983.

The *National Directory of Corporate Charity* lists a scant $140,000 in 1981 gifts from the company's Kendall foundation. This figure does not include direct corporate giving or other corporate foundations and may understate the company's total program.

Colgate-Palmolive operates three facilities in South Africa, which together employ approximately 1,200 persons, producing soap products, hospital supplies, and rice. They consistently received the highest rating for compliance with the Sullivan Principles for fair labor practices in that country from 1981 through 1984, although in 1985 its S. Wainstein & Company subsidiary slipped to second-highest ranking.

The company did not respond to CEP's questionnaires.

COLGATE-PALMOLIVE COMPANY											
	Women		Minorities				Contracts		PAC Contributions		
% to Charity	Directors	Officers	Directors	Officers	Social Disclosure	Sullivan Rating	% Military	Nuclear Weapons–Related	Dollar Amount	% to Republicans	% to Democrats
0.1%	1	0	?	?	F	I/IIA	None	None	None		

? = No information available
See also Appendix D for a listing of this company's products and services.

GILLETTE COMPANY

Best known in the marketplace for its safety razors, Gillette has also focused on safety in its products and the workplace. This Boston-based firm also produces cosmetics, deodorants, Paper Mate pens, Liquid Paper, and Braun small appliances.

Since 1974 Gillette has had a vice president for "product integrity," Robert Giovacchini. In 1975 the *Wall Street Journal* termed his position "a highly unusual corporate role" and stated that "the clout he wields within a major multinational company is even more surprising." Giovacchini reports directly to the chief executive officer and has a virtual carte blanche to pull any Gillette product off the market or out of production if he feels there are safety or quality problems. He reviews all advertising claims and product-labeling decisions. He vetoed use of vinyl chloride as a propellant in aerosol cans six years before the Food and Drug Administration banned its use, and pulled a newly introduced antiperspirant containing zirconium because test results showed potentially harmful long-term effects.

Giovacchini has also chaired Gillette's Occupational Medical Safety Committee since 1974. In 1979 the company set up a mandatory pilot training and education program for employees potentially exposed to hazardous chemicals in the workplace; in 1983 this program was extended to all domestic plants. Regular audits and surveys are part of this plan, which preceded workers' right-to-know laws in such states as Massachusetts, Minnesota, and Illinois.

Gillette's commitment to minority economic development goes back to 1973, when it helped found the New England Minority Purchasing Program. In 1985 it purchased $5.4 million in goods from minority vendors. Its small minority banking program has a $400,000 credit line.

GILLETTE COMPANY											
	Women		Minorities				Contracts		PAC Contributions		
% to Charity	Directors	Officers	Directors	Officers	Social Disclosure	Sullivan Rating	% Military	Nuclear Weapons–Related	Dollar Amount	% to Republicans	% to Democrats
1.0%	1	1	0	0	A	I/V	None	None	None		

See also Appendix D for a listing of this company's products and services.

In the Drugstore

As of 1984, its officials and managers comprised 19.3 percent women and 8.3 percent minorities. Approximately 11 percent of its work force is unionized.

Gillette's charitable giving program (primarily direct and not through its foundation) is a fairly strong one, with gifts totaling $2.5 million in 1985, equivalent to 1.0 percent of pre-tax earnings.

Gillette employs approximately 300 in South Africa, where it received the highest rating for compliance with the Sullivan Principles from 1981 through 1985 (with the exception of 1984, when it received the second-highest).

The company responded to CEP's questionnaires.

JOHNSON & JOHNSON

Johnson & Johnson's much praised commitment to social responsibility has been severely tested by two crises within four years involving Extra-Strength Tylenol capsules laced with poison after the product was on the shelves. Both times the company took prompt and comprehensive steps to assure public safety, although at considerable cost to itself. These actions were consistent with this decentralized company's general pattern of thorough and broad-reaching approaches to its social initiatives. In areas of controversy, it has a large South African operation.

Its chief executive officer, James E. Burke, was the only CEO to respond personally to our questionnaires. He believes that social responsibility should be a tenet of good management and integral to running a profitable company. In 1984 Burke announced the results of a study J&J had undertaken of 26 companies that followed a "social credo" in running their operations. The study found that for 15 companies that had been in existence for at least 30 years, an investment of $30,000 in their stock in 1954 would have grown to $1 million, as opposed to $134,000 in stock of the Dow Jones industrials.

Johnson & Johnson adopted a social credo in the 1940s clearly stating its commitment to consumers, employees, shareholders, and to the communities in which it operates. In practice, the company seems to have lived up to this credo. Among other credo-followers on the J&J list were Coca-Cola, General Foods, Gerber, IBM, Kodak, Procter & Gamble, R. J. Reynolds (now RJR Nabisco), Sun Company, and 3M.

Starting with its own particular area of expertise, for example, Johnson & Johnson has developed a comprehensive health care program for its employees. The program, "Live for Life," is available on a voluntary basis to employees at 43 of the J&J facilities. Participants receive an initial medical checkup and "lifestyle screen," followed by recommendations for specific health-related activities that would most benefit them. The company provides up-to-date, supervised exercise facilities; a 12-week course to help employees stop smoking; stress reduction, nutritional, and weight-loss clinics; and healthful foods in its cafeterias. As of early 1985, approximately 25,000 of J&J's 39,000 employees were taking part in this program.

In its headquarters community of New Brunswick, New Jersey, J&J has made a strong commitment to revitalization projects. J&J's decision to build its new corporate headquarters there in the mid-1970s was the cornerstone of a broad plan to reverse the declining economic condition of the city. The CEO of the company at that time, Richard Sellars, helped create and became chairman of New Brunswick Tomorrow (NBT), a citywide coalition promoting redevelopment efforts. After leaving the company, Sellars continued to head the development arm of NBT in the mid-1980s while another J&J executive, a native of New Brunswick, became the new NBT chairman. NBT is credited with many major revitalization projects, including a hotel and conference center, the expansion of Middlesex General Hospital, the opening of the Paul Robeson Community School, and the improvement of recreation, education, and housing in the city.

The company's efforts in minority economic development and affirmative action hiring and promotion appear to be comprehensive. They include a substantial minority purchasing program, which increased from $13 million in 1982 to $21 million in 1983, by far the highest among pharmaceutical companies profiled in this book. An additional $11 million in goods was purchased from women-owned businesses that year, up from $8 million in 1982.

Its minority banking program includes operating accounts for payrolls, a particularly important step for these banks. A venture capital company for minority-owned businesses headquartered at Rutgers University has received support from Johnson & Johnson. And J&J uses minority-owned companies for reinsurance on life insurance policies.

As of 1983, 12.8 percent women and 9.3 percent minority members were included among its officials and managers. There were no women and one minority among its top 20 officers, but two women (one of them black) on its 21-member board. *Savvy* magazine in 1982 rated the company as one of the best for women to work for.

Johnson & Johnson's charitable giving program was a moderate 0.7 percent of pre-tax earnings in 1983. But the company has made a concerted effort to increase its giving in recent years, up 31 percent from 1979 to 1982, reaching $5.4 million in 1983. This figure understates the full extent of the company's giving. J&J has a decentralized two-tier donations program, with subsidiaries contributing to the primary corporate fund, but free to make separate donations. These secondary gifts by the subsidiaries are "substantial," according to the company, but are not included in the $5.4 million figure.

The largest percentage (30 percent) of the company's gifts went to education in 1982. This included funding for a management training program for nurses at the Wharton School, and funding for pharmacy programs at four universities that together graduate about 50 percent of all black pharmacy students in the United States. Health care received 19 percent of the company's gifts, with major grants funding specific projects such as skin-cell cloning (used in treating severe burns) and the pharmacology of narcotic drugs. Civic involvement received 21 percent of the company's gifts, predominantly for federated fund drives. The company matched $1.3 million in employee gifts to nonprofit organizations.

The Robert Wood Johnson Foundation, established in 1968 with family money from the son of the company's founder, is one of the largest in the United States, having given over $600 million in its first 13 years to health care organizations and research. Waldemar Nielsen, in *The Golden Donors*, has highest praise for the innovative administration and enlightened giving of this foundation, which includes among its priorities health care projects for the elderly, the homeless, and those in rural regions. In 1986 the foundation initiated a four-year, $17.2 million project to provide health care for persons with AIDS, with a particular emphasis on out-of-hospital care.

The authors of *The 100 Best Companies to Work for in America* characterize Johnson & Johnson as a conservative, highly decentralized company, with "strong concern for its employees." Among its employee benefits are a tax-deferred savings plan inaugurated in 1982. Workers can contribute up to 15 percent of their salary, with the company matching half of the first 6 percent. In addition, J&J, like many others, has recently instituted a PAYSOP plan that distributes company stock to employees equal in value to ½ percent of the total payroll, for which the company receives a tax credit.

J&J's Ethicon division was recently involved in a bitter dispute with unions trying to organize a plant in New Mexico. Approximately 17 percent of J&J's work force is unionized.

The company has had its share of crises over its products, but its response has generally been swift and fully conscious of the public welfare. The most dramatic of these occurred in Chicago in 1982, when cyanide-laced Extra-Strength Tylenol capsules were purchased by consumers. Seven persons died. Even though the poisonings were in no way Johnson & Johnson's fault — the capsules had apparently been tampered with after they reached the stores — the firm voluntarily and immediately recalled the capsules at a cost of over $100 million. In 1986 another death occurred in Westchester County, New York, from arsenic in Tylenol capsules. The company swiftly decided at that point to stop all production of the capsule form of Extra-Strength Tylenol.

In 1983, Johnson & Johnson and the Food and Drug Administration determined that five persons had died from allergic reactions to the prescription

JOHNSON & JOHNSON											
	Women		Minorities				Contracts		PAC Contributions		
% to Charity	Directors	Officers	Directors	Officers	Social Disclosure	Sullivan Rating	% Military	Nuclear Weapons–Related	Dollar Amount	% to Republicans	% to Democrats
0.7%	2	0	1	1	A	I/IIA	None	None	$88,450	56%	44%

See also Appendix D for a listing of this company's products and services.

painkiller Zomax, which had been on the market for two years. While the FDA did not feel a recall was necessary, the firm voluntarily recalled the drug to include stronger warning labels, costing the company $20 million in after-tax earnings for the year. The recall extended to foreign countries as well, in sharp contrast to some other U.S. pharmaceutical companies that have continued overseas marketing of drugs banned in this country.

Johnson & Johnson is a substantial employer in South Africa, with approximately 1,400 workers, the largest of any U.S. drug company. For its major operations there, the company has consistently received the highest rating for compliance with the Sullivan Principles. Its Janssen Pharmaceutical company, which employs 95, has occasionally received the second-highest "making progress" Sullivan rating.

The company responded to CEP's questionnaires.

JOHNSON PRODUCTS CO., INC.

This Chicago-based maker of personal grooming products was the nation's first black-owned business to be listed on the stock exchange. Although it suffered losses in 1984 and 1985, in more profitable times it had a reputation as a "company with a conscience." The corporation has given generously to the United Negro College Fund and Rev. Jesse Jackson's Operation PUSH. It has sponsored programs and studies that raise the visibility of black achievers.

The company and its subsidiary, Debbie's School of Beauty Culture, have employee profit-sharing plans. The company's board of directors includes two women. Its top officers are racially diverse and include four women.

One flaw on the company's social record, however, was a U.S. District Court ruling in 1982 that the firm had discriminated against female sales employees in hiring, pay, and promotions. The judge noted, however, that the company had markedly improved its treatment of women since the suit was filed in 1974.

The company did not respond to CEP's questionnaires.

JOHNSON PRODUCTS CO., INC.											
	Women		Minorities				Contracts		PAC Contributions		
% to Charity	Directors	Officers	Directors	Officers	Social Disclosure	Sullivan Rating	% Military	Nuclear Weapons–Related	Dollar Amount	% to Republicans	% to Democrats
?	2	4	?	?	F	None	None	None	None		

? = No information available
See also Appendix D for a listing of this company's products and services.

MARY KAY COSMETICS, INC.

Mary Kay Ash's cosmetics empire has grown through the sales efforts of its female representatives, who as of 1984 reportedly outnumbered Exxon's worldwide payroll.

The company is known for its high commission rates as well as the pink Cadillacs, diamond rings, and mink coats with which Mary Kay Ash rewards her top sellers. According to *The 100 Best Companies to Work for in America*, more Mary Kay saleswomen earned over $50,000 in 1982 than women in any other U.S. company. The company also offers a particularly generous profit-sharing program.

Mary Kay Ash has turned the management reins over to her son. She remains the only woman on the board of directors and one of the firm's two top women officers. The company went private in 1985.

The company did not respond to CEP's questionnaires.

MARY KAY COSMETICS, INC.											
	Women		Minorities				Contracts		PAC Contributions		
% to Charity	Directors	Officers	Directors	Officers	Social Disclosure	Sullivan Rating	% Military	Nuclear Weapons–Related	Dollar Amount	% to Republicans	% to Democrats
?	1	2	?	?	F	None	None	None	None		

? = No information available
See also Appendix D for a listing of this company's products and services.

MILES LABORATORIES, INC.

In 1977 this Indiana-based producer of such well-known products as Alka-Seltzer, S.O.S. scrub pads, and Flintstones chewable vitamins was bought by the German company Bayer AG. Bayer is one of the largest pharmaceutical and chemical companies in the world, although its business in the United States had been sold to other companies after World War I. (Bayer aspirin is produced and marketed by Sterling Drug in this country, but by Bayer AG in other countries.)

The company's foundation gave a modest $200,000 in charitable contributions in 1982, according to the Taft *Corporate Giving Directory*. (The company suffered a loss in 1979 and had atypically low profits in 1980 and 1981.) This figure does not include direct corporate giving and may understate the company's total program.

Bayer has two subsidiaries in South Africa: Bayer South Africa, Ltd., and Chrome Chemicals, Ltd. Because Germany is a member of the European Economic Community (EEC), Bayer has presumably signed the EEC's code for labor practices in South Africa. This code is voluntarily enforced. (Miles itself was not a signatory of the Sullivan Principles, though it apparently had a South African operation which was sold before 1984.)

The company did not respond to CEP's questionnaires.

MILES LABORATORIES, INC.												
	Women		Minorities				Contracts		PAC Contributions		
% to Charity	Directors	Officers	Directors	Officers	Social Disclosure	Sullivan Rating	% Military	Nuclear Weapons–Related	Dollar Amount	% to Republicans	% to Democrats
*	1	0	1	1	F	None	None	None	None		

* = See profile
See also Appendix D for a listing of this company's products and services.

NOXELL CORPORATION

This Baltimore-based cosmetics company, best known for its Noxzema skin-care cream and Cover Girl cosmetics, is a member of the Baltimore Five-Percent Club, having pledged to increase pre-tax charitable giving to 5 percent within three years of joining. It gave $1 million in 1984 (up from $433,000 in 1983), or 2.8 percent of pre-tax earnings, one of the highest percentages for companies profiled in this book.

Although the company provided no detailed breakdown on the recipients of these funds, the Taft *Corporate Giving Directory* reports that in 1983 a notably high 25 to 30 percent went to arts and cultural organizations, along with gifts to education (35 percent) and welfare (20 percent, mostly to united fund drives).

Noxell's minority purchasing program bought over $1 million in goods in 1984. Although the company responded to CEP's questionnaires, it provided little detailed information on social initiatives.

NOXELL CORPORATION											
	Women		Minorities				Contracts		PAC Contributions		
% to Charity	Directors	Officers	Directors	Officers	Social Disclosure	Sullivan Rating	% Military	Nuclear Weapons–Related	Dollar Amount	% to Republicans	% to Democrats
2.8%	2	0	0	0	A	None	None	None	None		

See also Appendix D for a listing of this company's products and services.

PENNWALT CORPORATION

The charitable giving program of this Philadelphia-based chemical, precision instrument and pharmaceutical company is a generous one, with $987,000 in gifts in 1984, a healthy 1.8 percent of pre-tax earnings. According to the Taft *Corporate Giving Directory,* 40 percent of contributions went to education (two-thirds of that amount in matching gifts, one-quarter in scholarships in 1983); 35 percent to welfare organizations (nine-tenths of this amount going to united fund drives); and 15 to 20 percent to the arts and humanities (one-half of this amount going to public broadcasting).

Pennwalt purchased $1.1 million from minority businesses in 1984, a sharp increase from $461,000 in 1983. Among its highest officials and managers, 7.5 percent are women and 5.1 percent are minorities, one of the poorer records reported by pharmaceutical companies in this book.

Pennwalt was embroiled in a controversy in the early 1980s over mercury pollution at a Nicaraguan chemical plant in which it owned 40 percent interest. Pennwalt had entered this business during the Somoza regime. After the Sandinistas took power, they claimed that the plant was causing massive mercury pollution of Lake Managua in 1980. They also alleged that a substantial number of the plant's workers suffered symptoms of mercury poisoning.

The company asserted that the contamination of workers was not as bad as the Nicaraguan government claimed, and that conditions at the plant had deteriorated only during and after the revolution. The company further denied that it had control over the policies at the plant because of its limited ownership position. According to Pennwalt, it had recommended installing mercury recovery equipment well back into the 1970s; installation had been approved in 1978, but was delayed because of unrest and the impending revolution.

PENNWALT CORPORATION											
	Women		Minorities				Contracts		PAC Contributions		
% to Charity	Directors	Officers	Directors	Officers	Social Disclosure	Sullivan Rating	% Military	Nuclear Weapons–Related	Dollar Amount	% to Republicans	% to Democrats
1.8%	1	0	0	0	A	None	Negligible	None	$2,500	40%	60%

See also Appendix D for a listing of this company's products and services.

In the Drugstore

Pennwalt has several small operations in South Africa employing a total of 12 persons. A signatory of the Sullivan Principles, it received the second-highest rating for compliance in 1985, but sold its operations in that country in 1986.

Although Pennwalt is not rated here as a major military contractor, CEP found listings of $1.5 million in arms-related prime contracts to the company from the Department of Defense in 1984.

The company responded to CEP's questionnaires.

PFIZER INC.

This New York–based pharmaceutical company has a multifaceted, if moderate, commitment to social initiatives. Among its more adventuresome efforts is a joint project with the City of New York to develop an industrial park around one of its plants in the deteriorating East Williamsburg neighborhood of Brooklyn.

Its support for youth job-training programs has been thorough, with contributions to the Opportunities Industrialization Centers ($50,000), the Technical Training Project ($20,000), and Jobs for Youth ($10,000) in 1983.

In public policy grants for 1983, Pfizer favored conservative think tanks such as the American Enterprise Institute ($35,000) and the Heritage Foundation ($15,000) over more liberal organizations such as the Committee for Economic Development ($14,000) and the Brookings Institute ($10,000). Its support for conservative, business-oriented legal centers such as the Mid-Atlantic Legal Foundation totaled $19,000. Overall, its $3.8 million in cash giving in 1983 was a moderate 0.8 percent of pre-tax earnings, divided approximately equally among education, the United Way, and community service organizations.

The company matches employee gifts of up to $5,000 to most nonprofit organizations, and paid out a strong $400,000 in 1983. Pfizer has a volunteer program under which employees can take leave on company time to help nonprofit organizations, providing this leave does not interfere with work assignments.

Among employee benefits are flextime, child-care assistance, and an Employee Stock Ownership Program. Employees at the company headquarters have access to a child-care referral service as well as to various company-sponsored workshops on related issues. In 1984 the company established a

PFIZER INC.											
	Women		Minorities				Contracts		PAC Contributions		
% to Charity	Directors	Officers	Directors	Officers	Social Disclosure	Sullivan Rating	% Military	Nuclear Weapons–Related	Dollar Amount	% to Republicans	% to Democrats
0.8%	1	0	1	0	A	I	None	None	$134,450	55%	45%

See also Appendix D for a listing of this company's products and services.

free counseling service open to all employees. The service has a 24-hour-a-day hotline, and offers a wide range of counseling options.

The company purchased $8.0 million from minority-owned businesses in 1984 and $4.7 million from women-owned firms. Its minority banking program is small, with only $2 million in tax payments. In 1983 its officials and managers comprised 9.9 percent women and 6.8 percent minorities, one of the poorer records among pharmaceutical companies profiled in this book.

The company's Political Action Committee made more contributions to congressional candidates in the 1983–1984 election cycle ($134,000) than did the PAC of any other pharmaceutical company covered in this book.

Pfizer employs approximately 180 persons in South Africa, half of whom are white. It has received the highest rating, "making good progress," for compliance with the Sullivan Principles in recent years.

The company responded to CEP's questionnaire.

PROCTER & GAMBLE COMPANY

Traditional and responsible describes Cincinnati's Procter & Gamble, with its multitude of consumer products and long-standing reputation for quality goods. Over the past decade it has developed extensive family-oriented benefits for employees, and, despite a drawn-out dispute with unions in one plant, can claim a record of progressive employment policies.

In the mid-1970s, P&G adopted an innovative parental leave policy under which either parent could take up to six months off at the birth or adoption of a child, the first two months at full salary, the next four unpaid. The company also pays up to $1,000 in adoption expenses. Since 1982 P&G has offered a "flexible benefits" package including a dependent-care option. The package, over and above the company's already substantial regular benefits, is the equivalent of 2 to 4 percent of employees' salary, depending on length of time with the company. In 1982 the company set up a counseling service open to workers and their families, which can be used for child care–related problems.

In 1984 the company established a two-part child-care service open to the Cincinnati community. P&G provided the $35,000 start-up cost for a family day-care information and referral service — the Family Daycare Registry — in Cincinnati. Because Ohio has no system for licensing or monitoring family day-care, parents often find it difficult to locate these small, individually operated facilities and to evaluate their reliability. The registry establishes and monitors standards for child-care providers who register with it. Also in 1984, the company subsidized the start-up costs (reportedly $375,000) of two child-care centers near its largest work sites in town. These centers are run independently on a nonprofit basis, but P&G employees have access priority to three-quarters of the 140 slots.

According to *The 100 Best Companies to Work for in America*, P&G has long had a reputation for innovative employee benefits. For instance, it was one of the first companies in the country to set up profit-sharing and stock-purchase plans, both of which it established around the turn of this century. It is estimated that as much as 20 percent of the company's stock is owned by employees or retirees.

The company, however, was on the AFL-CIO boycott list from 1981 through 1984. Workers in a Kansas City plant manufacturing Ivory soap had voted for representation by the Steelworkers Union in 1980, but company and union representatives were unable to come to agreement on terms for a contract in the ensuing years. With no agreement in sight, the workers voted in March 1984 to reaffiliate themselves with the independent union that had previously represented them, and a contract with the company was almost immediately negotiated. About 25 percent of the company's total work force is unionized.

In Cincinnati, Procter & Gamble's reputation as a corporate citizen is excellent. Its $16.9 million 1985 charitable giving program, a fairly substantial 1.2 percent of pre-tax earnings, focused strongly on the region, with recent pledges to the University of Cincinnati, University of Miami, and other educational institutions, as well as the Cincinnati Fine Arts Fund. In addition, the company recently contributed $250,000 toward a summer jobs program in the city, and $100,000 to Investing in Neighborhoods, a coalition of neighborhood groups raising a $1 million endowment fund to provide a stable, ongoing source of support.

The company gave $521,500 in 1985 to public policy research, with its three largest grants going to conservative think tanks: the American Enterprise Institute ($125,000), the Heritage Foundation ($60,000), and the Hoover Institution ($50,000), although it also gave $42,500 to the more mainstream Committee for Economic Development. Additionally, the company funded several conservative law centers: the Capital Legal Foundation ($12,500), the National Legal Center for Public Interest ($10,000), and the Mid-America Legal Foundation ($5,000).

Volunteerism is strongly encouraged among P&G staff through a skills bank that matches employees' skills with the needs of local nonprofit groups. More than 200 employees participated in this service in 1984. The company will donate up to $1,000 to groups where employees volunteer. It gave out $40,000 through this program in 1984.

Support for minority economic development is channeled primarily through P&G's minority purchasing program, which came to $45 million in 1985. Its minority banking program has a moderate $1 million in certificates of deposit, but the company recently started up its own venture capital com-

PROCTER & GAMBLE COMPANY												
	Women		Minorities				Contracts		PAC Contributions		
% to Charity	Directors	Officers	Directors	Officers	Social Disclosure	Sullivan Rating	% Military	Nuclear Weapons– Related	Dollar Amount	% to Republicans	% to Democrats
1.2%	1	0	1	1	A	None	None	None	None		

See also Appendix D for a listing of this company's products and services.

pany for minority-owned businesses, the Sycamore Investment Company. In 1984 it appointed its first minority-group member, a Native American, to a vice presidential position.

Finding alternatives to the use of live animals in research and product testing is an area where Procter & Gamble has taken an innovative approach. The company's formal four-point policy commits P&G to eliminating the use of animals in testing wherever possible. Perhaps its most impressive action has been the development of an alternative to the widely used LD 50 test. In this test, groups of 50 to 200 animals are subjected to varying degrees of chemical exposure to determine the fatality point for at least 50 percent of the subjects. P&G has instead come up with an "up-down" testing method in which a single animal is given a single dose. If it survives, another test animal is given a higher dose, until the level of toxicity is determined. The company feels that equally valid results can be obtained in this way, using only six to eight animals per test. P&G's program has been called a model for the industry by the Coalition to Abolish the LD 50, led by Henry Spira, who also led animal rights campaigns concerning Revlon and Bristol-Myers. More radical animal rights groups continue to call for a boycott of P&G's products, along with those of virtually every other major cosmetic, drug, and detergent manufacturer, all of whom use animals in testing and research. (See also the Bristol-Myers and Revlon profiles.)

In 1980 the Centers for Disease Control found that P&G's Rely tampons had a higher correlation than other tampons to the often fatal toxic shock syndrome. The company quickly withdrew the product from the market and established a $75 million reserve to cover costs associated with the product. P&G has continued to maintain that the Rely tampons were no more liable to produce toxic shock syndrome than others, and funded $3 million in independent research on TSS.

In 1980 the company was criticized by environmentalists for its decision to reintroduce nitrilotriacetic acid (NAT), an alternative to pollution-producing phosphates, in its detergents. NAT had been voluntarily withdrawn by detergent manufacturers at the request of the Environmental Protection Agency in 1970 as a potential carcinogenic health hazard. In 1980, however, the agency ruled that NAT's dangers were negligible. Environmentalists worried that this chemical, which has caused bladder cancer in laboratory rats, will end up contaminating drinking water supplies. In 1982 Procter & Gamble stopped making detergents containing NAT pending resolution of this question.

In November 1985, Procter & Gamble acquired Richardson-Vicks. (See the Richardson-Vicks profile.)

The company responded to CEP's questionnaires.

RAPID-AMERICAN CORPORATION

The Rapid-American Corporation is the privately held creation of CEO Meshulam Riklis, who has received considerable press attention over the years both as an "empire builder" and for promoting the movie career of his wife, Pia Zadora. Rapid-American's holdings include Schenley Industries, distributors of Dewar's Scotch and other liquors; several retail store chains; and McGregor and other clothing manufacturers.

In 1984 Rapid-American acquired Fabergé, a personal care products company. Fabergé had a history of labor troubles. In 1979 the Oil, Chemical and Atomic Workers Union put Fabergé on its boycott list after the company closed a unionized New Jersey plant and moved its jobs to a non-union operation in North Carolina. Then in 1982 the unions lifted the boycott in an attempt to "re-establish decent labor-management relations" and assist negotiations at a second plant in St. Paul, Minnesota, according to the *AFL-CIO News*. But Fabergé shut down the St. Paul facility, moving this operation to the North Carolina plant as well. In 1983 the unions again called for a Fabergé boycott, which was still in effect as of early 1986.

The Rapid-American Foundation's 1984 gifts totaled $101,000. This figure does not include direct corporate giving and may understate the company's total program. Because the company is privately held, no comparison with profits is possible; however, this amount appears relatively meager in our opinion.

The company did not respond to CEP's questionnaires.

RAPID-AMERICAN CORPORATION											
	Women		Minorities				Contracts		PAC Contributions		
% to Charity	Directors	Officers	Directors	Officers	Social Disclosure	Sullivan Rating	% Military	Nuclear Weapons–Related	Dollar Amount	% to Republicans	% to Democrats
*	?	?	?	?	F	None	None	None	None		

* = See profile   ? = No information available
See also Appendix D for a listing of this company's products and services.

REVLON, INC.

Revlon has received positive publicity for its commitments to finding alternatives to animal experimentation in product research and testing. But information is scarce on other social initiatives by the company, which did not respond to CEP's questionnaires.

In November 1985, after a fierce takeover battle, Revlon, which was the creation of the hard-driving, high-living, and demanding Charles Revson, was acquired by Pantry Pride, a Florida-based supermarket and retail store company. Revlon's Norcliff Thayer division, which makes Tums antacids and Oxy acne medicines, was immediately sold by Pantry Pride to the Beecham Group, a British consumer products and pharmaceutical company.

In 1980 the company became the focus of a campaign by animal rights groups seeking to pressure the cosmetics and pharmaceutical industries to reduce the huge numbers of mammals used in product research and testing. An estimated total of 20 to 70 million animals are used worldwide each year by cosmetics companies; mice and rats are the most frequent subjects, along with substantial numbers of rabbits, monkeys, and others. Revlon was singled out by the activists primarily because of its high visibility within the cosmetics industry.

After initial private talks failed to bring meaningful company action, the animal rights groups ran full-page ads in the *New York Times* headlined, "How Many Rabbits Does Revlon Blind for Beauty's Sake?" At issue was the Draize test, in which potential irritants in new cosmetics and shampoos are dripped into rabbits' eyes.

The company eventually responded to this public campaign with a three-year, $750,000 grant (with subsequent contributions of $500,000) for the creation of a center at Rockefeller University to study alternatives to animal test-

REVLON, INC.											
	Women		Minorities				Contracts		PAC Contributions		
% to Charity	Directors	Officers	Directors	Officers	Social Disclosure	Sullivan Rating	% Military	Nuclear Weapons–Related	Dollar Amount	% to Republicans	% to Democrats
0.2%	1	0	?	?	F	V	None	None	None		

? = No information available
See also Appendix D for a listing of this company's products and services.

In the Drugstore

ing. In addition, Revlon announced in 1982 that it had reduced by 20 percent the number of rabbits it used for testing.

In that same year Avon responded with a $750,000 grant to the Cosmetics, Toiletries and Fragrances trade association toward the establishment of a similar center at Johns Hopkins University. The Estée Lauder cosmetics company also contributed $250,000 to this fund. (See the Procter & Gamble and Bristol-Myers profiles for further discussion of this issue.)

Revlon's record on charitable contributions does not appear to be strong. According to the Taft *Corporate Giving Directory*, it gave $500,000 through its foundation in 1983 (just 0.2 percent of pre-tax earnings), primarily to education and federated drives. This figure does not include direct corporate giving and may understate the company's total program.

The company has made several grants to Catalyst, a New York–based organization devoted to issues concerning women in the workplace. Revlon funds Catalyst's Corporate Board Resource, which helps companies interested in locating qualified women for their boards of directors. The company also gave grants of $61,000 for Catalyst's Maternity/Paternal Leave Project and $180,000 for its Upward Mobility Program.

Revlon employs approximately 300 persons (three-quarters of whom are white) in its South African operations. While a signatory of the Sullivan Principles in 1981 and 1982, the company did not report to the independent consultants evaluating American company operations. In 1983 it withdrew as a signatory rather than pay the fee for these independent evaluations. But in 1985 the company reversed this position and again became a signatory. In 1986 it announced plans to sell its operations there by the end of 1987.

RICHARDSON-VICKS INC.

In November 1985, Procter & Gamble acquired Richardson-Vicks, a large consumer products company with some moderate social initiatives. Previously, the company, although publicly held, had been largely owned and controlled by the Richardson family. At the time of the takeover, the *Wall Street Journal* described the five family members on the company's board of directors as "politically conservative, strongly Protestant, intensely private, genteel and charitable."

In its headquarters city of Wilton, Connecticut, the company took part in a business consortium that helped fund a community child-care center that opened in 1984. Also in that year the company, in an experimental program, lent $50,000 interest-free to a community group in nearby Norwalk that converted a former factory into moderate-income housing, and made a special grant to a Norwalk neighborhood housing group to fund low-interest revolving loans for rehabilitation.

Richardson-Vicks told CEP that it does not disclose dollar figures on its charitable contributions, but that in 1983, 41 percent of its gifts went to education, 38 percent to health and general welfare, 8 percent to civic programs, and 6 percent to cultural institutions. The company matched employee contributions to higher education dollar for dollar, but this amount totaled only $48,000 in 1982–1983. (The Smith Richardson family foundation has long been known as a major supporter of conservative policy study centers.)

Through 1985, 18.4 percent of the company's officials and managers were women and 6.7 percent minorities. Its minority purchasing program rose dramatically from $99,000 in 1983 to $4.25 million in 1984. But the company has no minority banking program. Approximately 5 percent of the company's work force is unionized.

RICHARDSON-VICKS INC.											
	Women		Minorities				Contracts		PAC Contributions		
% to Charity	Directors	Officers	Directors	Officers	Social Disclosure	Sullivan Rating	% Military	Nuclear Weapons–Related	Dollar Amount	% to Republicans	% to Democrats
?	1	0	0	0	A	IIA	None	None	$21,042	76%	24%

? = No information available
See also Appendix D for a listing of this company's products and services.

Prior to 1981, the Merrell pharmaceutical company was a part of the Richardson-Vicks operation, which was then known as Richardson-Merrell. (In 1981 Dow Chemical acquired Merrell.) Merrell had been involved in several major controversies surrounding its drugs, including Bendectin. (See the Dow Chemical profile for a brief description of the Bendectin controversy.)

Richardson-Vicks's rating for compliance with the Sullivan Principles climbed to the second-highest "making progress" category for 1984 and 1985 from the lower ranking — "needs to become more active" — which it had received from 1981 through 1983. The company employs about 280 workers in South Africa. In late 1986, Procter & Gamble announced that it would be selling Richardson-Vicks' South African operations.

The company responded to CEP's questionnaires.

A. H. ROBINS COMPANY, INC.

A. H. Robins faces a bitter, unprecedented, and highly controversial series of lawsuits concerning its intrauterine contraceptive device (IUD) known as the Dalkon Shield. Morton Mintz, writing in *At Any Cost*, asserts that the Dalkon Shield "created a disaster of global proportions," while the company denies any wrongdoing.

Through mid-1985, over 14,000 claims and suits had been filed alleging that the Dalkon Shield had caused sterility and even death among its users, primarily because those who accidentally became pregnant while wearing the shield may have been prone to septic abortions and serious pelvic inflammatory diseases. In addition, the company was charged with making inflated and unjustified claims for the efficiency of this IUD. Robins has vigorously denied these charges, and has consistently maintained that its product was safe and effective.

In August 1985, having settled 9,450 claims at a cost of $520 million and facing an additional 6,000 cases, A. H. Robins sought protection of the bankruptcy courts. Robins then successfully appealed to the courts to set a deadline after which no further Dalkon Shield suits could be filed. But by the April 1986 deadline, an overwhelming 1,000 new suits were reportedly being filed daily, with the total number of suits approaching 300,000.

In the meantime, in early 1986, the Internal Revenue Service took the unusual step of asking the courts to appoint a trustee to run the company because current management had made almost $7 million in payments, including some for executive compensation, without the required court approval. In June 1986, a further government investigation alleged that Robins had spent closer to $9 million without the court's permission. The company denied that it had been informed that such payments were improper and asserted that the executives had returned all unauthorized payments. In August 1986, a federal judge ordered an independent examiner appointed to monitor the company's bankruptcy proceedings.

Robins first marketed the Dalkon Shield in January 1971, and voluntarily withdrew it in June 1974. During this period it sold over 2 million devices in the United States and well over 1 million abroad, some of these through the U.S. Agency for International Development for use in developing nations. Reports of deaths among its users from accidental pregnancies complicated by severe infections prompted the company to cease Dalkon sales in 1974 and recommend that the device be removed from pregnant women. But it was not until six years later that the company sent a letter to doctors recommending removal of the Shield from nonpregnant, long-term users. In 1984 it launched a recall campaign to reach all users directly, offering to pay for the Shield's removal.

In the Drugstore

The company has been sharply criticized for its conduct during this time, particularly for its delay in the recall. Subrata Chakravarty, writing in *Forbes* magazine in 1984, stated that "Robins appears to have handled the Shield improperly, almost from the beginning," and that Robins "did not have a single obstetrician or gynecologist on its staff" when it entered the IUD market. Federal District Judge Miles Lord, in a Minnesota trial, described the Shield as "a deadly depth charge in [tens of thousand of women's] wombs, ready to explode at any time" and, in addressing Robins's chairman and two other officials, asserted that "It is not enough to say 'I did not know,' 'It was not me,' 'Look elsewhere.'" The judge's remarks were later stricken from the court record as having denied the defendant of due process of law and fundamental fairness.

A. H. Robins is run by the Robins family. Ironically, its current chairman, E. Claiborne Robins, Sr., is known for his philanthropic generosity in Richmond, Virginia. He has personally given over $50 million to the University of Richmond, and his family has given an additional $50 million. He co-chaired Businesses Who Care, a coalition of local companies founded in 1982 and devoted to increasing corporate philanthropy.

The company's recent record on charitable giving showed a fairly strong but traditional program; $788,000 in cash gifts in 1984, or 1 percent of pre-tax earnings, down from $937,000 in 1983. This amount went primarily to traditional recipients ($79,000 to the United Way, $60,000 for a mobile unit for the Richmond Blood Service, $40,000 to the 4-H Club). Approximately 43 percent of its gifts went to education.

In the promotion of minority group members to its ranks of officials and managers, Robins had the best record among the pharmaceutical companies profiled in this book — 10.1 percent in 1984. Women held 16.4 percent of the officials' and managers' positions. Its minority purchasing program is appar-

A. H. ROBINS COMPANY, INC.											
	Women		Minorities				Contracts		PAC Contributions		
% to Charity	Directors	Officers	Directors	Officers	Social Disclosure	Sullivan Rating	% Military	Nuclear Weapons— Related	Dollar Amount	% to Republicans	% to Democrats
1.0%	0	0	0	0	A	None	None	None	None		

See also Appendix D for a listing of this company's products and services.

ently just getting off the ground, with only $21,000 in 1984 purchases. The company planned to increase this figure to $1.2 million in 1985. Its minority banking program consisted of a $200,000 credit line and operating accounts.

Robins sold its South African operations in late 1985.

The company responded to CEP's questionnaires.

SCHERING-PLOUGH CORPORATION

The Schering pharmaceutical company merged with the Memphis-based Plough consumer products firm in 1971 to form Schering-Plough, headquartered in Madison, New Jersey. The company has taken some moderately innovative social initiatives.

In 1985, the firm made a $300,000 contribution toward the start-up of the new Puerto Rico Community Foundation, with Schering-Plough's chief executive officer heading the drive for further corporate contributions. The Ford Foundation's initial $2 million contribution made possible this joint business-community foundation, which will address the economic and social problems of the island. SmithKline and Warner-Lambert have contributed $300,000 each and Bristol-Myers, Johnson & Johnson, and Pfizer have contributed $150,000 apiece.

In Memphis, headquarters of the consumer products divisions, the company has instituted an innovative program to encourage volunteering. Each year all employees are given one day off with pay to work with nonprofit organizations of their choice. These are called Plough Days, after founding father Abe Plough, who was a major philanthropist in the Memphis region.

Among employee benefits is a profit-sharing plan, wherein up to 10 percent of the company's profits (after certain expenses such as research are deducted) is distributed to all workers including hourly and unionized staff. Individuals with three years at the company can receive a bonus payment of up to 15 percent of their base salary each year under this plan (7.5 percent for those with one or two years of service). The company also has a more usual employee stock-ownership program, with workers receiving the equivalent of ½ to ¾ percent of their salary in company stock each year; and a savings plan under which up to 4 percent of salary can be set aside on a pre-tax basis

SCHERING-PLOUGH CORPORATION											
	Women		Minorities				Contracts		PAC Contributions		
% to Charity	Directors	Officers	Directors	Officers	Social Disclosure	Sullivan Rating	% Military	Nuclear Weapons–Related	Dollar Amount	% to Republicans	% to Democrats
0.8%	1	0	0	?	A	IIA	None	None	$68,000	63%	37%

? = No information available
See also Appendix D for a listing of this company's products and services.

(although Schering-Plough does not match these savings as do many other companies).

Its charitable giving program is an average one — $1.9 million in 1985, or 0.8 percent of pre-tax earnings. Gifts are heavily weighted toward higher education (22 percent in 1984) and medical education (34 percent), with an additional 21 percent going to match employee contributions to hospitals and education. In 1984 the company completed a two-year, $50,000 grant to the conservative American Enterprise Institute economic think tank. The firm's foundation is particularly well endowed, with almost $14 million in assets in 1984.

The company's minority purchasing program is small, but apparently growing, up from $316,000 in 1983 to $1.2 million in 1985. Of Plough's officials and managers, 18 percent were women and 9 percent were minorities in 1985, about average for pharmaceutical companies profiled in this book. (In 1980 the company agreed to give $165,000 in back pay to 407 women, and $600,000 was spent on programs to accelerate the promotion of women at two New Jersey plants.)

From 1981 through 1985 its South African operations, which employ 260 workers, consistently ranked second-highest ("making progress") for compliance with the Sullivan Principles for nondiscriminatory labor practices in that country.

The company responded to CEP's questionnaires.

SMITHKLINE BECKMAN CORPORATION

SmithKline is a traditional pharmaceutical company, supportive of conservative public policy research centers, with charitable giving directed primarily to its native Philadelphia.

In 1906, Mahlon Kline, one of the company's founding fathers, advocated passage of the Pure Food and Drug Act. In 1979 the company voluntarily initiated a massive withdrawal of 1.2 million bottles of contaminated nasal spray. But its record was not helped by its failure in 1979 to withdraw from the marketplace a newly introduced antihypertensive drug, Selacryn, which had serious and sometimes fatal side effects. SmithKline pleaded guilty to criminal misconduct in this case.

Selacryn was introduced in May 1979, but withdrawn from the market in January 1980, by which time some 25 deaths due to liver damage had been linked to it. The Food and Drug Administration then filed criminal charges against SmithKline, alleging that it had delayed its reports on the drug's harmful side effects by substantial periods over the legal fifteen-day limit.

In late 1984, the company pleaded guilty and three of its employees pleaded no contest to these charges. Instead of paying a maximum $34,000 fine, the company agreed to contribute $100,000 to a Philadelphia child-abuse prevention program. The company was further sentenced to 500 hours of volunteer community service over a two-year period. The three employees were given five-year probationary sentences, and were required to put in 200 hours each in community service over two years. With regard to this case, the company wrote CEP that "several government agencies" investigating the incident "produced *absolutely no findings* that the company or its employees acted intentionally, recklessly or for commercial motive."

SMITHKLINE BECKMAN CORPORATION												
	Women		Minorities				Contracts		PAC Contributions			
% to Charity	Directors	Officers	Directors	Officers	Social Disclosure	Sullivan Rating	% Military	Nuclear Weapons–Related	Dollar Amount	% to Republicans	% to Democrats
0.9%	1	0	1	?	A	I/IIA	None	None	$69,050	57%	43%

? = No information available
See also Appendix D for a listing of this company's products and services.

In early 1986, the company promptly recalled its Contac cold remedy and two other over-the-counter medicines in capsule form when some were found to have been tampered with on the shelves. No deaths or injuries resulted from this incident.

SmithKline disbursed a moderate $5.7 million in 1984, 0.9 percent of pre-tax earnings, $2.5 million of which went to organizations in the Philadelphia area. Its giving is heavily weighted toward medical education and research projects (about $2 million of its total contributions). Education received 45 percent, distributed among higher education, public, and parochial schools. The company matched employee gifts in excess of $400,000 in 1984.

The firm's IMPACT program gave over $300,000 in public policy research grants in 1984, of which $135,000 went to conservative think tanks — $100,000 to the Heritage Foundation, $25,000 to the American Enterprise Institute, and $10,000 to the Hoover Institution. (The company's chairman, Robert F. Dee, is a member of the Heritage Foundation board of trustees.) In the early 1980s the company ran a series of advertisements on social issues including excessive government taxation of business, the virtues of nuclear power, and the threat to freedom from the Soviet Union.

SmithKline reports substantial progress in the promotion of minorities and women within the company, with representation of women among its officials and managers at an outstanding 20.5 percent as of 1984. Minorities were at 9.5 percent, one of the best overall records among pharmaceutical companies profiled in this book.

SmithKline has special programs providing on-the-job training for the handicapped, employment of the long-term unemployed, and work experience for minority high-school students. Among its employee benefits are adoption assistance, child-care support, full tuition reimbursement for education, and a tax-deferred savings and investment plan.

The company's operations in South Africa employ approximately 270 workers, two-thirds of whom are white. SmithKline has generally received the second-highest "making progress" rating for compliance with the Sullivan Principles, while its Beckman subsidiary, employing approximately 60 people in South Africa, was upgraded to the highest rating in 1985.

The company responded to CEP's questionnaires.

SQUIBB CORPORATION

We could locate no information on social initiatives by this New Jersey–based pharmaceutical company, which did not respond to CEP's questionnaires.

Its operations in South Africa, which employ about 190 persons, have received poor ratings for compliance with the Sullivan Principles in recent years, slipping from "making good progress" in 1981 and 1982 to "needs to become more active" in 1983 and 1984, below that for other U.S. drug companies. In 1985, the company was again ranked as "making good progress."

In late 1986, Squibb sold its cosmetics lines. (See addendum on page 500.)

SQUIBB CORPORATION											
	Women		Minorities				Contracts		PAC Contributions		
% to Charity	Directors	Officers	Directors	Officers	Social Disclosure	Sullivan Rating	% Military	Nuclear Weapons–Related	Dollar Amount	% to Republicans	% to Democrats
?	2	0	?	?	F	IIA	None	None	$34,548	53%	47%

? = No information available
See also Appendix D for a listing of this company's products and services.

STERLING DRUG INC.

With headquarters in New York City, this pharmaceutical and household products company has faced some controversy over its marketing practices at home and abroad. We could locate little information on social initiatives.

The company was involved in a lengthy dispute in the early 1970s and 1980s over advertising claims for Bayer aspirin, Cope, Midol, and Vanquish which the Federal Trade Commission (FTC) had ruled were misleading. (The FTC pursued similar cases against American Home Products and Bristol-Myers at that time.) The company appealed, but the FTC ruling was upheld in the courts.

In 1984 four church groups submitted a shareholder resolution to the company requesting that it stop marketing the painkiller dipyrone in developing nations. The U.S. Food and Drug Administration had withdrawn dipyrone from American markets in 1977 because of possible severe side effects related to blood disorders. The company opposed the resolution on the grounds that current research showed the drug was in fact safe, pointing out that it was licensed for sale in thirty countries, including Switzerland and West Germany. As of mid-1986 Sterling continued to maintain the safety of the drug and continued its marketing abroad.

According to the Taft *Corporate Giving Directory*, Sterling gave $1.3 million in direct grants in 1984, a moderate 0.5 percent of its pre-tax earnings. Approximately 53 percent of direct giving went to education, primarily in a limited number of large grants to higher education, along with scholarships for employees' children.

In South Africa, Sterling plants employ just over 400 workers and are evaluated as "making progress" (the second-highest rating) in complying with the Sullivan Principles.

The company did not respond to CEP's questionnaires.

STERLING DRUG INC.											
	Women		Minorities				Contracts		PAC Contributions		
% to Charity	Directors	Officers	Directors	Officers	Social Disclosure	Sullivan Rating	% Military	Nuclear Weapons– Related	Dollar Amount	% to Republicans	% to Democrats
0.5%	1	0	0	0	F	IIA	None	None	$19,150	90%	10%

See also Appendix D for a listing of this company's products and services.

WARNER-LAMBERT COMPANY

After a decade in which it was the subject of several controversies, Warner-Lambert has taken some strong social initiatives in the 1980s.

This New Jersey–based company, which produces an unusual mix of products including chewing gum, razor blades, and pharmaceuticals, now has a comprehensive minority economic development program. Minority purchasing totaled $6 million in 1984, with a goal of $7 million in 1985. The company placed $20 million in deposits with minority-owned banks in the United States and Puerto Rico that year, and made all FICA tax payments through the black-owned Freedom National Bank in New York. Various 1984 policies with minority-owned insurance companies accounted for 7 percent of its total life insurance (up from 6 percent the previous year) and included the workers' compensation for its headquarters.

Employee benefits are diverse, including child-care referral, the Entrepreneur Program (a pilot $250,000 fund for workers to pursue new product ideas), health and psychological counseling services (with a health care facility under construction), reimbursement for educational expenses ($874,000 in 1984), flextime, and an Employee Stock Ownership Plan.

Warner's charitable giving of $4.0 million in 1985 was a fairly strong 1.1 percent of pre-tax earnings, weighted toward education (35 percent) and health research and services (30 percent). Thirteen percent went to minority affairs. Warner-Lambert, along with several other companies, supports the Technical Training Project, a job-training center for inner-city youth in Newark, New Jersey. The company's foundation has also taken an interest in the issue of domestic violence.

Of its officers and managers in 1984, 15.9 percent were women and 8.9 percent minorities, roughly comparable with levels of other pharmaceutical companies covered in this book.

WARNER-LAMBERT COMPANY											
	Women		Minorities				Contracts		PAC Contributions		
% to Charity	Directors	Officers	Directors	Officers	Social Disclosure	Sullivan Rating	% Military	Nuclear Weapons–Related	Dollar Amount	% to Republicans	% to Democrats
1.1%	1	1	1	2	A	IIA/IIB	None	None	None		

See also Appendix D for a listing of this company's products and services.

In the 1970s, several controversies brought Warner-Lambert to the public's attention. An explosion in one of its chewing gum factories in 1976 killed 6 workers and injured 55 others.

With the acquisition of the Parke-Davis pharmaceutical company in 1970, Warner-Lambert inherited a controversy over one of its drugs, Chloromycetin. The drug had potentially serious side effects, and allegedly had been widely overprescribed in the United States and marketed without warning labels abroad. Warner-Lambert soon thereafter corrected these problems.

The company had a long-running battle with the Federal Trade Commission over the validity of its advertising claims for Listerine mouthwash. Warner-Lambert claimed that its product helped prevent or cure colds. The FTC ordered $10 million in corrective advertising by the company in 1975.

The company signed the Sullivan Principles in 1978, soon after they were promulgated. It now employs more than 500 persons there and received the second-highest "making progress" rating for compliance with the Sullivan Principles from 1981 through 1985.

The company responded to CEP's questionnaires.

Chapter 7

ON THE ROAD
Airline, Automobile, Hotel, and Oil Companies

AIRLINE COMPANIES

Comparisons among airlines on most social issues is difficult, in part because of a general lack of cooperation in disclosing information for this book. (Only Eastern and Republic cooperated fully.) Eastern, which reported strong minority economic development programs, was exceptional in having two minorities both in top management and on its board of directors. Texas Air had the most active Political Action Committee, followed by United Airlines. All others' PAC spending was under $50,000. United is the only airline with a substantial number of employees in South Africa (through its Westin Hotels subsidiary). Pan Am stands out as a major military contractor.

Deregulation of the airline industry in 1978, coupled with the ensuing price wars and the recession of the early 1980s, led to financial crises among many carriers. These crises in turn made labor relations and cost-cutting the primary social issues in the industry. How management handled these problems produced both innovative solutions and major controversies.

Among the older, unionized carriers, Eastern attempted the most far-reaching partnership between workers and management. Two other unionized airlines where financial crises produced innovative worker-management programs were Western and Republic. American has a profit-sharing plan. Pan Am has adopted a stock ownership plan as well.

Among non-union carriers, the upstart People Express, more than any other airline, pioneered no-frills discount air travel. Its use of profit sharing, widespread employee stock ownership, and job flexibility to motivate employees and to keep costs down has received plaudits. Delta, with its "family spirit" and no-layoffs jobs policy, has been much praised over the years.

Among the airlines most criticized by unions is Texas Air. Facing a financial crisis, Texas Air's Continental subsidiary elected to go into Chapter 11 bankruptcy and cut labor costs simply by canceling its union contracts.

Neither US Air nor Northwest Orient faced the major fiscal strains suffered by most other carriers around 1980. Both airlines avoided major confrontations with unions. US Air is active in promoting minority banking programs.

AIRLINES

Size of Charitable Contributions	Women Directors and Officers	Minority Directors and Officers	Social Disclosure	Brand Name	Company (Profile Page)	Involvement in South Africa	Conv. Weapons–Related Contracts	Nuclear Weapons–Related Contracts	Authors' Company of Choice
*	🚶🚶	🚶	No	American Airlines	AMR (p. 249)	No	✈✈	No	
$	🚶	🚶🚶	No	Delta	Delta Air Lines (p. 251)	No	No	No	
*	🚶	🚶🚶🚶	☞☞☞	Eastern	Eastern Airlines (p. 252)	No	No	No	
?	No	?	No	Northwest Airlines	NWA (p. 254)	No	No	No	
*	🚶	🚶	No	Pan American	Pan Am (p. 255)	No	✈✈✈	Yes	
?	🚶	?	No	People Express Britt Airways	People Express (p. 257)	No	No	No	
*	No	No	☞☞☞	Republic	Republic Airlines (p. 259)	No	No	No	
?	🚶	?	No	Continental New York Air Texas Air	Texas Air (p. 260)	No	No	No	

(Continued on next page)

Size of Charitable Contributions	Women Directors and Officers	Minority Directors and Officers	Social Disclosure	Brand Name	Company (Profile Page)	Involvement in South Africa	Conv. Weapons-Related Contracts	Nuclear Weapons-Related Contracts	Authors' Company of Choice
?	⋀⋀	⋀	No	TWA	Trans World Airlines (p. 262)	No	No	No	
✳	⋀⋀	⋀	No	United Airlines	UAL (p. 263)	Yes C	No	No	
?	⋀	No	✍✍	U.S. Air	US Air Group (p. 265)	No	No	No	
?	⋀	?	No	Western	Western Airlines (p. 266)	No	No	No	

✳ = See company profile
? = No information available
Single figure ($, ⋀) = Minimal
Double figure ($$, ⋀⋀, ✍✍, ⋀⋀) = Moderate
Triple figure ($$$, ⋀⋀⋀, ✍✍✍, ⋀⋀⋀) = Substantial

No = No involvement or participation
Yes = Involvement or participation. A, B, C in the South African column reflect the degree of compliance with Sullivan Principles and/or involvement in strategic industries.

See Chapter 4 for a detailed discussion of chart symbols.

AMR CORPORATION (AMERICAN AIRLINES)

Known as the vigorous competitor, this Dallas-based carrier is, with United, one of the top two airlines in the industry. Aside from a generous program of support for the Dallas public school system, we could locate little information on its social initiatives. It has recently faced some charges of unfair competitive practices.

In 1983 the Justice Department charged that American's chief executive officer, Robert Crandall, had attempted to persuade Braniff, its rival in the Dallas–Fort Worth market, to make a simultaneous, two-company, 20 percent hike in fairs. The antitrust suit was settled in 1985; the agreement stipulated that Crandall was prohibited from discussing fares with executives at other airlines for two years.

In 1984, 10 airlines sued American and United for allegedly providing travel agents with computerized reservations systems that favored their own flights. These are the two largest computerized reservations systems in the nation, and profitable operations in themselves for American and United. In 1985 American and United agreed to drop the features which had allegedly created a "bias" for their flights, although related suits continued into 1986.

In 1985 the Federal Aviation Administration (FAA) fined American $1.5 million for a series of maintenance violations, citing failures of maintenance procedures which had not kept pace with the company's rapid expansion.

American negotiated the difficulties of airline labor relations in the early 1980s by coming up with an innovative cost-cutting pact that kept full earnings and benefits for current workers while reducing wages for those hired in the future. In tough bargaining sessions in 1983 the company and unions hammered out a precedent-setting agreement under which employees were guaranteed lifetime job security and wage increases. In return, unions agreed

AMR CORPORATION											
	Women		Minorities				Contracts		PAC Contributions		
% to Charity	Directors	Officers	Directors	Officers	Social Disclosure	Sullivan Rating	% Military	Nuclear Weapons–Related	Dollar Amount	% to Republicans	% to Democrats
*	1	2	1	?	F	None	0.5%	None	$49,425	56%	44%

* = See profile   ? = No information available
See also Appendix D for a listing of this company's products and services.

that future staff could be hired at substantially lower salaries, more part-timers would be taken on, and there would be increased flexibility in job definitions. This meant that the company could hire new pilots at up to 50 percent less than the current rate, and permitted a 32 percent wage cut for new flight attendants. The company was able to offer this gradual cost-cutting plan because its losses were relatively small compared with those of most other carriers in the early 1980s.

American has also set up a profit-sharing plan that gave out $12 million to 35,000 employees in early 1985.

American has an innovative and generous contributions program supporting the Dallas–Fort Worth public schools. Starting in 1984 the company donated one dollar to the school system for every American flight made from the Dallas–Fort Worth airport, for a total of over $500,000 that year, with an additional $500,000 projected for 1985. According to the *National Directory of Corporate Charity*, American gave $533,000 in charitable contributions in 1983, but no meaningful correlation to earnings is possible because of company losses in previous years.

American received $29.3 million in Department of Defense contracts in 1984. The company provides flight training for the military, primarily for the KC-10 aerial tanker used for in-flight refueling of bomber or fighter aircraft.

AMR discontinued its South African operations in late 1985.

The company did not respond to CEP's questionnaires.

DELTA AIR LINES, INC.

In an industry characterized by labor disputes and tough contract negotiations, the non-union and profitable Delta stands out for its long history of harmonious relations with its workers. According to the authors of *The 100 Best Companies to Work for in America,* "One of the most publicized corporate love affairs is between Delta employees and their airline."

Among its policies for employees is near total job security. The company boasts of having kept this promise through good times and bad for over 25 years. Pay scales and benefits at Delta are reportedly as good as or better than other airlines. The company's management works hard to keep communications open with workers and to promote the "family" feeling for which the airline is famous.

This family spirit has served the airline well. Delta remained profitable in the years first following deregulation of the industry in 1978, when other airlines were racking up huge losses. In 1982, when the company succumbed to industry-wide losses, its top executives took a pay cut and 80 percent of its workers contributed a portion of their paychecks to finance the acquisition of a new airplane.

The work force is 99 percent non-union, and the company likes it that way. Management attributes part of the airline's profitability to the flexibility in duties which its workers accept in return for good wages and job security.

The company's charitable contributions appear to be minimal ($346,000 in 1983 — or 0.1 percent of pre-tax earnings — as reported in the Taft *Corporate Giving Directory*). This figure is for the company's foundation only and may understate the company's total program.

In late 1986, Delta acquired Western Airlines. (See addendum on page 500.)

The company did not respond to CEP's questionnaires.

DELTA AIR LINES, INC.											
	Women		Minorities				Contracts		PAC Contributions		
% to Charity	Directors	Officers	Directors	Officers	Social Disclosure	Sullivan Rating	% Military	Nuclear Weapons–Related	Dollar Amount	% to Republicans	% to Democrats
0.1%	1	0	1	1	F	None	None	None	$12,775	29%	71%

See also Appendix D for a listing of this company's products and services.

EASTERN AIRLINES, INC.

Eastern has had stormy relations with its unions for over ten years. In 1983, unions and management, faced with the possible bankruptcy of the airline, worked out what promised to be one of the most comprehensive labor-management partnerships in the airlines industry. But financial crises persisted, antagonisms resurfaced, and amid bitter charges on both sides, the carrier was acquired in 1986 by Texas Air. (See the Texas Air profile.)

This Miami-based company was the only airline to report substantial overall programs for minority economic development, although US Air and Republic both have made some efforts in that area.

Unions first gave wage concessions to Eastern's management, headed by ex-astronaut Frank Borman, in 1975, when pilots agreed to a wage freeze in return for profit sharing — a first in the airline industry. In 1976 Eastern workers agreed to a "variable earnings" plan, which meant profit sharing in good years, wage cuts in bad ones. The plan lost its popularity after 1980, when Eastern suffered a string of losses. In 1982 management unilaterally extended this plan through a legal technicality, a move unpopular with workers. Then in 1983, in a severely deteriorating financial situation, management came back to the unions for further, more substantial, concessions.

This time, with the airline hovering on the brink of bankruptcy, the unions demanded major concessions. In return for $360 million in wage cuts over a one-year period, employees received 25 percent of the airline's stock and representation on its 19-member board of directors. (Two board members were union officials and two others were designated by unions.) Unions also asked for and got a voice in future economic decisions. Eastern's employees have access to the company's financial performance records on a monthly basis and participate in the company's business decisions — a significant departure

EASTERN AIRLINES, INC.											
	Women		Minorities				Contracts		PAC Contributions		
% to Charity	Directors	Officers	Directors	Officers	Social Disclosure	Sullivan Rating	% Military	Nuclear Weapons–Related	Dollar Amount	% to Republicans	% to Democrats
*	0	1	2	2	A	None	None	None	$47,325	54%	46%

* = See profile
See also Appendix D for a listing of this company's products and services.

On the Road

from other airlines. In addition, Eastern established a companywide effort to increase worker participation through steering committees made up of equal numbers of management and union members, with the whole program overseen by an Employee Involvement Planning Council.

Continuing this partnership was not easy. In 1985 and again in early 1986, the company, shouldering a massive debt, teetered on the edge of insolvency. Unions faced the prospects of further wage concessions. There was talk of a union-backed buyout of the company, amid increasingly antagonistic union-management discussions. Finally failing to obtain wage concessions from all unions, Borman agreed to the sale of the airline to Texas Air.

The company has an active fair hiring program, with women in 14.3 percent of the company's managerial positions and minorities in 11.2 percent.

Eastern is one of only two airlines profiled in this book that reported having a minority purchasing program: $10.5 million in 1984, up from $8.9 million in 1983. It also made tax payments of $98 million through minority-owned banks in 1984.

Eastern's officials participate in numerous community-oriented organizations in the Miami region. For example, the company is represented on the board of directors of the Business Assistance Center (BAC), which was set up in 1980 after the race riots in the Liberty section of Miami. BAC has received $7 million from the Miami business community to provide financial and technical assistance to black businesses in the area. Eastern uses its minority purchasing program to support these fledgling or expanding enterprises.

In early 1986 the Federal Aviation Administration (FAA) proposed fining Eastern $9.5 million for safety role violations. Eastern's subsequent offer to settle the proposed penalties for $3.5 million was rejected by the FAA, and as of May 1986, the case remained unresolved.

Eastern made charitable contributions of $205,000 in 1983 and $336,000 in 1984. (Losses in previous years make comparisons with pre-tax earnings impossible to calculate.) In 1984, 43 percent of its gifts went to the United Way and similar federated campaigns, and 48 percent to other community health and welfare programs.

Eastern was acquired by Texas Air in mid 1986. (See addendum on page 500.)

The company responded to CEP's questionnaires.

NWA INC. (NORTHWEST AIRLINES)

A company with a reputation for tight cost control and tough bargaining with its unions in the 1970s, Northwest Airlines weathered the early 1980s without severe losses and hence without the dramatic labor confrontations that characterized many other unionized carriers at that time. Like various other airlines, it was the subject of sex discrimination cases in the 1970s, although the damages awarded to the plaintiffs, which Northwest ultimately paid, were the largest in the industry.

This Minnesota-based company's hard bargaining with its unions during the 1970s limited wage increases and was at least partially responsible for the carrier having the best worker productivity record in the airlines industry. This in turn helped the company during the difficult years following deregulation in 1978. Because Northwest did not suffer the huge losses of many other airlines, it did not have to ask its unions for wage and productivity concessions to remain afloat.

The company fought a class-action sex discrimination suit by flight attendants from 1970 to 1985. The courts initially ruled against Northwest in 1973, but the company appealed. In July 1984, a federal appeals court upheld lower court rulings in favor of the 3,362 flight attendants, and maintained the $60 million awarded in back pay — the second-largest award ever made in an employment discrimination suit at that time, according to the *Wall Street Journal*. The Supreme Court declined to review Northwest's appeal in 1985.

In January 1986, NWA announced its intention to acquire Republic Airlines, a move subsequently opposed by the U.S. Justice Department on anti-competitive grounds. The merger was approved in July 1986.

The company did not respond to CEP's questionnaires.

NWA INC.											
	Women		Minorities				Contracts		PAC Contributions		
% to Charity	Directors	Officers	Directors	Officers	Social Disclosure	Sullivan Rating	% Military	Nuclear Weapons–Related	Dollar Amount	% to Republicans	% to Democrats
?	0	0	?	?	F	None	None	None	None		

? = No information available
See also Appendix D for a listing of this company's products and services.

PAN AM CORPORATION

One of the oldest U.S. airlines, the New York–based Pan Am is unique in its industry as a major military contractor. It has had uneasy relations with its workers in recent years, economically difficult ones for the company. We could locate little information on social initiatives.

Pan American was the creation of the colorful Juan Trippe, who built up the airline in the 1930s through a total dominance of U.S. overseas air routes. Because of Trippe's connections with Washington politics and the airline's highly visible presence around the world, the Pan Am of those days "functioned practically as a branch of the State Department," according to the authors of *Everybody's Business*. However, the company no longer retains its monopoly on U.S. world travel. Other competitors have appeared, and Pan Am has sold off some of its major overseas routes during difficult financial times.

In 1985 Pan Am was the forty-third-largest Department of Defense prime contractor, with $520 million in awards, up from $459 million in 1984. According to the Investor Responsibility Research Center, Pan Am is in charge of "operation and maintenance of non-military functions" at the Trident nuclear submarine base in Bangor, Washington, and the Eastern Test Range at Patrick Air Force Base in Florida, where flight paths of missiles and space vehicles are tracked; it also provides similar services for several other military facilities around the country.

In order to increase domestic flights, Pan Am acquired National Airlines in 1979, immediately after the industry was deregulated. The move was considered unwise and partially responsible for the severe economic crisis that the company faced soon afterward. With the carrier on the verge of bankruptcy in 1981, its employees took a 10-percent wage cut for three years in exchange for one of the first Employee Stock Ownership Plans (ESOPs) in the industry.

PAN AM CORPORATION											
	Women		Minorities				Contracts		PAC Contributions		
% to Charity	Directors	Officers	Directors	Officers	Social Disclosure	Sullivan Rating	% Military	Nuclear Weapons–Related	Dollar Amount	% to Republicans	% to Democrats
*	1	0	1	0	F	None	12.5%	Yes	$40,375	44%	56%

* = See profile
See also Appendix D for a listing of this company's products and services.

Workers received approximately 13 percent of the company's stock and representation on its board of directors.

Despite these moves, relations between management and labor remained uneasy. In 1984 management angered unions by refusing to return wages to pre-1981 levels and implement raises, and disagreements with unions led to strikes in 1985.

In August 1986, Pan American agreed to pay nearly $2 million in fines to settle charges that it had violated various federal safety regulations, including the operation of unrepaired aircraft and failure to make required inspections.

In late 1985, Pan Am announced it would discontinue its South African operations entirely.

Pan Am did not respond to CEP's questionnaires.

PEOPLE EXPRESS AIRLINES, INC.

The "backpacker's airline," with headquarters in Newark, New Jersey, People Express was founded in 1980 by former employees of Texas Air. By 1986 it was among the largest airlines in the United States, although financially troubled at that time. It pioneered the concept of discount air travel, and deserves credit for its part in the dramatic drops in airline fares in the early 1980s. People is owned one-third by its employees, who are all called "managers." Upon starting work, everyone must buy at least 100 shares, at a 70 percent discount; these come with voting privileges. If a new employee can't afford the shares, the company will provide a no-interest loan.

People Express was established in the belief that if all employees are owners, their commitment ensures success. Initially, it seemed to have created a highly motivated and enthusiastic staff and a non-union shop. CEO Donald Burr put it this way: "We've gone to great lengths to avoid a unionized presence here because our competitive strategy depends upon free individuals doing what they freely enjoy. Bureaucratic unions telling their members . . . when, what, and how much they can do runs counter to that style."

Involvement and sharing were deeply imbedded in management style throughout the company. Everyone, including the president and the chief financial officer, takes a turn at other jobs with some regularity. No one has a secretary. However, the company contracts out baggage checking, maintenance, and reservations work, and hires college students as part-time ticket checkers. Burr explained to *Inc.* magazine in 1985 that these jobs involved "blue collar work . . . prone to unionization . . . [which is] antithetical to the business strategy of People Express."

The carrier started with low salaries by industry standards, although by now salaries at many other (unionized) airlines have been reduced sharply. A

PEOPLE EXPRESS AIRLINES, INC.											
	Women		Minorities				Contracts		PAC Contributions		
% to Charity	Directors	Officers	Directors	Officers	Social Disclosure	Sullivan Rating	% Military	Nuclear Weapons–Related	Dollar Amount	% to Republicans	% to Democrats
?	0	1	?	?	F	None	None	None	None		

? = No information available
See also Appendix D for a listing of this company's products and services.

profit-sharing plan paying up to 15 percent of base salaries makes up some of the difference in good years, as does a bonus-matching plan for stock purchases.

In 1985, after four years of successful expansion, the company began to experience losses, and its stock dropped sharply in value. This reportedly led to some unhappiness among employees, and underlies one of the possible drawbacks of employee stock ownership and profit-sharing plans as a means of motivation. In its profitable years, all full-time staff received one-third of company earnings; a third was reinvested in the firm, and a third went to stockholders. In addition, the company claims to make every effort to include "managers" in decision-making in this typically cyclical and risky industry.

In late 1985, People Express acquired the unionized Frontier Airlines. Frontier's unions had long been working to implement a worker buyout of the company, which was 45 percent owned by GenCorp. When Texas Air, known for strong anti-union moves at its Continental subsidiary, made a hostile takeover bid for Frontier, the unions quickly accepted People's rival offer. Frontier, which was losing money heavily in early 1986, proved a serious financial drain on People Express.

In late 1986, People Express was acquired by Texas Air. (See addendum on page 500.)

People Express did not respond to CEP's questionnaires, and we could locate no record of social initiatives.

REPUBLIC AIRLINES, INC.

Along with Eastern, Republic was one of the only two airlines to cooperate fully in providing information for this book. Social initiatives by this recently formed carrier, headquartered in Minneapolis, appear moderate.

Republic was in financial trouble almost from the moment of its creation in 1979. It was formed by the merger of two regional airlines — North Central Airlines and Southern Airways — and by the acquisition one year later of Hughes Airwest. Extreme financial difficulties forced Republic to seek a series of wage concessions from its unionized employees in exchange for substantial stock ownership in the company.

In 1981 the company first sought a 15 percent cut in one month's wages in exchange for the equivalent value of company stock. In 1982, when its financial situation hadn't improved, it asked most employees to defer one full month's salary. (Many later accepted stock in repayment.) Then, in July 1983, all workers were asked to accept a nine-month, 15 percent pay reduction and salary freeze. But when the company asked in early 1984 to have this agreement extended, the unions demanded sizable concessions. In exchange for an extension in the wage cut and freeze through 1986, as part of a "Partnership Plan" employees received 15 percent of the company's stock (they had asked for 25 percent) and one seat on the board of directors (they had asked for four). A profit-sharing plan was established for all workers.

Republic returned to profitability in 1984. The company attributes this turnaround in part to the Partnership Plan. In mid-1986 it was acquired by Northwest Airlines.

In 1984 the company gave $300,000 in charitable gifts, despite its previous years' losses. It had a small minority purchasing program of $700,000 in 1984. Among its top officials and managers as of 1985, 26.5 percent were women and 2.4 percent minorities.

REPUBLIC AIRLINES, INC.											
	Women		Minorities				Contracts		PAC Contributions		
% to Charity	Directors	Officers	Directors	Officers	Social Disclosure	Sullivan Rating	% Military	Nuclear Weapons— Related	Dollar Amount	% to Republicans	% to Democrats
*	0	0	0	0	A	None	None	None	$6,400	72%	28%

* = See profile
See also Appendix D for a listing of this company's products and services.

TEXAS AIR CORPORATION

Under CEO Frank Lorenzo, Texas Air has been the unions' nemesis within the airline industry. Unions first cried foul when the company created New York Air in 1980 as a non-union subsidiary to compete with Eastern Airlines in the Eastern seaboard market; because New York Air was not an independent airline, unions at other Texas Air subsidiaries viewed its creation as an attempt by management to evade their contracts, and called for a boycott.

In 1981 Texas Air moved to acquire Continental Airlines, which had good labor relations. Continental fought the takeover for eight months. At one point it looked as if the workers were going to buy the company themselves, which would have made Continental the largest worker-owned company in the country. At the last minute, bank financing for the workers fell through, the company's chairman committed suicide, and Texas Air won out in its acquisition bid.

Texas Air moved quickly to extract wage concessions from pilots in 1982, but the machinists' union balked at similar demands the following year. Texas Air, then in deep financial difficulties, offered Continental's workers ownership of 35 percent of the company's stock in exchange for further wage concessions. When the offer was refused, Lorenzo threw Continental into Chapter 11 bankruptcy, thereby canceling all its union contracts.

Thus began an extended series of suits and countersuits, accompanied by union charges that the company had sought bankruptcy protection solely to abrogate its union contracts. The company asserted that bankruptcy was indeed a necessity, and that the unions had simply failed to understand the seriousness of the financial crisis. The unions have lost most of their court cases against the company without proving union-busting charges. In September 1985, Texas Air announced a plan for bringing Continental out of

TEXAS AIR CORPORATION											
	Women		Minorities				Contracts		PAC Contributions		
% to Charity	Directors	Officers	Directors	Officers	Social Disclosure	Sullivan Rating	% Military	Nuclear Weapons–Related	Dollar Amount	% to Republicans	% to Democrats
?	0	1	?	?	F	None	None	None	$97,808	42%	58%

? = No information available
See also Appendix D for a listing of this company's products and services.

On the Road

bankruptcy within a year, although it still faced some lawsuits brought by the unions. By then it was operating with pilots and flight attendants who were paid salaries about half that of their predecessors. By 1986, Continental was thriving as a low-fare carrier. It had profit-sharing and gain-sharing plans for its pilots and employee morale was reportedly improving.

In 1986 the Federal Aviation Administration fined Continental $402,000 for safety violations, primarily involving inadequate training of flight engineers during the rebuilding of its operations under bankruptcy proceedings.

In this protracted battle Texas Air departed sharply from other financially troubled carriers by achieving labor-cost cuts through bankruptcy proceedings. While negotiations with unions at other airlines may have been difficult, Texas Air alone sought and effectively achieved the elimination of its union contracts. In 1985 it twice made offers for other airlines — TWA and Frontier — only to lose out both times when unions at these carriers threw their support behind rival bids. Then in early 1986, during a highly charged standoff between unions and management at Eastern Air Lines, Texas Air's offer to acquire the major, financially troubled carrier was accepted. This merger will make Texas Air one of the largest airlines in the industry. Later in 1986, Texas Air acquired People Express, making it the largest airline in the United States.

The company did not respond to CEP's questionnaires.

TRANS WORLD AIRLINES, INC.

This airline has a long and interesting history, including 20 years under the ownership of eccentric industrialist Howard Hughes. In 1985 it was bought out by investor Carl Icahn, after a protracted takeover battle with Frank Lorenzo of Texas Air. Although its past and present are colorful, we could find no record of charitable or other social initiatives by TWA.

One of the older airlines in the industry, TWA was taken over by Howard Hughes in 1939. Under his leadership, it became known as the airline of the Hollywood stars in the 1940s and 1950s. After Hughes's departure in 1960, the financially shaky carrier acquired a series of other businesses, including Hilton International Hotels, Century 21 real estate, and various food services. But in 1984 the TWA parent company spun off the airline from the other operations.

Union-management negotiations in 1983 and 1984 resulted in little in the way of wage concessions at TWA, which was losing money. But in 1985, in the face of competing bids to acquire the airline by investor Carl Icahn and Texas Air's anti-union Frank Lorenzo, unions sided with Icahn in his successful effort. Unions agreed to substantial wage cuts (30 percent for pilots, 15 percent for mechanics) in exchange for a 20 percent stake in the company and a 20 percent share of the company's future profits. But relations with at least one union deteriorated sharply in 1986, when flight attendants went on strike rather than agree to wage concessions demanded by Icahn as necessary for the financially troubled airline.

TWA discontinued its South African operations in 1985.

The company did not respond to CEP's questionnaires.

TRANS WORLD AIRLINES, INC.											
	Women		Minorities				Contracts		PAC Contributions		
% to Charity	Directors	Officers	Directors	Officers	Social Disclosure	Sullivan Rating	% Military	Nuclear Weapons–Related	Dollar Amount	% to Republicans	% to Democrats
?	2	1	1	?	F	None	None	None	$32,470	43%	57%

? = No information available
See also Appendix D for a listing of this company's products and services.

UAL, INC. (UNITED AIRLINES)

United, largest of the U.S. carriers, has a reputation (according to *Newsweek*) for "hardball tactics" as a competitor. It has also had some strained relations with its unions over the years.

United Airlines has experienced several strikes by its unions over the past 10 years. After the month-long pilots' strike in 1985, the company took a hard line with pilots and flight attendants who had refused to cross picket lines. The firm's refusal to hire some 500 new pilots who had completed training at United — but would not fly during the strike — reportedly extended this strike three weeks beyond its financial settlement. (Pilots agreed at that time to the establishment of a two-tier wage system similar to that at American, Republic, and Western Airlines. Maintenance workers had previously accepted a similar arrangement.) Management also wanted to give greater seniority to pilots who had flown during the strike. A federal court later ruled that the company must offer the new pilots jobs, and could not give extra seniority to non-striking pilots. This decision was overturned on further appeal. Flight attendants were similarly forced to go to court to win rehiring for 650 low-seniority attendants who had been replaced when they refused to cross picket lines.

In 1984, flight attendants employed during the 1960s and forced to quit upon marriage were awarded $38 million by the courts.

Also in 1984, 10 airlines filed a lawsuit charging that United and American had supplied travel agents with computerized reservation systems that favored their own flights over those of competitors. These are the two largest computer reservations systems in the nation, and profitable operations in themselves. In 1985 United and American agreed to drop the features which had allegedly created a "bias" for their flights, although related suits continued into 1986.

UAL, INC.											
	Women		Minorities				Contracts		PAC Contributions		
% to Charity	Directors	Officers	Directors	Officers	Social Disclosure	Sullivan Rating	% Military	Nuclear Weapons-Related	Dollar Amount	% to Republicans	% to Democrats
*	1	2	2	0	F	Non-sig.	None	None	$74,450	54%	46%

* = See profile
See also Appendix D for a listing of this company's products and services.

United Airlines' parent company owns Hertz, which has the largest share of the car rental market, and the Westin Hotel chain, which owns and operates such landmarks as New York's Plaza Hotel, Philadelphia's Bellevue-Stratford, and the St. Francis Hotel in San Francisco. *The 100 Best Companies to Work for in America* singled Westin out as exemplary within the hotel industry. It has a largely unionized work force and pays roughly 10 percent higher wages than the industry average, along with providing a thorough program of employee recognition, development, and promotion from within.

Westin operates hotels employing over 1,000 persons in South Africa. UAL signed the Sullivan Principles for fair labor practices only in 1984, and did not report on its efforts toward compliance in 1985. (By not reporting, the company becomes classed as a "non-signatory.") In 1986, it sold its ownership in hotels there, retaining two employees in the country, according to the Investor Responsibility Research Center.

United Airlines' foundation contributions dropped from $1 million in 1981 to $569,000 in 1982, undoubtedly due to its 1981 financial losses. Of its 1982 gifts, 76 percent went to the United Way. Grants to civic organizations, including community economic development groups, which had totaled $50,000 in 1981, were cut entirely in 1982. According to the Taft *Corporate Giving Directory*, the company's 1984 giving totaled $697,000. Because of losses in previous years, it is not possible to calculate charitable giving figures as a percentage of pre-tax earnings.

Minority Supplier News reports that United plans to award one-quarter of the contracts on its $400 million expansion project at O'Hare International Airport in Chicago to minority and women-owned businesses.

The company did not respond to CEP's questionnaires.

US AIR GROUP, INC.

Based in Pittsburgh and formerly known as Allegheny Airlines, US Air has been one of the most consistently profitable of U.S. airlines. During the early 1980s, when most other carriers were losing money, the company did not ask its employees for the wage cuts and givebacks that provoked major controversies at that time.

The only US Air social initiative about which we could locate information is a minority banking program set up by treasurer Juliette Heintze. While on the board of a minority-owned bank in Washington, D.C., she realized the importance of corporate accounts to small banks, which often operate in economically depressed neighborhoods. The US Air program has placed $2 million in below-market rate certificates of deposit; the carrier also makes its excise tax payments through minority banks in its route cities, along with some dormant deposits to keep up an ongoing relationship with certain banks. It has no lines of credit, in part because US Air has not had to borrow funds in recent years.

The company did not respond to CEP's questionnaires.

US AIR GROUP, INC.											
	Women		Minorities				Contracts		PAC Contributions		
% to Charity	Directors	Officers	Directors	Officers	Social Disclosure	Sullivan Rating	% Military	Nuclear Weapons–Related	Dollar Amount	% to Republicans	% to Democrats
?	1	1	0	0	C	None	None	None	$17,356	45%	55%

? = No information available
See also Appendix D for a listing of this company's products and services.

WESTERN AIR LINES, INC.

Since 1983, this Los Angeles–based carrier has embarked upon an innovative labor-management partnership.

In the early 1980s, after several changes in management and severe competitive pressures brought about by airline deregulation, Western found itself on the verge of bankruptcy. In 1983, in an effort to cut costs and increase productivity, Western established a Partnership Program with its unions, which turned over to employees 32 percent of the company stock, and set up a profit-sharing plan in return for wage concessions and job restructuring measures. In 1984 an additional Competitive Action Plan was instituted. Unions agreed to permanent wage reductions and received in exchange an expanded profit-sharing program, increased union representation on Western's board of directors (to 4 out of 16 members), and the establishment of an Employee Participating and Coordinating Committee (EPACC) to oversee the development of employee-involvement programs in management policies and practices.

Western's profit-sharing program now distributes 20 percent of the company's first $75 million in pre-tax earnings and 35 percent of profits thereafter. As of 1985, the stock distributed to employees is nonvoting except on mergers or other major matters, and had been diluted to approximately 17 percent of total stock. But, according to a union spokesman, negotiations were underway to obtain pass-through voting rights for the stock on all matters. A steering committee of top union and management representatives was overseeing the implementation of EPACC programs. While few were actually in effect as of late 1985, serious consideration was being given at that time to staff involvement throughout the company's operations, including such incentives as gain sharing — a partial distribution of savings from programs or suggestions

WESTERN AIR LINES, INC.											
	Women		Minorities				Contracts		PAC Contributions		
% to Charity	Directors	Officers	Directors	Officers	Social Disclosure	Sullivan Rating	% Military	Nuclear Weapons– Related	Dollar Amount	% to Republicans	% to Democrats
?	1	0	?	?	F	None	None	None	$5,400	58%	42%

? = No information available
See also Appendix D for a listing of this company's products and services.

On the Road

that increase productivity. Approximately 92 percent of the company's work force is unionized.

In 1982 Western responded to pressure from church groups, activists, and shareholders and stopped cooperating with U.S. Immigration and Naturalization officials in transporting undocumented aliens to Mexico City, where they would transfer to a foreign airline that would return them to their home countries. Critics labeled the rides "death flights" because many of the refugees faced the threat of execution or torture in their homelands. Western declined to characterize its decision as a political one, but attributed its suspension to the recognition of potential legal liabilities stemming from transporting refugees to Mexico City's airport without required documents.

In late 1986, Western was acquired by Delta Air Lines. (See addendum on page 500.)

The company did not respond to CEP's questionnaires.

AUTOMOBILE COMPANIES

An industry now in transition, U.S. auto manufacturing has been fighting, with some success, to overcome the staggering problems it faced in the late 1970s and early 1980s. Loss of market share to foreign competitors, a reputation for inferior quality, slow improvement of fuel efficiency and pollution control, and a severe worldwide recession in 1981–1982 all combined to force sweeping changes in the industry.

Moreover, auto manufacturing is rapidly becoming an international venture. General Motors and Toyota jointly manufacture cars in the United States, while Chrysler and Mitsubishi (in which Chrysler owns a 15 percent stake) announced plans in 1985 for joint production in the United States. Ford, which owns 25 percent of Mazda, will purchase half the cars Mazda produces at a new plant it is building in Michigan. Renault owns almost 50 percent of American Motors. Volkswagen, Honda, and Nissan produce their own trucks and cars in the United States.

Since there are only four companies profiled in this chapter, our overview offers general comments on each, rather than an issue-by-issue outline of the industry.

Chrysler, whose past financial troubles were the most dramatic and severe, can be singled out for certain initiatives that go beyond those of its competitors. The company was particularly innovative in appointing the United Auto Workers president to its board of directors and in giving substantial amounts of Chrysler stock to its workers. Whereas General Motors and Ford lobbied for and won a 1985 revision of government fuel efficiency regulations, Chrysler had already met previous deadlines (due in part to the smaller size of the cars in its fleet). The company has sold its interests in South Africa. Its cur-

**Minority Purchasing Programs
Reported by Profiled Automobile Companies**

	Purchases from Minority Vendors	Total Sales
	(millions of dollars)	
American Motors (1984)	$ 7.7	$ 4,215
Ford (1985)	163.0	52,774
GM (1985)	806.0	96,372

Source: Company responses to CEP inquiries.

rent involvement in military contracting is on a much smaller scale than that of GM or Ford.

Ford has received recognition for its commitments to employee-involvement programs and for its well-planned handling of plant shutdowns during the 1981–1982 recession. Its minority economic development programs are comprehensive; the company is reenforcing its already substantial efforts in these areas. Ford is one of only two companies profiled in this book to publish its fair hiring statistics by job category in its annual report.

Ford makes much of its current commitment to quality in manufacturing, although certain cars it produced in the 1970s have been subject to several major safety controversies, most notably involving the Pinto, in which the gas tank was allegedly prone to explode in rear-end collisions. (Ford no longer manufactures the Pinto.)

Ford is a partner in a vehicle manufacturing company in South Africa and faces continuing church criticism of its presence in that country.

Controversy swirls around General Motors, the rapidly diversifying giant of the industry. Some church groups attacked it as a primary "investor in apartheid" because of large operations in South Africa (subsequently sold). Ralph Nader and the Nader-affiliated Center for Auto Safety have had innumerable run-ins with the company over safety issues, and the National Highway Traffic Safety Commission is involved in an ongoing court battle with GM over the company's claims for the safety of certain X-car models.

By acquiring Hughes Aircraft in 1985, GM, already a substantial defense contractor, has now put itself among the top 10 U.S. military contractors.

The company, along with the city of Detroit, became the focus of a lengthy and bitter dispute in the early 1980s over the destruction of a neighborhood to build a new plant in that city.

However, in neighborhoods around its headquarters site in Detroit and in Pontiac, Michigan, it has contributed substantially to revitalization programs. While often criticized for poor labor relations, GM's plans for worker involvement at its new Saturn plant are among the most innovative in the U.S. auto industry. GM's minority economic development programs are impressive in size and scope; the company's minority purchasing program is by far the largest in the country, and continues to expand rapidly.

Little information was available on social programs at the financially struggling American Motors ($125 million in losses in 1985.)

AUTOMOBILES

AUTOMOBILES

Size of Charitable Contributions	Women Directors and Officers	Minority Directors and Officers	Social Disclosure	Brand Name	Company (Profile Page)	Involvement in South Africa	Conv. Weapons–Related Contracts	Nuclear Weapons–Related Contracts	Authors' Company of Choice
*	⚊	No	(x3)	AMC Jeep Renault	American Motors (p. 273)	No	No	No	
*	⚊	⚊	(x2)	Chrysler Dodge Plymouth	Chrysler (p. 274)	No	✈✈	No	
*	⚊⚊	⚊	(x3)	Ford Lincoln Mercury	Ford (p. 276)	Yes B	✈✈	Yes	
*	⚊⚊⚊	⚊	(x3)	Buick Cadillac Chevrolet Oldsmobile Pontiac, etc.	General Motors (p. 280)	No	✈✈	Yes	

* = See company profile
? = No information available
Single figure ($, ⚊) = Minimal
Double figure ($$, ⚊⚊, ⚑⚑, ✈✈) = Moderate
Triple figure ($$$, ⚊⚊⚊, ⚑⚑⚑, ✈✈✈) = Substantial

No = No involvement or participation
Yes = Involvement or participation. A, B, C in the South African column reflect the degree of compliance with Sullivan Principles and/or involvement in strategic industries.

See Chapter 4 for a detailed discussion of chart symbols.

CAR RENTAL AGENCIES

CAR RENTAL AGENCIES

Size of Charitable Contributions	Women Directors and Officers	Minority Directors and Officers	Social Disclosure	Brand Name	Company (Profile Page)	Involvement in South Africa	Conv. Weapons–Related Contracts	Nuclear Weapons–Related Contracts	Authors' Company of Choice
?	♦♦	?	No	National	Household International (p. 285)	No	No	No	
$ $ $	♦♦	?	No	Budget	Transamerica (p. 286)	No	No	No	✔
✱	♦♦	♦	No	Hertz	UAL (p. 263)	Yes C	No	No	

✱ = See company profile
? = No information available
Single figure ($, ♦) = Minimal
Double figure ($$, ♦♦, 🚗🚗, ♦♦) = Moderate
Triple figure ($$$, ♦♦♦, 🚗🚗🚗, ♦♦♦) = Substantial

No = No involvement or participation
Yes = Involvement or participation. A, B, C in the South African column reflect the degree of compliance with Sullivan Principles and/or involvement in strategic industries.

See Chapter 4 for a detailed discussion of chart symbols.

AMERICAN MOTORS CORPORATION

Smallest of the major U.S. car companies, AMC has apparently developed little in the way of social programs in recent years. It has yet to recover fully from a severe financial crisis that began in the late 1970s.

In 1979 Renault came to AMC's financial aid, investing a total of $545 million by 1984, and making Renault owner of 46 percent of the company's stock. Renault, controlled by the French government, is known for its politically radical unions in France.

AMC had what the *Wall Street Journal* termed in 1985 "decidedly confrontational" relations with its unions in the United States. Up until 1985, AMC's wages and benefits were the highest among U.S. automakers. Hard bargaining at that time resulted in a union agreement to trade wage concessions for job security. Three years earlier, unions had agreed to a wage and benefit freeze, but this has proved controversial, with disagreements over the repayment of foregone wages.

Like other U.S. car manufacturers, AMC has faced various suits over the safety of its cars.

AMC's Special Government Vehicles subsidiary was a supplier of military vehicles, primarily trucks, to the Department of Defense; it was sold to the LTV corporation in 1983.

The company's 1983 annual report cited "significant gains" in equal opportunity employment, but AMC would provide no specific figures for this book. The firm purchased $7.7 million from minority suppliers in 1984 and made $110,000 in charitable contributions that year. Because of losses in previous years, comparison with earnings are not possible.

The company responded to CEP's questionnaires.

AMERICAN MOTORS CORPORATION											
	Women		Minorities				Contracts		PAC Contributions		
% to Charity	Directors	Officers	Directors	Officers	Social Disclosure	Sullivan Rating	% Military	Nuclear Weapons–Related	Dollar Amount	% to Republicans	% to Democrats
*	1	0	0	0	A	None	None	None	$61,783	62%	38%

* = See profile
See also Appendix D for a listing of this company's products and services.

CHRYSLER CORPORATION

Under the aggressive and highly visible leadership of Lee Iacocca, and with the help of a $1.5 billion U.S. government loan-guarantee, Chrysler made a dramatic return from the brink of bankruptcy in 1979. While doing so, it undertook some of the most innovative labor relations initiatives in the auto industry, disposed of its military and South African interests, and built a fleet of cars that were generally more fuel efficient than those of GM or Ford.

Chrysler was the first major U.S. firm to establish an Employee Stock Ownership Plan (ESOP) for its workers in exchange for wage concessions. To get the unions to agree to $1.1 billion in wage cutbacks and benefit reductions, Chrylser set up the ESOP, which between 1979 and 1983 turned over 16 percent of the company's common stock to some 80,000 workers. (The company was required to set up this ESOP under the same federal legislation that gave the company its loan guarantees.) Chrysler's ESOP gives full voting rights with its shares, generally regarded as an important provision in developing a meaningful sense of participation for worker-shareowners. The union and company agreed in 1983 not to extend the plan, but to concentrate instead on restoring wage and benefit cuts. In 1985 the company repurchased some of these stocks from its workers.

At the same time, Chrysler set up a profit-sharing plan under which workers would get 15 percent of Chrysler profits in excess of 10 percent of the company's net worth. The firm agreed to pay quarterly wage bonuses as well during particularly profitable times. In the first quarter of 1985, for example, the bonus amounted to $500 apiece for everyone on the payroll.

Another first was Chrysler's appointment of the United Auto Workers union president, Douglas Fraser, to its board of directors. Various airlines have given over board seats to union representatives since then, but this re-

CHRYSLER CORPORATION											
	Women		Minorities				Contracts		PAC Contributions		
% to Charity	Directors	Officers	Directors	Officers	Social Disclosure	Sullivan Rating	% Military	Nuclear Weapons– Related	Dollar Amount	% to Republicans	% to Democrats
*	2	0	2	?	C	None	0.2%	None	$75,770	35%	65%

* = See profile   ? = No information available
See also Appendix D for a listing of this company's products and services.

On the Road

mains the most prominent example. Like Ford and General Motors, Chrysler has also worked jointly with the UAW to promote employee involvement throughout its manufacturing facilities.

The union also won the right to recommend to the company's pension fund that it divest itself of stocks in companies that have not signed the Sullivan Principles for nondiscriminatory labor practices in South Africa. (Each year since 1979, the unions have been permitted to make up to five recommendations.) Chrysler has also divested itself of its 25 percent stake in South Africa's major car manufacturer, Sigma. (GM and Ford both retain interests in that country.)

Chrysler reduced its involvement as a military contractor with the sale of its tank business in 1982. Nevertheless, it received $44 million in contracts, mostly arms-related, from the Department of Defense in 1984. In 1985 it bought Gulfstream Aerospace Corporation, primarily a commercial aircraft company, with some defense business. It was awarded a multimillion-dollar contract for C-20 aircraft by the U.S. Air Force in 1985.

Lee Iacocca broke ranks with his compatriots in the industry in 1984 by publicly criticizing the exorbitant bonuses they awarded themselves at a time when little had been done to restore workers' wage concessions. Chrysler kept its executives' bonuses to half of GM's and Ford's that year. In the financially rosier year of 1985, however, Chrysler's $5 million in bonuses led the industry. Iacocca signed full-page newspaper ads crediting employee concessions and dedication with having saved the company.

Chrysler had a better record than either General Motors or Ford in complying with federal gas efficiency requirements from 1981 through 1984 due in part to the smaller size of the cars in its fleet. It strongly objected when the Environmental Protection Agency revised its methods for calculating mileage in 1985, thus helping GM and Ford meet regulations. For 1986 models, however, Ford's Escort FS and GM's Chevette CS both tested more miles per gallon than any other U.S. car.

During its financial crisis Chrysler continued a limited charitable contributions program, primarily through its independently endowed foundation: $2.1 million in 1983, $1.7 million from the foundation. Of the foundation's contributions, almost $1 million went to social services, primarily united fund drives.

Minorities held 11.4 percent of Chrysler's officials and managers positions and women 5.2 percent, according to a 1986 *Black Enterprise* magazine article.

Chrysler had 42 black-owned car dealerships at the end of 1985. (Ford had 110 and GM 93.) There were approximately 4,000 Chrysler dealerships at that time. (Ford had 5,500 and GM had 9,800.)

The company did not respond to CEP's questionnaires.

FORD MOTOR COMPANY

The number-two automobile manufacturer in the United States, Ford has received considerable praise for its employee-involvement programs and for well-planned plant closing policies in recent years, and is in the process of revitalizing its already substantial minority development and affirmative action programs. At the same time the company finds itself involved in controversies over its South African operations, the past safety records of some of its cars, and its military contracting.

The gradual involvement of workers in production decisions through "quality circles" has been taking place throughout the auto industry since 1980, and Ford's initiatives have been singled out for particular praise. In 1984 *Business Week* found that Ford and the United Auto Workers Union had implemented "what may be the most extensive and successful worker participation process in a major, unionized company." Mark Green and John Berry, in *The Challenge of Hidden Profits,* credited Ford's employee-involvement programs with being "probably the most significant change at Ford" in increasing manufacturing efficiency, product quality, and helping regain profitability. In particular they found the commitment of the company's chairman, Philip Caldwell, to be crucial in assuring that these steps were meaningfully initiated. A voluntary program, employee involvement encompassed 20 to 30 percent of the company's work force by 1984.

In 1982, negotiating with the United Auto Workers, Ford agreed to set up a profit-sharing plan in exchange for certain wage concessions. (Under this plan Ford paid out about $340 million, or approximately $2,000 per worker, when the company returned to profitability in 1984.)

Also in 1982 Ford and the UAW agreed to create their joint Employee Development and Training Center, managed by a union-management committee and funded by company contributions of five cents for every union-member hour worked. Its dual goals are to aid in education and technical training for active workers, and to help in counseling and job retraining for those who have been laid off.

This joint effort has led to praise from both union and company sources. The "cooperative spirit" in the 1983 closing of Ford's plant in Milpitas, California, is an example. The automaker gave six months' notice of its intention to close the plant. During that time the company and union, in conjunction with state and local employment and education agencies, devised a series of counseling, job-training, skill development, and tuition-assistance programs, with an on-site training and education center. The firm's employee-involvement programs, which involved almost 100 percent of the plant's workers, continued to function, and the plant reportedly kept producing highest-quality goods up until its closing day.

In 1984 Ford set about increasing its already substantial minority purchasing program, which reached $163 million in 1985 (up from $113 million in 1983). These plans include a commitment to help those minority vendors providing the highest-quality goods to expand their businesses, and the creation of a Small Business Resource Center, which will provide technical and managerial assistance to any minority supplier. Ford already has a Minority Enterprise Small Business Investment Company, which provides venture capital funding for small minority-owned businesses.

Ford's minority banking program has a $25 million credit line, and uses minority institutions for $450 million in tax deposits annually. In 1986 the company will place $7.5 million in certificates of deposit in minority-owned banks. Employee insurance with $6 million in premiums was placed with minority-owned firms in 1985. Ford is working to increase the number of its black-owned car dealerships, which as of the end of 1985 stood at 110 (up from 29 in 1982; GM had 93 and Chrysler 42), with a goal of 320 by 1990. At the end of 1985, total Ford dealerships numbered approximately 5,500. (GM's numbered 9,800 and Chrysler's 4,000.)

In 1980 the Equal Employment Opportunity Commission settled a job discrimination suit filed against Ford in 1973 for $23 million. The number of women and minorities among the company's officials and managers grew from 2.5 percent and 8 percent respectively in 1982, to 3.7 percent and 9.6 percent in 1985. In June 1985, the company started a formal review of its affirmative action programs in order to accelerate their progress. (Ford and Sara Lee were the only companies profiled in this book to regularly publish complete EEOC statistics by job category in their annual report.)

Ford's charitable contributions totaled $11.6 million in 1984, of which $1,137,000 supported minority-oriented programs. Over $480,000 went to minority education and $360,000 to New Detroit, Inc., a coalition of the city's business and civic leaders founded in 1967 in response to race riots there. New Detroit works in four primary areas: improved race relations, minority economic development, crime prevention, and youth education.

Contributions from the Ford Motor Fund (the company's foundation) were primarily directed toward education (41 percent with $1.5 million in gifts matching employee contributions); health and welfare (31 percent, with $1.6 million to the United Foundation, Detroit's equivalent of the United Way); and civic and public-policy issues (19 percent, including $100,000 to the conservative American Enterprise Institute).

Ford family money established the Ford Foundation, which, with its $3.4 billion in assets as of 1984, is the largest private foundation in the United States. It has had a reputation for liberalism since the 1950s, and Waldemar Nielsen, writing in *The Golden Donors*, has termed it "the dominant liberal force among the large foundations." Since the late 1960s, it has been one of the foremost proponents of Program Related Investments — below-market-rate loans that supplement direct giving, going to community-revitalization and other organizations. A similar use of low-interest revolving loan funds is increasingly advocated by many in the social investment movement today.

Like other companies, Ford has been involved in numerous recalls of its cars and in disputes over their safety. The two most dramatic recent examples were accusations in the late 1970s that the gas tank of its Pinto model was liable to explode in rear-end collisions, and allegations that millions of other Fords from the 1970s with automatic transmissions had a tendency to slip from park into reverse. In a highly publicized trial in 1980, the company was acquitted of criminal liabilities in three deaths in a Pinto crash, on charges that it allegedly knew of the car's alleged dangers and failed to correct its defects or warn consumers when the Pinto was on the market. (Ford no longer manufactures the Pinto.)

In 1981 the company reached an agreement with the National Highway Traffic Safety Administration (NHTSA) under which it would send warning notices to owners of 23 million of its 1968–1980 Fords and Lincolns, alerting them to the dangers of possible transmission slippage problems. The company did so rather than face the monumentally expensive recall that had been urged by public-interest groups. In late 1985 the Nader-affiliated Center for Auto Safety sued the NHTSA to reopen its case against Ford, charging that the warning notices were not proving effective and that at least 80 deaths since 1981 were attributable to faulty Ford transmissions. In April 1986, this suit was disallowed by the courts on grounds that the courts did not have the power to force the regulatory agency to reopen this case.

Ford (like General Motors but unlike Chrysler) has had trouble recently in meeting federal goals for gas-mileage efficiency. In 1985 the Environmental Protection Agency altered its methods of calculating efficiency figures in such

FORD MOTOR COMPANY											
	Women		Minorities				Contracts		PAC Contributions		
% to Charity	Directors	Officers	Directors	Officers	Social Disclosure	Sullivan Rating	% Military	Nuclear Weapons–Related	Dollar Amount	% to Republicans	% to Democrats
*	1	1	2	0	A	V	2.1%	Yes	$78,044	66%	34%

* = See profile
See also Appendix D for a listing of this company's products and services.

a way that compliance was made easier for these two major manufacturers. For 1986 cars, Ford's Escort FS rated the best of U.S. models on miles per gallon.

Through its Aerospace division, Ford is substantially involved in military contracting. It was the twenty-eighth-largest Department of Defense prime contractor in 1985, with $1.0 billion in awards (down slightly from $1.1 billion in 1984). One of its main projects was an anti-aircraft gun system (subsequently canceled due to poor performance), but the company continues to do work on the Sidewinder and Chaparral missiles and on communications satellites.

According to the Investor Responsibility Research Center, $190 million of Ford's $1.1 billion awards from the Department of Defense in 1983 were for work on nuclear-related weapons systems, primarily for work on satellite communications. According to the Council on Economic Priorities, Ford Aerospace received $25 million for work on the "Star Wars" missile defense system in 1983 and was the thirty-third-largest military research and development contractor in 1985.

Ford has been a major U.S. employer in South Africa for many years, but in 1985 announced that it would become the 40 percent owner of an automobile-manufacturing operation there through a merger with a South African firm. This does not essentially change the size of Ford's investment there. Ford was singled out by a coalition of 50 church groups in 1985 as one of twelve U.S. corporate "key investors in apartheid" because of the company's continued sales to South African military and police.

Ford's 6,673 workers in that country made it the largest U.S. employer there in 1984. Its rating for compliance with the Sullivan Principles slipped from the top to the second-highest "making progress" rating in 1984. In 1985 it was ranked as a new signatory because of the transfer of ownership.

The company responded to CEP's questionnaires.

GENERAL MOTORS CORPORATION

Controversies have swirled about this giant of the industrial world ($96 billion in 1985 sales) while the company has taken certain social initiatives. Critics have faulted GM's involvement in military contracting and its presence in South Africa, its safety record, its hiring practices, and its part in the controversy over destruction of a portion of the Poletown neighborhood in Detroit for construction of a new plant. At the same time, GM has made commitments to minority economic development, has evolved an innovative working relationship with the United Auto Workers for its new Saturn plant, and has made commitments to urban revitalization projects in Detroit and Pontiac, Michigan.

GM has by far the largest minority purchasing program in the country. Its $806 million in 1985 purchases rose from $390 million in 1983 and $567 million in 1984. According to John Haines, the program's director, GM ultimately hopes to place 10 percent of its supply purchases with minority vendors. As of 1983 this figure stood at about 1 percent.

The company's program, formally established in 1968, began to make major progress in 1976 when GM adopted a goal-setting approach, with minority purchasing an integral part of every manager's responsibility. Purchases jumped from $19 million in 1975 to $50 million in 1976. GM now not only seeks out minority suppliers but also helps in company start-ups or expansions. Help includes making loans, giving equipment on consignment (GM owns the machinery, but the firm has an option to buy it), and loaning personnel to provide technical and administrative assistance. (The company also provides similar help to other suppliers but is more sensitive to promoting minority-owned businesses.) In 1985 GM's president headed the National Minority Supplier Development Council, which promotes these programs throughout industry.

The rest of GM's minority economic development initiative includes minority banking, which in 1985 used minority-owned institutions for tax deposits exceeding $1 billion; $2.3 million in term deposits; and demand deposit accounts with balances of $420,000. Of GM's total property damage insurance, 20 percent went to minority-owned brokers, and $350 million in group life insurance was reinsured with four minority-owned firms. Motor Enterprises, a GM venture capital company that funds start-ups or expansions of minority-owned businesses, made $7 million in loans to 226 businesses between 1970 and 1985. The company placed $5 million in 1985 ads in minority-owned media. Of its auto dealerships in 1985, 187 were owned by minorities and 152 by women. As of the end of 1985, 93 out of 9,800 GM dealerships were owned by blacks. (Ford had 110 out of 5,500 and Chrysler 42 out of 4,000.)

As GM rebounded from the recession of 1981 and 1982, its charitable cash giving rose from $40.3 million in 1983 to $60.4 million in 1984, with $12.4 million in in-kind contributions. GM's pre-tax earnings were atypically low in 1981 and 1982 ($22 million) as opposed to the more typical level of 1983 (4.9 billion). GM's gifts appear to have gone to largely traditional recipients in 1984, with support for urban programs declining despite the overall increase in funding. Education received 46 percent of total GM donations, health and welfare 19 percent, and urban development and community affairs 3 percent, down to $2.2 million from $2.4 million in 1983. GM has pledged $2.5 million to research on computer automation in manufacturing processes, and in 1984 gave $653,000 to Michigan Technology University's Technology Park. The United Way was awarded $5.1 million, cancer research $6 million, and hospitals $1.2 million. Grants from the GM foundation increased from $29.5 million in 1983 to $31.4 million in 1984.

Among GM's community development projects has been involvement in the New Center Development Partnership, which GM joined along with 14 other Detroit companies. This revitalization of an 18-square-block neighborhood just north of GM's world headquarters involved restoration of 125 single-family houses and 175 apartment units, plus construction of a 200-unit senior citizen complex and of 54 low- and moderate-income townhouses. The company has also been active in support of the Purdue Square Neighborhood Redevelopment Corporation's rehabilitation projects in Pontiac, to which its foundation has given several grants.

Overshadowing GM's involvement in community rehabilitation projects has been the Poletown controversy. In the late 1970s, GM and the mayor of Detroit announced the first plans in fifty years to build a new plant within the city limits. Jobs would be created to help this economically declining metropolis. But clearing the 362-acre plant site involved destroying some 1,500 homes and displacing 3,400 persons within an old neighborhood that had been known as Poletown since the 1870s, and was by 1980 half black and half white. An all-out battle ensued, with neighborhood activists fighting hard to stop the project. But the city, with its full weight behind the project, eventually prevailed.

GM's recent efforts to have its properties reassessed and taxes reduced, particularly in Michigan, have provoked considerable criticism. But, according to chairman Roger Smith, "We're not trying to pay less taxes than we should, we're trying *not* to pay *more* taxes than we should."

Fair hiring has been another area of controversy for GM. A $44.5 million settlement with the Equal Employment Opportunity Commission in 1983 put to rest job discrimination charges originally filed in 1973. But the settlement was criticized for not providing back pay. The heart of the settlement was a $15 million company commitment over five years to provide educational assistance for women and minorities employed by GM. In 1985 the Labor Department tightened the provisions of this accord to assure that the company met well-defined hiring and promotion goals. The percentage of women and minorities among GM's officials and managers rose to 8.9 and 11.1 respectively in 1985, from 6.5 and 9.5 in 1981.

Concern over poor labor relations in the auto industry in the 1970s, along with an increasing reputation for inferior quality in manufacturing, resulted in employee-involvement or quality circle programs to increase worker participation in production, and to facilitate communication between workers and management within the plant. Among unions, the United Auto Workers has been one of the leading advocates of employee involvement. Many other unions have remained more suspicious, or, as in the case of the International Association of Machinists, hostile; they see the cooperative aspects of these programs as undermining union solidarity at best, and at worst as outright union-busting efforts. In recent years the UAW has pursued joint labor-management initiatives within the auto industry not only in the workplace but to deal with plant closings and job training as well.

GM first initiated quality circles as early as 1973. It wasn't until contract negotiations with the UAW in 1982 and 1984, however, that a formal program was agreed upon. By the mid-1980s, virtually all GM plants had some form of employee-involvement program, although their substance varied widely. Advocates of more comprehensive European-style worker involvement in decision-making felt that these programs hadn't gone far enough. They have, however, won praise for having sharply reduced the number of worker grievance claims.

The most radical restructuring of management-worker relations at GM will come with its new Saturn plant, scheduled to open in 1989. Here GM and the UAW have negotiated what *Business Week* termed "the boldest experiment ever in self-management and consensus decision-making — going far beyond anything in Japanese or European factories." At the Saturn plant, blue-collar workers will be on salary; work in teams without foremen; be represented in policy-making committees at all levels, including those making salary and bonus decisions; and engage in decisions by consensus with management. And, for 80 percent of the work force, there will be guaranteed job security. In exchange, unions have agreed to greater job flexibility and an initial 20 percent reduction in wages.

At the same time, GM and the UAW have reached more general agreements on job security and retraining for workers, along with a profit-sharing plan that went into effect in 1983 and paid out $780 million in its first three years.

GM, along with Ford (but unlike Chrysler), has had trouble recently in meeting federal goals for gas-mileage efficiency. In 1985 the Environmental

Protection Agency altered its methods for calculating these figures in such a way as to make compliance easier for these two top automakers. GM's 1985 Chevette CS rated second-best among U.S. models on the EPA's miles-per-gallon tests.

Safety has been a major issue for GM, especially since Ralph Nader's best-selling 1965 exposé *Unsafe at Any Speed.* Among the most controversial of GM's recent problems with safety has been its 1979 and 1980 X cars. Complaints about their rear brakes locking up began within a year of their appearance on the market. The National Highway Traffic Safety Administration (NHTSA) began urging recalls as early as July 1981, and in 1982 and 1983 GM voluntarily recalled some cars, contending that the recalls corrected any problems that might have existed. But it refused to recall all X cars manufactured between 1979 and 1980, asserting that they were in no way defective. In August 1983 the NHTSA sued GM, alleging that the company knew about potentially defective brakes when it produced these cars, and had provided false and misleading information about them — charges that GM has denied. (In 1984 the NHTSA began a second investigation on an additional suspected defect in the brakes of these same cars. Again there were allegations of the company withholding information, and again GM refused to comply with the agency's request for a voluntary recall.) A long nonjury trial to force a recall began in March 1984, with a final judgment expected in mid-1986. The charges that GM provided misleading information are pending until after the ruling on the recall case.

In 1970, General Motors was the setting for the first major attempt to use shareholder resolutions to raise social issues. Although the company opposed the shareholders' request that it substantially increase minority and outside representation on its board of directors, it shortly thereafter appointed Leon Sullivan, a black minister from Philadelphia and founder of the Opportunities

GENERAL MOTORS CORPORATION											
	Women		Minorities				Contracts		PAC Contributions		
% to Charity	Directors	Officers	Directors	Officers	Social Disclosure	Sullivan Rating	% Military	Nuclear Weapons–Related	Dollar Amount	% to Republicans	% to Democrats
*	2	3	1	0	A	I	1.2%	Yes	$228,017	77%	23%

* = See profile
See also Appendix D for a listing of this company's products and services.

Industrialization Centers job training programs. Rev. Sullivan promptly requested that GM close down its large manufacturing facilities in South Africa; GM argued then, as it does now, that it could be most effective in dismantling apartheid by remaining in that country.

Sullivan created his principles for fair labor practices in 1977 as a means of assuring that business operations in South Africa were at least not racially discriminatory within the workplace. In 1985 Rev. Sullivan called for withdrawal of U.S. investments unless apartheid was ended within two years. GM, which has been in South Africa since 1926, employs the largest work force among U.S. companies (about 4,200 persons as of 1986) and has consistently received the highest rating for compliance with the Sullivan Principles. But because of its refusal to end all sales to South African military and police, and the general strategic importance of the auto industry to the country, a coalition of 50 church groups selected General Motors in May 1985 as one of twelve U.S. corporate "key investors in apartheid." In May 1986 GM announced it would cease all sales to the South African military and police, although it would continue sales to other governmental agencies. Later that year it agreed to sell off its operations and withdraw from South Africa.

Before acquiring Hughes Aircraft for $5 billion in 1985, General Motors was already a substantial military contractor, with $1.6 billion in Department of Defense prime contracts in 1985, up from $1 billion in 1984. Its work includes transmissions for the M-1 tank, as well as trucks and aircraft engines. According to the Investor Responsibility Research Center, $175 million of GM's $893 million in 1983 military contracts was for work on nuclear-related weapons systems, including the KC-135 aerial tankers used for refueling and support of the B-52 bomber fleet.

Hughes was the eighth-largest prime contractor for the Defense Department in 1985, doing more than $3.5 billion in military business. Hughes works on guided missiles, including the Maverick air-to-ground and TOW antitank missiles; radar systems; aircraft-bombing and tank fire control systems; and satellite and electronic warfare equipment. Hughes received $34 million for research done in 1983 and 1984 on the "Star Wars" Strategic Defense Initiative missile defense system. It was the tenth-largest contractor for military research and development in 1985.

The company responded to CEP's questionnaires.

HOUSEHOLD INTERNATIONAL, INC.

This diverse Chicago-based corporation is involved in finance, manufacturing, merchandising, and transportation. In 1984 it came under fire for alleged policies adversely affecting its customers.

In 1984 the Justice Department obtained a consent decree prohibiting the Household Finance Corporation (a unit of Household International) from discriminating against credit applicants on the basis of marital status, sex, or use of public assistance funds. The consent decree required the company to invite some 800 persons to reapply for credit, although Household Finance denied the allegations of discrimination.

In late 1986, Household International sold its National Car Rental subsidiary. (See addendum on page 500.)

The company did not respond to CEP's questionnaires.

HOUSEHOLD INTERNATIONAL, INC.											
	Women		Minorities				Contracts		PAC Contributions		
% to Charity	Directors	Officers	Directors	Officers	Social Disclosure	Sullivan Rating	% Military	Nuclear Weapons–Related	Dollar Amount	% to Republicans	% to Democrats
?	1	1	?	?	F	None	None	None	$107,700	62%	38%

? = No information available
See also Appendix D for a listing of this company's products and services.

TRANSAMERICA CORPORATION

More than two-thirds of Transamerica Corporation's business is in insurance and finance. But it also operates Budget Rent-a-Car, the Delaval industrial manufacturing operation, and its own airline. The company has recently become a leader in the corporate community in funding AIDS research.

Among other items, Delaval makes backup diesel engines for nuclear power plants. According to the *Wall Street Journal*, 13 electric utility companies had purchased 57 of these engines for use in 18 nuclear plants as of 1984. The engines have been alleged by the Nuclear Regulatory Commission to have major structural problems that threaten to delay the licensing of some plants.

Transamerica's insurance subsidiary contributed $100,000 to the American Foundation for AIDS Research in 1985, and was instrumental in obtaining an additional $100,000 contribution from the American Council of Life Insurance.

Transamerica has a fairly strong and flexible charitable giving program. Transamerica's 1985 contributions came to $2.4 million (or 1.3 percent of pre-tax earnings.) Its subsidiaries set their own priorities for grants. The company encourages employee involvement with organizations to which it gives.

In the latter half of 1986, Transamerica divested itself of its Budget Rent-a-Car subsidiary along with its Delaval division. (See addendum on page 500.)

The company did not respond to CEP's questionnaires.

TRANSAMERICA CORPORATION											
	Women		Minorities				Contracts		PAC Contributions		
% to Charity	Directors	Officers	Directors	Officers	Social Disclosure	Sullivan Rating	% Military	Nuclear Weapons–Related	Dollar Amount	% to Republicans	% to Democrats
1.3%	1	1	?	?	F	None	None	None	$76,450	33%	67%

? = No information available
See also Appendix D for a listing of this company's products and services.

HOTEL COMPANIES

Assessing the hotel industry is difficult because of the very limited information made available to CEP. Five of the nine companies approached did not respond to CEP's questionnaires. (Three of these five — Hilton, Holiday and Hyatt — are profiled in this chapter. Nestlé, which owns Stouffer's, and UAL, which owns Westin, are profiled elsewhere.) Social initiatives by the four cooperating companies (Best Western, Marriott, Ramada Inns, and Sheraton's parent company, ITT) are limited in scope. The fact that many of the major hotel chains are run in large part on a franchise basis also complicates appraisal of overall policies.

We have included a brief profile of Best Western, although it is not truly a hotel chain but a nonprofit trade association serving a network of hotel and motel operators.

CHARITABLE CONTRIBUTIONS AND COMMUNITY INVOLVEMENT

Hyatt Hotels are privately owned by the Pritzker family in Chicago, which has a reputation for generous philanthropy. None of the hotels has a particularly outstanding record on charitable giving, although ITT's is apparently the strongest.

REPRESENTATION OF WOMEN AND MINORITIES IN MANAGEMENT

Marriott was the only company profiled in this chapter to report at least one woman both in top management and on its board of directors. It has made a strong effort to hire and promote women, minorities, and the handicapped. The Kansas City–based Project Equality has undertaken a hotel-by-hotel evaluation of the policies of the major chains in the hiring and promotion of women and minorities. We have noted which chains cooperate with Project Equality in its evaluations.

INVOLVEMENT IN SOUTH AFRICA

Marriott recently sold its operations in South Africa. Sheraton's parent company, ITT, and Stouffer's parent company, Nestlé, have operations in that country.

CONVENTIONAL- AND/OR NUCLEAR-ARMS CONTRACTS

Sheraton's ITT parent company is a substantial military contractor.

POLITICAL ACTION COMMITTEE CONTRIBUTIONS

Holiday Inns and ITT have by far the most active PACs of companies profiled in this chapter.

HOTELS

HOTELS

Size of Charitable Contributions	Women Directors and Officers	Minority Directors and Officers	Social Disclosure	Brand Name	Company (Profile Page)	Involvement in South Africa	Conv. Weapons–Related Contracts	Nuclear Weapons–Related Contracts	Authors' Company of Choice
✳	No	No	✍ ✍ ✍	Best Western	Best Western (p. 291)	No	No	No	
?	No	No	No	Hilton Palmer House (Chicago) Waldorf Astoria (N.Y.)	Hilton Hotels (p. 292)	No	No	No	
$ $	🧍	🧍	No	Embassy Suites Hampton Inn Harrah's Holiday Inns	Holiday Corporation (p. 294)	No	No	No	
?	No	No	No	Hyatt	Hyatt (p. 295)	No	No	No	
$ $ $	🧍	🧍	✍ ✍ ✍	Sheraton	ITT (p. 296)	Yes B	✈ ✈ ✈	Yes	
$ $	🧍 🧍	🧍	✍ ✍ ✍	Marriott	Marriott (p. 298)	No	No	No	
✳	No	?	No	Stouffer's	Nestlé (p. 150)	Yes ?	No	No	

(Continued on next page)

Size of Charitable Contributions	Women Directors and Officers	Minority Directors and Officers	Social Disclosure	Brand Name	Company (Profile Page)	Involvement in South Africa	Conv. Weapons– Related Contracts	Nuclear Weapons– Related Contracts	Authors' Company of Choice
*	No	𝕏	✍✍✍	Ramada Inns Tropicana	Ramada Inns (p. 300)	No	No	No	
*	𝕏𝕏	𝕏	No	Westin	UAL (p. 263)	Yes C	No	No	

* = See company profile
? = No information available
Single figure ($, ♁) = Minimal
Double figure ($$, ♁♁, ✍✍, ♁♁) = Moderate
Triple figure ($$$, ♁♁♁, ✍✍✍, ♁♁♁) = Substantial

No = No involvement or participation
Yes = Involvement or participation. A, B, C in the South African column reflect the degree of compliance with Sullivan Principles and/or involvement in strategic industries.

See Chapter 4 for a detailed discussion of chart symbols.

BEST WESTERN INTERNATIONAL, INC.

Best Western is not truly a hotel chain, but a nonprofit association for hotel- and motel-owner members.

In 1981 Best Western's headquarters in Phoenix, Arizona, initiated a program to employ inmates at the Arizona Center for Women, a minimum-security prison seven miles from its offices. Best Western installed a complete reservations center at the prison at a cost of about $10,000, trained prisoners in computerized phone reservation work at a cost of $1,900 each, then hired them at salaries equivalent to those of reservation agents at its headquarters. One-third of the salary goes to the state to offset room-and-board costs; one-third is set aside in a trust fund for inmates when they are released; and one-third is paid out as disposable income, which can be sent outside for family support. Through mid-1985 the program had employed 134 inmates at the prison. Of those subsequently released, Best Western has hired approximately 30 as regular staff.

The headquarters offices in Phoenix and in Winston-Salem, North Carolina, have received local Employer of the Year awards for hiring the handicapped. In Phoenix, executives help a local halfway house for the mentally handicapped on company time.

The company has flextime arrangements for employees in reservations, customer relations, and data processing, and matches employee contributions to a saving plan. However, it has no formal charitable giving program.

The company responded to CEP's questionnaires.

BEST WESTERN INTERNATIONAL, INC.											
	Women		Minorities				Contracts		PAC Contributions		
% to Charity	Directors	Officers	Directors	Officers	Social Disclosure	Sullivan Rating	% Military	Nuclear Weapons–Related	Dollar Amount	% to Republicans	% to Democrats
*	0	0	0	0	A	None	None	None	None		

* = See profile
See also Appendix D for a listing of this company's products and services.

HILTON CORPORATION

Now under the leadership of Barron Hilton, son of this hotel chain's extravagant founder, Conrad Hilton, this was the first major hotel company to enter the casino business in the United States. (Holiday Inns and Ramada now also own casinos.)

In 1985 the New Jersey Casino Control Commission refused to grant a casino-operating license to Hilton, citing allegation of company associations with a lawyer with reputed ties to organized crime, and the alleged lack of candor of company executives during hearings. Commissioner Carl Zeitz stated: "I can conclude that the applicant [Hilton Corporation] has failed to demonstrate the good character, the honesty and integrity of certain corporate officials who appeared before us."

Of special concern to the commission was Hilton's retention of a Chicago labor lawyer, Sidney Korshak, as its outside counsel for 13 years. Mr. Korshak has been portrayed, according to the *New York Times*, as an associate of organized crime leaders.

Barron Hilton said he was "shocked and stunned" by the commission's decision and the company denied any wrongdoing. Hilton's $300 million Atlantic City casino-hotel was near completion at the time. The company did not appeal the commission's ruling, and instead sold the hotel to New York real estate developer Donald Trump. Hilton's casinos in Nevada and Australia generated approximately 45 percent of its income in 1985.

According to the Public Management Institute, Hilton "follows a fairly traditional pattern of [charitable] giving," but no specifics were provided on the size or nature of the gifts. Hilton Hotels has cooperated with Project Equality in its assessment of fair employment practices.

HILTON CORPORATION											
	Women		Minorities				Contracts		PAC Contributions		
% to Charity	Directors	Officers	Directors	Officers	Social Disclosure	Sullivan Rating	% Military	Nuclear Weapons–Related	Dollar Amount	% to Republicans	% to Democrats
?	0	0	0	0	F	None	None	None	None		

? = No information available
See also Appendix D for a listing of this company's products and services.

When Conrad Hilton died in 1979 he left most of his $300 million estate to the Conrad N. Hilton Foundation. Among its concerns as of 1984 were drug abuse, family violence, education and health care for the disadvantaged, and Catholic charities.

The company did not respond to CEP's questionnaires.

HOLIDAY INNS, INC.

Holiday Inns is the world's largest hotel chain, with more than 1,800 hotels in 53 countries. It entered the gaming world only over the strong religious objections of several top executives. It has not faced allegations of ties to organized crime.

Previously, Holiday Inns was known as a company that opened management meetings with a prayer, provided chaplains on call, required innkeepers to memorize the locations and hours of local church services, and did not allow bars in the inns until the early 1960s. In 1975 its largely Baptist board vetoed a concerted effort to involve the company in casinos. In 1978 the decision was reversed when the board voted to enter the gambling business. The company's president, L. M. Clymer, resigned because of "personal and religious convictions." In 1985 casinos accounted for 30 percent of the company's operating income.

The firm's $1 million in annual charitable giving is concentrated in its headquarters city of Memphis, Tennessee. According to the Public Management Institute, 33 percent of its 1982 disbursement went to education, 24 percent to civic and community organizations, 20 percent to human services, and 15 percent to arts and culture.

Holiday Inns has refused to cooperate with Project Equality's evaluations of hotel companies' employment practices, and did not respond to CEP's questionnaires.

HOLIDAY INNS, INC.											
	Women		Minorities				Contracts		PAC Contributions		
% to Charity	Directors	Officers	Directors	Officers	Social Disclosure	Sullivan Rating	% Military	Nuclear Weapons–Related	Dollar Amount	% to Republicans	% to Democrats
0.7%	1	0	1	?	F	None	None	None	$152,870	79%	21%

? = No information available
See also Appendix D for a listing of this company's products and services.

HYATT HOTELS CORPORATION

Hyatt is part of the large, diversified, private holdings of the Pritzker family of Chicago. Among the family's other businesses are *McCall's* magazine, a large interest in Braniff Airlines, timberland in California, and numerous industrial manufacturing companies.

The Pritzkers have a reputation for generous philanthropy in the Chicago area. In 1984 the Pritzker Foundation disbursed $2 million. Its recent gifts have reportedly included $12 million to the University of Chicago and $1.4 million for an ecology study at the Illinois Institute of Technology. The Pritzker Youth Foundation gives $50,000 each year for an after-school day-care program at a Chicago elementary school. The Hyatt Foundation awards an annual prize of $100,000 for architectural distinction to compensate for the absence of a Nobel prize in that field. Hyatt hotels are noted for their purchase of major original works of art for their interior designs.

The Pritzkers are known to keep a close eye on the multitude of family investments, with a concerted effort to keep management staff small and communications open. Hyatt Hotels hold special "gripe sessions" for their employees.

The Hyatt chain — 70 hotels in the United States and 42 abroad — has stayed out of gambling operations, although the Pritzkers reportedly hold a 21-percent stake in the Elsinore Corporation, which operates three casino hotels in Las Vegas, Lake Tahoe, and Atlantic City.

The Pritzker's Marmon Group employs approximately 400 persons in its South African operations and is not a signatory of the Sullivan Principles.

The company did not respond to CEP's questionnaires.

HYATT HOTELS CORPORATION											
	Women		Minorities					Contracts		PAC Contributions	
% to Charity	Directors	Officers	Directors	Officers	Social Disclosure	Sullivan Rating	% Military	Nuclear Weapons–Related	Dollar Amount	% to Republicans	% to Democrats
?	?	0	?	0	F	None	None	None	None		

? = No information available
See also Appendix D for a listing of this company's products and services.

ITT CORPORATION

Rarely has a corporation been the subject of such public controversy as ITT was in the early 1970s.

Between 1970 and 1973, ITT's activities in Chile were under close public scrutiny for possible cooperation with the CIA in opposing the election of the Marxist president of Chile, Salvador Allende. Apparently ITT funds were channeled to opposition candidates, although ITT at first denied the allegations. At the same time, in the United States, the company gave $400,000 to the city of San Diego to help underwrite the costs of the 1972 Republican presidential nomination convention. Allegedly, the gift was connected to company efforts to obtain a favorable antitrust settlement from the government at that time, allowing it to acquire The Hartford Insurance Company. The company denied this charge as well.

No wrongdoing on the company's part was found. But the U.S. Senate held lengthy public hearings that included such colorful personalities as Harold Geneen, who had built ITT's vast conglomerate empire, and the mysterious Dita Beard, ITT's Washington lobbyist.

In 1973 Anthony Sampson published his best-selling exposé, *The Sovereign State of ITT*, which presented the company as a multinational conglomerate operating beyond the control of national governments.

Ten years later, ITT had shed many of its diverse holdings, divesting its baking and industrial-products divisions, but remaining in the telecommunications, insurance, finance, hotel, and automotive parts industries.

Complaints about its insurance-selling policies have not helped its current public image. According to the *Wall Street Journal*, several states have charged ITT with "packing" — that is, selling customers unwanted and unexplained insurance policies as ad-ons. A 1984 out-of-court settlement with Wisconsin may result in up to $12 million in rebates. Iowa has reached a similar $500,000

ITT CORPORATION											
	Women		Minorities				Contracts		PAC Contributions		
% to Charity	Directors	Officers	Directors	Officers	Social Disclosure	Sullivan Rating	% Military	Nuclear Weapons– Related	Dollar Amount	% to Republicans	% to Democrats
1.1%	2	0	0	4	A	IIA/ IIB	9.0%	Yes	$161,075	65%	35%

See also Appendix D for a listing of this company's products and services.

settlement. A 1985 settlement with Colorado may mean as much as $2 million in refunds; in Minnesota $7 million may be returned to Minnesota residents.

The ITT of the mid-1980s is making an effort to portray itself as a socially responsible corporate citizen. It devoted a page to social issues in its 1984 annual report, and published a 22-page booklet, "Corporate Responsibility." But despite the space given to this issue, the company furnishes only select figures.

No totals on its current charitable giving program appear to be available, for example. The Taft *Corporate Giving Directory* lists a fairly generous $10.5 million in 1981, 1.1 percent of pre-tax earnings. Because ITT felt "U.S. Federal aid for communities has become more difficult to obtain," it began a Best Civic Idea program in 1981. These awards are for innovative self-help programs — for example, $25,000 to an emergency center for women and children in Seattle, Washington. Other projects have included a city program to improve handicapped access at a municipal airport, a job counseling and scholarship program for graduating high school students, and conversion of an abandoned school building into a youth and senior-citizen center.

In minority economic development, the company has several substantive programs: minority purchasing of $53 million in 1983; a minority banking program with a $5 million credit line; and an investment in a minority-oriented venture capital company operating out of Rutgers University. ITT reports that employment of the handicapped has long been one of its concerns. It would not, however, disclose figures on its employment record to CEP.

ITT's telecommunications work has made it the twentieth-largest U.S. military contractor in 1985, with $1.5 billion in Defense Department prime contracts, up from $1.1 billion in 1984. Its work includes communications satellites, air defense and shipboard radar, electronic warfare countermeasure systems, and radar for the Distant Early Warning system. According to the Investor Responsibility Research Center, $343 million of ITT's $603 million in 1983 contracts was for work on nuclear-related weapons systems. It was the twenty-fourth-largest military research and development contractor in 1985.

With its far-flung network of affiliated companies, it is not surprising to find ITT in South Africa. Its brake and radio manufacturing facilities there employ more than 280 persons, and received the second-highest "making progress" rating for compliance with the Sullivan Principles in 1984 and 1985.

The company responded to CEP's questionnaires.

MARRIOTT CORPORATION

The Marriott family founded and still runs this hotel and food-service company, headquartered in Washington, D.C. The Marriotts have been politically active, particularly in Republican circles; and their Mormon background has lent generally moral overtones to the company.

The Mormon influence may account for the company's decision not to involve its hotels in gambling. The company simply says that it has "no experience in gambling operations."

Using pep rallies to motivate employees, Marriott makes great efforts to imbue a "family" spirit in its workers, along with the work ethic of its devout founder, John Willard Marriott. Jobs are highly structured and tightly controlled. For example, maids reportedly must accomplish sixty-six tasks in room cleaning, from dusting picture tops to assuring that bibles are in good condition. A profit-sharing plan has matched $1.50 for every employee dollar contributed over the past 10 years. The company's work force is approximately 10 percent unionized.

Among its top managers, women hold a strong 29 percent of all positions and minorities 15 percent as of 1985; of its top 123 officers, three are women and four are minority group members. (This is an atypically large number of top officers compared with other companies in this book.) In 1986, *Black Enterprise* magazine ranked Marriott among the 25 best workplaces for blacks. Employment of the handicapped has long been a Marriott concern as well, with a substantial 5 percent of its current work force drawn from this group.

In South Africa, Marriott employs approximately 400 persons in its industrial and aviation catering service. This operation received poor grades ("needs to become more active") for compliance with the Sullivan Principles in 1983 and 1984, but rose to the second-highest "making progress" rating in 1985. In 1986, Marriott sold its operations there.

MARRIOTT CORPORATION											
	Women		Minorities				Contracts		PAC Contributions		
% to Charity	Directors	Officers	Directors	Officers	Social Disclosure	Sullivan Rating	% Military	Nuclear Weapons–Related	Dollar Amount	% to Republicans	% to Democrats
0.9%	1	3	0	4	A	IIA	None	None	$69,750	77%	23%

See also Appendix D for a listing of this company's products and services.

In the United States the firm has both a minority banking and purchasing program, but did not make figures on the size of either available for this book.

Marriott's 1984 charitable giving totaled $1.4 million, a moderate 0.9 percent of pre-tax earnings. No breakdown on the distribution of these funds was provided to CEP.

The company responded to CEP's questionnaires.

RAMADA INNS, INC.

Headquartered in Phoenix, Arizona, Ramada is one of the world's largest hotel chains, with more than 570 hotels worldwide as of 1985. Like the Hilton and Holiday Inn chains, the company owns casino hotels; but its gaming licenses have never been refused. In 1985, Ramada's Tropicana casino hotels brought in 40 percent of the company's profits. Social initiatives appear minimal, although women and minorities are well represented in its upper management.

Ramada acquired its first casino in 1979 with the purchase of the Tropicana in Las Vegas. When the company applied to open a second Tropicana in Atlantic City in 1981, the New Jersey Casino Control Commission issued a license after a lengthy investigation.

Representation of women and minorities among its officials and managers is strong — 32.7 percent and 14.3 percent respectively in 1984. Ramada cooperates with Project Equality in the latter's evaluation of fair hiring practices.

The firm has a minority purchasing program, although no dollar figures were made available, but does no minority banking. Its work force is 15 percent unionized.

Ramada's charitable cash giving totaled $337,000 in 1984, up from $198,000 the previous year. Almost half of the 1984 gifts went to the United Way. No meaningful comparison with previous years' profits is possible because of company losses in 1981 and 1982. The company recently created a program that matches worker contributions of up to $500 per employee to arts and educational organizations.

The company responded to CEP's questionnaires.

RAMADA INNS, INC.											
	Women		Minorities				Contracts		PAC Contributions		
% to Charity	Directors	Officers	Directors	Officers	Social Disclosure	Sullivan Rating	% Military	Nuclear Weapons–Related	Dollar Amount	% to Republicans	% to Democrats
*	0	0	0	1	A	None	None	None	None		

* = See profile
See also Appendix D for a listing of this company's products and services.

OIL COMPANIES

CHARITABLE CONTRIBUTIONS AND COMMUNITY INVOLVEMENT

Two companies stand out within the oil industry for their charitable and community involvement: Atlantic Richfield and Amoco.

Atlantic Richfield has a history of innovative and charitable giving programs that are particularly supportive of community development projects and minority-oriented causes. It has in the past published independent evaluations of its overall social responsibility performance. It was the only oil company profiled in this book with a charitable giving program of over 1.5 percent of pre-tax earnings. It remains to be seen, however, if recent reorganization at the company may weaken some of its social initiatives.

Since the mid-1970s, Amoco has made an exceptionally thorough commitment to a wide variety of minority economic development programs as well as to community revitalization projects in the Chicago area, far surpassing similar initiatives by other oil companies.

Exxon, Sohio, and Sun have taken some moderately strong steps to fund community revitalization efforts through their foundations.

REPRESENTATION OF WOMEN AND MINORITIES IN MANAGEMENT

Atlantic Richfield and Mobil were the only oil companies with at least one woman both in top management and on their board of directors. Compared to the other profiled oil companies for which we could locate statistics, Exxon has one of the stronger oil company records for the promotion of women and minorities.

Minority Purchasing Programs
Reported by Profiled Oil Companies

	Purchases from Minority Vendors	Total Sales
	(millions of dollars)	
Amoco (1984)	$145.0	$29,008
Atlantic Richfield (1983)	76.6	25,937
Exxon (1984)	88.0	85,415
Shell (1984)	61.0	20,898
Sun (1985)	69.2	14,435

Source: Company responses to CEP inquiries.

INVOLVEMENT IN SOUTH AFRICA

Chevron, Mobil, and Texaco have been sharply criticized by church groups for their willingness to continue selling to the South African military and police. Amoco, Atlantic Richfield, Occidental, and Sun have no operations there. Exxon and Phillips Petroleum recently withdrew.

CONVENTIONAL- AND/OR NUCLEAR-ARMS CONTRACTS

Tenneco is the oil company most heavily involved in military and nuclear arms contracting, through its Newport News subsidiary. Most oil companies have large contracts for fuel oil with the Department of Defense. These placed Amoco, ARCO, Chevron, Exxon, Mobil, Sun, and Texaco among the Defense Department's top one hundred prime contractors in 1985 along with British Petroleum and Royal Dutch Shell, parent companies of Standard Oil (Sohio) and Shell, respectively.

POLITICAL ACTION COMMITTEE CONTRIBUTIONS

The oil industry is one of the more aggressive lobbying forces in the country. This political activism is reflected in its PACs. The PACs of eight of the twelve companies profiled in this chapter each gave over $100,000 to federal candidates in the 1983–1984 election year. Sun's PAC was the most heavily oriented toward Republican candidates. Tenneco's and Amoco's PACs were the biggest spenders.

OTHER CONTROVERSIES

Oil companies, along with chemical companies, are at the center of innumerable controversies over air and water pollution, toxic and hazardous waste disposal, and worker safety, due to their drilling, refining, mining, and petrochemical manufacturing operations. Unfortunately, CEP could not locate reliable current comparative information on these vitally important issues, and had to depend on general accounts of individual controversies, along with CEP's decade-old comparative study of pollution control records of the refining industry. We have noted in the profiles for ARCO and Shell that they had the best records for air and water pollution control respectively among eight major refiners in the mid-1970s, according to CEP. Similarly, Texaco's profile notes its air pollution control record as being the worst in the industry during those years, and Gulf's (now owned by Chevron) as being the worst for water pollution control. The records for Amoco, Chevron, Exxon, and Mobil fell between these extremes and are not mentioned in their respective profiles.

Most of the oil companies in this book have been accused of oil price violations during the government price regulations imposed on the industry during the 1970s. The two largest of these accusations fell to Exxon, which was ordered to refund $2 billion, and Texaco, which is still fighting orders for refunds of $888 million. We have not detailed similar charges with other oil companies, although ARCO, Amoco, Chevron, and Mobil have reached lesser settlements.

In our opinion, oil companies with the poorest social records include Occidental, with its long history of severe environmental problems (as noted in its profile), notably at its Hooker Chemical subsidiary; and Texaco, with a relatively poor charitable giving record, a major presence in South Africa, and a dubious record on environmental affairs.

OIL COMPANIES

Size of Charitable Contributions	Women Directors and Officers	Minority Directors and Officers	Social Disclosure	Brand Name	Company (Profile Page)	Involvement in South Africa	Conv. Weapons–Related Contracts	Nuclear Weapons–Related Contracts	Authors' Company of Choice
$ $	No	☥	✍ ✍ ✍	Amoco	Amoco (p. 306)	No	✈ ✈	No	✔
$ $ $	☥ ☥	☥	✍ ✍ ✍	ARCO	Atlantic Richfield (p. 309)	No	✈ ✈	No	✔
$ $	☥	?	✍ ✍	Chevron Gulf	Chevron (p. 312)	Yes B	✈ ✈	No	
$ $	☥	☥	✍ ✍ ✍	Exxon	Exxon (p. 315)	No	✈ ✈	No	
$	☥ ☥	☥	✍ ✍	Mobil	Mobil (p. 318)	Yes B	✈ ✈	No	
$	☥	?	No	Cities Service	Occidental Petroleum (p. 321)	No	No	No	
$	☥	☥	✍ ✍	Phillips 66	Phillips Petroleum (p. 323)	No	✈ ✈	No	

On the Road

Size of Charitable Contributions	Women Directors and Officers	Minority Directors and Officers	Social Disclosure	Brand Name	Company (Profile Page)	Involvement in South Africa	Conv. Weapons–Related Contracts	Nuclear Weapons–Related Contracts	Authors' Company of Choice
$	No	?	✍ ✍ ✍	Shell	Shell (p. 325)	No	✈ ✈	No	
$	✦	No	✍ ✍	BP Sohio	Standard Oil (p. 327)	Yes B	No	No	
$ $ $	✦	✦	✍ ✍ ✍	Sunoco	Sun (p. 329)	No	✈ ✈	No	
$	No	?	No	Tenneco	Tenneco (p. 332)	Yes C	✈ ✈ ✈	Yes	
$	✦	No	No	Fire Chief Getty Sky Chief	Texaco (p. 334)	Yes B	✈ ✈	No	

* = See company profile
? = No information available
Single figure ($, ✦) = Minimal
Double figure ($$, ✦✦, ✍✍, ✈✈) = Moderate
Triple figure ($$$, ✦✦✦, ✍✍✍, ✈✈✈) = Substantial

See Chapter 4 for a detailed discussion of chart symbols.

No = No involvement or participation
Yes = Involvement or participation. A, B, C in the South African column reflect the degree of compliance with Sullivan Principles and/or involvement in strategic industries.

AMOCO CORPORATION

Amoco's long-standing commitment to minority economic development and community revitalization not only leads the oil industry, but is also the best among the corporations in its headquarters city of Chicago. At the same time, it has had some major environmental problems, and has one of the most active corporate Political Action Committees in the United States.

Since the late 1960s, Amoco's Corporate Social Policy Department, under the direction of Phillip Drotning, has developed one of the most extensive community-oriented social programs by a U.S. industrial corporation.

Its purchases from minority-owned businesses totaled $145 million in 1984, far surpassing those of other oil companies. (Exxon, the largest of the oil firms, purchased $88 million from minority suppliers that year.) Amoco formally launched its minority purchasing program in 1971, after an informal effort in the 1960s had little success. By requiring company managers to meet annually set goals, the company's purchases rose from $600,000 in 1970 to $75.3 million in 1979. Amoco sought out "qualifiable" as well as "qualified" minority vendors — that is, it provided technical and financial support to fledgling minority-owned suppliers.

In 1976 the company embarked on an exceptional program of direct investments in community redevelopment projects. These have included a $1 million commitment to Detroit's Renaissance Center, and $2.5 million pledged in risk capital in 1982 as part of a $20 million renovation of 304 low-income housing units in Chicago's deteriorating Rogers Park neighborhood. Amoco is reinvesting an anticipated $750,000 in profits from this project in athletic, day-care, medical, and other facilities in the same neighborhood.

In 1985, Amoco purchased a $1.5 million share in the Chicago Equity Fund, a unique project set up to pool corporate moneys for low- and moderate-income housing rehabilitation to be performed by non-profit groups. (The next-largest corporate contributors purchased $500,000 shares.) In addition, the company has provided a below-market mortgage loan of $230,000 to Chicago's Organization for the Northeast to rehabilitate an apartment house and restaurant.

Amoco has a sizable Minority Enterprise Small Business Investment Company (MESBIC), which invested $10 million between 1970 and 1984 in 60 minority-owned ventures. The company's minority banking program is a substantial one. Amoco's disbursement account for its Des Moines credit card office brought approximately $250 million through an operating account at Chicago's Highland Community Bank in 1983. Amoco processed $110 million in tax payments through minority-owned banks in 1984, and had $2 million in certificates of deposit.

The company's foundation makes a strong effort to support community development projects in Chicago. In 1983, for example, it gave $150,000 to People's Housing toward rehabilitation of 150 units; $50,000 to Good News Partners toward housing for 74 low-income residents; and $200,000 to two nonprofit groups in the Rogers Park neighborhood, in which it had directly committed company funds.

In 1983 Amoco's foundation began a three-year, $4.7 million energy conservation program aimed at reducing the energy bills of nonprofit organizations in the Chicago region through a combination of weatherization and increased heating efficiency. This program is being handled by Chicago's South Shore Bank, which in itself is a bank uniquely committed to community revitalization.

Overall, the company's foundation giving program increased from $16.6 million in 1983 to $19.4 million in 1984, with a projected $24 million in 1985. In 1984 the company gave an additional $2.5 million in direct contributions, for total contributions that year of $21.9 million or a moderate 0.7 percent of pre-tax earnings. The bulk of Amoco's giving goes to education (51 percent in 1983), particularly in science and engineering. Also included are two programs designed to improve math teaching in the Chicago public schools (run in conjunction with the University of Chicago) and to prepare talented minority high school students for college. An impressive 20 percent of the foundation's giving is dedicated to minority-oriented programs.

Amoco matched $1.4 million in employee gifts to education in 1984, and made over $100,000 in small grants to organizations with which its employees volunteer.

Amoco is a strong supporter of conservative economic think tanks, with $175,000 going to the American Enterprise Institute and $50,000 to the Heritage Foundation in 1984, along with over $80,000 to a network of conservative "public interest" law centers around the country.

AMOCO CORPORATION											
	Women		Minorities				Contracts		PAC Contributions		
% to Charity	Directors	Officers	Directors	Officers	Social Disclosure	Sullivan Rating	% Military	Nuclear Weapons-Related	Dollar Amount	% to Republicans	% to Democrats
0.7%	0	0	1	0	A	None	0.4%	None	$307,499	84%	16%

See also Appendix D for a listing of this company's products and services.

Progress in the hiring and promotion of women and minorities has been slow but steady. Of the twelve oil companies profiled in this book, Amoco was one of only three to report to CEP the percentage of women (up from 3.8 in 1981 to 4.5 in 1983) and minorities (up from 6.2 to 6.4) among its officials and managers.

In 1978, the company's tanker, the *Amoco Cadiz*, ran aground off Brittany, spilling some 68 million gallons of oil, creating an oil slick 80 miles long, and polluting 130 miles of the French seacoast. The French government and others sued for $1.9 billion in damages. In 1984, the U.S. courts ruled that Amoco was liable for damages from the spill, having failed to provide adequate backup systems and proper training of the ship's crew. The trial on actual damage awards was still underway as of mid-1986.

Amoco's $630,000 in 1983–1984 political spending topped the corporate PAC list. Of this amount, $307,000 went to federal congressional candidates, making it the fifth most active corporation in this category, surpassed only by Tenneco among the oil companies.

The company responded to CEP's questionnaires.

ATLANTIC RICHFIELD COMPANY (ARCO)

ARCO's social record throughout the 1970s and early 1980s was exceptional. It took innovative steps in its charitable giving and volunteer programs, in its compliance with environmental regulations, and in disclosure on and discussion of social issues, along with strong initiatives in minority economic development. It remains to be seen how well ARCO's social commitments will survive the major restructuring the company underwent in 1985.

The company's substantial charitable giving ($48.1 million in 1984, or 1.7 percent of pre-tax earnings) makes it the most generous of the oil companies profiled in this book. (Exxon gave more in total dollars, but less as a percentage of pre-tax earnings.) Its foundation program strongly supports community projects and the environment, is diverse in its aid to education, and is creative with its employees' community involvements.

In 1984, community programs received a substantial 36 percent of ARCO's grants. Just under half of this amount was channeled through the traditional United Way. Numerous smaller contributions went to a wide range of community revitalization organizations, minorities' and women's groups, and others working with the economically disadvantaged. In 1983, the company made over $1 million in large grants to three neighborhood revitalization organizations — $600,000 to the Enterprise Foundation, $300,000 to Neighborhood Housing Services, and $150,000 to the Local Initiatives Support Corporation.

Environmental groups received $1.8 million in 1984 and $1.6 million in 1983, including $200,000 to a migratory bird research program in Alaska, and $50,000 or more each to the Nature Conservancy, the Environmental Law Institute, the Conservation Foundation, the Peregrine Fund, and a Rutgers University toxicology program in 1983.

ARCO has a four-year, $5 million grant to support young faculty in science and engineering at thirty research universities, similar to programs of other companies with a strong interest in science. In addition, it gave $400,000 in liberal arts grants in 1983, and over $600,000 in gifts aimed at minorities in education. Its total $11.8 in education contributions (32 percent of total disbursements) included $2.6 million to match employee contributions.

In all, a hefty $4.4 million went out in company matches for employee gifts to nonprofit organizations in 1984. In 1984, $316,000 in special grants went to organizations with which its employees volunteer, under a program started in 1980. The company had one executive on loan to the Los Angeles school district and a second working with SER — Jobs for Progress, a Dallas-based network of training and technical support organizations for the Hispanic community.

The company has a formal volunteer program in twenty locations around the country. Its 1984 participation rate was 7 percent, up from 6 percent the year before. In Los Angeles, 150 employees volunteered an average of 32 hours each during the year on company release time to help out in four inner-city high schools.

The company, unlike many others, has not avoided debate about its social projects. In publishing a substantial and detailed description of its social programs (the last one in 1980), ARCO included outside assessments of the company's initiatives by independent critics from the corporate responsibility movement.

ARCO's commitments to minority economic development are substantial as well. Its $76.6 million in purchases from minority-owned businesses in 1983 was greater than Exxon's $60 million, but less than Amoco's $115 million that year. ARCO's minority banking program consists of a moderate $2.3 million in certificates of deposit and an operating account.

Among its officials and managers, women held 7.5 percent of the positions and minority group members 8.3 percent, according to a 1986 *Black Enterprise* magazine article.

In an industry characterized by frequent run-ins with environmental authorities, ARCO's record has generally been a good one. When the CEP analyzed the air and water pollution records of major oil refineries in the mid-1970s, ARCO's record was superior to other companies. (We were not able to locate a more recent overall comparison of ARCO's air and water pollution control records with the rest of the oil industry.) In 1980, Kirk Hanson of Stanford's Graduate School of Business asserted that ARCO's top management has been "willing to approve substantial expenditures for environmental control equipment above required minimums."

Despite ARCO's exceptional record in many areas, in others it has had its share of controversies. In 1980 its Anaconda Copper subsidiary (acquired in

ATLANTIC RICHFIELD COMPANY (ARCO)											
	Women		Minorities				Contracts		PAC Contributions		
% to Charity	Directors	Officers	Directors	Officers	Social Disclosure	Sullivan Rating	% Military	Nuclear Weapons–Related	Dollar Amount	% to Republicans	% to Democrats
1.7%	1	1	0	1	A	None	1.4%	None	$82,325	69%	31%

See also Appendix D for a listing of this company's products and services.

1977) shut down a major smelter in Anaconda, Montana, with little notice, prompting demonstrations and church-sponsored resolutions at the company's annual meetings over the next two years. ARCO set up a $3 million Community Adjustment Fund to help the small city of 10,000 affected by this closing. But continued Anaconda layoffs in the region, and the failure of the revitalization efforts, left church groups and others sharply critical of the company.

In 1985 ARCO underwent substantial changes. The company sold off most of its non-oil businesses, changed chief executive officers, and cut its work force by 20 percent (6,000 chose early retirement, and 1,900 were laid off). It remains to be seen whether ARCO under its new management will be as committed to social goals as was the old company under former CEOs Robert Anderson and Thornton Bradshaw. For example, the firm has not issued a report on its social activities since 1980; previously, these were published every three years. Nor would it provide CEP with the percentage of minorities and women among its officials and managers.

An ARCO refinery in Philadelphia and ARCO gas stations east of the Mississippi were sold to a Dutch international oil trader, John Deuss, in 1985.

The company responded to CEP's questionnaires.

CHEVRON CORPORATION

Everybody's Business describes San Francisco–based Chevron as "bring[ing] up the 'right wing' of the American oil industry," because of its overall conservative practices and policies and its reluctance to address environmental and fair hiring issues. Anthony Sampson, in *The Seven Sisters*, asserted in 1975 that Chevron made "a positive cult of conservatism."

Some of Chevron's recent initiatives in charitable giving have been moderately innovative. But the company did not respond to CEP's questionnaires, and we could locate little other information on this corporation's social programs.

Chevron acquired Gulf Oil in 1984 for $13 billion, in the largest merger in history. Gulf is headquartered in Pittsburgh, and has long been associated with the Mellon family. In late 1985, Chevron announced that it would be selling its gas station outlets in the Northeast to Cumberland Farms.

Chevron is co-partner with Texaco in the Caltex Petroleum Corporation, which employs approximately 2,100 persons in that country. (Approximately one-half of the workers are white.) Among U.S. oil companies, Mobil has a larger work force there. Caltex received the highest "making good progress" rating for its compliance with the Sullivan Principles from 1981 through 1984, but dropped to the second-highest in 1985. Along with Texaco and Mobil, Chevron was rated in May 1985 as one of the twelve corporate "key investors in apartheid" by a coalition of 50 church groups. They did so because of Caltex's sales to the South African military and police, its substantial role in the strategically important South African oil industry, and its refusal to place a moratorium on further investments in that country.

At the same time some conservatives have criticized the company's presence in Angola as aiding the Marxist government there. In early 1986 the Conservative Caucus called for a boycott of Chevron's Gulf subsidiary, which has been in Angola since the late 1960s.

Chevron created a series of eight Chevron Funds in 1982 to help compensate in part for federal cutbacks in social service programs. By channeling substantial grants to preestablished funding agencies in seven major cities around the country, Chevron sought to direct its aid most effectively to programs of greatest need. Its $3 million grant in 1982 to the California Community Foundation in Los Angeles, for example, increased that foundation's grant-making capabilities by 40 percent. In all, Chevron has committed $13 million to this program.

Chevron's $32.3 million in 1985 giving — or 1.0% pre-tax earnings — made it one of the more generous of the oil companies in this book. Its programs focused heavily on education with contributions totaling 46 percent, or $14.9 million. Federated drives, primarily the United Way, received $3.3 million and

YMCAS $2.4 million. Its gifts in the civic involvement category totaled $2.4 million. These went primarily to public policy research ($890,000), with the conservative research organizations American Enterprise Institute, Heritage Foundation, and Hoover Institute receiving $85,000, $40,000, and $32,500, respectively. The more mainstream research organizations, Conference Board, Committee for Economic Development, and Brookings Institute, received $55,000, $20,000 and $10,000, respectively. Of its $717,000 in environmental contributions, $250,000 went to Yosemite National Park. Arts grants came to $2.3 million or 7 percent of total giving.

In 1985 the Environmental Protection Agency won a $6 million penalty judgment for air pollution violations that had occurred between 1977 and 1979 at a Texas refinery. It was the largest penalty that the EPA had ever won in a civil suit. The *Wall Street Journal* quoted a company spokeswoman as saying at that time, "This is an old issue. We have solved our problems and are now in full compliance and have been since 1979."

In a negotiated settlement on a 1983 shareholder resolution, the company agreed to supply shareholders with an accounting of its political spending — indirectly through its Political Action Committee or directly on initiatives and referenda. Few companies make this information available to shareholders. (General Motors agreed to a similar resolution in 1980.)

Chevron's merger with Gulf Oil has brought with it Gulf's checkered history including price-fixing allegations in its supplying of uranium fuel and a 1983 out-of-court settlement with the Tennessee Valley Authority over this issue which cost Gulf $70 million. Gulf was also involved with major scandals over a $12 million slush fund kept for political contributions at home and abroad in the 1970s, which resulted in the resignation of the company's chairman and three other officials in 1976.

CHEVRON CORPORATION											
	Women		Minorities				Contracts		PAC Contributions		
% to Charity	Directors	Officers	Directors	Officers	Social Disclosure	Sullivan Rating	% Military	Nuclear Weapons–Related	Dollar Amount	% to Republicans	% to Democrats
1.0%	1	0	?	?	C	IIA	1.7%	None	$145,020	71%	29%

? = No information available
See also Appendix D for a listing of this company's products and services.

Oil Companies 313

Gulf's record on water pollution control was the worst among eight refiners evaluated by CEP in the mid-1970s. It fared better on air pollution at that time, having the fourth-best record. (We could locate no more recent overall comparison of Gulf's air and water pollution control records with the rest of the oil industry.)

According to the Investor Responsibility Research Center, Gulf's GA Technologies subsidiary works on gas-cooled nuclear reactors and on fusion research for the utility industry. The subsidiary's military contracts totaled less than $100,000 in 1983 for research and development work from the Army for ballistic missile defense and for other research and development from the Defense Nuclear Agency.

The company did not respond to CEP's questionnaires.

EXXON CORPORATION

Exxon is the second largest industrial corporation in the world ($86.7 billion in 1985 sales), with the second-highest profits ($4.9 billion in 1985 to IBM's $6.6 billion). The company has made substantial social commitments and in particular has one of the better oil industry records for employment of minorities and women, but seems to lack the leadership that might be expected from a company with such tremendous resources.

The company's charitable giving program is a major one. Its $69.6 million in 1984 contributions ($58.2 million in the United States and $11.4 million abroad) made it the second-largest corporate donor covered in this book. But it fell behind IBM's $90 million in cash contributions (and $60 million in donated products and services) that year. Exxon's program has a strong social component, but is neither as diverse and community-oriented as ARCO's, nor as large when compared with pre-tax earnings — a moderate 0.7 percent, less than half of ARCO's 1.7 percent.

The company's $5.2 million for civic and community service included grants to urban economic development projects: $500,000 to the Enterprise Foundation, $200,000 for management assistance to nonprofit organizations, $750,000 to New York City community groups, and $520,000 for summer jobs programs around the county. The company also gave out just over $550,000 in grants of up to $1,000 to groups with which Exxon staff volunteered in 1984. It matches three dollars for each employee dollar contributed to educational institutions.

In 1984 the company gave a total of $3.6 million to a wide range of public policy organizations. These included the conservative economic think tank Heritage Foundation ($30,000) and conservative law centers such as the Pacific and New England Law Foundations ($78,500 to eight of these), as well as the more liberal Brookings Institute ($85,000), the Scientists' Institute for Public Information ($15,000), and the Citizens Research Foundation ($10,000). In 1983 Exxon gave $200,000 to the conservative American Enterprise Institute, an economic research center.

Like many technology-dependent companies, Exxon's primary emphasis was on higher education, particularly scientific and engineering programs. A substantial 56 percent of its 1984 gifts in the United States went to education. Typical of its grants was the 1981 announcement that it would give $15 million over three years to support teaching fellowships and junior faculty salaries in "key engineering and science departments" at colleges and universities. Of its $32.8 million in educational grants in 1983, $2.4 million went to support minority colleges or students.

Other major areas of giving included health, welfare, and community programs, which received $11 million (19 percent of domestic contributions); the arts ($4.8 million); and public broadcasting ($4.5 million). Abroad, 39 percent of its $11.4 million in contributions went to Canada, and another 29 percent to the Far East (primarily Australia). Company grants in South Africa totaled approximately $19,000. Exxon and ARCO were the only two oil companies studied with substantial support for environmental groups, but one-third of Exxon's $1.5 million was the result of an out-of-court settlement (see below). Among its larger environmental gifts were $130,000 to the New York Zoological Society, $62,000 to the Brooklyn Botanical Garden, and $50,000 each to the Nature Conservancy, the Central Park Conservancy, and Cornell University's Laboratory of Ornithology.

The company has made strong commitments to minority purchasing: $88 million in 1984 — up from $60 million in 1983, but not as large as Amoco's $145 million in 1984, the largest program in the oil industry.

As of 1983, 7.2 percent of Exxon gas stations were owned or operated by minority group members. We could find no indication that the company has a minority banking program.

One of Exxon's strengths is its employment policies, according to *The 100 Best Companies to Work for in America,* which cited the company's excellent pay and benefits. Employees may contribute up to 6 percent of their annual salaries to a tax-deferred savings plan; the company will match these contributions dollar for dollar.

Exxon has one of the more successful affirmative-action employment and promotion programs in the oil industry. As of 1984, 8.2 percent of its officers and managers were women and 7.8 percent were minorities — both above the industry's discouraging national averages of 6.2 percent for women and 4.9 percent for minorities. *Black Enterprise* magazine termed Exxon's Upward Mobility Task Force, formed in 1981, "impressive" in its commitment of senior management and division heads to career development planning for

EXXON CORPORATION											
	Women		Minorities				Contracts		PAC Contributions		
% to Charity	Directors	Officers	Directors	Officers	Social Disclosure	Sullivan Rating	% Military	Nuclear Weapons–Related	Dollar Amount	% to Republicans	% to Democrats
0.7%	2	0	1	?	A	I/IIA	0.6%	None	$193,350	85%	15%

? = No information available
See also Appendix D for a listing of this company's products and services.

women and minorities. Exxon was one of four oil companies of the twelve profiled for which CEP could locate such statistics.

Of the oil companies, Exxon has been one of the most heavily involved in the uranium fuel cycle. For about four years, through 1983, it was the chief operator of the Idaho National Engineering Laboratory, which reprocesses spent fuel from nuclear submarines and research reactors for reuse, and for which it received $42 million in Department of Energy contracts in 1983. In 1984 Westinghouse took over operation of this plant from Exxon.

In 1986 Exxon paid $2.1 billion to the U.S. government in an oil price violations case, the largest fine or settlement paid in such a case as of that time.

Among its various environmental disputes, one was particularly bizarre. The company was accused of dumping oil-polluted waters between 1971 and 1983 from its tankers into the Hudson River, and then carrying fresh Hudson River water to Aruba in the Caribbean, where Exxon has a refinery and where there is a shortage of fresh water. The company reportedly sold the fresh water it didn't use in its refinery to the government of Aruba. While denying any wrongdoing, Exxon settled the case in 1984 with payments to New York State of $1.5 million, and made contributions of $250,000 each to two environmental groups (the Hudson River Foundation for Science and Environmental Research and the Open Space Institute), which had pursued the charges.

When, during the mid-1970s, many major U.S. companies were voluntarily disclosing questionable overseas payments, Exxon's $56.8 million exceeded all others. Most of these payments had been made in Italy, many of them in the form of political contributions.

Exxon's operations in South Africa employ fewer workers than most other major U.S. oil companies with a presence in that country — approximately 210 persons, one-half of whom are white. It has consistently received the highest rating, "making good progress," for its compliance with the Sullivan Principles. Exxon has publicly stated that it does not sell to the South African military or police. In 1986 it announced plans to sell its operations there.

Concern over Exxon's plans to double the operations of its copper-mining subsidiary in Chile prompted six church groups to file a shareholder resolution with the company in 1986. Citing the repressive human rights record of the military dictatorship there, and drawing parallels with current South African unrest, the groups asked the company to abandon its expansion plans. The resolution received a moderate 4 percent vote of approval from shareholders.

The company responded to CEP's questionnaires.

MOBIL CORPORATION

When it comes to political stands, Mobil fears no one, does as it pleases, and fights for its beliefs. It has been aggressive in the media, politics, and lobbying on governmental regulation. In 1980, President Carter publicly took on Mobil for its disregard of voluntary inflation-fighting wage and price standards, and columnist Jack Anderson wrote about "The Amazing Arrogance of Mobil Oil." The company asserted its prices at that time were justifiable and dismissed Carter's attack as "politically motivated."

Mobil is a great fan of "op-ads," quasi-editorial articles appearing in paid advertisements on the page facing a newspaper's editorial page. In its op-ads Mobil has, among other things, defended the PAC system and criticized organizations seeking its reform.

Former Mobil president William Tavoulareas, who retired in 1984, sued the *Washington Post* in 1979 for libel over a story reporting that he had set up his son in the shipping business. The original jury had awarded Tavoulareas $2 million; this verdict had been overturned by a federal judge on appeal, but later reinstated. Yet further appeals left the case unresolved as of May 1986. In 1983 the company took out insurance for its top executives covering up to $10 million in legal fees if they sued for libel.

In December 1984, Mobil announced that it would no longer cooperate with the *Wall Street Journal*. The company cited "troubles" with this newspaper as its reason for the boycott. The paper had, two weeks earlier, run a story reporting that the company's new 70-story office tower in Chicago would be built in conjunction with a firm employing the chairman's son-in-law.

Chairman Rawleigh Warner, Jr., wrote Mobil stockholders in 1984 asking them to contribute, automatically, a portion of their dividend checks to the company PAC, a precedent-setting, but perfectly legal request. Citing the PAC system as a "uniquely American democratic tradition," he encouraged stockholders' participation to help elect candidates who "share [their] beliefs and philosophy about government."

Despite the vocal public stances on political issues, Mobil's PAC is far from the most active in the oil industry. Its $138,000 in contributions to federal candidates in 1983–1984 was far surpassed by Tenneco's industry-leading $366,000, as well as by the PACs of Amoco, Exxon, Sun, Shell, and Chevron.

Mobil has been in South Africa since 1897, and employs over 3,000 workers in its operations there (of whom approximately one-half are white), more than any other U.S. oil company. In recent years it has consistently received the highest rating, "making good progress," for its compliance with the Sullivan Principles. But Timothy Smith, director of the Interfaith Center on Corporate Responsibility, states that in his opinion, Mobil is "America's foremost partner in apartheid." In 1985 a coalition of 50 church groups labeled Mobil one of twelve "key investors in apartheid," citing the company's continued sales to the South African military and police.

Mobil foundation's giving program appears to be moderate ($11.4 million in 1984 and $11.2 million in 1985). But this understates the company's total giving. The Investor Responsibility Research Center reports $27 million in total Mobil contributions worldwide in 1983, or 0.5 percent of pre-tax earnings. The foundation's gifts in all areas were numerous, small, and diverse in 1985. A strong 20 percent of giving went to support a wide variety of civic organizations. Among the foundation's larger grants in this area were $50,000 each to the Bedford-Stuyvesant Restoration Corporation and the NAACP, $60,000 to the National Urban League, and $25,000 to the SER — Jobs for Progress job-training centers. Of the rest of the foundation's giving, 42 percent went to education and 12 percent to united fund drives.

Mobil reports that the percentage of women and minorities among its highest officials, managers, and supervisors has grown from 4.4 percent and 4.8 percent respectively in 1977 to 7.4 and 7.3 percent in 1984, below Exxon's record but better than Amoco's. Mobil is one of only four oil companies profiled for which CEP could locate such statistics.

Minority purchasing and banking are among the company's activities, but no figures on the size of these programs were made available to us.

Mobil refused to respond to CEP's questionnaires. Moreover, after reviewing an initial draft of Mobil's profile, Herbert Schmertz, Mobil's vice president for public relations, wrote CEP, "Judging from past jousts with the CEP, we expected a biased, hostile report replete with inaccuracies and that's just what we got." Although criticizing CEP's "unsophisticated and shallow methodol-

MOBIL CORPORATION											
	Women		Minorities				Contracts		PAC Contributions		
% to Charity	Directors	Officers	Directors	Officers	Social Disclosure	Sullivan Rating	% Military	Nuclear Weapons–Related	Dollar Amount	% to Republicans	% to Democrats
0.5%	2	1	2	?	C	I	0.3%	None	$138,019	83%	17%

? = No information available
See also Appendix D for a listing of this company's products and services.

ogy," Schmertz declined our requests for information, stating, "In our best judgment, no useful purpose could be served by participating in your study. It clearly would not be in the best interests of our employees, shareholders, customers, or the general public." Despite this antagonistic stance, publications from Mobil's foundation and its affirmative action program provided some basic information on the company's social initiatives.

OCCIDENTAL PETROLEUM CORPORATION

Occidental, primarily because of its Hooker Chemical subsidiary, has faced dramatic and well-publicized environmental problems. We could locate little in the way of social initiatives.

Occidental acquired Hooker Chemical in 1968. Ten years later began the initial revelation of problems stemming from toxic wastes dumped by Hooker 25 years earlier at Love Canal in New York State. In 1980 the first charges were filed against Hooker in one of the first and most emotionally charged of the hazardous-waste site disputes that have since become a nationwide concern.

Hooker had used the abandoned Love Canal site for disposal of toxic wastes from 1942 to 1953. It sold the property to the local board of education, although it warned of possible hazards on the site at that time. An elementary school and housing development were subsequently built in the immediate region. In the late 1970s the New York Health Department began investigations of citizens' complaints of abnormal rates of birth defects, spontaneous abortions, and cancers in the Love Canal area. It uncovered a monumental problem in the leaking barrels of highly toxic chemical wastes it found there. Multimillion-dollar suits were filed against Hooker by government agencies to cover cleanup costs, and by residents for extensive damage to their property and lives.

Hooker defended itself by asserting that there was no concrete evidence of health problems at Love Canal, and that even if there were, the company was not responsible because it had initially warned of possible hazards, and its disposal of wastes had been proper. Company spokesmen claimed that the barrels were now leaking due to the subsequent installation of sewage sys-

OCCIDENTAL PETROLEUM CORPORATION											
	Women		Minorities				Contracts		PAC Contributions		
% to Charity	Directors	Officers	Directors	Officers	Social Disclosure	Sullivan Rating	% Military	Nuclear Weapons–Related	Dollar Amount	% to Republicans	% to Democrats
0.1%	1	0	?	?	F	None	None	None	$35,850	71%	29%

? = No information available
See also Appendix D for a listing of this company's products and services.

tems on the site. Occidental did not admit liability but ultimately settled the Love Canal claims in 1983 for between $5 and $6 million.

Hooker's environmental controversies did not stop with Love Canal. Three more of its hazardous-waste disposal sites in the Niagara region were also said to have major environmental problems. Hooker had used the large Hyde Park landfill from 1953, when it disposed of Love Canal, until 1974. After various charges and disputes, Occidental agreed to provide $10 million in cleanup costs there. The nearby S-Area dump was also allegedly linked to major pollution problems, and in 1984 the company agreed to pay $36 million toward its cleanup as well.

In addition, Hooker and Occidental faced major waste disposal problems in Lathrop, California, where a pesticide and fertilizer plant was alleged to be contaminating drinking water supplies, and in Michigan, where toxic pesticides were said to be leaking into a finger lake of Lake Michigan. In both cases the company agreed to multimillion-dollar settlements. The company also reached a $1.1 million settlement in Florida over air pollution charges relating to one of its fertilizer plants.

Occidental was a partner with Tenneco in the Cathedral Bluffs Oil Shale Project, one of the federally subsidized "synfuels" programs about which some environmentalists were concerned. The government has subsequently abandoned its synfuels program in the face of sharp drops in the price of oil.

In 1983–1984, Occidental's PAC contributions ($35,850) were the smallest among the oil companies covered in this book.

Occidental's charitable foundation gave only $291,000 in 1983 — well under 0.1 percent of pre-tax earnings. (This figure does not include direct corporate giving and understates the company's total program, much of which is made directly.) According to the Taft Corporate Giving Directory, 70 percent of these funds went to education and the rest primarily to federated fund drives. The firm's newly acquired Cities Service Company had a more substantial record, with $1 million in gifts from its foundation in 1983.

Occidental has for many years been headed by the outspoken and dynamic Armand Hammer, whose Armand Hammer Foundation is noted for its generous philanthropic giving, particularly to the arts.

The company did not respond to CEP's questionnaires.

PHILLIPS PETROLEUM COMPANY

In the 1970s an illegal campaign-contributions scandal brought control of its board to new, outside directors. But relations with employees and with the local community have remained good for this large company ($15.6 billion in 1985 sales), which remained in the small town of Bartlesville, Oklahoma (population 35,000), when other up-and-coming oil companies left.

It has contributed one-third of the construction costs for the town's $12.5 million community center, made a sizable donation toward the town's $3.5 million downtown revitalization program, and gave heavily to local schools, where it has an extensive volunteer program. One-third of the company is owned by employees under an Employee Stock Ownership Plan.

Nationwide, Phillips contributed 0.5 percent of pre-tax earnings to charity. Two-thirds of its $10.5 million in 1984 giving went to education. Almost $4 million went to support a massive program of educational films in which Phillips has been involved for over a decade. This Phillips-funded, but independently produced, multi-part film series promotes interest in science, mathematics, and the American economic system. Along with accompanying teaching materials, the films have been widely distributed and seen by millions of secondary-school children. Sheila Harty, in her book *Hucksters in the Classroom*, has criticized the general acceptance in public schools of corporate-provided educational material, which often contains commercial plugs for products or propaganda for specific political points of view.

Of Phillips's remaining $3.8 million in grants to education, approximately $1.2 million matched employee gifts, $600,000 went to fellowships and research grants, and $95,000 to minority scholarships. Of its $1.2 million in civic grants, $40,000 went to the American Enterprise Institute, a conservative economic think tank, $40,000 to conservative "public interest" law centers, and

PHILLIPS PETROLEUM COMPANY											
	Women		Minorities				Contracts		PAC Contributions		
% to Charity	Directors	Officers	Directors	Officers	Social Disclosure	Sullivan Rating	% Military	Nuclear Weapons–Related	Dollar Amount	% to Republicans	% to Democrats
0.5%	2	0	1	0	C	IIA	0.3%	None	$87,650	78%	22%

See also Appendix D for a listing of this company's products and services.

$143,000 to the Louisiana World Exhibition, and $58,000 to the Basketball Hall of Fame.

In a 1984 anti-takeover move, the company sold one-third of its outstanding shares to its employees under an Employee Stock Ownership Plan. This use of the ESOP differs from that of airline companies in recent years; when faced with huge losses, several airlines offered workers a share of the company in return for wage concessions and as an incentive to increase productivity. Phillips, in contrast, turned over part of a profitable company to its workers to keep it from the hands of outsiders — in this case, investor T. Boone Pickens.

In the late 1970s, as the result of a suit by shareholders, Phillips agreed in a court-approved settlement to turn over control of its board to outside directors. An earlier investigation by the Phillips board had discovered a $2 million fund of laundered corporate money for political campaign contributions. At least $500,000 had been used, including an illegal $100,000 contribution to President Nixon's 1972 reelection campaign, admitted by the company's chairman, William Keeler. The Center for Law in the Public Interest, representing shareholders, won the settlement whereby six outside directors were added to the company's board, three of them nominated by the Center. Although the company did not admit or deny allegations in the suit, rigorous safeguards were established to prevent dubious use of company funds in the future.

Phillips employs approximately 160 persons at its Carbon Black company in South Africa. Its rating for compliance with the Sullivan Principles was the second-highest ("making progress") from 1981 through 1985, except for 1984, when it received the highest rating ("making good progress"). It sold its operations in South Africa in 1986.

The company did not respond to CEP's questionnaires.

SHELL OIL COMPANY

This Houston-based company has a record of occasional controversy mixed with some fairly strong social initiatives.

In its mid-1970s study of the refinery records of eight major oil companies in the United states, CEP ranked Shell's record as best on water pollution control and fifth-best on air pollution. We could locate no more recent overall comparison of Shell's air and water pollution control record with that of other oil companies.

Shell has had an active minority purchasing program since 1971. It purchased $61 million from minority suppliers and $48 million from women-owned businesses in 1984. The company has a minority banking program which, as of 1981, had $2 million in deposits. It is also a founder and largest shareholder in the Minority Enterprise Small Business Investment Corporation of Houston, and a founder of the Houston Business Council, both of which provide financial and technical assistance to developing minority-owned businesses.

According to *The 100 Best Companies to Work for in America*, Shell's savings and investment plans are "the most generous in the petroleum industry." It will match up to 10 percent of employees' pay set aside in its Provident Fund. The company contributes to a stock-purchase plan for employees, and reimburses tuition for job-related education. For those nearing retirement, Shell reimburses tuition for education relating to planned retirement activities. The company would not provide statistics on its percentages of women and minorities in top management for publication in this book.

Shell Oil's charitable program is moderate and traditional. Its total giving of $18.2 million in 1984 ($15.3 million from its foundation and $2.9 million directly) represented 0.6 percent of pre-tax earnings, average for the oil com-

SHELL OIL COMPANY											
	Women		Minorities				Contracts		PAC Contributions		
% to Charity	Directors	Officers	Directors	Officers	Social Disclosure	Sullivan Rating	% Military	Nuclear Weapons–Related	Dollar Amount	% to Republicans	% to Democrats
0.6%	0	0	?	?	A	None	0.6%	None	$174,220	81%	19%

? = No information available
See also Appendix D for a listing of this company's products and services.

panies covered in this book. In recent years its foundation's giving has been heavily weighted toward education — approximately 65 percent of contributions, including matching gifts from employees. About 15 percent of its giving goes to traditional federated fund drives. Between 5 and 10 percent go to the arts and to civic projects.

The company promotes volunteerism among its employees through its SERVE program. Along with Exxon, it sponsored a "Volunteer Houston" drive in 1985, encouraging local residents and businesses to aid volunteer organizations in the city.

Shell's most serious environmental suit was filed by the U.S. government in 1983. It was "the largest suit by any federal agency that seeks damages for natural resources," according to the Department of Justice. The suit seeks $1.9 billion to cover cleanup costs at the Army's Rocky Mountain arsenal in Colorado, which the company had leased since 1947. Shell had produced numerous herbicides and pesticides there, including products such as aldrin and dieldrin, which were later banned by the Environmental Protection Agency as potentially carcinogenic or capable of causing birth defects. The Army asserted that chemical dump sites left by Shell were dangerously polluting the land, water, and wildlife on and near the arsenal. The Army had spent some $50 million simply to determine the extent of this pollution. This lawsuit has been combined with one by the state of Colorado suing both the Army and Shell for the cleanup costs.

The British Shell International Petroleum Company has a major presence in South Africa. Its 5,161 employees in 1984 substantially outnumbered those employed by U.S. oil companies in that country. (Mobil had the most at that time, with 3,342 workers.)

In 1986 the anti-apartheid Free South Africa Movement called for a boycott of Shell in the United States because of Royal Dutch Shell's strategically important role in the coal and oil industries in South Africa. Shell disclaims any influence over its parent company's policies or practices in South Africa.

The company responded to CEP's questionnaires.

STANDARD OIL COMPANY

Just over 50 percent of the stock of this Cleveland-based oil company is controlled by British Petroleum (BP), half of which in turn is controlled by the British government. Essentially a small regional oil company until the 1960s, Standard Oil Company (familiarly called Sohio) was catapulted into the ranks of major petroleum producers the following decade, when it went into partnership with BP in Alaska's oil-rich North Slope. It is a proponent of ethical business behavior, but is a major presence in South Africa through its mining operations there.

According to Sohio's former chairman Alton W. Whitehouse, the firm developed its code of ethics — called Principles of Business Conduct — in response to rapid growth in the 1970s. These principles were seen as one means of communicating the corporation's ideals to a rapidly expanding work force.

Since the mid-1970s most major U.S. corporations have adopted similar codes. At that time highly publicized revelations of illegal political contributions at home and questionable payments abroad (e.g., bribes, kickbacks, political contributions) promoted growing concern for ethics questions in the business community. While codes vary substantially, among issues frequently included are bribery and the acceptance of gifts, the divulging of confidential business information, outside employment, and unethical conduct in the workplace.

Business ethics codes are occasionally faulted as window dressing, ineffectively communicated to employees, unmonitored and unenforced. Elements making for effective programs include the full support of top management, promotion of codes through special company seminars, and ethics committees or ombudsmen empowered to deal with specific cases. Professor Michael Hoffman of Bentley College found in a 1985 survey that of 280 *Fortune* 1,000

STANDARD OIL COMPANY											
	Women		Minorities				Contracts		PAC Contributions		
% to Charity	Directors	Officers	Directors	Officers	Social Disclosure	Sullivan Rating	% Military	Nuclear Weapons–Related	Dollar Amount	% to Republicans	% to Democrats
0.5%	1	0	0	0	C	IIA	None	None	$66,850	74%	26%

See also Appendix D for a listing of this company's products and services.

companies that responded, 93 percent had written codes of ethics, but only 8 percent has an ombudsman to ajudicate complaints; only three companies had a judiciary board to rule on violations.

Sohio's moderate charitable giving program (0.5 percent of pre-tax earnings) is substantially committed to energy conservation and urban redevelopment. A full $1 million of its $16.9 million given in 1984 went to nonprofit urban redevelopment organizations such as the Enterprise Foundation ($200,000), Neighborhood Housing Services ($320,000), and the National Trust for Historic Preservation ($110,000). The company has committed an additional $1.2 million to a Cleveland weatherization program initiated by the Ford Foundation and supported by a range of public and private groups. Sohio matched federal funds to weatherize the houses of qualifying low-income families, and for energy conservation in buildings owned by nonprofit groups. Minority affairs received $327,000, including $60,000 for the Cooperative Assistance Fund, a loan and venture capital fund for minority businesses.

The remainder of Sohio's charitable program is traditional and moderate by oil industry standards. Just over 50 percent went to education, much of this under a five-year, $10 million "scientific excellence" program. Under this program, grants of approximately $2 million each went to five universities for projects of immediate interest to Sohio, such as computer simulation of petroleum reservoirs, or improvement of longwall mining systems. The American Association for the Advancement of Science received $1.7 million from Sohio to promote science education in junior high schools in a three-year period. Slightly over $1.1 million went to Sohio employees in a tuition reimbursement plan, an expense included by many other companies in their benefit — not charitable giving — programs.

While the city of Cleveland was pleased with Sohio's decision to build its new headquarters downtown, Cincinnati was much less happy about the company's 1985 plans for the temporary storage of the highly toxic chemical benzene in that city. (The chemical would eventually be loaded onto barges headed down the Ohio River.) Despite considerable public concern, railroad shipments got underway in February, only to have the first carload spring a leak. Amid an immediate public outcry, the mayor of Cincinnati banned all further storage of benzene in the city's terminals.

Sohio Chemical is a part-owner of Richards Bay Mineral, which employs over 1,500 persons in South Africa. It received the second-highest "making progress" rating for compliance with the Sullivan Principles in 1984 and 1985. In 1985 British Petroleum had a large presence in South Africa (4,500 employees), larger than that of any American oil company.

The company did not respond to CEP's questionnaire.

SUN COMPANY, INC.

Sun was founded and long controlled by the Pew family, noted for its involvement in Republican politics. Its legacy can be seen in Sun's current PAC, which gives almost exclusively to Republican candidates. But the company in recent years has spoken out publicly on the virtues of social investments, set up a Minority Enterprise Small Business Investment Company, and runs a generous charitable giving program with a strong emphasis on community revitalization and minority economic development.

Sun's $183,000 in Political Action Committee contributions to congressional candidates in 1983–1984 was the most heavily weighted toward Republican candidates (91 percent) among the oil companies profiled in this book. Sun takes the unusual step of publishing an annual report on its PAC activities, and solicits shareholders, as well as employees, for contributions. In 1975 it obtained a precedent-setting ruling from the Federal Election Commission permitting corporations to spend their own funds to set up and run PACs, thus allowing them to spend as much corporate funds as they choose to solicit PAC funds from non-corporate sources. Sun's network of 50 Responsible Citizenship Program Councils encourages employees around the country "to be involved in the process of government," although these councils do not endorse candidates.

Sun gave a fairly substantial 1.3 percent of pre-tax earnings to charity in 1985, second only to ARCO among oil companies in this book. It uses an unusual decentralized dual-tier grant system similar to Pillsbury's. Overall social initiatives are supervised by a staff of three at company headquarters in Radnor, Pennsylvania. But each of the company's six principal locations has its own budget for charitable giving, allocated at the discretion of local committees composed of a cross section of employees.

The company's 1983 Citizenship Report does not give a complete breakdown of grants, but does show major commitments to community revitalization and job-training programs, with a stated emphasis on promoting "self-sufficiency." For example, it made a $200,000 grant to the Philadelphia Clearinghouse toward setting up the Management Assistance Program (MAP). Working with the Wharton School of Economics and LaSalle University, MAP provides management and technical assistance to nonprofit organizations throughout the Delaware Valley region, enabling them to increase their fundraising and to stretch their resources through more efficient management.

Grants to community revitalization included $100,000 to the Philadelphia chapter of the Local Initiatives Support Corporation, as well as to Neighborhood Housing Services in Philadelphia and in Tulsa, Oklahoma. In Parkside and Chester, Pennsylvania, Sun has supported revolving loan funds for community housing efforts, a relatively new and innovative mechanism to help local groups finance rehabilitation and construction costs.

A $60,000 Sun grant went to Philadelphia's Opportunities Industrialization Center job training program. In Dallas, the local Sun office has given to the Hispanic SER — Jobs for Progress organization, and to the Mexican American Legal Defense and Education Fund's leadership training program.

In all, a strong 21 percent of Sun Company's $12 million given in 1983 went to community economic development, with education receiving 36 percent, the United Way 12 percent, and health and human services 17 percent. Its cash contributions have held steady at $12 million from 1983 through 1985.

Where other companies have occasionally lent top executives to annual United Way drives, Sun has loaned an executive to the Philadelphia public school system for two years, where he oversees all plant operations and personnel relations. As of 1983, Sun had seven executives on social leave working at a variety of locations, including Philadelphia's Academy of Applied Automotive and Mechanical Science, a "magnet" technical training school within the city's school system; and a redevelopment corporation set up in Chester to help cushion the sale of Sun's large shipyard in that city.

Sun and Amoco are the only oil companies profiled in this book to have their own Minority Enterprise Small Business Investment Company venture capital fund for minority-owned businesses. In 1985 Sun purchased $69 million from minority-owned businesses.

The company has had some recent labor relations problems. The Oil, Chemical and Atomic Workers union called a boycott of Sun products when workers at its Philadelphia and Toledo refineries went on strike in March 1984. The Toledo union accused Sun of having used its newly instituted, $2 million Quality of Work Life program (set up to increase worker productivity, involvement, and cooperation with management) to undercut the union's po-

SUN COMPANY, INC.											
	Women		Minorities				Contracts		PAC Contributions		
% to Charity	Directors	Officers	Directors	Officers	Social Disclosure	Sullivan Rating	% Military	Nuclear Weapons–Related	Dollar Amount	% to Republicans	% to Democrats
1.3%	1	0	0	3	A	None	1.1%	None	$183,150	91%	9%

See also Appendix D for a listing of this company's products and services.

sition in the months prior to the strike. By the year's end the strike had been resolved.

The Pew family's seven foundations, with assets of $2 billion as of 1984, have been until recently "reactionary in spirit and inferior in performance," according to Waldemar Nielsen, writing in *The Golden Donors*. However, changes since the late 1970s have improved and updated the nature and quality of the foundations' giving program.

The company responded to CEP's questionnaires.

TENNECO INC.

This huge, diverse, Houston-based conglomerate is primarily an oil and natural gas company, but it is also in the auto parts business (Speedy Muffler King, among others), real estate, and farm equipment. Its $1.2 billion in defense contracts in 1985 made it the twenty-fourth largest military contractor in the United States (up from thirty-first in 1984), and it is a major presence in California agribusiness, specializing in nut farming. Its social initiatives center primarily on a volunteer program in the Houston area.

Tenneco's Newport News Shipbuilding and Dry Dock subsidiary, the nation's largest shipyard, is heavily involved in nuclear-related work. According to the Investor Responsibility Research Center, the shipyard received $3.2 billion in Defense Department contracts for work on Nimitz-class nuclear-powered aircraft carriers in 1983. These ships are the largest warships in the world, and are designed to carry nuclear-capable aircraft. The shipyard also contracts for attack submarines carrying nuclear-capable missiles. In 1984 Tenneco's military contracts dropped to $749 million from $3.7 billion in 1983.

In 1985 a church-sponsored shareholder resolution requested that management establish a permanent standing committee to review its military contracting practices and policies. The resolution received the support of 11 percent of those shares voted, a strong level of support for a resolution opposed by management.

Tenneco has one of the most active Political Action Committees among U.S. corporations. Its $366,700 in 1983–1984 spending was the second-highest (after Philip Morris) among companies profiled in this book, and placed Tenneco second on the Federal Election Commission's list of top PAC corporate contributors to candidates.

TENNECO INC.											
	Women		Minorities				Contracts		PAC Contributions		
% to Charity	Directors	Officers	Directors	Officers	Social Disclosure	Sullivan Rating	% Military	Nuclear Weapons–Related	Dollar Amount	% to Republicans	% to Democrats
0.6%	0	0	?	?	F	IIIA	5.0%	Yes	$366,700	83%	17%

? = No information available
See also Appendix D for a listing of this company's products and services.

On the Road

In the 1970s, with rapidly rising petroleum prices, many oil companies became involved in the federally subsidized and environmentally controversial "synfuels" projects to extract oil from shale, Tenneco particularly so. With Occidental Petroleum, it undertook construction of the Cathedral Bluffs Oil Shale Project, which, according to the Investor Responsibility Research Center, has received federal subsidies of $2.2 billion and could ultimately cost close to $3 billion. With four other companies, Tenneco also built the Great Plains Coal Gasification plant, which the *Wall Street Journal* described in mid-1985 as a "financial disaster." At that time, the federal government, which had already put up $1.5 billion in loans for the plant, refused to supply over $700 million in gas price subsidies that the plant owners said was necessary to make its operation viable. The owners predicted the plant would close. The government's Synthetic Fuels Corporation was shut down in 1986. Sharp drops in 1985 and 1986 oil prices, along with a drying up of federal subsidies, have forced many oil companies to abandon their synfuels programs as economically unfeasible.

Tenneco's best-known social project is its volunteer program in Houston. Begun in 1978, Volunteers In Assisting (VIA) was recruiting 1,500 volunteers annually (employees, retirees, and family members) by 1983. VIA works with more than 60 groups in a variety of capacities. Its volunteers provide companionship to the elderly, to abused children, and to the retarded; run phone banks for fund-raising events by public television, the American Heart Association, and others; provide teaching and counseling in the public schools; and participate in fund-raising walkathons for medical and other causes. The company matches two dollars for every employee dollar contributed to such groups.

The company's $7 million in charitable giving in 1984 (a moderate 0.6 percent of pre-tax earnings) went in large part to traditional causes, according to the Taft *Corporate Giving Directory.*

In South Africa, Tenneco's J. I. Case farm equipment facility employs 400 workers. Its rating for compliance with the Sullivan Principles was the second-highest ("making progress") in 1984, but fell to third-highest ("needs to become more active") in 1985. Tenneco is also the majority owner of SA Paper Chemicals Ltd., with 30 employees in that country.

The company did not respond to CEP's questionnaires.

TEXACO INC.

In his book on the oil industry, *The Seven Sisters*, Anthony Sampson writes, "Texaco has always taken pride in being the meanest of the big companies, refusing to contribute anything except for profit (apart from their patronage of opera). . . ." The company's record seems to bear out this assertion. The $7.9 million (0.3 percent of pre-tax earnings) charitable contributions from Texaco's foundation in 1984 made it one of the least generous of the oil companies profiled in this book. (This figure, however, may understate the company's full program, as it does not include direct giving by the company.)

Texaco's 1983 annual report stated, "As Federal funds to support the arts, education, health and welfare programs have been cut, President Reagan asked the nation's leading corporations to help 'bridge the gap.' At Texaco, his request has been taken seriously." Yet in relative terms Texaco's claim does not appear to be justified. Not only is the size of its contributions apparently meager but its giving program is directed primarily toward sponsorship of the Metropolitan Opera's radio and television broadcasts. *Corporate Foundation Profiles* lists $3.1 million of Texaco's $7.7 million going to the Metropolitan Opera in 1983, with an additional 21 percent of its gifts to education.

Among the eight largest oil refiners examined by CEP in the mid-1970s, Texaco held the worst record for air pollution control and the fifth-worst for water pollution control. CEP described the company at that time as having "a record of intransigence in the face of regulation." We could locate no more recent overall comparison of Texaco's air and water pollution control records with that of the rest of the oil industry.

Among oil companies charged with price-control violations in the 1970s, Texaco and Exxon were accused of greater overcharges than others. In 1983 the courts upheld rulings that Texaco must refund $888 million in overcharges

TEXACO INC.											
	Women		Minorities				Contracts		PAC Contributions		
% to Charity	Directors	Officers	Directors	Officers	Social Disclosure	Sullivan Rating	% Military	Nuclear Weapons–Related	Dollar Amount	% to Republicans	% to Democrats
0.3%	1	0	0	0	F	IIA	0.9%	None	$125,410	80%	20%

See also Appendix D for a listing of this company's products and services.

from the previous decade. The company has continued to fight this ruling before the Department of Energy's Office of Hearings and Appeals.

Texaco had two serious run-ins with its unions in the early 1980s. A seven-month strike by the Oil, Chemical, and Atomic Workers union in 1982 centered around the company's methods of calculating workers' pension benefits. In 1984 unions called a boycott of the company (which lasted several months) during two lengthy strikes by West Coast workers.

Texaco's Caltex operation in South Africa (jointly owned with Chevron) employs over 2,100 workers, approximately one-half of whom are white, and received the highest rating for its compliance with the Sullivan Principles from 1981 through 1984, but dropped to the second-highest in 1985. Just behind Mobil, Caltex has the second-largest U.S. oil company presence in South Africa. Along with Mobil and Chevron, Texaco was chosen in May 1985 by a coalition of 50 church groups as one of twelve U.S. corporate "key investors in apartheid." Church groups view Caltex's involvement in South Africa as strategically important to the government there because of the company's sales to the military and police. Caltex has refused to place a moratorium on further investments there.

Texaco's purchase of Getty Oil in 1984 for $10 billion led to the largest civil judgment in history a year later, when a Texas jury awarded $10.5 billion to Pennzoil, which had also sought to purchase Getty. Pennzoil argued successfully in the courts that Texaco had improperly seized ownership of Getty after Pennzoil had an oral but legally binding contract to purchase the company. In the highly dramatic aftermath of this stunning decision, Texaco — the third-largest U.S. oil company — was pushed to the brink of bankruptcy. The case was still in the courts as of mid-1986, and it is unclear at this time how much of an impact it will have on Texaco.

The company did not respond to CEP's questionnaires.

Chapter 8

AROUND THE HOUSE
Appliance and Household Product Companies

APPLIANCE COMPANIES

The coverage of companies manufacturing household appliances, home entertainment equipment, cameras, and typewriters is incomplete, primarily because of the major role in these industries played by foreign companies not covered in this book.

CHARITABLE CONTRIBUTIONS AND COMMUNITY INVOLVEMENT

Polaroid has long had numerous innovative policies, including a generous, diverse, and decentralized charitable giving program, excellent employee relations, and a for-profit youth job training subsidiary. Xerox has a comprehensive set of social programs, and encourages volunteering among its employees. Eastman Kodak, whose annual meetings were the site of protests by civil rights groups in the 1960s, has initiated several social programs in its headquarters city of Rochester, New York, where it has a good reputation as an employer. IBM and GE have undertaken major steps in job training and minority education, respectively. RCA was a pioneer in promoting social responsibility in the corporate community. Polaroid, RCA, and United Technologies are the three companies in this section with charitable giving at 1.5 percent of pre-tax earnings or above, by CEP's calculations.

REPRESENTATION OF WOMEN AND MINORITIES IN MANAGEMENT

General Electric and Xerox, both known for their progressive programs in hiring and promoting of women and minorities, were the only companies profiled in this chapter to have at least one woman and one minority both in top management and on their board of directors.

Minority Purchasing Programs
Reported by Profiled Appliance and Household Product Companies

	Purchases from Minority Vendors	Total Sales
	(millions of dollars)	
Clorox (1985)	$ 4.4	$ 1,079
Eastman Kodak (1985)	11.5	10,631
GE (1984)	50.5	27,947
IBM (1985)	150.0	50,056
Kimberly-Clark (1985)	2.5	4,073
Polaroid (1984)	3.4	1,272
Procter & Gamble (1985)	45.0	13,552
RCA (1984)	38.9	10,112
Reynolds Metals (1985)	16.0	3,416
3M (1984)	14.0	7,705
United Technologies (1984)	80.0	14,992
Whirlpool (1984)	2.1	3,138
Xerox (1984)	29.5	8,792

Source: Company responses to CEP inquiries.

INVOLVEMENT IN SOUTH AFRICA

More than half the companies profiled in this industry had operations in South Africa as of 1985. Allegheny International employs more persons there than other companies profiled in this section. Polaroid was exceptional in expressing concerns about apartheid early on, and withdrawing from South Africa on principle in 1977. Black & Decker, Eastman Kodak, General Electric, IBM, and Scovill all sold, or announced plans to sell, their operations in South Africa during 1986. Hoover has a particularly poor record for compliance with the Sullivan Principles.

CONVENTIONAL- AND/OR NUCLEAR-ARMS CONTRACTS

A substantial proportion of companies in the appliance industry are heavily involved in both nuclear and conventional arms work. GE, GTE, IBM, Litton, Raytheon, RCA, and United Technologies are all major military contractors. Eastman Kodak Company has faced church criticism over its work on the "Star Wars" missile defense system.

POLITICAL ACTION COMMITTEE CONTRIBUTIONS

General Electric, Litton, and United Technologies all had PACs contributing over $200,000 to Congressional candidates in the 1983–1984 election cycle.

OTHER CONTROVERSIES

Litton has had the most highly publicized problems with labor, with a national labor campaign against the company over unionizing disputes, which have subsequently been resolved. White Consolidated and Magic Chef have also had confrontations with unions in recent years.

In contrast, Maytag is known for long-standing excellent labor relations, as well as for the high quality of its products and service, and a cordial relationship with the small Iowa town in which it is based.

Not dealt with here but of particular concern for purchasers of refrigerators and air conditioners should be their energy efficiency ratings, which indicate how effectively specific models use electricity.

APPLIANCES, LARGE

AIR CONDITIONERS

Size of Charitable Contributions	Women Directors and Officers	Minority Directors and Officers	Social Disclosure	Brand Name	Company (Profile Page)	Involvement in South Africa	Conv. Weapons–Related Contracts	Nuclear Weapons–Related Contracts	Authors' Company of Choice
$ $ $	♦ ♦	♦ ♦	🖐 🖐 🖐	G.E.	General Electric (p. 353)	No	✈ ✈ ✈	Yes	
$	No	?	No	Magic Chef	Magic Chef (p. 362)	No	No	No	
$ $	No	?	No	Amana	Raytheon (p. 367)	Yes B/C	✈ ✈ ✈	Yes	
$ $ $	♦ ♦	♦	🖐 🖐 🖐	Carrier	United Technologies (p. 374)	Yes B	✈ ✈ ✈	Yes	
$ $	No	No	🖐 🖐 🖐	Whirlpool	Whirlpool (p. 377)	No	No	No	✔
$ $	No	?	No	Frigidaire Gibson Kelvinator White-Westinghouse	White Consolidated (p. 378)	No	No	No	

✳ = See company profile
? = No information available
Single figure ($, ♦) = Minimal
Double figure ($$, ♦♦, 🖐🖐, ✈✈) = Moderate
Triple figure ($$$, ♦♦♦, 🖐🖐🖐, ✈✈✈) = Substantial

No = No involvement or participation
Yes = Involvement or participation. A, B, C in the South African column reflect the degree of compliance with Sullivan Principles and/or involvement in strategic industries.

See Chapter 4 for a detailed discussion of chart symbols.

APPLIANCES, LARGE

OVENS, RANGES, AND MICROWAVE OVENS

Size of Charitable Contributions	Women Directors and Officers	Minority Directors and Officers	Social Disclosure	Brand Name	Company (Profile Page)	Involvement in South Africa	Conv. Weapons–Related Contracts	Nuclear Weapons–Related Contracts	Authors' Company of Choice
$ $ $	[person] [person]	[person] [person]	[hand] [hand] [hand]	G.E. Hotpoint	General Electric (p. 353)	No	[plane] [plane] [plane]	Yes	
$	[person]	?	No	Litton	Litton (p. 360)	No	[plane] [plane] [plane]	Yes	
$	No	?	No	Magic Chef Toastmaster	Magic Chef (p. 362)	No	No	No	
$ $	No	No	[hand] [hand] [hand]	Hardwick Jenn-Air Maytag	Maytag (p. 363)	No	No	No	✔
$ $	No	?	No	Amana Caloric Glenwood Modern Maid	Raytheon (p. 367)	Yes B/C	[plane] [plane] [plane]	Yes	
$ $	No	No	[hand] [hand] [hand]	Kitchen Aid Whirlpool	Whirlpool (p. 377)	No	No	No	✔
$ $	No	?	No	Frigidaire Kelvinator White- Westinghouse Vesta	White Consolidated (p. 378)	No	No	No	

APPLIANCES, LARGE

REFRIGERATORS AND FREEZERS

Size of Charitable Contributions	Women Directors and Officers	Minority Directors and Officers	Social Disclosure	Brand Name	Company (Profile Page)	Involvement in South Africa	Conv. Weapons-Related Contracts	Nuclear Weapons-Related Contracts	Authors' Company of Choice
$ $ $	♟♟	♟♟	✍ ✍ ✍	G.E. Hotpoint	General Electric (p. 353)	No	✈ ✈ ✈	Yes	
$	No	?	No	Admiral	Magic Chef (p. 362)	No	No	No	
$ $	No	?	No	Amana	Raytheon (p. 367)	Yes B/C	✈ ✈ ✈	Yes	
$ $	No	No	✍ ✍ ✍	Whirlpool	Whirlpool (p. 377)	No	No	No	✔
$ $	No	?	No	Frigidaire Gibson White-Westinghouse	White Consolidated (p. 378)	No	No	No	

* = See company profile
? = No information available
Single figure ($, ♟) = Minimal
Double figure ($$, ♟♟, ✍✍, ✈✈) = Moderate
Triple figure ($$$, ♟♟♟, ✍✍✍, ✈✈✈) = Substantial

No = No involvement or participation
Yes = Involvement or participation. A, B, C in the South African column reflect the degree of compliance with Sullivan Principles and/or involvement in strategic industries.

See Chapter 4 for a detailed discussion of chart symbols.

APPLIANCES, LARGE

VACUUM CLEANERS

Size of Charitable Contributions	Women Directors and Officers	Minority Directors and Officers	Social Disclosure	Brand Name	Company (Profile Page)	Involvement in South Africa	Conv. Weapons–Related Contracts	Nuclear Weapons–Related Contracts	Authors' Company of Choice
?	🚶🚶	?	No	Black & Decker	Black & Decker (p. 349)	Yes C	No	No	
✱	No	?	No	Hoover	Hoover (p. 356)	Yes C	No	No	
$ $ $	🚶	🚶	🖐🖐🖐	Electrolux	Sara Lee (p. 167)	No	No	No	✔

✱ = See company profile
? = No information available
Single figure ($, 🚶) = Minimal
Double figure ($$, 🚶🚶, 🖐🖐, 🚶🚶) = Moderate
Triple figure ($$$, 🚶🚶🚶, 🖐🖐🖐, 🚶🚶🚶) = Substantial

No = No involvement or participation
Yes = Involvement or participation. A, B, C in the South African column reflect the degree of compliance with Sullivan Principles and/or involvement in strategic industries.

See Chapter 4 for a detailed discussion of chart symbols.

APPLIANCES, LARGE

WASHERS AND DRYERS

Size of Charitable Contributions	Women Directors and Officers	Minority Directors and Officers	Social Disclosure	Brand Name	Company (Profile Page)	Involvement in South Africa	Conv. Weapons– Related Contracts	Nuclear Weapons– Related Contracts	Authors' Company of Choice
$ $ $	✶ ✶	✶ ✶	🖐 🖐 🖐	G.E. Hotpoint	General Electric (p. 353)	No	✈ ✈ ✈	Yes	
$	No	?	No	Admiral Norge	Magic Chef (p. 362)	No	No	No	
$ $	No	No	🖐 🖐 🖐	Maytag	Maytag (p. 363)	No	No	No	✔
$ $	No	?	No	Amana Speed Queen	Raytheon (p. 365)	Yes B/C	✈ ✈ ✈	Yes	
$ $	No	No	🖐 🖐 🖐	Whirlpool	Whirlpool (p. 377)	No	No	No	✔
$ $	No	?	No	Frigidaire Gibson Kelvinator White- Westinghouse	White Consolidated (p. 378)	No	No	No	

✶ = See company profile
? = No information available
Single figure ($, ✶) = Minimal
Double figure ($$, ✶✶, 🖐🖐, ✈✈) = Moderate
Triple figure ($$$, ✶✶✶, 🖐🖐🖐, ✈✈✈) = Substantial

No = No involvement or participation
Yes = Involvement or participation. A, B, C in the South African column reflect the degree of compliance with Sullivan Principles and/or involvement in strategic industries.

See Chapter 4 for a detailed discussion of chart symbols.

Around the House

APPLIANCES, SMALL

KITCHEN APPLIANCES

Size of Charitable Contributions	Women Directors and Officers	Minority Directors and Officers	Social Disclosure	Brand Name	Company (Profile Page)	Involvement in South Africa	Conv. Weapons–Related Contracts	Nuclear Weapons–Related Contracts	Authors' Company of Choice
$ $	No	No	No	Oster Sunbeam	Allegheny International (p. 348)	Yes C	No	No	
?	♀ ♀	?	No	Black & Decker	Black & Decker (p. 349)	Yes C	No	No	
$ $	♀ ♀	♀	✍ ✍ ✍	West Bend	Dart & Kraft (p. 130)	Yes B	No	No	
?	No	No	No	Waring	Dynamics Corp. of America (p. 350)	No	No	No	
$ $	♀ ♀	No	✍ ✍ ✍	Braun	Gillette (p. 212)	Yes A	No	No	✔
$	No	?	No	Magic Chef Toastmaster	Magic Chef (p. 362)	No	No	No	
$ $	No	?	✍ ✍	Hamilton-Beach	Scovill (p. 372)	No	No	No	

* = See company profile
? = No information available
Single figure ($, ♀) = Minimal
Double figure ($$, ♀♀, ✍✍, ♀♀) = Moderate
Triple figure ($$$, ♀♀♀, ✍✍✍, ♀♀♀) = Substantial

No = No involvement or participation
Yes = Involvement or participation. A, B, C in the South African column reflect the degree of compliance with Sullivan Principles and/or involvement in strategic industries.

See Chapter 4 for a detailed discussion of chart symbols.

APPLIANCES, SMALL

TYPEWRITERS

Size of Charitable Contributions	Women Directors and Officers	Minority Directors and Officers	Social Disclosure	Brand Name	Company (Profile Page)	Involvement in South Africa	Conv. Weapons–Related Contracts	Nuclear Weapons–Related Contracts	Authors' Company of Choice
$ $ $	𝍫 𝍫	𝍫	✍ ✍ ✍	IBM	IBM (p. 357)	No	✈ ✈ ✈	Yes	
$ $ $	No	?	No	Smith Corona	SCM (p. 371)	No	No	No	
$ $	𝍫 𝍫	𝍫	✍ ✍ ✍	3M	3M (p. 425)	Yes A	No	No	
$ $ $	𝍫 𝍫	𝍫 𝍫	✍ ✍ ✍	Xerox	Xerox (p. 379)	Yes A	No	No	✔

* = See company profile
? = No information available
Single figure ($, 𝍫) = Minimal
Double figure ($$, 𝍫𝍫, ✍✍, ✈✈) = Moderate
Triple figure ($$$, 𝍫𝍫𝍫, ✍✍✍, ✈✈✈) = Substantial

No = No involvement or participation
Yes = Involvement or participation. A, B, C in the South African column reflect the degree of compliance with Sullivan Principles and/or involvement in strategic industries.

See Chapter 4 for a detailed discussion of chart symbols.

Around the House

ENTERTAINMENT

CAMERAS AND PHOTOGRAPHIC EQUIPMENT

Size of Charitable Contributions	Women Directors and Officers	Minority Directors and Officers	Social Disclosure	Brand Name	Company (Profile Page)	Involvement in South Africa	Conv. Weapons–Related Contracts	Nuclear Weapons–Related Contracts	Authors' Company of Choice
$ $	🧍	🧍 🧍	✍ ✍ ✍	Kodak	Eastman Kodak (p. 351)	No	✈ ✈	No	
$ $ $	🧍	🧍	✍ ✍ ✍	Polaroid	Polaroid (p. 365)	No	No	No	✔

ENTERTAINMENT

RADIOS AND TELEVISIONS

Size of Charitable Contributions	Women Directors and Officers	Minority Directors and Officers	Social Disclosure	Brand Name	Company (Profile Page)	Involvement in South Africa	Conv. Weapons–Related Contracts	Nuclear Weapons–Related Contracts	Authors' Company of Choice
$ $ $	🧍 🧍	🧍 🧍	✍ ✍ ✍	G.E.	General Electric (p. 353)	No	✈ ✈ ✈	Yes	
$ $ $	🧍	🧍	✍ ✍ ✍	RCA	RCA (p. 369)	No	✈ ✈ ✈	Yes	
*	No	🧍	No	Zenith	Zenith (p. 381)	No	✈ ✈	No	

ALLEGHENY INTERNATIONAL, INC.

Formerly a major steel company, this Pittsburgh-based conglomerate now produces a variety of items, including razor blades, small home appliances, specialty metals, matches, railroad wheels, exercise equipment, patio furniture, computer disc drives, fire-extinguishing systems, hardware, thermostats, pollution control equipment, and robotics.

Allegheny's majority ownership in the Lion Match Company in South Africa makes it the eighth-largest U.S. employer in that country, with 2,025 workers there. Allegheny did not sign the Sullivan Principles until 1985 and had previously been the largest nonsignatory U.S. employer.

Although Allegheny is not rated here as a major military contractor, CEP found $5.2 million listed in Department of Defense prime contracts for bombs and pyrotechnic devices in 1984 for Allegheny's Kilgore Corporation subsidiary and an additional $3.3 million in arms-related prime contracts for its HTL subsidiaries. HTL makes fire detection and suppression systems for aircraft, armored vehicles, and missiles.

The company has a moderate charitable giving program, with $563,000 in 1984 gifts, according to the Taft *Corporate Giving Directory,* or 0.8 percent of pre-tax earnings. (This figure does not include direct corporate giving and may understate the company's total program.) It concentrates heavily on the Pittsburgh area, with diverse but largely traditional grant recipients.

The company did not respond to CEP's questionnaires.

ALLEGHENY INTERNATIONAL, INC.											
	Women		Minorities				Contracts		PAC Contributions		
% to Charity	Directors	Officers	Directors	Officers	Social Disclosure	Sullivan Rating	% Military	Nuclear Weapons—Related	Dollar Amount	% to Republicans	% to Democrats
0.8%	0	0	0	0	F	V	Negligible	None	$39,175	89%	11%

See also Appendix D for a listing of this company's products and services.

BLACK & DECKER MANUFACTURING COMPANY

Black & Decker dominates the power tool market worldwide. In 1984 it bought General Electric's small-appliance division, and has undertaken a drive to become a major player in this product market as well.

To cut its costs in 1985, the company announced several large plant closings and plans to move some manufacturing operations overseas. When it closed a unionized GE toaster-manufacturing plant in Allentown, Pennsylvania, union workers charged the company with union-busting, but Black & Decker asserted this plant closing, along with its others, was part of overall restructuring.

With plants in 14 countries and sales operations in 50, it is not surprising to find B&D in South Africa. It employs approximately 75 workers there. In 1984 the company was classed as a nonsignatory of the Sullivan Principles because it refused to pay the fee for monitoring the implementation of the principles. In 1985 the company reversed this position and is now a signatory. In early 1987, the company announced plans to look for a buyer for its South African operations.

As of 1985, the firm was a member of the Baltimore Five-Percent Club, meaning that it was currently giving at least 1 percent of its pre-tax earnings to charitable causes, and has pledged to raise this figure to 5 percent within three years. We could locate no firm figures on its cash giving.

The company did not respond to CEP's questionnaires.

BLACK & DECKER MANUFACTURING COMPANY											
	Women		Minorities				Contracts		PAC Contributions		
% to Charity	Directors	Officers	Directors	Officers	Social Disclosure	Sullivan Rating	% Military	Nuclear Weapons–Related	Dollar Amount	% to Republicans	% to Democrats
?	1	1	0	?	F	V	None	None	None		

? = No information available
See also Appendix D for a listing of this company's products and services.

DYNAMICS CORPORATION OF AMERICA

This Connecticut-based conglomerate manufactures industrial air-conditioning equipment, agricultural machinery, electronics equipment, and generators, as well as Waring kitchen appliances.

Some of its electronics work has military applications, and CEP found $1.3 million in prime contracts listed by the Department of Defense in 1984, although we have not rated the company here as a major military contractor.

The company did not respond to CEP's questionnaires, and we could find no indications of social initiatives on its part.

DYNAMICS CORPORATION OF AMERICA											
	Women		Minorities				Contracts		PAC Contributions		
% to Charity	Directors	Officers	Directors	Officers	Social Disclosure	Sullivan Rating	% Military	Nuclear Weapons–Related	Dollar Amount	% to Republicans	% to Democrats
?	0	0	0	0	F	None	Negligible	None	None		

? = No information available
See also Appendix D for a listing of this company's products and services.

EASTMAN KODAK COMPANY

At the heart of the economic life of Rochester, New York, Eastman Kodak has had a long record of generosity to its employees, strongly supported various minority economic development programs, and maintained a moderate record on charitable contributions. Weak sales in the face of stiff competition forced Kodak cutbacks in its work force in 1985 and 1986, undermining somewhat its positive record in the community. Some church groups have lately questioned the company's ethical criteria for accepting "Star Wars" research work.

Kodak's generous employee benefits have won praise. These benefits include flextime and job-sharing options, full reimbursement for work-related tuition expenses (the company reimbursed $2.2 million under this program in 1982), and an annual profit-sharing wage dividend, which averaged $3,000 for each employee in 1983. The company's employee suggestion plan for cost-saving ideas disbursed over $1.5 million annually in the early 1980s. In 1984 Eastman Kodak created a "venture panel" to fund employee suggestions for new product development. But James O'Toole, in *Vanguard Management*, has criticized Kodak's "generous paternalism," asserting that it "creates a sense of destructive psychological dependency."

Eastman Kodak experienced confrontations between corporate management and civil rights activists demanding more jobs for minorities in its annual meetings in the mid-1960s, following summer race riots in Rochester. Since that time the company has developed a comprehensive program supporting minority-owned businesses. Its purchasing from minority-owned firms stood at $11.5 million in 1985, a $3.5 million increase over 1984. It processed $22.5 million in tax payments through minority-owned banks in 1984, and had a $200,000 operating account with one. It has invested $300,000 in the local Ibero American Investors venture capital fund for minority busi-

EASTMAN KODAK COMPANY											
	Women		Minorities				Contracts		PAC Contributions		
% to Charity	Directors	Officers	Directors	Officers	Social Disclosure	Sullivan Rating	% Military	Nuclear Weapons–Related	Dollar Amount	% to Republicans	% to Democrats
1.0%	1	0	1	1	A	I	1.6%	None	$51,650	91%	9%

See also Appendix D for a listing of this company's products and services.

nesses. Kodak annually supports the Rochester Business Opportunities Corporation (RBOC), which was founded in 1968 as a financial and technical support organization for fledgling minority-owned enterprises. One of Kodak's executives serves as an officer of RBOC. In 1984, of Kodak's officials and managers, 6.7% were women and 4.2% minorities.

Eastman Kodak's founder, George Eastman, was known as a major philanthropist. The company has a fairly strong, though apparently traditional, giving program, with $15.6 million disbursed in 1985 or 1.0 percent of pre-tax earnings. Its gifts were focused primarily on higher education (49 percent in 1984), with an emphasis on scientific scholarships. An additional 28 percent went to health and human services, 13 percent to cultural groups, and 7 percent to civic and community causes. Kodak's strong support for minority scholarships and schools totaled $690,000 in 1982.

In 1985 Kodak participated in a task force that recommended the creation of a "Rochester Alliance" to improve the city's public schools. (See the Clorox profile for a further discussion of a similar alliance.)

The company encourages volunteering by executives to the United Way (11 in 1984), and publicizes volunteering opportunities with nonprofit organizations in its company newspaper.

Department of Defense contracts for Eastman Kodak totaled $163 million in 1985 (holding steady from $166 million in 1984), making it the ninety-third-largest prime contractor for the Department of Defense that year. Recently, some church groups have been especially concerned about the company's involvement in research for the "Star Wars" space missile defense system. The company refused church groups' requests to disclose the nature of this military work in 1984. (According to a study by the Council on Economic Priorities, this work is related to optical mirrors and laser technology.) In 1985 Kodak opposed a shareholder resolution asking for the establishment of a committee to evaluate the ethical considerations surrounding military contracts.

Kodak's photographic sales operation in South Africa employs 650 workers. The company consistently received the highest rating for compliance with the Sullivan Principles from 1981 through 1985. It announced plans to sell its operations there in 1986.

The company responded to CEP's questionnaires.

GENERAL ELECTRIC COMPANY

This huge manufacturing conglomerate has a particularly strong record for fair hiring practices within the company, and for promoting minority education programs. Of the consumer products companies covered in this book, it is the largest military contractor, as well as the most heavily involved in nuclear arms and nuclear power plant manufacturing. GE was the fourth-largest military contractor in the United States in 1985. In 1986 it acquired RCA, another large consumer products company and defense contractor. (See the RCA profile.)

The career track most likely to lead to top management positions at General Electric is engineering, a fact that has led the company to create one of its more interesting social initiatives: PIMEG (Program to Increase Minority Engineering Graduates).

Most high-technology companies today support programs for increasing the numbers of minority members and women in engineering, but General Electric was among the first to offer assistance to these groups so they might improve opportunities to enter the field. GE sought to hire more minority engineers in the late 1960s as one means of ultimately increasing minority representation in its highest ranks. But the company was soon confronted with the fact that less than 1 percent of graduating engineers were minorities. (By 1984, just over 5 percent of graduating engineers were black, Hispanic or Native American, according to GE.) GE's initial studies traced the problem to secondary schools, where little or no effort was made to channel minority students into engineering careers.

To address this shortage, GE began a comprehensive program, working with others and on its own. Internally, GE formally initiated PIMEG in 1972. The company's facilities across the nation were encouraged to assist local school systems in promoting engineering as a viable career for minorities. GE began summer job-training programs for minorities, and funded minority scholarships at regional colleges and universities. The GE Foundation also began funding an increasing number of minority scholarships directly, and supporting the national and regional organizations that were springing up around the country to pursue these same goals.

In 1974, GE, along with several other corporations, was instrumental in founding the National Action Council for Minorities in Engineering (NACME). NACME now comprises both an association of several hundred corporate CEOs committed to promoting engineering as a minority career, and a separate nonprofit organization with its own scholarship fund. (NACME gave over $2 million in scholarships to new and continuing minority engineering students in 1980.) GE's chief executive officer was the first to head NACME.

PIMEG was in many ways a natural outgrowth of GE's long interest in career counseling and in promoting science education at a secondary-school level. GE's efforts in these areas continue with its Educators in Industry program, which brings secondary-school guidance counselors and teachers to the workplace to see which educational skills are most useful for various careers. GE funds this program in cities where the company has plants.

In fact, education is very much a part of GE's corporate culture. According to *The 100 Best Companies to Work for in America*, as many as 50 percent of GE employees are in a company-funded job or career education program at any given time.

These programs seem to have benefited women and minority employees. *Savvy* magazine ranked the company as one of the best for women workers in 1983 and *Black Enterprise* magazine included the company among 25 best workplaces for blacks in 1986. In 1985, 6.3 percent of the company's officials and managers were women (up from 5.7 percent the previous year), and 4.9 percent were minorities (up from 4.8 percent in 1984). The company's minority purchasing program was $50.5 million in 1984, down from $60.8 million in 1983. (In 1978, however, GE settled a job discrimination suit brought by the U.S. Equal Employment Opportunity Commission for $32 million. Of this amount, $7 million went for back pay to women and minorities, $10 million for job training, and $11 million for special promotion incentive bonuses.)

GE's foundation strongly supports education, with donations of $7.6 million, or 48 percent of $15.8 million disbursed in 1984. Its wide variety of programs includes $2 million in matching employee gifts; $1 million for minorities in engineering and for black colleges; $1.6 million for young faculty in the sciences and engineering; $1 million for business studies; and $850,000 to improve the teaching of mathematics and science at pre-college levels. Another 28 percent of foundation giving ($4.4 million) went to united fund

GENERAL ELECTRIC COMPANY											
	Women		Minorities				Contracts		PAC Contributions		
% to Charity	Directors	Officers	Directors	Officers	Social Disclosure	Sullivan Rating	% Military	Nuclear Weapons–Related	Dollar Amount	% to Republicans	% to Democrats
1.1%	2	1	1	1	A	None	16.2%	Yes	$226,550	47%	53%

See also Appendix D for a listing of this company's products and services.

Around the House

drives in 1984. The company's full giving program in 1984 totaled $31.2 million, or a fairly strong 1.1 percent of pre-tax earnings.

General Electric was the fourth-largest military contractor in the country in 1985, with $5.9 billion in contracts (up from $4.5 billion in 1984), as well as a major manufacturer of nuclear power plants. Aircraft engines are the backbone of its military work, although it also performs substantial work on nuclear propulsion systems for the Navy and the MX missile's reentry vehicle. According to the Investor Responsibility Research Center, $2.2 billion of GE's $4.5 billion in 1983 military contracts were for work on nuclear-related weapons systems. For the Department of Defense, GE also manages the plant in Pinellas, Florida, at which nuclear warheads are manufactured. It was also the fourth-largest contractor for military research and development in 1985.

General Electric is a major producer of nuclear power plants in the United States and abroad. For many years the company has received shareholder resolutions questioning the moral and economic wisdom of its heavy dependence on nuclear contracting. In 1980, Rev. Daniel Berrigan and seven other peace activists broke into the company's facility in King of Prussia, Pennsylvania, and damaged several nuclear missile nose cones. They were prosecuted by the state and convicted for this act of civil disobedience for which they faced a prison term of three to ten years. Their convictions were overturned in 1984. This decision, however, was appealed by the state and had not been resolved as of April 1986.

In May 1985, GE was fined approximately $1 million for defrauding the government on military and space contracts. It paid the fine in civil penalties after admitting guilt to overcharging the Pentagon by $800,000 on Minuteman missile contracts.

The company's South African operations employed 850 workers, and had consistently received the second-highest "making progress" rating for compliance with the Sullivan Principles from 1981 through 1985. In May 1985, a coalition of church groups singled out General Electric as one of twelve U.S. corporate "key investors in apartheid" because of the apparent strategic nature of that company's investments in South Africa. In 1986 GE sold its South African operations.

The company responded to CEP's questionnaires.

HOOVER COMPANY

Headquartered in North Canton, Ohio, Hoover has eight overseas manufacturing facilities. One of these is in South Africa, where it employs approximately 250 persons. Hoover consistently received the third-highest "needs to become more active" rating for compliance with the Sullivan Principles from 1982 through 1985, a lower rating than most U.S. corporations.

According to the Taft *Corporate Giving Directory*, Hoover's charitable contributions totaled more than $1.1 million in 1984, with giving concentrated locally in North Canton, supporting such projects as computer education in public schools and a medical foundation. The company had a loss in 1981, making comparison with pre-tax earnings impossible to calculate.

In late 1985, Hoover was bought out by Chicago Pacific Corporation, a holding company that has been overseeing the liquidation proceedings for the bankrupt Chicago, Rock Island and Pacific Railroad.

The company did not respond to CEP's questionnaires.

HOOVER COMPANY											
	Women		Minorities				Contracts		PAC Contributions		
% to Charity	Directors	Officers	Directors	Officers	Social Disclosure	Sullivan Rating	% Military	Nuclear Weapons–Related	Dollar Amount	% to Republicans	% to Democrats
*	0	0	?	?	F	IIIA	None	None	None		

* = See profile   ? = No information available
See also Appendix D for a listing of this company's products and services.

INTERNATIONAL BUSINESS MACHINE CORPORATION

IBM is one of the largest corporations in the world, and the most profitable, with $6.6 billion in after-tax profits in 1985. The legendary Thomas Watson led the company on its astonishing road to success in the early years of this century. It has fought charges of monopolistic and unfair marketing practices along the way, successfully defending itself in court.

The company has been aggressive in pursuing charitable giving, fair hiring and promotion practices, child-care, and other benefits for employees, and job training for the economically disadvantaged. These programs are among the largest and most progressive reported in this book. But at the same time the company is a major military contractor, and because of its sales of computers in South Africa was singled out by some church groups in 1985 as a "key investor in apartheid."

IBM's job training program for disadvantaged youth is one of the most comprehensive efforts by a U.S. corporation. It began in 1968 as a joint effort of the National Urban League, the Bank of America, and IBM's Los Angeles office, with a single training center for computer programmers and operators. During the 1970s, IBM offices in other cities, seeing the Los Angeles effort as a logical and appropriate social initiative for the company, established similar centers. By 1981, when there were approximately eight such training centers, IBM's upper management decided to make a major, formalized commitment to these centers, and by 1984, 57 were in operation around the country.

For each center, IBM selects as a partner a local community service organization such as the Hispanic SER — Jobs for Progress, or the Opportunities Industrialization Centers. IBM then undertakes the renovations necessary to create the center, provides computer and office equipment, and lends training personnel. No cash subsidies are provided by IBM, and the understanding is that after three years the center should be economically self-sufficient. The centers can keep their IBM equipment providing they maintain the original goals of the program and place at least 80 percent of their graduates. On the average, 100 to 125 students graduate from each of these centers annually; there were 4,000 graduates in 1985, bringing the total number since the program began to 14,000. In 1984 IBM began a supplemental youth work/study summer session through these same centers. (In addition, IBM supports 32 training projects serving the handicapped around the country. Begun in 1974, this program has trained more than 1,700 persons.)

Employee benefits at IBM are reputedly among the best in the country. Especially noteworthy is a child-care information and referral service open to IBM employees throughout the country. Free to all 240,000 IBM workers, this referral system is also set up to strengthen overall local child-care networks.

IBM pays $1,750 toward adoption expenses for employees, and up to $50,000 for the care of handicapped children.

One of the more dramatic potential benefits in working for IBM comes from its employee suggestion program, which gave out $18 million in 1985 for cost-saving ideas. The maximum award for an individual is $150,000. But James O'Toole, writing in 1985 in *Vanguard Management*, asserts that IBM "has probably done the *least* of all major U.S. manufacturers to implement genuine worker participation."

The company's commitments to minority economic development are substantial. Its purchasing program did more than $150 million in business with minority-owned companies in 1985, up from $133 million in 1984, and obtained $83 million in goods and services from women-owned firms, up from $74 million the previous year. Its minority banking program apparently relies only on tax deposits ($600 million in 1984), although this is not, in CEP's opinion, the most useful form of patronage for minority banks. The company underwrites a portion of its group life insurance with minority-owned firms, and has invested in minority-oriented venture capital companies in New York and Dallas.

As of 1985, IBM had a substantial percentage of women and minorities among its officials and managers (16.2 percent and 10.9 percent, respectively), up from 9.8 percent and 9.5 percent in 1981. IBM appointed a woman vice president in 1985. It told CEP that it had 483 women and 280 blacks in the top 20 percent of its 32,000 officials and managers, up 30 percent and 26 percent from 1984, respectively. In 1986, *Black Enterprise* magazine ranked it among the 25 best places for blacks to work.

IBM's charitable cash contributions in 1985 were approximately $113 million, with additional donations of $76 million in products and services. Its $90 million in 1984 cash gifts made it the most generous corporate giver among companies in this book. Of this amount, $59 million went to educational insti-

INTERNATIONAL BUSINESS MACHINES CORPORATION											
	Women		Minorities				Contracts		PAC Contributions		
% to Charity	Directors	Officers	Directors	Officers	Social Disclosure	Sullivan Rating	% Military	Nuclear Weapons– Related	Dollar Amount	% to Republicans	% to Democrats
1.2%	1	1	1	0	A	I	3.4%	Yes	None		

See also Appendix D for a listing of this company's products and services.

tutions, much in support of computer education and research. For example, the company has given $50 million in grants and equipment to 22 universities to promote "excellence in manufacturing systems engineering education." IBM has given out 50 two-year grants ($30,000 each year) to subsidize untenured computer science professors at 25 universities. Few other details on recipients of IBM's extensive giving program were available.

IBM will contribute two dollars for each employee dollar contributed to most nonprofit organizations, up to $5,000 per organization. Its Fund for Community Service gave out $3.9 million in small grants in 1984 to organizations with which its workers were volunteering. The company has also had a social service "leave" program since 1971. Through 1984, 800 IBM employees had taken full or partial leave at full pay to work with various nonprofit, community-oriented groups.

IBM was the fifteenth-largest military contractor in 1985, with $1.8 billion in prime contracts, up from $1.6 billion in 1984. It was also the seventh-largest contractor for military research and development work in 1985. Its computers and electronics systems are used by all branches of the military. Its work includes radar, sonar, communications, and electronic warfare systems. According to figures compiled by the Investor Responsibility Research Center, $923 million of IBM's total $1.42 billion in military contracts in 1983 went toward weapons systems either primarily or secondarily supporting U.S. nuclear fighting capability.

IBM has had operations in South Africa since 1952. It was the ninth-largest U.S. employer there in 1986, with about 1,500 employees, approximately 1,150 of whom are white. Its operations are essentially in marketing. In 1985 a coalition of 50 church groups labeled IBM one of the twelve U.S. corporate "key investors in apartheid" because of its strong role in the South African computer market and its refusal to stop sales to certain South African government agencies, although the company has a policy of no sales to the military and police or to government agencies administering apartheid laws.

In a March 1985 op-ed piece in the *New York Times,* the company's CEO, John F. Akers, pointed out that IBM could leave South Africa with "very little financial sacrifice," but said the company is convinced that "the right thing to do is to remain and redouble our efforts to advance social equality." IBM has consistently received the highest rating for compliance with the Sullivan Principles. Among the benefits it has provided, the company cites contributions of approximately $10 million toward black education projects from 1974 to 1984. In late 1986, IBM announced plans to withdraw from South Africa.

The company responded to CEP's questionnaires.

LITTON INDUSTRIES, INC.

Headquartered in Beverly Hills, California, this conglomerate has moved increasingly into the military, geophysical-exploration, and industrial-automation businesses, while selling off its interests in office furnishings, paper supplies, and industrial tools. It derives more than half its sales from Department of Defense contracts, primarily related to nuclear-capable weapons systems. In the early 1980s, Litton had an extended face-off with unions over its labor practices. We could locate little information on any social initiatives.

In the early 1980s, labor organizations began a highly publicized campaign aimed at Litton that centered around a unionizing dispute at a South Dakota microwave oven plant. Unions accused the company of a consistent pattern of union busting throughout its subsidiaries. This campaign involved petitioning the National Labor Relations Board to treat all Litton subsidiaries as a single employer; demonstrating at colleges where Litton directors were on the faculty; and lobbying for the "Litton Law," which would have forced the company to conform with labor laws or lose defense contracts. Litton defended itself by claiming that its labor practices were set at the subsidiary or division level, not by the parent company.

In 1983 the company proposed a joint committee, consisting of two labor representatives, two Litton representatives, and a neutral chairperson, to study its labor situation. On the committee's recommendations, Litton subsequently renegotiated its contract with unions at its South Dakota microwave oven plant.

Litton was the tenth-largest Department of Defense contractor in 1984, with over $2.4 billion in awards accounting for 53 percent of its sales. In 1985 it dropped to nineteenth, with $1.5 billion in military contracts. Much of its recent work has been for the Navy on nuclear-capable *Ticonderoga*-class

LITTON INDUSTRIES, INC.							Contracts		PAC Contributions		
	Women		Minorities								
% to Charity	Directors	Officers	Directors	Officers	Social Disclosure	Sullivan Rating	% Military	Nuclear Weapons–Related	Dollar Amount	% to Republicans	% to Democrats
0.1%	1	0	?	?	F	None	53.0%	Yes	$227,500	78%	22%

? = No information available
See also Appendix D for a listing of this company's products and services.

guided-missile cruisers, and on renovation of the battleship *Iowa*. Other Litton work has included inertial navigation and guidance systems, communications systems, and electronic warfare work. These various components are used in missiles, artillery, and aircraft. According to the Investor Responsibility Research Center, $1.5 billion of the company's $2 billion military contracts in 1983 were for work on nuclear-related weapons systems.

In July 1986, Litton agreed to pay $15 million in penalties and restitution to the Department of Defense. It had pleaded guilty to defrauding the Pentagon of $6.3 million in its military work at that time.

Corporate Foundation Profiles reports $734,000 in charitable contributions from Litton's foundation in 1984, representing 0.1 percent of the company's pre-tax earnings. Approximately 30 percent of this amount went to higher education. This figure does not include direct corporate giving and may understate the company's total program.

The company did not respond to CEP's questionnaires.

MAGIC CHEF, INC.

Magic Chef is the fourth-largest appliance manufacturer in the United States, behind General Electric, Whirlpool, and White Consolidated (now owned by the Swedish company Electrolux). Like White Consolidated, Magic Chef has attained this position by acquiring unprofitable appliance lines from other companies (e.g., Admiral from Rockwell International and Norge from Fedders Corporation) and restoring them to profitability.

In 1983 Magic Chef fought an unusually bitter strike with the International Molders and Allied Workers Union at its Cleveland, Tennessee, plant. When the union struck for higher pay, the company hired non-union workers. A fierce battle raged for several months, with accusations of violence by both sides; the union ultimately lost. In response to anti-union charges at the time, the company asserted that it had good relations with its unions at four other plants.

The company's foundation gave $48,000 in 1983, but this figure does not include direct corporate giving and may understate its total program.

In early 1986, Maytag announced that it would acquire Magic Chef.

The company did not respond to CEP's questionnaires.

MAGIC CHEF, INC.											
	Women		Minorities				Contracts		PAC Contributions		
% to Charity	Directors	Officers	Directors	Officers	Social Disclosure	Sullivan Rating	% Military	Nuclear Weapons– Related	Dollar Amount	% to Republicans	% to Democrats
0.3%	0	0	?	?	F	None	None	None	$25,700	100%	0%

? = No information available
See also Appendix D for a listing of this company's products and services.

MAYTAG COMPANY

In 1984 Maytag held its annual meeting in the Newton, Iowa, High School Performance Center. The company's relationship with the small farm community in which it is headquartered is much like a mutual admiration society. That holds true for its relations with employees as well. Represented by the United Auto Workers, Maytag workers often describe themselves as "Maytaggers," proud to share the commitment to quality that has earned Maytag a reputation for making some of the most durable machines on the market. The company pays premium wages in the area and within the industry, and its benefit packages are among the most attractive.

One of the reasons for the company's good relations with its unions, in an industry frequently marked by labor problems, may be its long-time commitment to employee participation and communication. While other companies discovered "quality circles" in the 1980s, Maytag began its similar Work Simplification program back in 1947. It consists of an employees' idea plan, which pays up to $7,500 dollars for cost-saving ideas from nonsupervisory staff, and a training program for supervisors in productivity improvement.

The Maytag foundation gave a moderate $402,000 in 1984, or 0.7 percent of pre-tax earnings. The company gave an additional $160,000 directly. Of its foundation's gifts, 59 percent went to education (including $118,000 in college scholarships for employees' children, $31,000 in vocational school scholarships, and $29,000 in matching contributions to higher education) and 9 percent to the United Way. Of its $180,000 in additional contributions, $46,000 went to the Des Moines Symphony Orchestra, $10,000 to the Iowa National Heritage Foundation, and $20,000 each to the Living History Farms Foundation and the Iowa Historical Museum.

MAYTAG COMPANY											
	Women		Minorities				Contracts		PAC Contributions		
% to Charity	Directors	Officers	Directors	Officers	Social Disclosure	Sullivan Rating	% Military	Nuclear Weapons–Related	Dollar Amount	% to Republicans	% to Democrats
0.7%	0	0	0	0	A	None	None	None	$27,250	77%	23%

See also Appendix D for a listing of this company's products and services.

The company reports that it subcontracts work to women-owned businesses, but does not have much opportunity to do business with minority-owned firms because of the scarcity of such businesses in its region.

In early 1986 Maytag announced that it would acquire Magic Chef. (See the Magic Chef profile.)

The company responded to CEP's questionnaires.

POLAROID CORPORATION

Founded and built by independent inventor Edwin Land, Polaroid's strong commitment to social programs and ideas has a twenty-year history. Whether it concerns involvement in South Africa, employee relations, charitable giving, or job training for youth, Polaroid's initiatives have been imaginative, innovative, and forceful. The company, which produces cameras, film, and other photographic equipment, is headquartered in Cambridge, Massachusetts.

The first U.S. company to take a public stand on sales of its products to the South African government, Polaroid initially considered discontinuing sales in that country through its South African distributor in 1971; but rather than withdraw at that time, it required that its distributor refrain from sales to the government and military, and that it improve the working conditions for its black employees. Then, in 1977, the company discovered that its equipment was being sold secretly to the government by the distributor. Despite praise for the improvement in employment practices that the distributor had implemented there, the company chose to formally withdraw.

At home, Polaroid's employment policies have been exceptional in everything from benefits to severance pay. When the company had to reduce its work force in the early 1980s in the face of hard financial times, the incentives it offered for retirement were remarkable — up to 30 months' full pay. The company offers an Employee Stock Ownership Plan and two profit-sharing plans. It is also one of the few companies in the country to directly subsidize its employees' child-care expenses. It will reimburse 20 to 80 percent of these costs, on a sliding scale for workers with salaries under $25,000. About 100 employees participate per year. (Most other companies that provide reimbursement do so through a "flexible benefit" program in which child-care is one of several options.)

Polaroid prides itself on its generous support of education for its workers through its Tuition Assistance Program (100 percent reimbursement) as well as its own numerous training courses.

The company was a supporter of workers' "right-to-know" laws in Massachusetts before they were made state law in 1984. These require that workers be informed of any toxic chemicals being used in the workplace, and of any potential dangers associated with them.

In 1968 Polaroid created a wholly owned subsidiary, Inner City, which was both a manufacturing facility and a youth job training center. Inner City remains highly unusual in that it is a self-sustaining, for-profit operation. Located in the Roxbury section of Boston, Inner City serves the unemployed, the underemployed, and the poor, providing work and training in five- to six-month cycles. Employees are given basic job training for the first six weeks in the manufacturing of various goods sold to Polaroid and other companies. In the second phase of the program, trainees are required to attend (on their own time) a series of seminars and counseling sessions given by Polaroid workers and other professional staff. Inner City then arranges job interviews for the trainees. The program is a relatively small one — only about 100 persons participate each year. But the company considers it highly successful, because 70 percent of those it places stay at their first job for at least a year.

The company's commitment to other minority economic development programs is moderate. It purchased $3.4 million in goods from minority vendors in 1984, and Inner City has an operating account with Boston's only minority-owned bank.

Polaroid's foundation is exceptional in several respects. Its grants are given out in a notably decentralized fashion. Decisions on grant applications are made by four committees of volunteer employees (about 50 persons altogether). Each committee specializes in a given area (community, cultural, education, and one for the city of New Bedford). One result is that the company gives a high percentage of its grants in small amounts to local community and arts organizations. It will also make short-term interest-free loans. Of its total $1.9 million given in 1984, an impressive 2.4 percent of pre-tax earnings, 43 percent went to social and human services organizations, 39 percent to education, and 14 percent to the arts. Traditional sources still received substantial support ($280,000 to the United Way, $58,000 to MIT). But much of its funding went out in grants of $250 to $5,000 to local Massachusetts organizations such as La Alianza Hispanica (Roxbury), the National Consumer Law Center (Boston), the Somerville Media Action Project (Somerville), and Aid to Incarcerated Mothers (Boston). The company matches two dollars for each employee dollar donated to most nonprofit groups, up to $500. It also has a Volunteers Skill Bank to pair employees with local nonprofit organizations.

The company responded to CEP's questionnaires.

POLAROID CORPORATION											
	Women		Minorities				Contracts		PAC Contributions		
% to Charity	Directors	Officers	Directors	Officers	Social Disclosure	Sullivan Rating	% Military	Nuclear Weapons–Related	Dollar Amount	% to Republicans	% to Democrats
2.4%	1	0	2	0	A	None	None	None	None		

See also Appendix D for a listing of this company's products and services.

RAYTHEON COMPANY

This Massachusetts-based corporation manufactures missiles. Awards from the Department of Defense in 1985, totaling $3.0 billion, made it the ninth-largest military contractor that year. According to the Investor Responsibility Research Center, of $2.7 billion in 1983 military contracts, $268 million was for work on nuclear-related systems, including the ballistic missile early warning system and the Trident missile guidance system. Its major military work consists of the Patriot and Hawk air-defense missile systems, Sparrow and Sidewinder air-to-air missiles, and sonar, radar, and electronic warfare countermeasures.

Raytheon's United Engineers and Constructors subsidiary is involved in the design and engineering of nuclear power plants.

In 1965 Raytheon acquired the Amana Corporation, an Iowa-based appliance manufacturer. For nearly thirty years Amana was primarily owned by the Amana Society, which in turn was owned by the residents of the seven communal Amana villages, descendants of the original members of the Amana religious sect who emigrated from Germany in the mid-1800s. Their communal corporation, the Amana Society, and their business activities (ranging from woolen mills and furniture manufacturing to refrigeration) exemplified a kind of corporate commitment to employees, consumers, and the community. The society's founding credo stated that "each member is to bear his burden, according to his ability, for the common good of the community." The company's chairman, George C. Foerstner, has been known to refuse awards because when "people tell you how great you are . . . you start believing it."

Amana was exceptional among large, twentieth-century American corporations in its cooperative-ownership and operation. While the Amana Society

RAYTHEON COMPANY											
	Women		Minorities				Contracts		PAC Contributions		
% to Charity	Directors	Officers	Directors	Officers	Social Disclosure	Sullivan Rating	% Military	Nuclear Weapons– Related	Dollar Amount	% to Republicans	% to Democrats
0.8%	0	0	?	?	F	IIB/ IIIA	51.6%	Yes	$138,125	50%	50%

? = No information available
See also Appendix D for a listing of this company's products and services.

Appliance Companies 367

continues today, the company has lost some of its unique qualities in becoming part of a larger conglomerate.

Raytheon was one of four corporate founding members of the New England Minority Purchasing Council in 1973 (along with Gillette, the Norton Company, and Digital), and, according to Michael J. Merenda in *Research in Corporate Social Performance and Policy*, had a thoroughly institutionalized minority vendor program by 1978.

The company phased out its charitable foundation in recent years, but makes moderate contributions directly. Its 1983 giving totaled $4.5 million, including $1 million from subsidiaries for a moderate 0.8 percent of pre-tax earnings. Approximately one-third went to united fund drives, one-third to education (including matching employee gifts), and the remainder to health, social services, and the arts.

Raytheon's two subsidiaries in South Africa employ 74 persons and received the second- and third-highest rating for compliance with the Sullivan Principles in 1985.

The company did not respond to CEP's questionnaires.

RCA CORPORATION

Headquartered in New York City, RCA is among companies pioneering corporate social responsibility. Information provided for this book shows a solid effort on minority economic development. However, with electronics and communications at the heart of its business, RCA is also involved in defense contracting. In 1986 RCA merged with GE. (See the General Electric profile.)

RCA was the twenty-third-largest military prime contractor in 1985, with $1.3 billion in military business (up from $1.1 billion in 1984). The bulk of this work is on the Navy's Aegis shipboard fire-control and air defense system. RCA also makes meteorological satellites for military as well as for civilian customers, electronics, and radar. According to the Investor Responsibility Research Center, approximately $609 million of the company's $1.2 billion military work was on nuclear-related weapons systems, the bulk of this going toward the Aegis air defense system being built for the *Ticonderoga*-class guided-missile cruisers.

Vice president for corporate relations Samuel Convissor was among the earliest advocates of corporate social responsibility. RCA has a reputation as a company supportive of community development projects and organizations. Along with Campbell Soup, it has supported revitalization efforts in Camden, New Jersey. In 1985 it made a commitment to deposit $100,000 in community-oriented credit unions. Although not a large sum, it is unusual in that few companies have made deposits with credit unions, concentrating instead on banks. Of this amount, $50,000 will go to two credit unions in Indianapolis, where the company has a plant. The remaining $50,000 is pledged to the Community Development Central Credit Union (CDCCU), established by the National Federation of Community Development Credit Unions. CDCCU will serve as a central source of capital for credit unions that make community

RCA CORPORATION											
	Women		Minorities				Contracts		PAC Contributions		
% to Charity	Directors	Officers	Directors	Officers	Social Disclosure	Sullivan Rating	% Military	Nuclear Weapons–Related	Dollar Amount	% to Republicans	% to Democrats
1.9%	1	0	1	0	A	None	11.0%	Yes	None		

See also Appendix D for a listing of this company's products and services.

economic revitalization a priority. RCA reports that it has a minority banking program and uses minority-owned insurance companies, but gave no details.

The company has a long-standing commitment to minority purchasing; in 1984 it placed $38.9 million of its subcontracted work with minority vendors. This figure compares favorably with other companies in RCA's industry. For example, the much larger United Technologies — with $14.8 billion in 1983 sales, compared to RCA's $8.9 billion — purchased approximately the same amount from minority suppliers that year.

Since 1975 the company has had a Minorities in Engineering Program active at thirteen plants. It works with 250 to 300 minority high school students each year, selecting those with aptitudes appropriate to an engineering career, but who have not made a final commitment. The company then brings them to its plants for ten to twelve half-days to gain hands-on engineering experience. In 1980 the firm surveyed 536 previous participants, and found that about half planned or were embarked on engineering or physical science careers.

RCA reports that 25 out of the company's 557 highest officers are women, and that women occupied 19.1 percent of its combined managers and professionals categories in 1984. The company did not provide a figure for minorities either in its managers or professionals category, but reported 17 minorities among its top 557 officers. Its work force is approximately 45 percent unionized.

RCA disbursed $5.5 million in 1985 contributions, a strong 1.9 percent of pre-tax earnings. The company has a Volunteer Incentive Program that provides small grants to nonprofits with which its employees volunteer.

The company responded to CEP's questionnaires.

SCM CORPORATION

SCM, a diverse chemical, paper, and consumer product corporation, donated $600,000 in charitable gifts in 1984, or 1.2 percent of pre-tax income. According to the Taft *Corporate Giving Directory*, approximately 40 percent of this amount went to education.

After a lengthy takeover battle, SCM was acquired in early 1986 by the British conglomerate Hanson Trust PLC. As of 1984, Hanson had operations in South Africa employing approximately 1,800 persons, according to the Investor Responsibility Research Center. Because it is a British company, Hanson does not receive a Sullivan rating.

SCM did not respond to CEP's questionnaires.

SCM CORPORATION											
	Women		Minorities				Contracts		PAC Contributions		
% to Charity	Directors	Officers	Directors	Officers	Social Disclosure	Sullivan Rating	% Military	Nuclear Weapons–Related	Dollar Amount	% to Republicans	% to Democrats
1.2%	0	0	?	?	F	None	None	None	$2,200	77%	23%

? = No information available
See also Appendix D for a listing of this company's products and services.

SCOVILL INC.

This is one of the oldest companies in America, founded in 1802 in Waterbury, Connecticut, where it has kept its headquarters, although it closed its major manufacturing operations there some time ago. Scovill, which started out in the brass business, is now a diverse worldwide corporation, making home appliances, car parts, locks, zippers, and door chimes. It has apparently retained a commitment to its plant communities and employees, according to the information we were able to obtain.

Scovill has made low-cost loans for housing revitalization projects, helped organize a neighborhood low-cost housing service in Waterbury, and provided seed capital for a minority-owned bank. It encourages volunteering by employees on company time to help in community activities, and has loaned an executive to help administer a job-training program.

The company reports that its charitable giving regularly exceeds 1 percent of pre-tax earnings, but did not provide specific dollar amounts. The Taft *Corporate Giving Directory* lists the company's foundation giving in 1983 at $346,000, or 0.7 percent of pre-tax earnings, by CEP's calculations. This foundation figure may understate the full company program.

The company states that it was among the first to establish pre-retirement and alcohol counseling programs for its workers. It provides guaranteed student loans, and has a savings plan matching employees' contributions on a 50 percent basis. It claims "good success" in promoting women and minorities, but does not make figures public on its hiring record.

Scovill's South African operation employs 130 workers in car-parts manufacturing. It told CEP that it adheres to the Sullivan Principles, although it is not a signatory "because of the detailed reporting that is required of even a

SCOVILL INC.											
	Women		Minorities				Contracts		PAC Contributions		
% to Charity	Directors	Officers	Directors	Officers	Social Disclosure	Sullivan Rating	% Military	Nuclear Weapons–Related	Dollar Amount	% to Republicans	% to Democrats
0.7%	0	0	?	?	C	Non-sig.	None	None	None		

? = No information available
See also Appendix D for a listing of this company's products and services.

small-sized operation like ours, and the fact that employment goals are not realistic if business turns down as ours has on occasion." The company sold its South African operations in 1986.

In 1985 the company was purchased by First City Investing, Inc., owned by the Belzbergs, Canadian investors. In late 1986, Scovill sold its Hamilton-Beach lines. (See addendum on page 500.)

The company responded in a limited way to CEP's questionnaires.

UNITED TECHNOLOGIES CORPORATION

United Technologies, with headquarters in Hartford, Connecticut, is one of the country's largest military contractors. Its recent social initiatives have centered around a rapidly increasing charitable giving program, which reached a strong 1.5 percent of pre-tax earnings in 1985. The company grew dramatically during the 1970s through a series of hard-fought takeovers under the leadership of Harry Gray, although in 1985 it was in the process of selling off some of these acquisitions.

United Technologies was the seventh-largest military contractor in the nation in 1985, with $3.9 billion in prime awards (up from $3.2 billion in 1984), and the sixteenth-largest contractor for military research and development. Its Pratt & Whitney division produces engines for the nuclear-capable F-15 and F-16 jet fighters. Its Sikorsky division makes transport helicopters for the Army and antisubmarine helicopters for the Navy and Air Force. The company manufactures propulsion systems for missiles, and computers for military satellite communications systems. According to the Investor Responsibility Research Center, $1.9 billion of the firm's $3.9 billion in military contracts in 1983 was nuclear-related, primarily for engines and components for nuclear-capable aircraft. United Technologies received slightly over $1 million in 1983 contracts for research on President Reagan's "Star Wars" missile defense system.

In 1983 the Air Force announced that it planned a $1.4 million deduction from new United Technologies contracts to compensate for overcharges on jet-aircraft engine work in 1977. The company confirmed that it too had found "errors" in its accounting, although it put the discrepancy at $1 million.

In February 1985 its Otis Elevator subsidiary agreed to pay $900,000 to the federal government in a settlement over allegations of overcharging on a mass transit project.

United Technologies' charitable giving program has increased from $3 million in 1977 to $12.8 million in 1985, a strong 1.5 percent of pre-tax earnings.

The company's support for the arts was a particularly strong 25 percent of its total 1984 charitable giving. Major grants went to Boston's Museum of Fine Arts, New York's Metropolitan Opera, and to the Museum of American Folk Arts, as well as to arts organizations in Hartford, Connecticut. Much of the rest of the company's giving goes to traditional recipients such as education (40 percent) and the United Way and health organizations (12 percent). Of its $207,000 grants to public policy organizations in 1984, $25,000 and $15,000 went to such conservative think tanks as the American Enterprise Institute and the Heritage Foundation, respectively. Additional support went to the more liberal Committee for Economic Development ($12,500), and $5,000 went to the Ethics Resource Center, which develops codes of ethics and helps integrate them into corporate management.

Its matching gifts program contributed two dollars for every employee dollar donated to education and cultural organizations, totaling an impressive $2.4 million in 1984.

The company purchased a strong $80 million from minority vendors in 1984, up sharply from $39 million in 1983. But it has not supported other minority economic development efforts, such as banking.

The company told CEP that it "considers itself one of the forerunners in the Equal Employment Opportunity movement" and that in the years prior to the 1960s, United Aircraft (United Technologies' forerunner) was one of the first ten employers to voluntarily commit itself to fair hiring practices. But it declined to make available to CEP Equal Employment Opportunity data by job category, although it did report one woman and two minorities among its top 52 officers.

In the early 1980s the company was involved in a highly publicized dispute with the city of Yonkers, New York, over the closing of one of its plants. At that time its Otis Elevator subsidiary closed a facility it had built on land Yonkers had purchased, cleared, and then sold to the company during the 1970s. The mayor of Yonkers, Angelo Martinelli, angered that the city had spent $14 million on redeveloping the land for Otis, demanded compensation from the company. The company would not pay the city, asserting that it had bought the land from the city at fair market value, spent $10 million building its plant, and then, through no fault of its own, the parts which the plant manufactured had become obsolete. The city sued the company but, through mid-1986, had been unsuccessful in the courts.

Otis Elevator employs approximately 1,000 persons in South Africa, and received the second-highest "making progress" rating for compliance with the Sullivan Principles in 1985. United Technologies' Carrier Corporation subsid-

UNITED TECHNOLOGIES CORPORATION											
	Women		Minorities				Contracts		PAC Contributions		
% to Charity	Directors	Officers	Directors	Officers	Social Disclosure	Sullivan Rating	% Military	Nuclear Weapons–Related	Dollar Amount	% to Republicans	% to Democrats
1.5%	2	1	0	2	A	IIA/IIIA	19.6%	Yes	$285,280	64%	36%

See also Appendix D for a listing of this company's products and services.

iary employs an additional 200 workers in air conditioning and refrigeration equipment plants. Its rating for compliance with the Sullivan Principles was a poor third-highest, "needs to become more active." Overall, approximately one-half of the company's South African employees are white.

The company responded to CEP's questionnaires.

WHIRLPOOL CORPORATION

A dominant force in the major appliance industry (along with General Electric), Whirlpool is particularly proud of energy-use reductions it has brought about since 1972 in refrigerators (down 44 percent), air conditioners (down 18 percent), and dishwashers (down 42 percent). In the 1960s and 1970s it embarked on several community-oriented social initiatives which have lapsed. Approximately 40 percent of its 1984 sales went to Sears, Roebuck for resale under Sear's Kenmore brand name.

In the late 1960s and 1970s, Whirlpool founded Highland House and Highland Development Center in its hometown of Benton Harbor, Michigan. Company-paid employees served as staff for this neighborhood revitalization agency, which initiated housing renovations, the development of day-care facilities, and various counseling services. Whirlpool also participated in the Area Resources Improvement Council (ARIC), a coalition of business executives in Benton Harbor concerned with economic revitalization. In addition, Whirlpool Opportunities Inc., a business organization employing the handicapped, was originally staffed and financed by Whirlpool, but now operates independently. Both Highland House and ARIC have been phased out.

Minority vendors accounted for $2.1 million in work subcontracted by Whirlpool in 1984, a level it plans to maintain in 1985. Of its officials and managers in 1984, 6.9 percent were women and 3.7 percent minorities.

The firm has a fairly strong traditional charitable giving program concentrating on its plants' localities. Of its $2.2 million in 1984 foundation gifts (plus $300,000 in additional direct giving by the company), 40 percent went to education, including $233,000 for scholarships for employees' children and $109,000 in matching gifts; 44 percent to health and human services, primarily for the United Way and hospitals; and 11 percent to the arts.

The company responded to CEP's questionnaires.

WHIRLPOOL CORPORATION								Contracts		PAC Contributions		
	Women		Minorities									
% to Charity	Directors	Officers	Directors	Officers	Social Disclosure	Sullivan Rating	% Military	Nuclear Weapons–Related	Dollar Amount	% to Republicans	% to Democrats
1.0%	0	0	0	0	A	None	None	None	$51,000	99%	1%

See also Appendix D for a listing of this company's products and services.

WHITE CONSOLIDATED INDUSTRIES, INC.

This Cleveland-based company entered the household appliance business in 1969; it is now number three in the industry, behind General Electric and Whirlpool. This rapid rise was achieved by purchasing failing but well-known brand name lines from other companies (Westinghouse, for example) and restoring them to profitability through drastic cost-cutting measures.

Its personnel cuts have reportedly been sometimes as high as 40 percent, when it first takes over a company. And *Business Week* described the firm in 1980 as one "never known for a go-easy labor relations policy," in part because of its tough negotiating with unions and willingness to "take" strikes.

Its foundation's charitable giving program, while only moderate, has seen a rapid increase from $400,000 in 1981 to an estimated $700,000 in 1984. It concentrates its giving on united fund drives (30 percent), and, according to the Taft *Corporate Giving Directory,* limits its contributions to education to 15 percent of its total, through matching employee gifts. It makes some grants to economic and urban development, safety, and environmental protection projects. This figure does not include direct corporate giving and may understate the company's total program.

In 1986 White was purchased by Electrolux, the giant Swedish consumer product company. Electrolux already owns the Tappan appliance company in the United States. (Confusingly enough, Electrolux vacuum cleaners are made in the United States by Sara Lee Corporation.)

White did not respond to CEP's questionnaires.

WHITE CONSOLIDATED INDUSTRIES, INC.											
	Women		Minorities				Contracts		PAC Contributions		
% to Charity	Directors	Officers	Directors	Officers	Social Disclosure	Sullivan Rating	% Military	Nuclear Weapons–Related	Dollar Amount	% to Republicans	% to Democrats
0.7%	0	0	?	?	F	None	None	None	$9,050	89%	11%

? = No information available
See also Appendix D for a listing of this company's products and services.

XEROX CORPORATION

Xerox has an impressive, long-standing commitment to social initiatives, with a particular emphasis on volunteering. Except for disputes with some church groups over its business dealings in South Africa, the company has stayed relatively clear of controversy.

One of the firm's more unusual programs is a social service "leave," open to all employees. Going significantly beyond programs elsewhere that loan executives to nonprofit groups, Xerox's is open to all workers. A committee made up of a cross section of company staff reviews applications for these leaves, which can range from one month to a year. Those on leave receive full salary, benefits, and vacations. The program, which began in 1971, had twelve Xerox employees on leave in 1984 and twelve in 1985. Work done recently includes job placement for newly released prisoners, legal aid for the poor, finding adequate shelter for the homeless, and training women in skills for nontraditional jobs.

In addition, Xerox's volunteer program is exceptionally active and strongly supported by the company. Officially inaugurated in 1974, nine years later the Xerox Community Involvement Program included 10,500 volunteers working in projects ranging from community theater to job training for the disadvantaged. The company sets yearly goals for involvement (11,000 volunteers in 1984), and supports projects with grants from its foundation. Also in 1983 the company gave out $512,000 under this program, averaging out to a strong $1,300 per project supported, and making it one of the most generous initiatives for supporting volunteers by companies profiled in this book.

Its charitable giving for 1984 totaled $10 million, a fairly substantial 1.2 percent of pre-tax earnings. Of its foundation's $8.5 million in grants, $3.4 million went to higher education, with diverse support of science, liberal arts, and minorities; $2.6 million to the United Way; $2 million to other community organizations; $800,000 to national affairs programs, with a $30,000 grant to the conservative American Enterprise Institute, balanced by a $25,000 grant to the more liberal Brookings Institute; and $800,000 to the arts and to cultural organizations.

The company's matching gift program has an unusual twist. To encourage substantial contributions, the company matches, dollar for dollar, gifts of up to $100, but between $100 and $1,000, the company will contribute $1.50 for each employee dollar donated.

Its support of minority economic development is strong, with $29.5 million in purchases from minority-owned vendors in 1984, and $17.4 million from women-owned businesses. It has strong representation by women and minorities among its top officials and managers (23 percent and 14.6 percent, respectively, in 1984), and one woman and one minority among its top 37 officers. In 1986, *Black Enterprise* magazine singled out Xerox as the best workplace in the country for blacks.

The company appears to have generally good relations with its workers, despite having to reduce its work force in recent years. (A number of age discrimination suits were filed in relation to these layoffs.) In the 1970s Xerox took the innovative step of setting up an "ombudsman" to handle worker complaints. Reportedly it also involves its workers in policy decisions regarding production and safety problems, run in conjunction with its unions. Approximately 11 percent of the company's work force is unionized.

Some church groups have waged an ongoing battle with Xerox over its South African business. The company employed 790 workers in that country as of 1986 (approximately two-thirds of whom were white), and consistently received the best rating for compliance with the Sullivan Principles from 1981 through 1985. But it opposed shareholder proposals that the company prohibit new investments there or refrain from sales to the South African military or police. In 1982 and 1983, two Xerox stock owners joined church groups in sponsoring these resolutions: the California teachers' and public service workers' pension funds, two of the largest pension funds in the country. Support for the resolutions totaled approximately 10 percent of shares voted in 1982 and 7 percent in 1983. Vernon Jordan, a member of Xerox's board of directors, publicly supported the ban on company sales to the South African military and police, despite management's opposition to a formal policy at that time. Since then, however, the company has decided not to sell to the police or military or government agencies enforcing apartheid.

Xerox has been a major military contractor in the past, but sold its primary military businesses to the Loral Corporation in 1983. By CEP's calculations, its arms-related contracts dropped to $7 million out of $106 million in total contracts with the Department of Defense in 1984.

The company responded to CEP's questionnaires.

XEROX CORPORATION											
	Women		Minorities				Contracts		PAC Contributions		
% to Charity	Directors	Officers	Directors	Officers	Social Disclosure	Sullivan Rating	% Military	Nuclear Weapons–Related	Dollar Amount	% to Republicans	% to Democrats
1.2%	1	1	1	1	A	I	Negligible	None	None		

See also Appendix D for a listing of this company's products and services.

ZENITH ELECTRONICS CORPORATION

Zenith's social commitments include programs for minority banking and purchasing; investment in a Minority Enterprise Small Business Investment Corporation (MESBIC); membership in Chicago United, a coalition of major corporations and minority-owned businesses devoted to social issues; a profit-sharing retirement plan for employees; and $430,000 in charitable contributions in 1984. (According to the Taft *Corporate Giving Directory,* Zenith's giving goal is 1 percent of pre-tax earnings. But this Chicago-based company, which has been facing recent financial struggles, did not provide information for this book, and an analysis of its initiatives was not possible.)

Since the early 1970s Zenith has led a long and still unresolved court battle against Japanese companies, which it asserts have been using unfair competitive practices in marketing televisions in the United States.

Over the past decade, hard financial times have provoked substantial lay-offs by this company, and in the early 1980s it experienced labor unrest at a Mexican plant.

The Department of Defense listed $36 million in arms-related contracts with Zenith in 1984.

The company did not respond to CEP's questionnaires.

ZENITH ELECTRONICS CORPORATION											
	Women		Minorities				Contracts		PAC Contributions		
% to Charity	Directors	Officers	Directors	Officers	Social Disclosure	Sullivan Rating	% Military	Nuclear Weapons–Related	Dollar Amount	% to Republicans	% to Democrats
*	0	0	1	0	F	None	2.2%	None	None		

? = No information available
See also Appendix D for a listing of this company's products and services.

HOUSEHOLD PRODUCT COMPANIES

CHARITABLE CONTRIBUTIONS AND COMMUNITY INVOLVEMENT

Dow Chemical has one of the most active charitable giving programs of any company in this book, with 3.0 percent of pre-tax earnings channeled to charity in 1985. It is directed primarily toward educational institutions. Clorox gave 1.4 percent of pre-tax earnings, with a major commitment to bettering its economically depressed headquarters city of Oakland, California, and a particular emphasis on minority youth programs. S. C. Johnson and Son has a reputation for generous philanthropy, with an annual commitment of 5 percent of pre-tax earnings to charity, the best record of any company in the book.

REPRESENTATION OF WOMEN AND MINORITIES IN MANAGEMENT

None of the household product companies in this section has at least one woman and minority both on its boards of directors and among top management. Four others — American Home Products, Greyhound, GTE, and 3M — have at least one woman both on their board and among top officers.

INVOLVEMENT IN SOUTH AFRICA

Presence in South Africa is not as much an issue in the household products industry as it is for the oil, auto, and pharmaceutical companies. Only one-third of the household products companies profiled in this chapter have South African operations. Kimberly-Clark is the only paper products company with investments in that country. 3M has received high grades on its compliance with the Sullivan Principles, but has been criticized by some church groups for its unwillingness to limit sales to the South African military and police.

POLITICAL ACTION COMMITTEE CONTRIBUTIONS

Dow and GTE have the most active PACs among the companies profiled in this chapter with at least $285,000 and $229,000, respectively, going to Congressional candidates. Greyhound's PAC was also a substantial player with $146,000 in contributions. Georgia-Pacific, Bristol-Myers, and 3M have PACs that were moderately active during the 1983–1984 election cycle.

OTHER CONTROVERSIES

Environmental issues have plagued Dow Chemical over the past twenty years.

On the positive side, 3M's pollution prevention program has been widely publicized, and Scott has been praised for some of its recent environmental efforts in Maine.

American Cyanamid, Greyhound, and Sterling Drug have various controversies in their recent past and little apparent record on social initiatives. American Cyanamid faced controversies over a policy in the 1970s, requiring the sterilization of women potentially exposed to harmful chemicals in one of its plants. Some church groups have criticized Sterling Drug for overseas sales of a drug banned in the United States. Greyhound has recently had confrontations with some of its unionized workers.

Mixtures of strong social programs and controversies characterize various other companies: Sara Lee (owner of Kiwi brand waxes and polishes), known for its charitable giving, has had labor problems at its Hanes textile subsidiary; American Home Products, once known as secretive and criticized for its aggressive marketing of infant formula at home and abroad, asserts it has adopted a more open and socially conscious stance, although its current programs still appear minimal.

Certain household products can pose health threats if not used properly, or can contribute to indoor air pollution. Both the Center for Science in the Public Interest and the Consumers Federation of America have done work on these potential hazards.

CLEANING AIDS

AIR FRESHENERS

Size of Charitable Contributions	Women Directors and Officers	Minority Directors and Officers	Social Disclosure	Brand Name	Company (Profile Page)	Involvement in South Africa	Conv. Weapons-Related Contracts	Nuclear Weapons-Related Contracts	Authors' Company of Choice
*	🧍🧍	No	✍✍✍	Wizard	American Home Products (p. 406)	Yes A/B	No	No	
$$$	🧍🧍	?	✍✍✍	Renuzit	Bristol-Myers (p. 208)	Yes B	No	No	
$$$	🧍	🧍	✍✍✍	Twice as Fresh	Clorox (p. 409)	No	No	No	✔
$$$	🧍	🧍	✍✍✍	Glade	S. C. Johnson & Son (p. 420)	Yes C	No	No	
$	🧍	No	No	Lysol	Sterling Drug (p. 242)	Yes B	No	No	

* = See company profile
? = No information available
Single figure ($, 🧍) = Minimal
Double figure ($$, 🧍🧍, ✍✍, 🧍🧍) = Moderate
Triple figure ($$$, 🧍🧍🧍, ✍✍✍, 🧍🧍🧍) = Substantial

No = No involvement or participation
Yes = Involvement or participation. A, B, C in the South African column reflect the degree of compliance with Sullivan Principles and/or involvement in strategic industries.

See Chapter 4 for a detailed discussion of chart symbols.

CLEANING AIDS

BATHROOM CLEANING AIDS

Size of Charitable Contributions	Women Directors and Officers	Minority Directors and Officers	Social Disclosure	Brand Name	Company (Profile Page)	Involvement in South Africa	Conv. Weapons–Related Contracts	Nuclear Weapons–Related Contracts	Authors' Company of Choice
*	♀♀	No	✍✍✍	Sani-Flush	American Home Products (p. 406)	Yes A/B	No	No	
$$$	♀♀	?	✍✍✍	Vanish	Bristol-Myers (p. 208)	Yes B	No	No	
$$$	♀	♀	✍✍✍	Tilex	Clorox (p. 409)	No	No	No	✔
$$$	♀	?	✍✍✍	Dow Bathroom Cleaner Tough Job Fantastik	Dow Chemical (p. 411)	Yes B	No	No	
$$$	♀	♀	✍✍✍	Bloo Johnny Mop	Sara Lee (p. 167)	No	No	No	
$	♀	No	No	Lysol	Sterling Drug (p. 242)	Yes B	No	No	

* = See company profile
? = No information available
Single figure ($, ♀) = Minimal
Double figure ($$, ♀♀, ✍✍, ♀♀) = Moderate
Triple figure ($$$, ♀♀♀, ✍✍✍, ♀♀♀) = Substantial

No = No involvement or participation
Yes = Involvement or participation. A, B, C in the South African column reflect the degree of compliance with Sullivan Principles and/or involvement in strategic industries.

See Chapter 4 for a detailed discussion of chart symbols.

CLEANING AIDS

CARPET CARE PRODUCTS

Size of Charitable Contributions	Women Directors and Officers	Minority Directors and Officers	Social Disclosure	Brand Name	Company (Profile Page)	Involvement in South Africa	Conv. Weapons–Related Contracts	Nuclear Weapons–Related Contracts	Authors' Company of Choice
✳	♀ ♀	No	🖐 🖐 🖐	Woolite	American Home Products (p. 406)	Yes A/B	No	No	
?	♀	No	No	Arm & Hammer	Church & Dwight (p. 408)	No	No	No	
$ $ $	♀	♀	🖐 🖐 🖐	Glory	S. C. Johnson & Son (p. 420)	Yes C	No	No	✔
$ $ $	♀	No	🖐 🖐 🖐	Lestoil	Noxell (p. 221)	No	No	No	✔
$	♀	No	No	Love My Carpet Resolve	Sterling Drug (p. 242)	Yes B	No	No	
$ $	♀ ♀	♀	🖐 🖐 🖐	Scotch Guard Carpet Cleaner	3M (p. 425)	Yes A	No	No	✔

✳ = See company profile
? = No information available
Single figure ($, ♀) = Minimal
Double figure ($$, ♀♀, 🖐🖐, ♀♀) = Moderate
Triple figure ($$$, ♀♀♀, 🖐🖐🖐, ♀♀♀) = Substantial

No = No involvement or participation
Yes = Involvement or participation. A, B, C in the South African column reflect the degree of compliance with Sullivan Principles and/or involvement in strategic industries.

See Chapter 4 for a detailed discussion of chart symbols.

Around the House

CLEANING AIDS

DISHWASHING DETERGENTS

Size of Charitable Contributions	Women Directors and Officers	Minority Directors and Officers	Social Disclosure	Brand Name	Company (Profile Page)	Involvement in South Africa	Conv. Weapons–Related Contracts	Nuclear Weapons–Related Contracts	Authors' Company of Choice
$	🯅	?	No	Ajax Crystal White Octagon Palmolive	Colgate-Palmolive (p. 211)	Yes A/B	No	No	
$$$	🯅	🯅🯅	✍✍✍	Cascade Dawn Ivory Joy	Procter & Gamble (p. 226)	No	No	No	✔
$	No	No	No	All Dove Lux Sunlight	Unilever (p. 171)	Yes ?	No	No	

* = See company profile
? = No information available
Single figure ($, 🯅) = Minimal
Double figure ($$, 🯅🯅, ✍✍, 🯅🯅) = Moderate
Triple figure ($$$, 🯅🯅🯅, ✍✍✍, 🯅🯅🯅) = Substantial

No = No involvement or participation
Yes = Involvement or participation. A, B, C in the South African column reflect the degree of compliance with Sullivan Principles and/or involvement in strategic industries.

See Chapter 4 for a detailed discussion of chart symbols.

CLEANING AIDS

DRAIN OPENERS

Size of Charitable Contributions	Women Directors and Officers	Minority Directors and Officers	Social Disclosure	Brand Name	Company (Profile Page)	Involvement in South Africa	Conv. Weapons–Related Contracts	Nuclear Weapons–Related Contracts	Authors' Company of Choice
$ $ $	☧ ☧	?	✍ ✍ ✍	Drāno	Bristol-Myers (p. 208)	Yes B	No	No	
$ $ $	☧	☧	✍ ✍ ✍	Liquid Plumr	Clorox (p. 409)	No	No	No	✔

* = See company profile
? = No information available
Single figure ($, ☧) = Minimal
Double figure ($$, ☧☧, ✍✍, ☧☧) = Moderate
Triple figure ($$$, ☧☧☧, ✍✍✍, ☧☧☧) = Substantial

No = No involvement or participation
Yes = Involvement or participation. A, B, C in the South African column reflect the degree of compliance with Sullivan Principles and/or involvement in strategic industries.

See Chapter 4 for a detailed discussion of chart symbols.

CLEANING AIDS

FLOOR CARE PRODUCTS

Size of Charitable Contributions	Women Directors and Officers	Minority Directors and Officers	Social Disclosure	Brand Name	Company (Profile Page)	Involvement in South Africa	Conv. Weapons–Related Contracts	Nuclear Weapons–Related Contracts	Authors' Company of Choice
✳	⚲ ⚲	No	✍ ✍ ✍	Aerowax	American Home Products (p. 406)	Yes A/B	No	No	
?	⚲ ⚲	⚲	No	Bruce	Greyhound (p. 416)	No	No	No	
$ $ $	⚲	⚲	✍ ✍ ✍	Beautifloor Brite Future Klear Stepsaver	S. C. Johnson & Son (p. 420)	Yes C	No	No	✔
$ $ $	⚲	⚲	✍ ✍ ✍	WoodPreen	Sara Lee (p. 167)	No	No	No	✔
$	⚲	No	No	Beacon Mop & Glo Perk	Sterling Drug (p. 242)	Yes B	No	No	

✳ = See company profile
? = No information available
Single figure ($, ⚲) = Minimal
Double figure ($$, ⚲⚲, ✍✍, ⚲⚲) = Moderate
Triple figure ($$$, ⚲⚲⚲, ✍✍✍, ⚲⚲⚲) = Substantial

No = No involvement or participation
Yes = Involvement or participation. A, B, C in the South African column reflect the degree of compliance with Sullivan Principles and/or involvement in strategic industries.

See Chapter 4 for a detailed discussion of chart symbols.

CLEANING AIDS

FURNITURE POLISHES AND WAXES

Size of Charitable Contributions	Women Directors and Officers	Minority Directors and Officers	Social Disclosure	Brand Name	Company (Profile Page)	Involvement in South Africa	Conv. Weapons–Related Contracts	Nuclear Weapons–Related Contracts	Authors' Company of Choice
?	🚶🚶🚶	No	No	Kleen Guard	Alberto-Culver (p. 204)	No	No	No	
*	🚶🚶	No	✍✍✍	Old English	American Home Products (p. 406)	Yes A/B	No	No	
$ $ $	🚶🚶	?	✍✍✍	Behold Endust	Bristol-Myers (p. 208)	Yes B	No	No	
$ $ $	🚶	🚶	✍✍✍	Favor Pledge	S. C. Johnson & Son (p. 420)	Yes C	No	No	✔
$ $ $	🚶	🚶	✍✍✍	Preen	Sara Lee (p. 167)	No	No	No	✔

* = See company profile
? = No information available
Single figure ($, 🚶) = Minimal
Double figure ($$, 🚶🚶, ✍✍, 🚶🚶) = Moderate
Triple figure ($$$, 🚶🚶🚶, ✍✍✍, 🚶🚶🚶) = Substantial

No = No involvement or participation
Yes = Involvement or participation. A, B, C in the South African column reflect the degree of compliance with Sullivan Principles and/or involvement in strategic industries.

See Chapter 4 for a detailed discussion of chart symbols.

CLEANING AIDS

GENERAL PURPOSE CLEANERS

Size of Charitable Contributions	Women Directors and Officers	Minority Directors and Officers	Social Disclosure	Brand Name	Company (Profile Page)	Involvement in South Africa	Conv. Weapons–Related Contracts	Nuclear Weapons–Related Contracts	Authors' Company of Choice
$ $ $	No	No	No	Pine Sol	American Cyanamid (p. 205)	Yes A	No	No	
$ $ $	🯅 🯅	?	✍ ✍ ✍	Windex	Bristol-Myers (p. 208)	Yes B	No	No	
$ $ $	🯅	🯅	✍ ✍ ✍	Formula 409 Soft Scrub Tackle	Clorox (p. 409)	No	No	No	✔
$	🯅	?	No	Ajax	Colgate-Palmolive (p. 211)	Yes A/B	No	No	
$ $ $	🯅	?	✍ ✍ ✍	Fantastik Glass Plus Grease Relief Janitor in a Drum Pine Magic	Dow Chemical (p. 411)	Yes B	No	No	
?	🯅 🯅	🯅	No	Bab-O Old Dutch Parsons Ammonia	Greyhound (p. 416)	No	No	No	
$ $ $	🯅	No	✍ ✍ ✍	Lestoil	Noxell (p. 221)	No	No	No	✔

(Continued on next page)

GENERAL PURPOSE CLEANERS *(cont'd.)*

Size of Charitable Contributions	Women Directors and Officers	Minority Directors and Officers	Social Disclosure	Brand Name	Company (Profile Page)	Involvement in South Africa	Conv. Weapons–Related Contracts	Nuclear Weapons–Related Contracts	Authors' Company of Choice
$ $ $	⚣	⚣ ⚣	✍ ✍ ✍	Comet Mr. Clean Spic & Span Top Job	Procter & Gamble (p. 226)	No	No	No	✔
$	⚣	No	No	Lysol	Sterling Drug (p. 242)	Yes B	No	No	

* = See company profile
? = No information available
Single figure ($, ⚣) = Minimal
Double figure ($$, ⚣⚣, ✍✍, ⚣⚣) = Moderate
Triple figure ($$$, ⚣⚣⚣, ✍✍✍, ⚣⚣⚣) = Substantial

No = No involvement or participation
Yes = Involvement or participation. A, B, C in the South African column reflect the degree of compliance with Sullivan Principles and/or involvement in strategic industries.

See Chapter 4 for a detailed discussion of chart symbols.

CLEANING AIDS

LAUNDRY AIDS

Size of Charitable Contributions	Women Directors and Officers	Minority Directors and Officers	Social Disclosure	Brand Name	Company (Profile Page)	Involvement in South Africa	Conv. Weapons–Related Contracts	Nuclear Weapons–Related Contracts	Authors' Company of Choice
?	♀♀♀	No	No	Static Guard	Alberto-Culver (p. 204)	No	No	No	
*	♀♀	No	✍✍✍	Easy-On starch	American Home Products (p. 406)	Yes A/B	No	No	
$$$	♀	♂	✍✍✍	Clorox bleach	Clorox (p. 409)	No	No	No	✔
$	♀	?	No	Axion	Colgate-Palmolive (p. 211)	Yes A/B	No	No	
$	♀	♂	No	Niagara Starch	CPC International (p. 129)	Yes B	No	No	
$$$	♀	?	✍✍✍	Spray & Starch Spray & Wash Vivid	Dow Chemical (p. 411)	Yes B	No	No	
?	♀♀	♂	No	Fleecy Magic Sizing Sta-Puf	Greyhound (p. 416)	No	No	No	
$$$	♀	♂	✍✍✍	Shout	S. C. Johnson & Son (p. 420)	Yes C	No	No	

(Continued on next page)

LAUNDRY AIDS *(cont'd.)*

Size of Charitable Contributions	Women Directors and Officers	Minority Directors and Officers	Social Disclosure	Brand Name	Company (Profile Page)	Involvement in South Africa	Conv. Weapons–Related Contracts	Nuclear Weapons–Related Contracts	Authors' Company of Choice
$ $ $	♦	♦ ♦	✎ ✎ ✎	Bounce Downy Solo	Procter & Gamble (p. 226)	No	No	No	✔
$ $ $	♦	♦	✎ ✎ ✎	Miracle White	Sara Lee (p. 167)	No	No	No	
$	No	No	No	Final Touch Snuggle	Unilever (p. 171)	Yes ?	No	No	

* = See company profile
? = No information available
Single figure ($, ♦) = Minimal
Double figure ($$, ♦♦, ✎✎, ♦♦) = Moderate
Triple figure ($$$, ♦♦♦, ✎✎✎, ♦♦♦) = Substantial

No = No involvement or participation
Yes = Involvement or participation. A, B, C in the South African column reflect the degree of compliance with Sullivan Principles and/or involvement in strategic industries.

See Chapter 4 for a detailed discussion of chart symbols.

CLEANING AIDS

LAUNDRY DETERGENTS

Size of Charitable Contributions	Women Directors and Officers	Minority Directors and Officers	Social Disclosure	Brand Name	Company (Profile Page)	Involvement in South Africa	Conv. Weapons–Related Contracts	Nuclear Weapons–Related Contracts	Authors' Company of Choice
*	[figure] [figure]	No	[hand] [hand] [hand]	Woolite	American Home Products (p. 406)	Yes A/B	No	No	
?	[figure]	No	No	Arm & Hammer	Church & Dwight (p. 408)	No	No	No	
$	[figure]	?	No	Ajax Cold Power Dynamo Fab Fresh Start	Colgate-Palmolive (p. 211)	Yes A/B	No	No	
$ $ $	[figure]	?	[hand] [hand] [hand]	Yes	Dow Chemical (p. 411)	Yes B	No	No	
?	[figure] [figure]	[figure]	No	Dutch Purex Trend	Greyhound (p. 416)	No	No	No	
$ $ $	[figure]	[figure] [figure]	[hand] [hand] [hand]	Bold Cheer Dash Ivory Snow Oxydol Tide, etc.	Procter & Gamble (p. 226)	No	No	No	✔
$	No	No	No	All Wisk	Unilever (p. 171)	Yes ?	No	No	

CLEANING AIDS

OVEN CLEANERS

Size of Charitable Contributions	Women Directors and Officers	Minority Directors and Officers	Social Disclosure	Brand Name	Company (Profile Page)	Involvement in South Africa	Conv. Weapons–Related Contracts	Nuclear Weapons–Related Contracts	Authors' Company of Choice
*	♀ ♀	No	✍ ✍ ✍	Easy-Off	American Home Products (p. 406)	Yes A/B	No	No	
$ $ $	♀ ♀	?	✍ ✍ ✍	Mr. Muscle	Bristol-Myers (p. 208)	Yes B	No	No	✔
?	♀	No	No	Arm & Hammer	Church & Dwight (p. 408)	No	No	No	✔
$ $ $	♀	?	✍ ✍ ✍	Oven Cleaner	Dow Chemical (p. 411)	Yes B	No	No	

* = See company profile

? = No information available

Single figure ($, ♀) = Minimal

Double figure ($$, ♀♀, ✍✍, ♀♀) = Moderate

Triple figure ($$$, ♀♀♀, ✍✍✍, ♀♀♀) = Substantial

See Chapter 4 for a detailed discussion of chart symbols.

No = No involvement or participation

Yes = Involvement or participation. A, B, C in the South African column reflect the degree of compliance with Sullivan Principles and/or involvement in strategic industries.

CLEANING AIDS

SPONGES AND SCRUB PADS

Size of Charitable Contributions	Women Directors and Officers	Minority Directors and Officers	Social Disclosure	Brand Name	Company (Profile Page)	Involvement in South Africa	Conv. Weapons–Related Contracts	Nuclear Weapons–Related Contracts	Authors' Company of Choice
?	✦	No	No	Scrunge	Church & Dwight (p. 408)	No	No	No	
$ $ $	✦ ✦ ✦	✦ ✦	🖐 🖐 🖐	O-Cel-O sponges	General Mills (p. 135)	No	No	No	✔
?	✦ ✦	✦	No	Brillo	Greyhound (p. 416)	No	No	No	
*	✦ ✦	✦ ✦	No	SOS Tuffy	Miles Labs (p. 220)	No	No	No	
$ $	✦ ✦	✦	🖐 🖐 🖐	Scotch Brite Reserve	3M (p. 425)	Yes A	No	No	

* = See company profile
? = No information available
Single figure ($, ✦) = Minimal
Double figure ($$, ✦✦, 🖐🖐, ✦✦) = Moderate
Triple figure ($$$, ✦✦✦, 🖐🖐🖐, ✦✦✦) = Substantial

No = No involvement or participation
Yes = Involvement or participation. A, B, C in the South African column reflect the degree of compliance with Sullivan Principles and/or involvement in strategic industries.

See Chapter 4 for a detailed discussion of chart symbols.

HOME AND PAPER PRODUCTS

BATHROOM TISSUES

Size of Charitable Contributions	Women Directors and Officers	Minority Directors and Officers	Social Disclosure	Brand Name	Company (Profile Page)	Involvement in South Africa	Conv. Weapons–Related Contracts	Nuclear Weapons–Related Contracts	Authors' Company of Choice
$	⚤	No	✍✍	Coronet	Georgia-Pacific (p. 414)	No	No	No	
?	No	?	No	Marina Nice 'n Soft Northern Vanity Fair	James River (p. 419)	No	No	No	
$$	⚤	⚤	✍✍✍	Delsey	Kimberly-Clark (p. 422)	Yes C	No	No	
$$$	⚤	⚤⚤	✍✍✍	Banner Charmin White Cloud	Procter & Gamble (p. 226)	No	No	No	✔
$$	⚤	⚤⚤	✍✍✍	Cottonelle Soft-Weve Waldorf	Scott Paper (p. 429)	No	No	No	

✱ = See company profile
? = No information available
Single figure ($, ✱) = Minimal
Double figure ($$, ✱✱, ✍✍, ⚤⚤) = Moderate
Triple figure ($$$, ✱✱✱, ✍✍✍, ⚤⚤⚤) = Substantial

No = No involvement or participation
Yes = Involvement or participation. A, B, C in the South African column reflect the degree of compliance with Sullivan Principles and/or involvement in strategic industries.

See Chapter 4 for a detailed discussion of chart symbols.

Around the House

HOME AND PAPER PRODUCTS

BATTERIES

Size of Charitable Contributions	Women Directors and Officers	Minority Directors and Officers	Social Disclosure	Brand Name	Company (Profile Page)	Involvement in South Africa	Conv. Weapons–Related Contracts	Nuclear Weapons–Related Contracts	Authors' Company of Choice
$ $	🏃 🏃	🏃	✍ ✍ ✍	Duracell	Dart & Kraft (p. 130)	Yes B	No	No	
$ $	🏃	?	✍ ✍	Energizer Eveready	Ralston Purina (p. 162)	No	No	No	

* = See company profile
? = No information available
Single figure ($, 🏃) — Minimal
Double figure ($$, 🏃🏃, ✍✍, 🏃🏃) = Moderate
Triple figure ($$$, 🏃🏃🏃, ✍✍✍, 🏃🏃🏃) = Substantial

No = No involvement or participation
Yes = Involvement or participation. A, B, C in the South African column reflect the degree of compliance with Sullivan Principles and/or involvement in strategic industries.

See Chapter 4 for a detailed discussion of chart symbols.

HOME AND PAPER PRODUCTS

FACIAL TISSUES

Size of Charitable Contributions	Women Directors and Officers	Minority Directors and Officers	Social Disclosure	Brand Name	Company (Profile Page)	Involvement in South Africa	Conv. Weapons–Related Contracts	Nuclear Weapons–Related Contracts	Authors' Company of Choice
?	No	?	No	Vanity Fair	James River (p. 419)	No	No	No	
$ $	↑	↑	✍ ✍ ✍	Kleenex	Kimberly-Clark (p. 422)	Yes C	No	No	
$ $	↑	↑ ↑	✍ ✍ ✍	Lady Scott Scotties	Scott Paper (p. 429)	No	No	No	✔

* = See company profile
? = No information available
Single figure ($, ↑) = Minimal
Double figure ($$, ↑↑, ✍✍, ↑↑) = Moderate
Triple figure ($$$, ↑↑↑, ✍✍✍, ↑↑↑) = Substantial

No = No involvement or participation
Yes = Involvement or participation. A, B, C in the South African column reflect the degree of compliance with Sullivan Principles and/or involvement in strategic industries.

See Chapter 4 for a detailed discussion of chart symbols.

HOME AND PAPER PRODUCTS

INSECTICIDES AND REPELLENTS

Size of Charitable Contributions	Women Directors and Officers	Minority Directors and Officers	Social Disclosure	Brand Name	Company (Profile Page)	Involvement in South Africa	Conv. Weapons–Related Contracts	Nuclear Weapons–Related Contracts	Authors' Company of Choice
$$$	No	No	No	Combat	American Cyanamid (p. 205)	Yes A	No	No	
*	🏃🏃	No	✍✍✍	Black Flag	American Home Products (p. 406)	Yes A/B	No	No	
$$$	🏃	🏃	✍✍✍	Raid	S. C. Johnson & Son (p. 420)	Yes C	No	No	✔
*	🏃🏃	🏃🏃	No	Cutter	Miles Labs (p. 220)	No	No	No	
$	🏃	No	No	d-Con Four/Gone	Sterling Drug (p. 242)	Yes B	No	No	

* = See company profile
? = No information available
Single figure ($, ↟) = Minimal
Double figure ($$, ↟↟, ✍✍, ↟↟) = Moderate
Triple figure ($$$, ↟↟↟, ✍✍✍, ↟↟↟) = Substantial

No = No involvement or participation
Yes = Involvement or participation. A, B, C in the South African column reflect the degree of compliance with Sullivan Principles and/or involvement in strategic industries.

See Chapter 4 for a detailed discussion of chart symbols.

HOME AND PAPER PRODUCTS

KITCHEN BAGS, FOILS, AND WRAPS

Size of Charitable Contributions	Women Directors and Officers	Minority Directors and Officers	Social Disclosure	Brand Name	Company (Profile Page)	Involvement in South Africa	Conv. Weapons–Related Contracts	Nuclear Weapons–Related Contracts	Authors' Company of Choice
$ $ $	♀	?	✍✍✍	Handi-Wrap Saran Wrap Ziploc	Dow Chemical (p. 411)	Yes B	No	No	
$	♀♀ ♀	♀	✍✍	Baggies Hefty Kordite	Mobil (p. 318)	Yes B	✈ ✈	No	
*	No	No	✍✍✍	Cut-Rite waxed paper Diamond Wrap freezer paper Reynolds Wrap aluminum foil	Reynolds Metals (p. 428)	No	No	No	✔

* = See company profile
? = No information available
Single figure ($, ♀) = Minimal
Double figure ($$, ♀♀, ✍✍, ✈✈) = Moderate
Triple figure ($$$, ♀♀♀, ✍✍✍, ✈✈✈) = Substantial

No = No involvement or participation
Yes = Involvement or participation. A, B, C in the South African column reflect the degree of compliance with Sullivan Principles and/or involvement in strategic industries.

See Chapter 4 for a detailed discussion of chart symbols.

HOME AND PAPER PRODUCTS

LIGHT BULBS

Size of Charitable Contributions	Women Directors and Officers	Minority Directors and Officers	Social Disclosure	Brand Name	Company (Profile Page)	Involvement in South Africa	Conv. Weapons–Related Contracts	Nuclear Weapons–Related Contracts	Authors' Company of Choice
$ $ $	⋀ ⋀	⋀ ⋀	✍ ✍ ✍	G. E.	General Electric (p. 353)	No	✈ ✈ ✈	Yes	
$ $	⋀ ⋀	?	✍ ✍	Sylvania	GTE (p. 417)	No	✈ ✈ ✈	Yes	

✷ = See company profile
? = No information available
Single figure ($, ⋀) = Minimal
Double figure ($$, ⋀⋀, ✍✍, ✈✈) = Moderate
Triple figure ($$$, ⋀⋀⋀, ✍✍✍, ✈✈✈) = Substantial

No = No involvement or participation
Yes = Involvement or participation. A, B, C
in the South African column reflect the degree of compliance with Sullivan Principles
and/or involvement in strategic industries.

See Chapter 4 for a detailed discussion of chart symbols.

HOME AND PAPER PRODUCTS

PAPER TOWELS AND NAPKINS

Size of Charitable Contributions	Women Directors and Officers	Minority Directors and Officers	Social Disclosure	Brand Name	Company (Profile Page)	Involvement in South Africa	Conv. Weapons–Related Contracts	Nuclear Weapons–Related Contracts	Authors' Company of Choice
?	No	?	No	Brawny Earth Tone Spill Mate Vanity Fair Zee	James River (p. 419)	No	No	No	
$ $	✦	✦	✍ ✍ ✍	Hi-Dri	Kimberly-Clark (p. 422)	Yes C	No	No	
$ $ $	✦	✦ ✦	✍ ✍ ✍	Bounty	Procter & Gamble (p. 226)	No	No	No	✔
$ $	✦	✦ ✦	✍ ✍ ✍	Job Squad Scot Towels Viva	Scott Paper (p. 429)	No	No	No	

✳ = See company profile
? = No information available
Single figure ($, ✦) = Minimal
Double figure ($$, ✦✦, ✍✍, ✦✦) = Moderate
Triple figure ($$$, ✦✦✦, ✍✍✍, ✦✦✦) = Substantial

No = No involvement or participation
Yes = Involvement or participation. A, B, C in the South African column reflect the degree of compliance with Sullivan Principles and/or involvement in strategic industries.

See Chapter 4 for a detailed discussion of chart symbols.

HOME AND PAPER PRODUCTS

SHOE POLISH

Size of Charitable Contributions	Women Directors and Officers	Minority Directors and Officers	Social Disclosure	Brand Name	Company (Profile Page)	Involvement in South Africa	Conv. Weapons–Related Contracts	Nuclear Weapons–Related Contracts	Authors' Company of Choice
*	⚐⚐	No	✍✍✍	Griffin	American Home Products (p. 406)	Yes A/B	No	No	
$ $ $	⚐	⚐	✍✍✍	Kiwi	Sara Lee (p. 167)	No	No	No	✔

* = See company profile
? = No information available
Single figure ($, ⚐) = Minimal
Double figure ($$, ⚐⚐, ✍✍, ⚐⚐) = Moderate
Triple figure ($$$, ⚐⚐⚐, ✍✍✍, ⚐⚐⚐) = Substantial

No = No involvement or participation
Yes = Involvement or participation. A, B, C in the South African column reflect the degree of compliance with Sullivan Principles and/or involvement in strategic industries.

See Chapter 4 for a detailed discussion of chart symbols.

AMERICAN HOME PRODUCTS CORPORATION

American Home Products (AHP) is a pharmaceutical and consumer products company once known for its passion for secrecy. (Until the early 1980s, its corporate headquarters answered the phone with a phone number rather than its name.) Although consumers are not generally familiar with AHP's name, they know its products well: Anacin, Chef Boy-ar-dee, and Woolite, among others.

AHP has now abandoned its secretive stance, left several controversies in the past, and enjoys excellent relations with its unions. But as of 1985 it had not undertaken a number of social initiatives common at other companies, such as minority purchasing or banking programs.

Two unions — the Oil, Chemical, and Atomic Workers and the United Food and Commercial Workers (UFCW) — singled out AHP in 1984 and 1985 for its particularly good labor relations. The UFCW noted that the company had agreed to coordinated bargaining, which permits simultaneous negotiation with different unions representing employees at several plants.

Along with Abbott Labs and Bristol-Myers, AHP was involved in a controversy over the marketing of infant formula in developing nations during the late 1970s. It began to implement a series of modifications in its policies in 1978, culminating with compliance with the World Health Organization (WHO) code adopted in 1983 that restricted this marketing, although AHP had previously opposed the guidelines.

In 1985 some church groups criticized AHP for promotional policies in the United States; the company had obtained sole rights to distribute its infant formulas in New York City hospitals. In exchange, the Health and City Corporation, which runs the hospitals, received a $1 million grant from the firm, an additional $400,000 in special services, and the full range of AHP formula

AMERICAN HOME PRODUCTS CORPORATION											
	Women		Minorities				Contracts		PAC Contributions		
% to Charity	Directors	Officers	Directors	Officers	Social Disclosure	Sullivan Rating	% Military	Nuclear Weapons–Related	Dollar Amount	% to Republicans	% to Democrats
*	1	1	0	0	A	I/IIA	None	None	$20,650	72%	28%

* = See profile
See also Appendix D for a listing of this company's products and services.

products (including packets to be given to mothers upon discharge from the hospital) at no cost. Church groups were concerned that this kind of marketing encouraged new mothers to choose a source of nutrition potentially less healthful — and more expensive — than their own milk. In response to a 1985 resolution of these church groups, the company agreed to publish a special report to shareholders on its marketing practices for infant formula at home and abroad. In 1986 these same groups again filed a resolution with AHP, calling on it to reaffirm its commitment to the WHO guidelines, particularly regarding distribution of free samples in hospitals. The resolution received a moderate 4.6 percent vote of support from shareholders.

In 1984 some church groups submitted a shareholder resolution to AHP, asking the company to discontinue marketing the drug clinquinol as an ingredient in dry products sold in Pakistan and other developing nations. This anti-diarrhea drug had not been sold in the United States for some time because of possible links to side effects to the nervous system. The company promptly agreed to withdraw the drug from all markets.

AHP is a major advertiser (sixteenth-largest in the United States in 1985). Throughout the 1960s and 1970s and on into the 1980s, AHP fought a running battle with the Federal Trade Commission (FTC) over the validity of its claims for Anacin. FTC claims of misleading advertising by the company were upheld by the courts. (See the Bristol-Myers and Sterling Drug profiles for discussions of similar claims.)

AHP reports cash and in-kind charitable contributions of $6.3 million in 1984, up from $2.6 million in 1983. The company did not provide a figure for cash contributions alone for this book. Unlike many other pharmaceutical and consumer product companies, it has no formal programs supporting minority economic development, and would not supply fair hiring statistics to CEP.

The company employs approximately 500 workers (one-half of whom are white) in South Africa, and became a signatory of the Sullivan Principles in 1983; in 1984 it received the second-highest rating for compliance with the Sullivan Principles. AHP reports that in South Africa it has undertaken initiatives to support its nonwhite workers, including loans for homes, job training, and tuition support for children. The company also purchases goods from nonwhite businesses, and supports legal services and educational institutions. In 1985 the Sullivan rating for its Wyeth Laboratories subsidiary, employing 300, was upgraded to the highest category, while its Ayerst and Whitehall subsidiaries received the second-highest rating.

The company responded to CEP's questionnaires.

CHURCH & DWIGHT CO., INC.

Headquartered in New Jersey, Church & Dwight is a publicly traded company; however, it is estimated that about 70 percent of outstanding stock is owned by employees or by the descendants of its founding fathers, Dr. Austin Church and John E. Dwight.

In 1970, when there was great concern about harm done to rivers and streams from detergents high in phosphates, the company scored high points with environmentalists when it introduced nonpolluting laundry detergent.

Its charitable giving program supports health-related research at various universities, including research on the possible health benefits of baking soda, one of its major products.

The company did not respond to CEP's questionnaires.

CHURCH & DWIGHT CO., INC.											
	Women		Minorities				Contracts		PAC Contributions		
% to Charity	Directors	Officers	Directors	Officers	Social Disclosure	Sullivan Rating	% Military	Nuclear Weapons–Related	Dollar Amount	% to Republicans	% to Democrats
?	1	0	0	0	F	None	None	None	None		

? = No information available
See also Appendix D for a listing of this company's products and services.

CLOROX COMPANY

Clorox, based in Oakland, California, has made a substantial and innovative commitment to its economically troubled headquarters city, choosing to locate its new offices downtown at a time when most corporations were seeking suburban settings. Along with Kaiser Aluminum, Clorox invested over $1 million in the construction of a new hotel and convention center that were an integral part of plans to revitalize the community. Again with Kaiser, it became a limited partner in the rehabilitation of a historic Oakland area known as Victorian Row.

One of the most unusual aspects of Clorox's social program is its commitment to Oakland's youth. Former CEO Robert Shetterly threw the full weight of the company behind construction of the East Oakland Youth Development Center (EOYDC). This job training and counseling facility opened in 1978 in a neighborhood where over 50 percent of the families live at or below the poverty level, and unemployment among minority youth runs at 60 percent. By 1983 the EOYDC programs were finding 150 jobs annually for local teenagers and providing in-depth counseling for 115. The center also has recreational, art, and sewing activities.

In order to provide long-term financial stability and independence for EOYDC, Clorox and Shetterly (now retired) headed a $3.5 million endowment drive, with Clorox providing $1.5 million in matching funds. (More than $1.4 million had been raised by 1986 to match Clorox's contribution.) In addition, a substantial portion of Clorox's charitable gifts go directly to EOYDC ($127,000 in 1985).

In 1985 the company extended its youth program beyond Oakland with seven $10,000 grants to plants in other cities for the development of youth-oriented projects of their own design, up from three in 1984.

CLOROX COMPANY											
	Women		Minorities				Contracts		PAC Contributions		
% to Charity	Directors	Officers	Directors	Officers	Social Disclosure	Sullivan Rating	% Military	Nuclear Weapons-Related	Dollar Amount	% to Republicans	% to Democrats
1.4%	2	0	0	2	A	None	None	None	$15,500	94%	6%

See also Appendix D for a listing of this company's products and services.

Clorox is active in Oakland high school education. It has "adopted" a school in one of the city's most economically depressed neighborhoods. Along with Kaiser Aluminum and Equitec Financial, the company helps fund that city's Quality Education Project, which works primarily to increase parent's involvement in school curricula and in assisting their children with schoolwork.

It has also joined with other businesses in supporting the Oakland Alliance. This "partnership" among the city's school system, various California state and private colleges and universities, and Oakland's business community, is working to upgrade the city's public school system. The coalition has pledged to find jobs for those who graduate from the high schools, to increase corporate volunteering in the school system, to raise the level of professional career counseling, and to work to establish special "academies" for job-oriented education for selected students in health, computer sciences, and the media.

Clorox's $1.6 million given in 1985 represented a strong 1.4 percent of pretax earnings. A substantial 33 percent of this went to youth organizations, 18 percent to civic and social welfare groups, 10 percent to united fund drives, and 10 percent to education.

In 1982 the company initiated a formal volunteer program to encourage its employees to take part in community activities. By 1984, 150 were participating.

The company supports minority economic development as well, with operating accounts in minority-owned banks, and some $4.4 million in goods purchased from minority-owned suppliers in 1985 (up from $3 million in 1983).

Salaried Clorox employees enjoy substantial benefits, including a tax-reduction savings plan (the company contributes one dollar for each four-dollar employee deposit), a profit-sharing plan, and a PAYSOP plan (the company gives employees company stock equivalent to one-half percent of their annual salary each year, for which it in turn receives a federal tax credit). Its workers have access to a counseling program and a child-care information and referral service. In 1984 Clorox contributed $25,000 to a $700,000 drive headed by Chevron and the Bank of America to train child-care providers and create facilities in key California cities.

The company responded to CEP's questionnaires.

DOW CHEMICAL COMPANY

In a 1983 *Fortune* article, Dow's chairman, Robert W. Lundeen, characterized the company as being perceived as "prickly, difficult, and arrogant." This reputation is attributable in part to Dow's handling of the numerous environmental controversies in which it has been involved over the years. Recently, however, the firm is making efforts to improve its social image. Its foundation contributions, for example, were 3.0 percent of pre-tax earnings in 1985, one of the highest among companies profiled in this book.

For twenty years, claims concerning the hazards of dioxin have dogged Dow. Dioxin is a contaminant found in the herbicide 2,4,5-T, which was used for many years in Vietnam in a defoliant code-named Agent Orange. In the United States the herbicide was used for weed control in agriculture until 1970, and in forestry until 1979. Dow was one of the major manufacturers of 2,4,5-T.

Dow has consistently maintained that there is no scientific proof that this herbicide poses any threat to human health if properly used. The company has held fast to this position despite the anguished outcry of Vietnam veterans and their families, who allege that their psychological, physical, and birth-defect problems stem from exposure to Agent Orange. In a 1984 court-approved settlement, seven manufacturers of the herbicide set up a $180 million fund to pay for medical expenses incurred by some of these veterans.

A parallel battle raged throughout the 1970s over use of 2,4,5-T in forestry. The Environmental Protection Agency (EPA) suspended the herbicide's forestry uses in 1979. Residents near heavily sprayed areas had claimed unusually high rates of miscarriage and other damages, although these claims had been disputed.

There is little doubt that dioxin is one of the most toxic chemicals known. The debate centered around the question of whether the chemical would affect human health in the minute quantities in which it appears in herbicides and in the manner in which these herbicides were applied. Dow eventually abandoned its campaign to have the herbicide reinstated, at which point the EPA ceased its studies of the chemical's health effects. (For a more complete analysis of these issues, see the CEP study *Forests, Herbicides and People*.)

Dow has also been at the center of controversies surrounding possible pollution in and around its headquarters in Midland, Michigan. Following questions raised by a citizens' coalition, the Environmental Congress of Mid-Michigan (ECOMM), the state's Department of Natural Resources discovered 14 spills in Dow's brine waste disposal operations during a three-month period at the beginning of 1984. Dow downplayed the significance of these spills, but subsequently agreed to modernize its brine system, which, according to *Chemical Week*, occupies nearly 250 square miles in and around Midland.

For several years prior to 1984, the company also disputed the right of the Environmental Protection Agency (EPA) to monitor potential dioxin pollution in and around its Midland Plant. The company had refused to turn over to the EPA environmentally related information on its manufacturing operations on the grounds that they were "trade secrets." The EPA sued for release of the data in 1983 and a year later reached a settlement with the company providing for access to the information.

Ralph Nader and William Taylor, writing in *The Big Boys* in 1986, find this combative stance when it comes to government regulations typical of Dow, particularly under its CEO Paul Oreffice, whom they portray as a "hard-nosed political fighter." But they also note that, as in its 1984 settlement with the EPA, the company seems to have "slowly begun to smooth over some of its roughest corporate edges."

In 1983 Dow bowed out of a different sort of controversy. It announced that its pharmaceutical division would stop making the anti-nausea drug Bendectin, which had been used by millions of women since the mid-1950s. Dow had acquired rights to Bendectin in 1981, when it purchased the Merrell drug company from Richardson-Vicks (then Richardson Merrell). Numerous suits had been filed in the late 1970s, charging that the drug caused birth defects if taken during early pregnancy. Many, but not all, of these suits had been decided in the favor of the manufacturers of Bendectin. But Dow, while maintaining that the drug was entirely safe, decided to cease its production rather than face possible future litigation.

Dow is a politically active company. According to CEP's analysis of Federal Election Commission records, its numerous Political Action Committees contributed a substantial $285,000 to congressional candidates in the 1983–1984 election cycle. But the company informed CEP that its total PAC contributions

DOW CHEMICAL COMPANY											
	Women		Minorities				Contracts		PAC Contributions		
% to Charity	Directors	Officers	Directors	Officers	Social Disclosure	Sullivan Rating	% Military	Nuclear Weapons–Related	Dollar Amount	% to Republicans	% to Democrats
3.0%	1	0	?	?	A	IIA	None	None	$284,700	92%	8%

? = No information available
See also Appendix D for a listing of this company's products and services.

Around the House

for this period was $397,000, making it one of the largest corporate contributors in the nation.

The company is now apparently becoming more attuned to public concerns. It published a public interest report for the first time in its history in 1984, and announced its intention to publish a second such report in 1986. The firm purchased $16.5 million from minority-owned businesses in 1985. Dow told CEP that as of mid-1985 it was "just getting started" on a minority banking program, and plans to invest in venture capital funds supporting minority-owned businesses. As of late 1985, minorities represented 7.0 percent of the company's officials and managers, and women 7.3 percent, up from 6.6 percent and 5.3 percent the previous year.

The company's charitable giving program is a very generous one, with $14.3 million in 1985 gifts (up from $11.9 million in 1984), or 3.0 percent of its average pre-tax earnings. The company does not publish details on who receives these funds, but reported in 1984 that 45 percent went to education, 26 percent to health, 19 percent to community organizations, and 3 percent to the arts.

In South Africa, Dow employs 200 workers at its facilities, approximately two-thirds of whom are white. The company consistently received the second-highest "making progress" rating for compliance with the Sullivan Principles from 1981 through 1985. In early 1987 the company announced plans to sell its operations in South Africa.

The company responded to CEP's questionnaires.

GEORGIA-PACIFIC CORPORATION

This huge wood-products company ($6.7 billion in 1985 sales), based in Atlanta, disclosed limited information regarding social initiatives to CEP, stating that the "company's decentralized structure makes it impractical to provide . . . company-wide statistics in some areas. . . ."

Georgia-Pacific has been involved in recent environmental controversies in California, Louisiana, and Maine. In California, the company is involved in a ten-year battle with environmental groups to prevent it from logging 75 acres of redwoods in Mendocino County. The company has offered to sell this land to the state at fair market value if funds are approved for its purchase. In Louisiana, it paid a $625,000 civil penalty in 1986 to settle a lawsuit regarding air pollution violations at one of its plants. It is also facing class-action suits for $350 million in damages resulting from an alleged discharge of phenol into the Mississippi River in 1981. In Maine, the company settled state environmental lawsuits with fines of $120,000 from 1979 through 1984. (Scott Paper, in contrast, received a Conservation Award from the Natural Resources Council of Maine.)

In a 1972 study of air and water pollution control records conducted by CEP, Georgia-Pacific ranked a moderate, but not exceptional, eighth out of twenty-one companies evaluated. (Scott ranked seventh and Kimberly-Clark eleventh.) The company had a partcularly strong record on air pollution, but a relatively poor one on water pollution control. We could not locate a more recent assessment of Georgia-Pacific's overall air and water pollution control records.

Despite its share of controversies, Georgia-Pacific, along with Scott Paper, has received several awards from the American Paper Institute for innovative environmental projects in recent years, and has made many contributions of land to conservation groups.

GEORGIA-PACIFIC CORPORATION											
	Women		Minorities				Contracts		PAC Contributions		
% to Charity	Directors	Officers	Directors	Officers	Social Disclosure	Sullivan Rating	% Military	Nuclear Weapons–Related	Dollar Amount	% to Republicans	% to Democrats
0.5%	0	1	0	0	C	None	None	None	$93,975	56%	44%

See also Appendix D for a listing of this company's products and services.

The company's charitable giving program appears to be smaller than those of the three other paper companies covered in this book. The Taft *Corporate Giving Directory* listed the G-P foundation's 1983 giving at $1.0 million, or 0.5 percent of pre-tax earnings. (This figure does not include direct corporate giving and may understate the company's total program.) Georgia-Pacific would not make total contribution figures available for this book. It told CEP that "it is our philosophy that our shareholders should make their own decisions about how to make their charitable contributions and that Georgia-Pacific should help them to do this through increased value of their investment in G-P." It reported $660,000 in scholarships to employees' children, $170,000 to the United Way and Egleston Hospital for Children, and $1 million toward establishment of a branch of the Atlanta High Museum of Art at the company's downtown headquarters building (shared with Metropolitan Life). Along with four other companies, it helped establish a child-care center in downtown Atlanta in 1985.

Although it has a minority purchasing program, the company provided no figures on its size.

The company responded in a limited way to CEP's questionnaires.

GREYHOUND CORPORATION

Headquartered in Phoenix, Arizona, Greyhound has been reshaping itself in recent years. It is cutting back on the bus service for which it is best known, and concentrating increasingly on the food, household products, mortgage insurance, and capital equipment leasing businesses.

A number of its recent restructuring moves have brought it into conflict with some of its unions. In 1983, after negotiations with workers at thirteen unionized meat-packing plants in its Armour Meats division failed to produce wage concessions, Greyhound shut the plants down and sold them to Con-Agra. This move in effect canceled Greyhound's contracts with unions at these plants. ConAgra reopened them with non-union workers, who were then paid approximately half the previous salaries.

Also in 1983, Greyhound saw a bitter strike by drivers on its bus lines, which had been losing money. The drivers eventually accepted a 15 percent wage cut. But with fewer people riding buses after airline deregulation brought sharply lower air fares, Greyhound invoked further "cutthroat cost-cutting" (in the words of *Business Week*), with layoffs of supervisory personnel and demands of further wage concessions.

Although we have not rated Greyhound as a defense contractor, the Department of Defense lists just over $1 million in arms-related prime awards for the company in 1984.

The company did not respond to CEP's questionnaires.

GREYHOUND CORPORATION											
	Women		Minorities				Contracts		PAC Contributions		
% to Charity	Directors	Officers	Directors	Officers	Social Disclosure	Sullivan Rating	% Military	Nuclear Weapons–Related	Dollar Amount	% to Republicans	% to Democrats
?	1	1	1	?	F	None	Negligible	None	$146,250	63%	37%

? = No information available
See also Appendix D for a listing of this company's products and services.

GTE CORPORATION

This Connecticut-based communications company is a substantial military contractor with a moderate, and apparently growing, commitment to social initiatives with an emphasis on educational programs.

Over the years GTE has supported two urban revitalization projects. Along with four other companies, the firm invested $500,000 in a housing project in Stamford, Connecticut, site of its corporate headquarters. This project was aimed at expanding the middle-class housing stock. In addition, it joined with banks, churches, and other corporations (including Bristol-Myers and Xerox) to capitalize a $1.6 million revolving loan fund for New Neighborhoods, Inc., a housing construction agency specializing in low-income housing development in Stamford.

GTE's charitable giving program has grown rapidly, up from $8.6 million in 1982 to $15.9 million in 1984 (or 1.0 percent of pre-tax earnings), with $18.7 million projected for 1985. Two innovative education-oriented giving projects are now underway: GIFT, which makes special $2,500 development grants to outstanding high school mathematics teachers ($800,000 committed in 1984); and FOCUS, which will allocate some $1.4 million between 1985 and 1987 to 45 colleges and universities that come up with innovative proposals for recruiting and retaining minority students. Of its 1984 giving, $2.4 million went to the United Way, and $1.24 million to minority- and women-oriented organizations, many relating to education.

GTE's Volunteer Initiatives Program (VIP) helps match employee volunteers with local organizations, and provides additional grants of up to $1,000 to those organizations. GTE estimates it will give out a substantial $500,000 in VIP grants in 1985.

GTE CORPORATION											
	Women		Minorities				Contracts		PAC Contributions		
% to Charity	Directors	Officers	Directors	Officers	Social Disclosure	Sullivan Rating	% Military	Nuclear Weapons–Related	Dollar Amount	% to Republicans	% to Democrats
1.0%	1	1	?	?	C	None	4.9%	Yes	$228,790	50%	50%

? = No information available
See also Appendix D for a listing of this company's products and services.

GTE was the thirty-ninth-largest military contractor in 1985, with $611 million in defense business, down from $707 million in 1984. According to the Investor Responsibility Research Center, a total of $276 million of GTE's $674 million in 1983 defense contracts were primarily or secondarily related to nuclear-capable weapons systems. These included the MX and Minuteman missiles and the Project ELF submarine communications system. Other GTE works include the Worldwide Military Command and Control Information System, carrier-fighter linkups for the Navy, battlefield communications equipment, and electronic-warfare work for the Army.

In September 1985 its Government Systems division pleaded guilty to improperly obtaining internal Pentagon planning documents, and agreed to pay $580,000 to the Department of Defense for the costs of the investigation.

It was only in 1985 that GTE became a signatory to the Sullivan Principles, and hence was not rated. According to the Investor Responsibility Research Center, it has sold its Valenite-Modco subsidiary in South Africa.

The company responded to CEP's questionnaires.

JAMES RIVER CORPORATION OF VIRGINIA

Through a series of acquisitions since its founding in 1969, this Virginia-based paper products company has grown rapidly, and is now a major player in consumer markets. However, we found little information on social initiatives by the firm.

Since 1974 it has had a stock purchase plan open to all workers, who can contribute up to 5 percent of yearly earnings toward purchase of shares in the company. The company will match this amount on a sliding scale, from 60 percent to 33 percent, diminishing as the employee's contribution increases. In its annual reports the company stresses its commitment to employee participation programs in the workplace.

The company did not respond to CEP's questionnaires.

JAMES RIVER CORPORATION OF VIRGINIA											
	Women		Minorities				Contracts		PAC Contributions		
% to Charity	Directors	Officers	Directors	Officers	Social Disclosure	Sullivan Rating	% Military	Nuclear Weapons–Related	Dollar Amount	% to Republicans	% to Democrats
?	0	0	?	?	F	None	None	None	None		

? = No information available
See also Appendix D for a listing of this company's products and services.

S. C. JOHNSON & SON, INC.

Although it occasionally maintains the relative secrecy available to privately held firms, S. C. Johnson & Son (better known as Johnson Wax) is among the most socially progressive of companies, with the exception of its failure to become a signatory of the Sullivan Principles until 1985.

A mostly non-union firm, the company pioneered paid vacations for employees in 1900, profit-sharing and group life insurance in 1917, and pension and medical plans before World War II. It introduced the 40-hour work week a decade before federal law required it, and had a no-layoff policy during the Great Depression. (The company has yet to face a major layoff, though it has frozen wages in hard times.) Overseas employees are eligible for its profit-sharing plans. Pay scales are reputed to be high, especially for Racine, Wisconsin, where the company is headquartered in a building by Frank Lloyd Wright. (Three of its buildings are registered historical landmarks.)

Since at least 1959, Johnson Wax has contributed to charity the maximum 5 percent of pre-tax earnings for which companies can then receive tax credit. This is an unusual policy and makes the company the most generous among those corporations covered in this book. According to the Taft *Corporate Giving Directory*, the Johnson Wax Fund contributed $1.7 million in 1984. Fifty percent of this went to education, half in the form of scholarships and fellowships primarily for employees' children. (The foundation matches employee gifts to education of up to $2,000.) Some 30 to 35 percent went to united fund drives. The fund reports that it has a "prevailing interest" in environmental programs devoted to wildlife preservation, and a general policy of not contributing to health organizations.

	Women		Minorities				Contracts		PAC Contributions		
% to Charity	Directors	Officers	Directors	Officers	Social Disclosure	Sullivan Rating	% Military	Nuclear Weapons–Related	Dollar Amount	% to Republicans	% to Democrats
5.0	?	1	0	1	A	V	None	None	None		

S. C. JOHNSON & SON, INC.

* = See profile   ? = No information available
See also Appendix D for a listing of this company's products and services.

In 1975, when the National Academy of Science found a possible link between fluorocarbons and depletion of the Earth's protective ozone layer, the company announced it was no longer using fluorocarbons in its aerosol spray cans. In 1976, company president Samuel C. Johnson declared the move a success, and challenged other companies to follow its example. "There are some companies who were not very happy with us, but sometimes we do our own thing, and this time we did our own thing," commented Johnson.

According to the American Association of MESBICS, Johnson has made a substantial investment in at least one Minority Enterprise Small Business Investment company.

The company has a South African subsidiary, which employs approximately 150 persons. It did not become a signatory of the Sullivan Principles until 1985.

KIMBERLY-CLARK CORPORATION

This paper products company (Kleenex, Huggies) provides substantial benefits for its employees. It has moderate minority banking and purchasing programs. It is the only U.S. paper products company with an investment in a South African paper company, but its affiliate in that country was the first major South African company to sign the Sullivan Principles.

Notable among K-C's benefits is a comprehensive Health Management Program, started in 1977, now serving some 5,800 employees at its former headquarters in Wisconsin. Employees have access to a $2.5 million health center, with an indoor and outdoor track, 25-meter pool, exercise equipment, and saunas. Also available are comprehensive physical examinations and "lifestyle screens," many health education and exercise classes, and a closely supervised "cardiac rehabilitation" program (one of the few such in-house programs in the country, according to the company). As of 1982 these facilities were also open to the spouses of current and retired employees, with the spouses paying a $100 annual fee. The company has subsequently set up a similar health facility and program at its Roswell, Georgia, operations headquarters.

Integrated into the Health Management Program is the company's Employee Assistance Program (EAP), a counseling service aimed primarily at alcohol- and drug-abuse, but also available for marital, financial, or other problems. From 1977 to 1984 the program had served 5,400 workers, about half of these for alcohol or chemical dependence. The company reports a reduction of absenteeism by 43 percent and of accident rates by 70 percent among employees with substance-abuse problems, and a high rehabilitation rate for alcoholics. The EAP is run in cooperation with the United Paperworkers International Workers and other unions. (Approximately 40 percent of the company's work force is unionized.) Health services are free to all employees.

Among other employee benefits, the company offers an education fund; a sum of $650 per worker per year is available for courses or publications, not necessarily job-related, and an additional $150 annually in an accumulating account for family educational expenses. Kimberly-Clark has a savings plan under which both salaried and hourly workers can set aside up to 12 percent of their wages, with the firm matching the first 6 percent in company stock. This is done either on a 50 percent basis for investments in a savings plan tied to company stock, or on a 20 percent basis for other plans.

The company's matching gift program is a strong one. It puts in two dollars for each employee dollar. Almost one-third of its 1985 giving ($879,000 of $2.8 million) went to these matches. Company gifts to education totaled $1.3 million, and $353,000 went to the United Way.

Minority economic development initiatives are moderate with a $2.5 million minority purchasing program in 1985 and $29 million in tax payments made through minority-owned banks in 1985. The company had 11.2 percent women and 5.2 percent minorities among its officials and managers, up from 8.4 percent and 4.5 percent respectively in 1984.

Kimberly-Clark holds a 39 percent interest in the Carlton Paper Corporation, which employs approximately 1,700 workers in South Africa. The remaining 61 percent of Carlton is controlled by South African companies and investors. Kimberly-Clark and Carlton did not become signatories to the Sullivan Principles until 1985. A shareholder resolution urging K-C to sign received a strong 15 percent vote of support that year. It signed after successfully urging Carlton to become the first major South African company to sign the Sullivan Principles.

The company takes the unusual step of publishing a lengthy annual report evaluating and assessing its involvement with Carlton. For example, it reported that Carlton's facilities were partially desegregated in 1984, and completely desegregated by early 1985; that the company paid equal wages for comparable work, but that blacks held the vast majority of lower-paying jobs; that it was providing special loans for the purchase or improvement of housing, primarily to blacks; and that its foundation would be providing $50,000 each year for five years toward a vocational and technical training school for blacks. Since 1978 the company has had a policy of no further investments in South Africa under an apartheid government, but it argues strongly for continuing its current presence in that country as a means of bettering conditions and gradually dismantling apartheid.

In a 1972 study of the air and water pollution control records of twenty-one pulp and paper companies, Kimberly-Clark ranked a moderate, but not exceptional eleventh. (Scott was seventh and Georgia-Pacific eighth.) At that time its water pollution record was excellent, whereas it rated very poorly in

KIMBERLY-CLARK CORPORATION											
	Women		Minorities				Contracts		PAC Contributions		
% to Charity	Directors	Officers	Directors	Officers	Social Disclosure	Sullivan Rating	% Military	Nuclear Weapons–Related	Dollar Amount	% to Republicans	% to Democrats
1.0%	2	0	3	0	A	V	None	None	$38,450	86%	14%

See also Appendix D for a listing of this company's products and services.

controlling air pollution. We could not locate a more recent overall assessment of the company's air and water pollution control records. But the company told CEP that it brought the plant responsible for its previous poor air pollution control record into compliance with federal standards in 1977.

In 1982 Kimberly-Clark caused a stir by not renewing its ads on the television series "Lou Grant" starring Ed Asner, as a result of Asner's statements supporting the shipment of medical supplies to leftist factions fighting the government in El Salvador. Kimberly-Clark was one of several companies to discontinue its spots on the show, which had been under attack by Rev. Jerry Falwell of the Moral Majority, among others.

The company responded to CEP's questionnaires.

MINNESOTA MINING & MANUFACTURING COMPANY (3M)

3M has joined other companies in the Minneapolis–St. Paul area in taking various social initiatives, receiving particular credit for its pollution-prevention programs. The authors of *The 100 Best Companies to Work for in America* praised the company for fostering independent research by its scientists, involving production workers in employee-participation programs, and making a commitment to small towns in siting its factories.

3M initiated 3P — "Pollution Prevention Pays" — in 1975 as part of its environmental engineering department's cost-cutting effort. The general approach within industry had been to attack pollution problems after their appearance with a conventional barrage of control devices. But 3M's vice president for environmental engineering and pollution controls at the time, Joseph Ling, decided that it would be more cost effective to eliminate pollutants from the manufacturing process at the outset, or, failing that, recycle wastes before they left the workplace.

Two years later, *Business Week* reported, "EPA officials maintain that the 3M program is the most thorough they have seen." By 1984 the company had implemented 1,500 3P projects and claimed a total program savings of $235 million. Projects in the program include recycling solvent-filled air to a boiler, where it is incinerated, providing a substantial source of heat for a plant; substituting brush-and-pumice for environmentally dangerous chemical solvents in cleaning copper sheeting in an electronics production plant; and capturing ammonium sulfate discharges and converting them into marketable fertilizers.

The company attributes most of its savings under this program to the elimination of the need for new pollution control equipment, and to a reduction in raw materials and operating costs. Company spokesmen have actively promoted this program among other firms as well.

In another environmental effort, 3M was among the first companies to install a fleet of commuter vans. Starting with six vans in 1973, 3M had 125 on the road by 1979. This number has remained more or less constant since then. The vans average 11 persons each for a total of 1,300 employees, who get door-to-door service and pay about $50 per month. The company estimates that it keeps seven cars off the highways for each of its vans, and has saved $3 million by eliminating the need for 1,000 extra parking spaces at its headquarters facilities. Numerous other companies now have similar programs. Aetna, for example, has 215 vans operating in Hartford.

3M is a strong supporter of the Metropolitan Economic Development Association (MEDA) in Minneapolis, which aids the setup and expansion of minority-owned businesses in the region. The company received MEDA's Corporation of the Year award in 1985. 3M is a promoter of minority purchasing, both nationally and in the Minneapolis region; its 1983 purchases from minority vendors totaled $12.9 million. It has adopted a comprehensive "goal setting" approach to these purchases with a 1984 goal of $14 million. 3M's minority banking program is small relative to that of many other companies profiled in this book, consisting of $500,000 in certificates of deposit.

The company has undertaken an aggressive affirmative action hiring and promotion program since 1982, when it settled a job discrimination case for $2 million and promised to set up various job training and affirmative action programs. Its Affirm project provides multi-session training for supervisory personnel in the hiring and promotion of women and minorities. Through 1983, 8,500 had participated in this program. The company has also strengthened its long-standing policy of promoting from within on the basis of companywide searches for excellence. This approach drew praise from *Savvy* magazine as beneficial for female employees, although it is not aimed particularly at women or minorities.

Benefits for 3M workers include company stock at 85 percent of market value; a retirement savings plan to which the company will contribute one dollar for every four dollars employees save, up to 6 percent of earnings; and a PAYSOP plan, under which the equivalent of one-half of 1 percent of the company's payroll is distributed in stock equally among all employees. In 1985 it reportedly had a pilot child-care program, which subsidizes up to 75 percent of the costs of health-care workers who stay at the homes of parents with sick children.

3M's charitable cash contributions were $8.6 million in 1984, a moderate 0.8 percent of pre-tax earnings. Of this, just over 50 percent went to education, 6.5 percent to community and civic causes, 10 percent to the United Way, 14 percent to the arts, and 9 percent to health. Recent major grants included $1

3M											
	Women		Minorities				Contracts		PAC Contributions		
% to Charity	Directors	Officers	Directors	Officers	Social Disclosure	Sullivan Rating	% Military	Nuclear Weapons–Related	Dollar Amount	% to Republicans	% to Democrats
0.8%	1	2	0	1	A	I	Negligible	None	$86,350	67%	33%

See also Appendix D for a listing of this company's products and services.

million to computer sciences at the University of Minnesota's Institute of Technology, $1.5 million to the Ordway Music Theater in St. Paul, and $250,000 to Junior Achievement.

3M has an exceptionally strong in-kind giving program, with $10.4 million in goods and services in 1984. These included typewriters, medical supplies, and media services. The company also encourages volunteering among its employees, and for many years has had a job skills bank that matches employees' skills with the needs of local nonprofits. In 1983 it initiated a retirees' volunteer program and in 1984 established a Community Service Executive Program.

Two private foundations created by the family wealth of 3M's founders have become active in Minnesota within the past two decades. The larger of the two, the McKnight Foundation, is described by Waldemar Nielsen in *The Golden Donors* as displaying an imaginative and adventuresome pattern of giving. This has included a particularly innovative $10 million revolving loan fund for housing rehabilitation in the Twin Cities area. A less imaginative agenda has characterized the giving of the Bush Foundation, which favors grants for improving the administrative and fiscal structures of recipient organizations.

Although 3M is not rated here as a major military contractor, CEP located listings of $4.3 million in prime contracts for electronics equipment classified as arms-related in 1984 for the company, out of a total of $43 million in awards from the Department of Defense.

The company is a substantial employer in South Africa, where it employs approximately 1,200 workers, half of whom are white. Although it has consistently received the highest rating for compliance with the Sullivan Principles for fair labor practices, 3M has faced considerable criticism from some church groups for its unwillingness to stop sales to the South African police and military and for its refusal to place a moratorium on new investments there.

The company responded to CEP's questionnaires.

REYNOLDS METALS COMPANY

Recent years have been difficult ones for the aluminum industry, but Reynolds Metals, despite pre-tax losses in 1982 and 1983, has managed to make some moderate social commitments. (Among aluminum companies, Kaiser has strong community commitments in Oakland, California, and Alcoa is particularly strong in charitable giving.)

Reynolds has a nationwide aluminum recycling subsidiary, with some 1,500 collection points around the country. The company's Reynolds Metals Development Company (RMDC) was set up in 1959 to participate in federally sponsored urban renewal projects; it has served as a partner, along with the Korman Corporation, in the New Eastwick development in Philadelphia, one of the largest urban renewal projects in the country. RMDC also takes part in a wide range of traditional industrial and residential commercial development ventures.

Its 1983 charitable giving amounted to $585,000, a reduction from just over $1 million in 1982. (Because of the losses in previous years, comparisons with pre-tax earnings are not possible.) The company gave to traditional recipients: 30 percent to education, 30 percent to united fund drives, and 20 percent to health organizations. Its minority purchasing program totaled $16 million in 1985, up from $11.8 million the previous year.

In an unusual corporate effort, Reynolds Metals sponsors a yearly contest to find the restaurant in the United States offering the most authentic black cooking. Its Preservation of Black Heritage Award went to restaurants in Memphis, Tennessee, Atlanta, Georgia, and Petersburg, Virginia, in recent years.

The company responded to CEP's questionnaires.

REYNOLDS METALS COMPANY											
	Women		Minorities					Contracts		PAC Contributions		
% to Charity	Directors	Officers	Directors	Officers	Social Disclosure	Sullivan Rating	% Military	Nuclear Weapons–Related	Dollar Amount	% to Republicans	% to Democrats
*	0	0	0	0	A	None	None	None	$24,500	48%	52%

* = See profile
See also Appendix D for a listing of this company's products and services.

SCOTT PAPER COMPANY

This Philadelphia-based company has a consistent, if moderate, record of commitment in social areas, while staying relatively free of controversies.

Along with Georgia-Pacific, Scott has received numerous awards from the American Paper Institute and the National Forest Products Association for its creative steps in addressing environmental problems. One consistent effort has been in building mills that can use wood chips as fuel. In a 1972 study of the environmental records of the pulp and paper industry, CEP ranked Scott a moderate, but not exceptional, seventh out of twenty-one companies studied. (Georgia-Pacific was eighth and Kimberly-Clark eleventh.) We could not locate a more recent assessment of Scott's overall air and water pollution control records.

In 1982 the Natural Resources Council of Maine gave one of its five Conservation Awards to Scott for the "outstanding environmental design and operation" of its Somerset Mill in Hinckley. An unusual degree of openness and cooperation on Scott's part prompted the Council to give this award to a corporation for the first time in its twenty-year history. (In contrast, Georgia-Pacific had settled six separate environmental cases with the state's attorney general, carrying some $120,000 in penalties from 1979 through 1984; and James River had settled two cases with $41,000 in penalties.)

The company has had a long-standing minority economic development program, although it did not provide figures on its size. The company reports that it does business with minority-owned vendors, banks, and insurance companies. It offers technical assistance and occasionally will guarantee loans for expanding or strengthening some of those minority-owned ventures. It also works to develop minority-owned distributors for Scott products, who either have exclusive rights to distribute the items in a given region, or work with the master distributors in a region. Among the company's officials and

SCOTT PAPER COMPANY												
	Women		Minorities				Contracts		PAC Contributions		
% to Charity	Directors	Officers	Directors	Officers	Social Disclosure	Sullivan Rating	% Military	Nuclear Weapons–Related	Dollar Amount	% to Republicans	% to Democrats
0.7%	1	0	1	1	A	None	None	None	$41,800	72%	28%

See also Appendix D for a listing of this company's products and services.

managers, women held 6.6 percent of the positions and minorities 4.7 percent as of 1984.

Scott's $1.2 million in charitable giving for 1984 was a moderate 0.7 percent of pre-tax earnings. It gave largely to traditional causes: united fund drives received 28 percent of this amount; 40 percent went to education (including $114,000 to a scholarship program); hospitals and other health organizations received 14 percent; 7 percent went to the arts, and 9 percent to community organizations. The company has budgeted $1.5 million for 1985 giving.

The company's work force is approximately 57 percent unionized.

The company responded to CEP's questionnaires.

APPENDIXES

Appendix A

METHODOLOGY AND SOURCES OF INFORMATION

CEP Questionnaires

In December 1984, CEP sent the companies to be profiled questionnaires requesting quantitative information on several social issues, along with a cover letter explaining our purpose in gathering this information and a description of our book. A second approach to those who had not responded was made in March 1985 through their public relations firms. Eventually, 30 companies returned our full questionnaire. An initial draft of the company profiles was sent to all 130 firms for review and comment in June 1985. For those companies that still had not responded, we also sent a shorter questionnaire as a final opportunity to provide information. An additional 24 companies answered the shorter questionnaire. Approximately a dozen other companies, while not returning our actual questionnaires, provided substantial social information in correspondence with CEP or by sending special corporate publications. In February 1986, a further request for updated information was sent to all companies that had responded to our questionnaires. (See the end of Appendix A for the text of these questionnaires.)

Press and Specialized Publications Searches

CEP conducted an extensive search of newspapers, magazines, and other publications for accounts of controversies or positive initiatives relating to the companies covered. The files at the Data Center in Oakland, California, were particularly valuable in this regard. In addition, we contacted organizations such as Volunteer, the Minority Supplier Development Council, and the National Bankers Association, which specialize in promoting and monitoring specific initiatives. From these organizations we obtained newsletters, along with listings of corporate awards. Similarly, we drew on information from the President's Task Force on Private-Sector Initiatives in Washington, D.C.; and Civitex, a computerized data base for public- and private-sector community-oriented programs maintained by the New York–based Citizens Forum on Self-Government/National Municipal League.

Charitable Contributions and Community Involvement

Gathering and analyzing information on charitable contributions posed several difficulties, as no single source exists for current comparable figures. In addition, calculating the size of charitable contributions, both in absolute dollars and in relation to company profits, has complexities of its own.

We drew on several secondary sources for information on those firms that did not provide data: The Taft *Corporate Giving Directory* (1986 edition); the *National Directory of Corporate Charity,* published by the Regional Young Adult Project in 1984; the Public Management Institute's *Corporate 500* (1984 edition); the Investor Responsibility Research Center's *Corporate Giving in the Reagan Years;* and the *National Data Book,* put out by the Foundation Center in New York (1985 edition).

Most companies contribute to charities both directly from corporate funds and indirectly through a company foundation. Legally, their foundation's contributions must be disclosed, but direct donations need not be. Whenever possible, we have used total figures for both types of contributions, although for some companies only the foundation's figures were available. We did not include in-kind contributions in our figures. Exceptionally generous in-kind programs are credited in the profiles. Data in the company profiles came directly from the company or its publications, unless an alternative source is noted.

The dollar figures for contribution totals are for the most recent year for which we could locate totals, but this is not always the same year for each company.

In order to compare the size of giving programs at larger and smaller companies, total charitable giving is often calculated as a percent of pre-tax earnings. Unfortunately, there is no generally accepted method of calculating this figure. Donations in a given year can be compared with corporate earnings from the same year, or from the previous year, or from an average of several previous years' earnings. We have chosen for this book comparisons with three previous years' average pre-tax net earnings. This is a method often used within the corporate community in setting its yearly contribution budgets. Averaging three years' earnings offsets atypically high or low company profits in a single year.

A further question arises as to whether this comparison should be made with *worldwide* pre-tax net earnings or with *domestic* earnings only. The corporate community often chooses domestic earnings, presumably on the grounds that a comparison is being made with domestic giving programs. This choice usually yields a higher percentage figure, because many U.S. companies give proportionally more at home than abroad. For this book we have chosen worldwide company profits for our comparison. We did so in part because this figure is readily available in annual reports and financial reference sources, while domestic earnings figures are not; and because we felt that giving abroad should be encouraged. Correspondingly, we have included details and figures on international giving wherever possible.

For an excellent presentation of arguments for and against various methods of calculation, and of the intricacies therein, see Hayden W. Smith's *A Profile of Corporate Contributions* (Council for Financial Aid to Education, New York, 1983).

Descriptions of *the nature* of giving programs are wherever possible drawn directly from company publications. When other sources are used, they are cited in the text.

Representation of Women and Minorities in Management

All information on minority group members on boards of directors and in upper management came directly from the companies. For figures on women in these two categories, we relied first on direct company responses to CEP's inquiries; for those companies that failed or refused to respond, we turned to annual reports, 10-K forms, and proxy statements for this information.

After careful consideration, we chose as our definition of "upper management" corporate staff officers at a vice-presidential level or higher, and heads of domestic subsidiaries or divisions.

Overall equal employment hiring figures by job category, which all companies with federal contracts must file with the U.S. Equal Opportunity Employment Commission, are considered proprietary and are not available to the public through the federal government. Where reported in company profiles, these figures for the "officials and managers" job category come directly from companies themselves. For most of the companies providing CEP with this information, officials and managers, which is the highest of the five white-collar job categories, constituted between 10 and 15 percent of their total work force.

Conventional- and/or Nuclear-Arms Contracts

Figures for this category came from three sources: the Department of Defense's annual listing of its top 100 prime contractors; its microfiche listing of all contractors with prime contracts of over $25,000; and the Investor Responsibility Research Center's *Stocking the Arsenal: A Guide to the Nation's Top Military Contractors* (Washington, D.C., 1985). For conventional arms contracting we have used 1984 figures; for nuclear arms contracting we have relied on IRRC's classifications, using 1983 data. (The world of defense contracting is relatively stable with major contracts, and their work usually does not change dramatically from year to year.)

For nuclear contracting, IRRC's publication distinguishes between work on "primary" nuclear weapons systems, intended solely to deliver nuclear warheads (such as intercontinental ballistic missiles), and "secondary" nuclear weapons systems, capable of delivering nuclear warheads as well as conventional weapons (e.g., a jet fighter capable of carrying nuclear-armed missiles). We have indicated the nature of a company's nuclear work in its profile.

Total figures on prime defense contracts are drawn from Department of Defense publications. Many companies profiled in this book have contracts with the Department of Defense for supplies, or have a limited number of arms-related defense contracts (totaling less than $10 million). If a company had between $1 million and $10 million in arms-related contracts, we did not rate it as a major weapons contractor in the product charts, although we did note these figures in the company profiles. (We did not note those few companies for which arms-related contracts were under $1 million.)

Much work on nuclear weapons is contracted by the Department of Energy. Companies profiled in this book with such nuclear arms-related contracts in 1983 were Exxon and General Electric. We have included brief descriptions of this work and its dollar value in the profiles of these companies.

We considered arms-related those Department of Defense contracts labeled A1 (aircraft), A2 (missiles), A3 (ships), A4 (combat vehicles), A5 (weapons), A6 (ammunition), A7 (electronics), and A8 (petroleum). Service contracts, where work was clearly related to weapons systems (such as Pan Am's maintenance of nuclear-submarine and missile-tracking facilities), were also classed as arms-related.

For calculating arms-related contracts as a percentage of company sales, we have used 1984 fiscal year figures both for the Department of Defense and the company. These fiscal years do not always coincide exactly.

Description of the nature of a company's military work was drawn from corporate annual reports, IRRC's and CEP's publications, Defense Department contract lists, or press accounts of defense contract awards.

Involvement in South Africa

We used several sources for information on corporate involvement in South Africa.

Assessing the compliance of companies that are signatories of the Sullivan Principles, the International Council for Equality of Opportunity Principles publishes an annual evaluation conducted by the Arthur D. Little consulting company. We have used the 1985 edition. (See Chapter 3 for a description of this rating system.) The Investor Responsibility Research Center's *U.S. and Canadian Investment in South Africa*, published in June 1986, gives employment figures for U.S. companies, as well as a brief description of the nature of their business. Additional information was drawn from the *Unified List of United States Companies with Investments or Loans in South Africa and Namibia*, published by the Africa Fund in 1985.

Political Action Committee Contributions

Information on PAC contributions for all corporations came directly from the U.S. Federal Election Commission.

We used figures on total PAC contributions to federal candidates for 1983 and 1984. Other figures were also available, including total PAC funds raised and spent in the same time period. We chose to focus on federal candidate contributions as the single most prominent and influential PAC activity. (Total funds spent can include money allocated to raising further funds for the PAC or contributions to other PACs, and are therefore not as relevant to the concerns in this book.) We have included PAC figures for company subsidiaries in the companies' totals. For Dow, for example, we located eight related PACs, bringing its total to just under $300,000. (Subsidiaries are not reflected in the table on page 42, which was compiled by the Federal Election Commission.)

Social Disclosure

CEP's criteria for the adequacy of social disclosure for the purposes of this book are found in Chapter Four. Companies that responded to our questionnaires or otherwise publish accounts of charitable and other social initiatives received highest grades, while those that failed to respond and for which we could locate no other sources of substantive social information received the lowest.

Disclosure ratings have long been a usual fixture in CEP's comparative corporate research.

December 5, 1984

Q̲U̲E̲S̲T̲I̲O̲N̲N̲A̲I̲R̲E̲ (I)

Special Social Initiatives By Your Company

This questionnaire is broad and general. Its purpose is
to ascertain what programs or policies best exemplify
your company's commitment to the well-being of its employees,
the communities in which it operates and society more generally.

We have already sent a separate questionnaire to your company
on charitable contributions. We have also sent a questionnaire
on affirmative action commitments. Please do not include
information on these here.

This information will be used for profiling your company in
Better Buying, a "product guide for the socially sensitive
consumer."

Please complete information for as many of the areas listed
below as possible.

                    *   *   *   *

COMPANY NAME_____

ADDRESS_____

         _____

         _____

CONTACT PERSON_____

PHONE (   )_____   DATE_____

                    (Continued on next page)

1. Has your company published any special reports detailing
   its involvement with the community or on other social
   responsibility issues in recent years?

   Yes ☐   No ☐

   Please send a copy of these.

2. Does your company have a volunteer program to "lend" executive
   or other employees to non-profit organizations and projects?

   Yes ☐   No ☐

   How many people participated:

	Latest Fiscal Year 198___	Previous Fiscal Year 198___
On company time full time	_____	_____
Part time	_____	_____
Through company program	_____	_____
On their own time	_____	_____

   Please send descriptions of these. We'd especially appreciate
   any document describing to your employees how they can participate.

3. Does your company have a special program for purchasing goods or
   services from minority-owned companies?

   Yes ☐   No ☐

	Latest Fiscal Year 198___	Previous Fiscal Year 198___
How much was purchased?	$_____	$_____

   Please send any descriptions or news stories you may have.

   (Continued on next page)

4. Does your company have a special program for banking with minority-owned or community oriented banks?

Yes ☐   No ☐

Types of Accounts:

☐ Tax Accounts (TT&L) - Yearly amount $_____

☐ CD's - Amount $_____

☐ Lines of Credit - Total $_____

☐ Operating Accounts

5. Does your company commit funds (not counting charitable contributions) to community projects:

through low-interest loans?   Yes ☐   No ☐

through sponsorship of a Minority
Enterprise Small Business Investment   Yes ☐   No ☐
Company (MESBIC)?

Other_____

Please send any descriptions or news coverage you may have.

6. Has your company established special programs to deal with toxic waste and environmental problems in recent years?

Yes ☐   No ☐

Please send details of these programs.

7. Has your company established innovative programs to monitor and improve worker safety in recent years?

Yes ☐   No ☐

(Continued on next page)

8. Has your company received any awards for outstanding
    performance in the community, environment, product
    or worker safety, etc.?

    Yes ☐   No ☐

    If yes, please cite:_____

    _____

    _____

9. Does your company offer uncommon benefits for its employees such as:

    Flextime   Yes ☐   No ☐

    Child care assistance   Yes ☐   No ☐

    Profit sharing   Yes ☐   No ☐

    Employee stock ownership programs   Yes ☐   No ☐
    in which over 10% of your employees
    participate

    Other _____

    Please send descriptions.

10. Does your annual report cite injuries from accidents?

    Yes ☐   No ☐

    Please disclose number of workdays lost per 200,000 hours worked
    and fatalities.

	Latest Fiscal Year 198___	Previous Fiscal Year 198___
Workdays lost	_____	_____
Fatalities	_____	_____

    We would greatly appreciate a copy of your OSHA Form 200.

For any questions about this questionnaire, contact Alice Tepper Marlin,
Sean Strub or Steven Lydenberg at 212/420-1133.

Return Questionnaire to: Council on Economic Priorities
                                Att: Steven D. Lydenberg
                                30 Irving Place
                                New York, NY 10003

December 5, 1984

Q̲U̲E̲S̲T̲I̲O̲N̲N̲A̲I̲R̲E̲ (II)

Fair Employment

COMPANY NAME _____

ADDRESS _____

_____

_____

CONTACT PERSON _____

PHONE ( ) _____ DATE _____

*　　*　　*　　*

1. Does your company have women among its top corporate
    officers (excluding subsidiaries and foreign operations)?

    Yes ☐   No ☐

    How many top officers are there in your company? _____

    Of these, how many are women? _____

(Continued on next page)

2. Does your company have minority members among its top corporate officers (excluding subsidiaries and foreign operations)?

   Yes ☐   No ☐

   How many minority group members?_____

3. Does your company have women on its Board of Directors?

   Yes ☐   No ☐

   How many Board Members does your company have?_____

   Of these, how many are women?_____

4. Does your company have minority group members on its Board of Directors (Blacks, Hispanics, Asians)?

   Yes ☐   No ☐

   How many minority group members are on your board?_____

5. Does your company make public information on the percentages of women and minorities employed in domestic operations for the firm as a whole?

   Yes ☐   No ☐

   By job category?

   Yes ☐   No ☐

(Continued on next page)

How are these made available?

In your Annual Report?   Yes ☐   No ☐

In special reports?   Yes ☐   No ☐

On specific request of
shareholders or others?   Yes ☐   No ☐

6. Would your company provide CEP with your most recent
report listing percentages of women and minorities
employed in domestic operations by job category?

Yes ☐   No ☐

If yes, please enclose. We would especially appreciate
full EEOC forms, or listing by job categories as defined
by the EEOC.

7. Does your company have any special training programs
specifically for women or minorities and their supervisors?

Yes ☐   No ☐

If so, please enclose a general description of these programs.

8. What percentage of your domestic labor force is unionized?_____%

9. Send any other information you think relevant to your
company's commitment to affirmative action and the
employment of women and minorities.

For any questions about this questionnaire, contact Alice Tepper
Marlin, Sean Strub or Steven Lydenberg at 212/420-1133

Return Questionnaire to: Council on Economic Priorities
Att: Steven D. Lydenberg
30 Irving Place
New York, NY 10003

December 5, 1984

Q̲U̲E̲S̲T̲I̲O̲N̲N̲A̲I̲R̲E̲ (III)

Charitable Contributions

COMPANY NAME _____

ADDRESS _____

_____

_____

CONTACT PERSON _____

PHONE ( ) _____ DATE _____

*   *   *   *

1. Does your company have a charitable foundation?

Yes ☐   No ☐

2. What were your foundation's charitable contributions
    for its two most recent fiscal years?

Amount $_____ Year _____

Amount $_____ Year _____

Please enclose a copy of your foundation's most recent
report if available.

(Continued on next page)

3. Does your company have a policy of matching charitable
    contributions by employees?

        Yes ☐   No ☐

        Dollar for dollar?   Yes ☐   No ☐

        If not dollar for dollar, what ratio? _____

    Can any charity recognized by the IRS qualify?

        Yes ☐   No ☐

    If only certain charities qualify, please send list and/or
    criteria for qualification.

4. What was the total company match for employees' contributions
    for your two most recent fiscal years?

        Amount $_____   Year _____
        Amount $_____   Year _____

5. Is the amount in (4) included in the total of foundation
    contributions listed in (2)?

        Yes ☐   No ☐   It is over and above the
                             amount in (2).

(Continued on next page)

Methodology and Sources of Information   445

6. Does your company make additional charitable cash
   contributions through other programs?

   Yes ☐   No ☐

7. What was the total of these other charitable cash
   contributions for your two most recent fiscal years?

   Amount $_____ Year_____

   Amount $_____ Year_____

8. Does your company make non-cash contributions through
   in-kind goods or services?

   Yes ☐   No ☐

   What was the amount of such non-cash contributions
   for your two most recent fiscal years?

   Amount $_____ Year_____

   Amount $_____ Year_____

   Please describe:_____

   _____

   _____

10. Please enclose any other information you feel is essential
    to a complete picture of your company's charitable activites.

    _____

For any questions about this questionnaire, contact Alice Tepper
Marlin, Sean Strub or Steven Lydenberg at 212/420-1133.

Return questionnaire to: Council on Economic Priorities
                              Att: Steven D. Lydenberg
                              30 Irving Place
                              New York, NY 10003

Appendix A

Appendix B

REFERENCES

American Association of Fund-Raising Counsel. *Giving USA, Annual Report 1985.* New York: American Association of Fund-Raising Counsel, 1985.

Bertsch, Kenneth A. *Corporate Giving in the Reagan Years.* Washington, D.C.: Investor Responsibility Research Center, 1986.

Black Enterprise. "In Good Company: 25 Best Places for Blacks to Work." Volume 16, number 7, February 1986.

Bowers, Cathy, and Cooper, Alison. *U.S. and Canadian Investment in South Africa.* Washington, D.C.: Investor Responsibility Research Center, 1986.

Council for Financial Aid to Education, *CFA Corporate Handbook of Aid-to-Education Programs.* New York: Council for Financial Aid to Education, 1984.

DeGrasse, Robert G. *Military Expansion, Economic Decline: The Impact of Military Spending on U.S. Economic Performance.* Armonk, N.Y.: Sharpe — Council on Economic Priorities, 1983.

Foundation Center. *Corporate Foundation Profiles,* 4th edition. New York: Foundation Center, 1985.

————. *National Data Book, Ninth Edition.* New York: Foundation Center, 1985.

Green, Kass. *Forests, Herbicides and People: A Case Study of Phenoxy Herbicides in Western Oregon.* New York: Council on Economic Priorities, 1983.

Green, Mark, and Berry, John. *Challenge of Hidden Profits: Reducing Corporate Bureaucracy and Waste.* New York: William Morrow, 1985.

Harty, Sheila. *Hucksters in the Classroom: A Review of Industry Propaganda in Schools.* Washington, D.C.: Center for the Study of Responsive Law, 1979.

Kaufman, Joel, and Rabinowitz-Dagi, Linda. *Over-the-Counter Pills That Don't Work.* Washington, D.C.: Public Citizen, Inc., 1983.

Kanter, Rosabeth Moss. *The Change Masters: Innovation and Entrepreneurship in the American Corporation.* New York: Simon and Schuster, 1983.

Kerlin, Gregg, and Rabovsky, Daniel. *Cracking Down: Oil Refining and Pollution Control.* New York: Council on Economic Priorities, 1975.

Levering, Robert; Moskowitz, Milton; and Katz, Michael. *The 100 Best Companies to Work for in America.* Reading, Mass.: Addison-Wesley, 1984.

Little, Arthur D., and Co. *Ninth Report on the Signatory Companies to the Sullivan Principles.* Philadelphia: International Council for Equality of Opportunity Principles, 1985.

Merenda, Michael J. "The Process of Corporate Social Involvement: Five Case Studies." In *Research in Corporate Social Performance and Policy,* edited by Lee J. Preston. Greenwich, Conn.: JAI Press, 1981.

Mintz, Morton. *At Any Cost: Corporate Greed, Women and the Dalkon Shield.* New York: Pantheon, 1985.

Moskowitz, Milton; Katz, Michael; and Levering, Robert. *Everybody's Business, An Almanac: The Irreverent Guide to Corporate America.* New York: Harper and Row, 1980.

Nader, Ralph, and Taylor, William. *The Big Boys: Power and Position in American Business*. New York: Pantheon, 1986.

Newman, Anne, and Bowers, Cathy. *Foreign Investments in South Africa and Namibia*. Washington, D.C.: Investor Responsibility Research Center, 1984.

Nielsen, Waldemar. *The Big Foundations*. New York: Columbia University Press, 1972.

———. *The Golden Donors: A New Anatomy of the Great Foundations*. New York: Dutton, 1985.

O'Toole, James. *Vanguard Management: Redesigning the Corporate Future*. Garden City, New York: Doubleday, 1985.

Peters, Thomas J., and Waterman, Robert H. *In Search of Excellence: Lessons from America's Best-Run Companies*. New York: Harper and Row, 1982.

Peters, Thomas J., and Austin, Nancy K. "Diamonds in the Rough." *Savvy*, June 1984.

Public Management Institute. *Corporate 500: The Directory of Corporate Philanthropy*. San Francisco: Public Management Institute, 1984.

Rothenberg, Stuart, and Becker, David. *Business PACs and Ideology, 1984*. Washington, D.C.: Institute for Government and Politics, 1985.

Sampson, Anthony. *The Seven Sisters: The Great Oil Companies and the World They Made*. New York: Viking, 1976.

———. *Sovereign State of ITT*. New York: Stein and Day, 1973.

Savvy. "The Savvy Sixteen." *Savvy*, May 1982.

Scholl, Jay. "Savvy Corporations of the Year." *Savvy*, June 1983.

Shane, Douglas. *Hoofprints on the Forest*. Washington, D.C.: U.S. Department of State, Office of Environmental Affairs, 1980.

Shaw, Linda S.; Knopf, Jeffrey W.; and Bertsch, Kenneth A. *Stocking the Arsenal: A Guide to the Nation's Top Military Contractors*. Washington, D.C.: Investor Responsibility Research Center, 1985.

Sternberg, Sam. *National Directory of Corporate Charity*. San Francisco: Regional Young Adult Project, 1984.

Taft Group, Inc. *Taft Corporate Giving Directory: Comprehensive Profiles and Analyses of Major American Corporate Philanthropic Programs*, revised edition. Washington, D.C.: The Taft Group, Inc., 1986.

Taylor, Peter. *The Smoke Ring: Tobacco, Money and International Politics*. New York: Pantheon, 1984.

Useem, Michael, and Kutner, Stephen. "Corporate Contributions to the Nonprofit Sector: The Organization of Giving and the Influence of the Chief Executive Officer and Other Firms on Company Contributions in Massachusetts." Boston: Center for Applied Social Science at Boston University, 1985.

Walker, Roger, and Knight, Richard. *Unified List of United States Countries with Investments or Loans in South Africa or Namibia*. New York: The Africa Fund, 1985.

Appendix C

RESOURCES AND RELATED PUBLICATIONS

General Information on Corporate Social Responsibility and Related Issues

Center for Corporate Public Involvement
1850 K Street, N.W.
Washington, DC 20006
(202) 862-4047

Founded in the early 1970s, this organization serves as an association for insurance companies concerned with corporate social involvement. It publicizes members' efforts, promotes greater involvement throughout the insurance industry, and publishes the monthly newsletter *Response*.

Civitex
Citizens Forum/National Municipal
  League
55 West 44th Street
New York, NY 10036
(212) 730-7930
(800) 223-6004

This computerized data base contains approximately 1,500 profiles of innovative community-sponsored projects including public/private partnerships with corporate involvement.

Council on Economic Priorities
30 Irving Place
New York, NY 10003
(212) 420-1133

CEP conducts research on corporate social responsibility, hazardous waste disposal, the relationship between toxic wastes and the incidence of cancer, "Star Wars" missile defense contracting, the economics of defense spending, ver-

ification of arms-control agreements, and other issues. It publishes the monthly *CEP Newsletter*, along with numerous other reports, studies, and books.

Data Center
464 19th Street
Oakland, CA 94612
(415) 835-4692

This organization maintains a vast library of newspaper and magazine clippings on the financial and social records of thousands of companies, as well as files organized separately by issue. The library's services and researchers are available to members, but the Data Center will perform specific searches upon request by nonmembers as well. It publishes several monthly digests: *Social Responsibility Monitor; Plant Closing Monitor; Central American Monitor;* and *Information Service for Latin America*.

Interfaith Center on Corporate Responsibility
475 Riverside Drive #566
New York, NY 10115
(212) 870-2936

This group coordinates the annual filing of church resolutions on corporate responsibility issues, publishes a monthly newsletter, *The Corporate Examiner*, and coordinates a Clearinghouse on Alternative Investments for church groups seeking to place investments with socially creative organizations working for the poor. Its 1985 *Directory of Alternative Investments* is an excellent compendium of such projects.

Investor Responsibility Research Center
1755 Massachusetts Avenue, N.W.,
  Suite 600
Washington, DC 20036
(202) 939-6500

The IRRC provides institutional investors with research and background on issues being raised each year through shareholder resolutions at corporate annual meetings. It publishes a monthly newsletter, *News for Investors,* as well as studies on corporate involvement in South Africa, the defense industry, the nuclear power industry, history of shareholder activism, corporate philanthropy, and other topics.

Public Citizen
2000 P Street, N.W., Suite 605
Washington, DC 20036
(202) 293-9142

This is the umbrella organization for Ralph Nader's various consumer advocacy groups, including the Health Research Group, Congress Watch (lobbying), Critical Mass Energy Project (energy issues), Tax Reform Research Group, Litigation Group, and Buyers Up (fuel-purchasing cooperative). The *Public Citizen* newsletter is published quarterly. On a state level, the Nader-affiliated Public Interest Research Groups work through advocacy and public education campaigns on issues similar to Public Citizen's national concerns.

Charitable Contributions and Community Involvement

The Council on Foundations
1828 L Street, N.W., Suite 1200
Washington, DC 20036
(202) 466-6512

The long-time trade association for foundations, it published an excellent collection of essays on corporate philanthropy in 1982 entitled *Corporate Philan-*

thropy. The Council publishes the journal *Foundation News.*

Independent Sector
1828 L Street, N.W., Suite 1200
Washington, DC 20036
(202) 223-8100

This association of businesses, foundations, volunteer organizations, and other individuals and groups was founded in 1980 and is devoted to actively promoting increased and more professional charitable giving. It publishes the bimonthly *Corporate Philanthropy* newsletter.

National Committee for Responsive Philanthropy
2001 S Street, N.W. #620
Washington, DC 20009
(202) 387-9177

NCRP works for greater openness and disclosure in charitable giving and increased funding directed toward organizations working with minorities, women, the elderly, and the economically disadvantaged. It publishes the *Responsive Philanthropy* newsletter, as well as studies and reports.

Volunteer — The National Center
1111 North 19th Street, Suite 500
Arlington, VA 22209
(703) 276-0542

This organization promotes greater volunteering by members in and out of the corporate community, and publishes the newsletter *Volunteering* and other publications.

Representation of Women and Minorities in Management

American Association of MESBICS
915 15th Street, N.W., Suite 700
Washington, DC 20005
(202) 347-8600

This trade association for Minority Enterprise Small Business Investment Companies provides legislative advocacy and professional development services for members.

Catalyst
250 Park Avenue South
New York, NY 10003
(212) 777-8900

Catalyst works with the corporate community to encourage the placement and promotion of women to upper management and boards of directors. It also publishes various research papers.

National Bankers Association
122 C Street, N.W., Suite 240
Washington, DC 20001
(202) 783-3200

A trade association for minority- and women-owned banks, the NBA's Corporate Advisory Board actively promotes minority banking programs within the corporate community.

National Minority Supplier Development Council
1412 Broadway, 11th Floor
New York, NY 10018
(212) 944-2430

This group promotes minority purchasing programs among the corporate community, publishes *Minority Supplier News* six times a year, and coordinates the activities of regional minority supplier councils around the country.

Involvement in South Africa

American Committee on Africa
198 Broadway
New York, NY 10038
(212) 962-1210

ACOA conducts research on South African issues. It provides numerous publications, including *Unified List of United States Companies with Investments or Loans in South Africa and Namibia.*

Interfaith Center on Corporate Responsibility
475 Riverside Drive, #566
New York, NY 10115
(212) 870-2936

This coalition of Protestant and Roman Catholic church groups has since the early 1970s coordinated the filing of church resolutions urging corporate disengagement from South Africa.

International Council for Equality of Opportunity Principles
1501 North Broad Street
Philadelphia, PA 19122
(215) 236-6757

Associated with the Rev. Leon Sullivan, this group monitors the compliance of U.S. signatories of the Sullivan Principles and publishes an annual assessment and ranking of corporate performance in South Africa.

Investor Responsibility Research Center
1755 Massachusetts Ave., N.W., Suite 600
Washington, DC 20036
(202) 939-6500

This group reviews U.S. corporate involvement in South Africa and has published *Foreign Investment in South Africa.* It also focuses on questions of divestment by institutional investors.

Conventional- and/or Nuclear-Arms Contracts

There are thousands of local and national groups that work on military contracting and nuclear arms issues. Among them are:

Center for Defense Information
1500 Massachusetts Avenue, N.W.
Washington, DC 20005
(202) 862-0700

Founded in 1972, CDI is an authoritative, independent source of background information on military issues and policies. It publishes the *Defense Monitor* newsletter.

Institute for Defense and Disarmament Studies
2001 Beacon Street
Brookline, MA 02146
(617) 734-4216

Originators of the first "freeze" proposals for limiting future development or testing of nuclear weapons, this group has published the *Peace Resource Book, 1986* (Ballinger, 1986), listing some 5,700 national and local organizations working on issues of peace and disarmament.

Nuclear Free America
325 East 25th Street
Baltimore, MD 21218
(301) 235-3575

Advocates of "nuclear-free zones" — towns and municipalities that have no businesses with nuclear-weapons contracts — NFA also promotes boycotting consumer goods produced by the top 50 nuclear arms contractors.

SANE: Committee for a Sane Nuclear Policy
711 G Street, S.E.
Washington, DC 20003
(202) 546-7100

Founded in 1957 to work for a nuclear test ban treaty, SANE is one of the oldest and largest of groups focusing on disarmament issues through public education. Its newsletter, *Sane World*, is published monthly.

The *Socially Responsible Buyer's Guide* lists consumer products made by top nuclear contractors, along with alternative products in each category. The guide is available from: Committee for a Sane Nuclear Policy, 1416 Hill Street, Ann Arbor, MI 48104.

Union of Concerned Scientists
26 Church Street
Cambridge, MA 02138
(617) 547-5552

Some of the most prominent scientists in the country have worked with UCS, which is now particularly concerned with nuclear disarmament and the militarization of space. It provides numerous publications, including a quarterly newsletter, *Nucleus*.

Political Action Committee Contributions

Citizens Against PACs
2000 P Street, N.W., Rm. 408
Washington, DC 20036
(202) 463-0465

An independent research and advocacy organization headed by Philip Stern.

Common Cause
2030 M Street, N.W.
Washington, DC 20036
(202) 833-1200

This citizens' lobbying organization has spearheaded the drive against the influence of corporate PACs as part of its overall concern with reform of political processes. It publishes a bimonthly journal, *Common Cause*.

Institute for Government and Politics
721 2nd Street, N.E.
Washington, DC 20002
(202) 546-3004

This organization publishes research and monthly newsletters on congressional campaigns (*The Political Report*) and on state and local ballot measures (*Initiative and Referendum Report*), as well as studies of the ideological orientation of business PAC spending (*Business PACs and Ideology*, 1984).

Product Safety and Reliability

Any decision on whether to purchase a particular product should involve careful consideration of its safety, quality, and reliability. A partial listing of publications and organizations providing detailed information on these issues is included here for further reference in shopping decisions.

Center for Auto Safety
2001 S Street, N.W., Suite 410
Washington, DC 20009
(202) 328-7700

A Nader-affiliated organization, this advocacy group publishes the bimonthly newsletter *Impact* and the quarterly newsletter *Lemon Times*; acts as a clearinghouse for consumer complaints on automobile-related problems; and frequently urges recalls of models that it views as hazardous.

Center for Science in the Public Interest
1501 16th Street, N.W.
Washington, DC 20036
(202) 332-9110

The focus of CSPI is advocacy and public education on health issues relating to food and diet. It publishes *Nutrition Action Newsletter* ten times yearly, along with numerous other publications on hazards associated with diet, food additives, household products, and other items.

Consumer Federation of America
1424 16th Street, N.W., Suite 604
Washington, DC 20036
(202) 387-6121

This coalition of consumer organizations around the country works through advocacy and public education programs. It has published *The Product Safety Book: The Ultimate Consumer Guide to Product Hazards*, by Stephen Brobeck and Anne C. Averyt (Dutton, 1983), a listing of 1,200 potentially hazardous consumer products. It also publishes listings of state and local consumer organizations, and the *CFAnews* newsletter.

Consumer Interpol
International Organization of
Consumers Union
PO Box 1045
Penang, Malaysia
Telephone: 885072

This international information network of consumer and citizens' groups is concerned with hazardous products and substances around the world, particularly pharmaceuticals, agricultural chemicals, toys, and household items. It publishes a bimonthly newsletter, *Focus*.

Consumers Union of the United States
256 Washington Street
Mount Vernon, NY 10553
(914) 667-9400

Consumers Union publishes the monthly magazine *Consumer Reports* and the annual *Buying Guide Issues* compendium, which rate products on price and quality, as well as evaluate safety features. CU conducts extensive testing on these products.

Health Research Group
2000 P Street, N.W., Suite 700
Washington, DC 20036
(202) 872-0320

Associated with Ralph Nader's Public Citizen organization, this research and advocacy group has issued numerous publications on food, drug, and occupational health and safety concerns, including *Pills That Don't Work* (Farrar, Straus & Giroux, 1980), a guide to 600 prescription drugs that lack evidence of effectiveness. It also published *Over-the-Counter Pills That Don't Work* (Public Citizen, Inc., 1983), as well as a bimonthly newsletter, *Health Letter.*

Social Investing

Center for Economic Revitalization
Box 363
Worcester, VT 05682
(802) 223-3911

This group publishes *Good Money: The Newsletter for Social Investing, Catalyst,* and *Netbacking* as well as analyses of specific industries.

Franklin Research and Development
711 Atlantic Avenue
Boston, MA 02111
(617) 423-6655

Investment advisors specializing in socially responsive investing, Franklin publishes the newsletter *Insight,* along with analyses of the social and financial records of individual companies, and similar overviews of various industries.

Social Investment Forum
711 Atlantic Avenue
Boston, MA 02111
(617) 423-6655

SIF is a coalition of institutional and individual investors, research, community, and church groups concerned with the possibilities of social investing. SIF publishes a vendors' guide to socially responsible brokers and funds.

General Books on Corporate Social Issues

There are numerous books on various aspects of corporations' relations to society and social accountability issues. The following is a brief list of titles of particular interest to readers of this book.

Domini, Amy L., and Kinder, Peter. *Ethical Investing,* Reading, MA: Addison-Wesley, 1984.

Green, Mark, and Berry, John F. *The Challenge of Hidden Profits: Reducing Corporate Bureaucracy and Waste.* New York: William Morrow, 1985.

Levering, Robert, Moskowitz, Milton, and Katz, Michael. *The 100 Best Companies to Work for in America,* Reading, MA: Addison-Wesley, 1984.

Moskowitz, Milton, Katz, Michael, and Levering, Robert, eds. *Everybody's Business: An Almanac. The Irreverent Guide to Corporate America.* New York: Harper & Row, 1980.

O'Toole, James. *Vanguard Management: Redesigning the Corporate Future.* Garden City, NY: Doubleday, 1985.

Vogel, David. *Lobbying the Corporation: Citizen Challenges to Business Authority.* New York: Basic Books, 1978.

Appendix D

COMPANY PRODUCTS AND SERVICES

This list does not reflect sales or announced plans of sales of product lines after July 1986.

ABBOTT LABORATORIES

Personal care: Murine eye care; Selsun Blue shampoo.
Infant formula: Similac, Isomil.
Nutritional supplements: Ensure.
Pharmaceuticals
Hospital and laboratory products

ALBERTO-CULVER

Personal care: Alberto VO5 products.
Foods: Mrs. Dash salt substitute; Sugar Twin sugar substitute.
Household: Kleen Guard furniture polish; Static Guard.
Wholesale food and beauty-care products

ALLEGHENY INTERNATIONAL

Personal care: Wilkinson razors.
Household: Sunbeam and Oster appliances; Northern Electric blankets; Hanson scales; Allmet/Lawnlite lawn furniture; barbecue grills; exercise equipment.
Other manufacturing: Aerospace; semiconductors; magnets; refrigeration equipment; thermostats; pollution control equipment; railroad wheels, axles; robotics; tungsten carbide cutting tools; patient-care products; computer tapes and disk drives; pyrotechnic and signaling devices; industrial metal products; welding equipment; combustion equipment; and others.

AMERICAN BRANDS

Tobacco: Pall Mall, Lucky Strike, Carlton, and Tareyton cigarettes; Antonio y Cleopatra, Roi-Tan, and La Corona cigars; Half and Half, Paladin Black Cherry, and Bourbon Blend pipe tobaccos.

Liquors: Jim Beam bourbon, Chateaux cordials, and Dark Eyes vodka; importer of Spey Royal scotch, Kamora coffee liqueur, Aalborg Akvavit.
Foods: Sunshine crackers and cookies — Krispy, Cheez-It, HiHo, Vienna Fingers, Hydrox, Bell Brand, Humpty Dumpty; Mr. and Mrs. "T" Bloody Mary mix.
Personal care: Jergens soaps and lotions.
Household and office: Master locks; Regal china; Case cutlery; Marvel light bulbs; Swingline staplers; Wilson Jones stationery and supplies.
Leisure: Titleist and Pinnacle Golf Products.
Financial: Franklin and Southland insurance companies.
Other: Pinkerton security agency.

AMERICAN CYANAMID

Personal care: Breck and Ultra Swim shampoos; Old Spice, Blue Stratos, and Mandate men's toiletries; Lady's Choice antiperspirant; La Prairie skin care; Centrum and Stresstab vitamins; Footwork athlete's foot aid.
Perfumes and fragrances: L'Air du Temps; Niki de St. Phalle; Pierre Cardin; Gray Flannel; Geoffrey Beene; CIE.
Household: Pine-sol cleaners.
Pharmaceuticals
Agricultural products and feed additives

AMERICAN HOME PRODUCTS

Nonprescription drugs: Advil, Anacin, and Arthritis Pain Formula; Dristan; Primatene; Dry and Clear acne medicine; Infrarub; Neet hair remover; Preparation H antihemorrhoid; Anbesol; Riopan antacid; Sleep-Eze; Denorex shampoo.

Foods: Chef Boy-ar-dee pasta; Brach candies; Gulden's mustard; Pam cooking oil; Dennison's chile; Ranch Style beans; Jiffy Pop popcorn; Franklin snacks; SMA, Nursoy, S-26, and Promil infant formula.
Household: Aerowax; Sani-Flush; Griffin shoe polish; Noxon metal polish; Old English furniture polish; Easy-Off oven cleaner; Woolite detergents; Easy-On starch; Wizard air fresheners; Black Flag insecticides; 3 in 1 oil.
Agricultural products
Pharmaceuticals
Hospital supplies

AMERICAN MOTORS
Automobiles: AMC, Renault, and Jeep.

AMOCO
Petroleum: Amoco gas; petroleum; natural gas.
Chemicals

AMR
Airlines: American.
Other: American Airlines Training Corporation for flight training.

ANDERSON CLAYTON
Foods: Chiffon margarine; Seven Seas salad dressing; Woodys', Maybud, and Hoffman specialty cheeses; Avoset dessert toppings; Gaines pet foods.
Household: Igloo ice chests and coolers.

ANHEUSER-BUSCH
Beverages: Budweiser, Busch, Michelob, LA, and King Cobra beers; Sante and Saratoga mineral waters.
Foods: Eagle snacks; Campbell Taggart bakeries (Colonial, Rainbo, Kilpatricks, Earth Grains, Grant's Farms); El Charrito Mexican foods.
Real estate: Busch Garden theme parks; Busch baseball stadium.
St. Louis Cardinals baseball team
Aluminum can manufacturing and recycling

ATLANTIC RICHFIELD
Petroleum: ARCO gas and oil.
Chemicals
Solar energy

AVON PRODUCTS
Personal care: Avon, Nurtura, and Louis Feraud lines.
Clothing: Avon, Bright Creek, and James River Traders lines.
Medical-care products

BEATRICE
Foods: Tropicana juices; Hunt's tomato products; Swift meat and turkey products; Wesson and Sunlite cooking oils; La Choy oriental foods; Peter Pan peanut butter; Fisher nuts; Swiss Miss cocoa mixes; Orville Redenbacher's popcorn; Rosarita Mexican foods; Country Line, Pauly, Treasure Cave, and Swissrose cheeses; Martha White flours; Eckrich and Lowrey's meat products; Meadow Gold, Viva, Louis Sherry, and Mountain High dairy products; Arrowhead, Great Bear, and Ozarka bottled drinking water; Reddi-Whip whipped cream; Aunt Nellie's sauces; Bonkers cat treats; and Soup Starter.
Personal care: Jhirmack hair care; Max Factor and Almay cosmetics; Halston/Orlane fragrances and skin care.
Clothing: Playtex; Danskin; Round-the-Clock and Givenchy hosiery; Halston III fashion clothing.
Household: Samsonite and Lark luggage; Stiffel lamps; Del Mar and Louver Drape window shades; Samsonite furniture; Aristokraft cabinets.
Other: Rusty Jones Automobile rustproofing; Jensen Audio equipment.

BEST WESTERN INTERNATIONAL
Hotels and motels: Best Western.

BLACK & DECKER
Appliances: Black & Decker power tools and small home appliances.

BORDEN

Foods: Borden dairy products; Eagle condensed milk; Wise snack foods; Cracker Jacks; Bama juices and jellies; Cremora nondairy creamer; Kava instant coffee; Wylers and Lite Line drink mixes; ReaLemon concentrated lemon juice; Snow's chowders; Creamette and Ronco pastas; Haviland candies.

Household: Elmer's glues; Krylon spray paints; Rain Dance, Rally, Sun Shield car wax; Engine Cleaner; Gas Booster; Wall-Tex wallpapers; Sterling school and office supplies.

Commercial chemical products

BRISTOL-MYERS

Personal care: Clairol and Condition shampoos and hair care; Clairol, Son of a Gun, and Crazycurl hair-care appliances; Ban, Tickle, Ultra Ban, and Mum antiperspirants; Vitalis men's hair care; Sea Breeze and Keri skin care; PreSun suntan lotion.

Nonprescription drugs: Bufferin, Excedrin, Nuprin, and Datril pain relievers; Comtrex, 4-Way, and Congespirin cold medicines; No-Doz; Ammens medicated powders; Vi-Sol, Vi-Flor, and Natalins vitamins for infants; Colace laxative; Sustacal and Isocal adult nutritionals.

Infant formula: Enfamil and ProSobee.

Household: Windex glass cleaner; Renuzit air freshener; Vanish toilet cleaner; Endust and Behold furniture polish; O-Cedar mops; Mr. Muscle oven cleaner; Fleecy fabric softener, Javex bleach; Drano; Good Measure laundry products.

Pharmaceuticals

Health-care products

CAMPBELL SOUP

Foods: Campbell soups; Pepperidge Farm baked goods; Swanson and Le Menu frozen dinners; V-8 and Juice Works juices; Franco-American pastas; Prego spaghetti sauce; Mrs. Pauls frozen foods; Snow King frozen foods; Vlasic pickles and condiments; Plump & Juicy poultry; Godiva chocolates; fresh mushrooms; many other foods.

Pet foods: Recipe dog food.

Restaurants: Pietro's, Annabelle's, and H. T. McDoogal's.

CASTLE & COOKE

Foods: Dole canned and fresh fruits and juices; Dole sorbet and frozen juice bars; Bud of California produce.

Pet foods: Figaro cat food.

Real estate

In 1985 Castle & Cooke was acquired by Flexi-Van, a transportation-equipment leasing company.

CHESEBROUGH-POND'S

Personal care: Vaseline; Q-tips; Cutex cosmetics; Pond's skin care; Rave hair care.

Perfumes and fragrances: Prince Matchabelli (Aviance, Aziza, Beret, Cachet, Chimere, Erno Laszlo, Matchabelli, and Wind Song).

Foods: Adolph's meat tenderizer; Ragu spaghetti sauce.

Clothing: Bass shoes.

Sporting: Prince tennis racquets.

Hospital products

Chemicals, including the Stauffer Chemical company.

CHEVRON

Petroleum: Chevron and Gulf gas and oil.

Chemicals: Ortho garden products.

Minerals

Geothermal energy

CHRYSLER

Automobiles: Chrysler, Dodge, and Plymouth.

Financial: Chrysler Financial Corporation.

Aerospace: Gulfstream aircraft.

CHURCH & DWIGHT

Household: Arm & Hammer detergents, carpet cleaners, baking soda; Scrunge scrub pads.

CLOROX

Household: Clorox bleach; Formula 409, Tilex, and Soft Scrub cleansers; Twice As Fresh air freshener; Kingsford charcoal; Olympic, Lucite, and Carver Tripp paints and stains.

Foods: Hidden Valley Ranch salad dressings; Kitchen Bouquet meat sauce.

Pet care: Fresh Step cat litter.

Restaurants: Emil Villa's Original Hick'ry Pit.

Restaurant equipment

COCA-COLA

Soft Drinks: Coca-Cola, Tab, Sprite, Ramblin' Root Beer, Fanta, Mello Yello.

Other beverages: Minute Maid orange juice; Hi-C and Five Alive fruit drinks; Maryland Club and Butter-Nut coffees; Belmont Springs bottled water.

Entertainment: Columbia Pictures television and films; Mylstar Electronics video games.

COLGATE-PALMOLIVE

Household: Ajax, Axion, Cold Power, Dynamo, Fab, Punch, and Fresh Start laundry detergents; Palmolive, Ajax, Dermasage, and Crystal White Octagon dishwashing detergents; Ajax cleanser.

Personal care: Palmolive, Cashmere Bouquet, and Irish Spring soaps; Colgate and Ultra-brite toothpastes; Colgate shaving cream; Curity and Curad first-aid strips, gauzes, tapes, etc.; Wildroot hair grooming; Wash 'N Dri hand wipes; Curity baby products.

Hospital and dental supplies and equipment

Other: Sterno canned heat.

CONAGRA

Foods: Banquet, Patio, Chun King, and Morton frozen foods; Singleton, Sea Alaska, and Country Skillet Catfish fish; Country Pride and Country Skillet poultry; Armour foods (Classic frozen dinners, Armour meats; Golden Star meats and poultry; Cloverbloom, Miss Wisconsin); Home Brand jellies.

Restaurants: Taco Plaza.

Retail stores: Peavey, Northwest Fabrics.

Agricultural: Grains and grain products; feed; fertilizers; pesticides.

CPC INTERNATIONAL

Foods: Hellmann's and Best Foods mayonnaise; Mazola and Nucoa margarines and oils; Skippy peanut butter; Thomas's muffins and Sahara breads; Mueller's pastas; Karo, Old Tyme, and Golden Griddle syrups; Argo corn starch; Knorr soups and sauces.

Household: Rit dyes; Niagara starches.

Corn milling: Corn starches, syrups, high fructose syrups, and dextrose.

DART & KRAFT

Foods: Kraft brand cheese; Philadelphia cream cheese; Cracker Barrel, Cheez Whiz, and Velveeta cheeses and cheese spreads; Breakstone sour cream and cottage cheese; Sealtest ice cream and dairy products; Breyers ice cream and yogurt; Miracle Whip salad dressing; Parkay margarine; Light 'n Lively ice milk and dairy products; Lender's bagels; Celestial Seasonings teas.

Household: Tupperware containers; Duracell batteries; Durabeam lighting products; Borg scales; Total Gym and Precor exercise systems.

Appliances: West Bend kitchen appliance; Hobart commercial food service equipment.

Other: Wilsonart decorative laminates; Seamless health-care products.

In mid-1986 the company announced that it would split into two firms, with Kraft retaining the food and Duracell battery business and the second, smaller company keeping the remaining lines.

DELTA AIR LINES

Airlines: Delta.

DOW CHEMICAL

Household: Handi-Wrap and Saran Wrap; Ziploc food storage bags; Tough Act; Dow Bathroom Cleaner, Fantastik, Glass Plus, and Pine Magic cleaners; Vivid bleach; Yes, and Spray 'n Wash detergents.

Nonprescription drugs: Novahistine cough and cold medicines; Cepacol mouthwash and cough medicines; Nicorette antismoking aid.

Pharmaceuticals

Industrial and Agricultural Chemicals

DYNAMICS CORP

Appliances: Waring.

Other manufacturing: Agricultural equipment; semiconductors; quartz crystal products; engine generators; air conditioning and refrigeration equipment; air distribution equipment

EASTERN AIRLINES

Airlines: Eastern.

In 1986 Texas Air announced that it would acquire Eastern.

EASTMAN KODAK

Photographic: Kodak cameras, films, and video equipment.

Office: Copiers and information systems.

Medical: Blood analyzers; X-ray films.

Chemicals and fibers

EXXON

Petroleum: Exxon oil and gas; petroleum; natural gas.

Mining: Coal, uranium.

Industrial: Reliance Electric.

Chemicals

FORD

Automobiles: Ford, Lincoln, and Mercury.

Tractors

Aerospace: Ford Aerospace — satellites.

Financial: Ford Motor Credit Company; First Nationwide Financial Corporation.

GENERAL ELECTRIC

Lighting: GE light bulbs.

Appliances: GE and Hotpoint appliances.

Aerospace and electronics: Aircraft engines; radar; semiconductors.

Industrial: Motors; turbines; diesel-electric locomotives; construction equipment; factory automation equipment; specialized materials, nuclear power plant construction.

Medical equipment

Petroleum

Financial: General Electric Credit Corporation; Kidder, Peabody investment banking.

Other: General Electric Information Systems.

In 1985 General Electric acquired RCA. See separate listing.

GENERAL FOODS

Coffees: Maxwell House, Yuban, Sanka, Brim, and General Foods International.

Other beverages: Kool-Aid and Crystal light soft-drink mixes; Country Time and Tang drink mixes; Postum cereal beverage.

Foods: Post cereals; Entenmann's baked goods; Oroweat breads; Oscar Mayer meats; Louis Rich and Chef's Pantry meat and turkey products; Bird's Eye frozen vegetables; Ronzoni pasta; Claussen pickles; Log Cabin syrups; Jell-O, D-Zerta, and Minute Tapioca desserts; Cool Whip and Dream Whip dessert toppings; Baker's chocolate products, Calumet baking powder; Certo & Sure-Jell fruit pectins; Stove Top stuffing mix; Shake 'n Bake; Open Pit barbecue sauce; Good Seasons salad dressing mixes.

Food services
In 1985 General Foods was acquired by Philip Morris. See separate listing.

GENERAL MILLS
Cereals: Cheerios, Wheaties, Total, Trix, Kix, Buc* Wheats, Golden Grahams, Lucky Charms, and other cereals.
Other foods: Nature Valley granola bars and snacks; Fruit Roll-Ups; Gold Medal, La Pina, and Red Brand flours; Bisquick; Betty Crocker mixes; Potato Buds instant mashed potatoes; Gorton's frozen foods; Yoplait yogurts; Hamburger Helper, Tuna Helper, and Chicken Helper; Bac*Os salad garnish.
Household: O-Cel-O sponges.
Restaurants: Red Lobster; York's Choice; The Olive Garden.
Retail outlets: Eddie Bauer clothing and camping equipment; The Talbots clothing.
Furniture: Kittinger; Pennsylvania House.

GENERAL MOTORS
Automobiles: Chevrolet, Pontiac, Buick, and Cadillac.
Automobile products: Delco.
Aerospace: Aircraft engines, radar, missile guidance, fire-control systems. (GM acquired Hughes Aircraft in 1985.)
Data processing: Electronic Data Systems.
Robotics
Financial: General Motors Acceptance Corporation.

GEORGIA-PACIFIC
Paper: Coronet, Mr. Big, Delta, and M-D tissues and paper towels; containers, packaging, and specialty paper products.
Building materials: Plywood, lumber, roofing, gypsum products.
Resins and formaldehyde

GERBER PRODUCTS
Foods: Gerber baby foods.
Appliances and accessories: Hankscraft humidifiers; Nuk nipples; Century car seats and strollers; Wooltex quilts and pillows.
Clothing: Buster Brown; Weather Tamer.
Furniture: Bilt-Rite; Nod-A-Way.
Transportation: CW Transport.
Gerber Children's Centers
Financial: Gerber Life Insurance Company.

GILLETTE
Personal care: Gillette, Trac II, and Good News razors; Right Guard, Dry Idea, and Soft & Dri deodorants/antiperspirants; Silkience, Mink Difference, and White Rain shampoos; Body Elegance; Toni hair care products; Foamy shaving cream; Aapri and Jafra skin care; Oral-B toothbrushes.
Office: Paper Mate, Flair, Eraser Mate, S. T. Dupont, and Accu-Point pens; Liquid Paper correction fluid; Misco computer supplies.
Appliances: Braun.

GREYHOUND
Transportation: Greyhound bus lines.
Personal care: Dial, Tone, SweetHeart, and Pure & Natural soaps; Dial antiperspirant.
Household: Purex, Trend, and Dutch detergents; Parson's and Bo-Peep ammonias; Bruce floor wax; Brillo scrub pads; Old Dutch and Bab-O cleanser; Magic Spray starch; Toss 'n Soft and Sta-Puf fabric softeners; Hilex bleach; Bruce floor polishes.
Foods: Ellio's frozen pizza; Appian Way pizza mixes; Armour and Treet canned meats.
Financial: Verex; Greyhound Leasing & Financial Corporation; Greyhound Capital Corporation.
Transportation manufacturing: Buses.
Services: Premier Cruise Lines cruises; Travelers Express money orders; aircraft, food, and exhibition services.

GTE

Consumer: Sylvania light bulbs; Sprint long-distance telephone service.

Other businesses: Telephone services; satellite and other telecommunications services; Yellow Pages telephone directories; communications equipment; military communications and reconnaissance systems; specialty metals.

H. J. HEINZ

Foods: Heinz brand catsup, pickles, beans, etc.; Ore-Ida frozen potatoes; Weight Watchers brand foods; Heinz baby foods; Star-Kist tuna; Alba mixed drinks; Steak-ummm meats.

Pet foods: 9-Lives cat food; Meaty Bones and Jerky Treats dog food.

Other: Commercial corn starches and syrups.

HERSHEY FOODS

Candies: Hershey's, Reese's, Mr. Goodbar, KitKat, Y&S licorice, Twizzlers, Skor, and other candies.

Foods: San Giorgio, Skinner, Delmonico, P&R, Light 'N Fluffy, and American Beauty pastas; New Trail granola bars; Hershey's cocoa and chocolate syrup.

Restaurants: Friendly's.

HILTON

Hotels: Hilton.

HOLIDAY INNS

Hotels: Holiday Inns; Crown Plaza; Embassy Suites; Hampton Inn; Harrah's.

HOOVER

Appliances: Hoover vacuum cleaners.

In late 1985, Hoover was acquired by the Chicago Pacific Corporation.

HOUSEHOLD INTERNATIONAL

Transportation: National car rentals.

Household: Thermos and Structo cooler chests and barbecue grills.

Financial: Consumer loans; banking (Household and Valley National banks), commercial loans; life insurance (Alexander Hamilton).

Manufacturing: Schwizter engine components; gears; Eljer plumbing products; Halsey Taylor water coolers; Simonds, Thorsen, Atrax, and Newcarb tools.

HYATT HOTELS

Hotels: Hyatt.

Hyatt is privately owned by the Pritzker family, whose holdings also include the Marmon Group of manufacturing companies; McCall's magazine; timberland and real estate; interests in other hotels, including the Elsinore Corporation's casinos and Playboy's Atlantic City casino; and Braniff Airlines.

IC INDUSTRIES

Foods: Old El Paso Mexican foods; Downyflake frozen waffles; Whitman's chocolates; Pet-Ritz frozen pie shells; Underwood meat spreads; B&M and Friend's baked beans; Ac'cent flavor enhancer; Sego liquid diet foods; Aunt Fanny's baked goods; Pet condensed milk.

Automotive: Midas mufflers and accessories.

Industrial: Landing gear and flight control equipment for aircraft; refrigeration equipment; hydraulic pumps, motors, and servo-valves; wheels; bearings; switches.

Illinois Central Gulf Railroad

INTERNATIONAL BUSINESS MACHINES

Consumer and office: Typewriters; computers; word processors; printers; office and information systems; telecommunications.

Industrial: Telecommunications; computers and information systems.

Satellite Business Systems — joint venture with Aetna Life and Casualty.

International Market Net — joint venture with Merrill Lynch & Co.

INTERNATIONAL MULTIFOODS

Foods: Robin Hood flour; Kretschmer wheat germ; Sun Country granola cereals; Kaukauna specialty cheese; Adams Old Fashioned and All American peanut butter and nut snacks; Reuben, Smoke Craft, Trail Blazer, and Deli Gourmet specialty meats; La Crosta pizza mix; Morey's smoked and frozen fish; Sherwood Forest bird food.

Restaurants: Mister Donut, Boston Sea Party.

Commercial: Flours and prepared bakery mixes.

Agricultural: Animal feeds, drugs, and health-care products; Lynx corn seed.

ITT

Hotels: Sheraton.

Financial: Consumer and industrial financial services; Hartford Insurance company.

Forest products: ITT Rayonier.

Industrial and office: Computers; telecommunications; semiconductors; electronics; military air defense systems; radar maintenance; night-vision equipment.

JAMES RIVER

Household: Northern, Vanity Fair, Aurora, Gala, Brawny, Zee, and Bolt bathroom tissue, towels and napkins.

Commercial paper products: Bathroom tissues and towels (Marathon, Nibroc, Dorsette, Heather, and Protex); specialty industrial and packaging papers; disposable food and beverage products (Dixie and Papermaid); cartons and packaging; specialty papers.

JOHNSON & JOHNSON

Personal care: Affinity and J&J Baby Shampoo; Sundown sunscreen; Stayfree, Modess, Silhouettes, and Sure & Natural sanitary napkins; Assure and Carefree feminine protective pads; "o.b." tampons; Coets cosmetic squares; Shower-to-Shower deodorant powder; J&J baby oils, soaps, powders, and creams; J&J dental floss; Reach toothbrushes.

Nonprescription drugs: Tylenol pain reliever; CoTylenol cold medicine; Sine-Aid sinus tablets; Band-Aids; Ortho-gynol contraceptive products.

Pharmaceuticals

Hospital supplies and equipment

Other commercial: Sausage casings; veterinary products.

JOHNSON PRODUCTS

Personal care: Ultra Sheen, Ultra Wave, Classy Curl, Gentle-Treatment, Afro Sheen, Bantu, and Mellow Touch hair care products; Ultra Sheen and Moisture Formula cosmetics.

Debbie's School of Beauty Culture

S. C. JOHNSON & SON

Household: Brite, Future, Klear, Stepsaver, and Beautiflor floor waxes and polishes; Favor and Pledge furniture polishes; Shout stain remover; Glade air freshners; Glory carpet care; Raid insecticides; Kit and Sprint car waxes.

KELLOGG

Cereals: Corn Flakes, Special K, Rice Krispies, Froot Loops, Nutri-Grain, Frosted Flakes, Honey Smacks, Product 19, Crispix, and others.

Other foods: Whitney's yogurt; Pop-Tarts; Mrs. Smith's pies; Eggo frozen waffles; Junket desserts; Crouettes croutons; Dutch Maid pancake batter and nondairy topping; Le Gout institutional foods.

Beverages: Salada tea.

KIMBERLY-CLARK

Personal care: Kleenex tissues; Hi-Dri paper towels and napkins; Delsey bathroom tissues; Huggies disposable diapers; Kotex, Light Days, and New Freedom sanitary napkins and protective pads; Depend incontinence products.

Commercial: Newsprint and specialty papers; pulp.

Transportation: Commercial airline service; truck transportation service.

LITTON INDUSTRIES

Appliances: Microwave ovens.

Shipbuilding: Military and commercial ships at the Ingalls Shipyards.

Advanced electronics: Military and commercial systems, including inertial navigation; command, control, and communications; electronic warfare and optical systems; laser systems; digital processing.

Geophysical exploration and services

Industrial automation systems

McCORMICK

Foods: McCormick and Schilling spices; Tio Sancho Mexican foods.

Food services and processing

Real estate

Commercial packaging

McDONALD'S

Restaurants: McDonald's.

MAGIC CHEF

Appliances: Magic Chef; Admiral; Norge; Toastmaster; Gaffers & Sattler; Dixie; Edison heaters, humidifiers, and fans; Ingraham clocks.

Soft drink vending equipment: Dixie-Narco.

Magic Chef was acquired by Maytag in early 1986.

MARRIOTT

Hotels: Marriott; Courtyard by Marriott.

Restaurants: Roy Rogers; Bob's Big Boy; Howard Johnson's.

Food services: Airline catering; operation of food concessions at airports through Host International; Saga food services.

Resorts: American Resorts Group.

MARS

Candies: M&Ms, Mars Bars, Snickers, 3 Musketeers, Milky Way, and Twix.

Foods: Uncle Ben's rice.

Pet foods: Kal Kan and Mealtime pet foods.

MARY KAY

Personal care: Mary Kay cosmetics.

MAYTAG

Appliances: Maytag; Jenn-Air; Hardwick.

Commercial appliances: Power ventilation equipment.

Maytag acquired Magic Chef in early 1986.

MILES LABORATORIES

Household: S.O.S. and Tuffy scrub pads; Cutter insect repellent.

Nonprescription drugs: Alka-Seltzer; One-A-Day, Bugs Bunny, and Flintstones vitamins.

Hospital supplies and equipment

Pharmaceuticals

MINNESOTA MINING & MANUFACTURING

Household: Scotchgard fabric protector; Scotch transparent tapes; Scotch Brite scrub pads; Scotch recording and video tapes; photographic films and supplies.

Office: Post-it note pads; copying and printing equipment; graphic arts supplies; electrical, electronics, and telecommunications equipment.

Industrial: Abrasives; polyester films; granules for roofing products; specialty chemicals; reflective materials for traffic signs, markers, etc.; signaling and lighting devices.

Hospital supplies and equipment

MOBIL

Petroleum: Mobil gas and oil, Superior.

Retail stores: Montgomery Ward department stores.

Household: Kordite trash bags; Hefty trash bags and microwave containers; Baggies food bags.

Chemicals

NESTLÉ

Beverages: Nescafé, Taster's Choice, Chase & Sanborn, Hills Brothers, and MJB coffees; Nestea instant tea; Nesquik and Carnation Quick cocoa mixes; Carnation evaporated milk.

Foods: Stouffer's and Lean Cuisine frozen foods; Libby's canned fruits and juices; Nestlé chocolates and candies; Sno-Caps, Oh Henry!, Goobers and Raisinet candy bars; Beech-Nut baby foods; Crosse & Blackwell soups and sauces; Coffee-Mate nondairy creamer; Contadina canned tomato products; Albers corn meal and grits; Slender diet foods; Lactogen infant formula.

Pet foods: Carnation brands — Mighty Dog, New Breed, Come 'N Get It, Friskies dog foods; Bright Eyes, Chef's Blend, Fancy Feast, Fish Ahoy, and Friskies cat foods.

Hotels: Stouffer's.

Restaurants: Stouffer; Rusty Scupper; J. B. Winberie; Cheese Cellar; and Top Restaurants.

Wines: Beringer; Los Hermanos; C&B Vintage Cellars.

Personal care: Alcon Prescription and nonprescription eye-care products; Paloma Picasso, Gloria Vanderbilt, Polo, and Ralph Lauren perfumes; minority interest in L'Oreal.

Pharmaceuticals

NOXELL

Personal care: Cover Girl cosmetics; Noxema skin care products.

Household: Lestoil cleaning products.

Foods: Wick Fowler's 2-Alarm Chili ingredients.

NWA

Airlines: Northwest; Republic.

OCCIDENTAL PETROLEUM

Petroleum: Cities Service gas; petroleum and natural gas.

Coal mining: Island Creek Coal Company.

Foods: A major beef packer through IBP (Iowa Beef Processors).

Agricultural: Phosphate fertilizers.

Chemical products

OGDEN

Foods: Progresso brand soups, sauces, and canned goods; Hain brand crackers, dressings, and oils; Hollywood oil; Las Palmas Mexican foods.

Services: Maintenance services for office buildings, health-care facilities, and industrial plants; airport cargo handling; food services for airports, convention centers, sports facilities, etc.; security services; racetrack operations; logistical support for oil rigs and remote industrial sites.

Industrial: Construction and operation of waste-to-energy plants; scrap metal brokerage and processing; railroad-car construction.

PAN AM

Airlines: Pan American World Airways.

Services: Aerospace, technical, and management services for commercial, government bases, and military projects in the U.S. and abroad.

PENNWALT

Nonprescription drugs: Allerest, Sinarest, Cruex, Cold Factor 12, and Ting decongestants and cold remedies; Desenex foot products; Caldesene diaper rash treatments; Calecort skin ointment.

Personal care: Fresh deodorants and antiperspirants.

Chemicals
Pharmaceuticals
Specialized equipment: Navigation signals; vacuum pumps; centrifuges; chlorination equipment; flow meters; etc.

PEOPLE EXPRESS

Airlines: People Express; Britt Airways; Provincetown-Boston Airline.

PEPSICO

Soft drinks: Pepsi-Cola, Diet Pepsi, Pepsi Free, Mountain Dew, Slice, Teem.
Foods: Frito-Lay snacks — Fritos, Doritos, Chee-tos, O'Grady's, etc.; Grandma's brand cookies.
Restaurants: Pizza Hut; Taco Bell; La Petite Boulangerie. (PepsiCo purchased the Kentucky Fried Chicken restaurants from RJR Nabisco in July 1986.)

PFIZER

Personal care: Coty fragrances — Emeraude, Wild Musk, Sophia, Nuance, Sweet Earth, Muguet, L'Aimant, L'Origan for women, and Stetson and Musk for Men; Pacquin skin care; Desitin skin care; Barbasol shaving cream and men's toiletries; Visine eye drops; Ben-Gay pain relief ointment; Desitin baby care products; Unisom sleep aid.
Pharmaceuticals
Agricultural, including antibiotic and vitamin feed additives.
Specialty chemicals, including food additives.
Hospital supplies and equipment
Specialty metal products

PHILIP MORRIS

Tobacco: Marlboro, Benson & Hedges 100s, Merit, Virginia Slims, Parliament, Players, Saratoga, and Cambridge cigarettes.
Beers: Miller High Life, Lowenbrau, Meister Brau, and Milwaukee's Best.
Soft drinks: 7-Up.

Real estate: Mission Viejo real estate development company.
In late 1985 Philip Morris acquired General Foods. See separate listing for General Foods' products.

PHILLIPS PETROLEUM

Petroleum: Phillips 66 gas; petroleum and natural gas.
Chemicals

PILLSBURY

Foods: Pillsbury flours; Pillsbury refrigerated doughs for baked goods; Farina cereal; Hungry Jack pancake mix; Milk Break Milk Bars; Green Giant and LeSueur canned and frozen vegetables; Stir Fry Entrees and Van de Kamp's frozen foods; Totino and My Classic frozen pizzas; Häagen-Dazs and Seduto ice creams; Azteca corn products; Apollo ethnic foods.
Restaurants: Burger King; Steak & Ale; Bennigan's; JJ Mugg's; Häagen Dazs Shoppes; Godfather's pizza.
Commercial agricultural: Grain merchandizing; flour milling; rice milling; feed ingredients.

POLAROID

Photographic: Polaroid films, cameras and video equipment.

PROCTER & GAMBLE

Household: Tide, Cheer, Ivory Snow, Oxydol, Bold, Dash, and Dreft detergents; Downy, Bounce, Era, Solo, and Dawn laundry products; Biz bleach; Joy, Cascade, and Ivory detergents; Comet, Spic and Span, Mr. Clean, and Top Job cleansers; Charmin, White Cloud, Banner, and Bounty paper towels and tissues.
Personal care: Ivory, Camay, Coast, Lava, Safeguard, and Zest soaps; Prell, Pert, and Head & Shoulders shampoos; Lilt hair care; Crest and Gleem toothpastes; Sure and Secret antiperspirants and deodorants; Wondra skin

care; Scope mouthwash; Always feminine protection pads; Pampers and Luvs disposable diapers; Attends incontinence products.

Foods: Citrus Hill orange juice; Crush and Hires sodas; Duncan Hines mixes; Jif peanut butter; Folgers and High Point coffees; Tender Leaf teas; Crisco and Puritan oils; Pringle snacks.

Nonprescription drugs: Encaprin and Norwich pain relievers; Chloraseptic sore throat products; Head & Chest cold medicine; Pepto-Bismol.

QUAKER OATS

Foods: Quaker Oatmeals hot cereals; Quaker cold cereals — Life, Cap'n Crunch, Halfsies, Mr. T; Aunt Jemima pancake mixes, frozen pancakes, and syrups; Flako pie crust mixes; Quaker Chewy Granola Bars and Dipps; Van Camp's canned beans; Gatorade drink; Celeste frozen pizzas; Wolf chili; Arden rice cakes.

Pet foods: Ken-L Ration, Kibble, and Love Me Tender dog foods; Puss 'n Boots cat foods.

Food services

Children's toys: Fisher-Price.

Retail stores: Jos. A. Bank Clothiers; Brookstone tools; Herrschners needle crafts; Eyelab eyewear.

RALSTON PURINA

Foods: Ralston breakfast cereals — Chex, Donkey Kong, Cracker Jack; Rainbow Bright, Gremlins; S'mores snack bars; Continental Bakery breads — Wonder, Home Pride, and Beefsteak; Hostess snacks — Twinkies, Ding Dongs, Sno Balls, and Choco-diles; Drake's baked goods; Chicken of the Sea tuna.

Pet foods: Cat Chow, Thrive, Meow Mix, and Tender Vittles cat foods; Dog Chow, Hi-Pro, and Bonz dog foods.

Agricultural: Animal and poultry feeds.

RAMADA INNS

Hotels: Ramada Inns; Tropicana hotels-casinos.

RAPID-AMERICAN

Personal care: Fabergé Organics shampoos; Brut deodorants, aftershave and other toiletries; Aqua Net hair care.

Liquors: Dewar's, I. W. Harper, J. W. Dants, and Schenley whiskies; Stock vermouths; Fratelli Lambrusco wines; and other wines and liquors.

Retail outlets: T. G. & Y.; McCrory; Zodys; McLellan; H. L. Green; J. J. Newberry; and S. H. Kress.

Clothing: Jody-Tootiques; McGregor; Botany; Worsted-Tex; Bert Pulitzer; Gilead; and Gillies.

RAYTHEON

Appliances: Amana, Caloric, Speed Queen, Modern Maid, and Glenwood.

Electronics: Military and civilian work, including radar systems; missile guidance and fire control; missile systems; air traffic control equipment; sonar; communications; electronic countermeasures; microwave components.

Publishing: Heath textbooks.

Commercial aircraft: Beechcraft airplanes.

Energy services: Seismograph Service Corporation for geophysical oil searches; Badger for petroleum and chemical processing plants and services; United Engineers & Constructors for power plant and industrial plant construction.

Other: Raytheon Service Company for engineering and maintenance primarily on government and military bases; Iowa Manufacturing for construction equipment.

RCA

Appliances: RCA televisions and video equipment; information systems for use on home computers.

Entertainment: National Broadcasting Company (NBC) television network; RCA records.

Commercial electronics: Television and broadcasting equipment and components; leasing and servicing of communications equipment.

Communications: Various satellite-based communication services.

Government electronics: Military and space systems, primarily shipboard defense and fire-control systems; satellites; and semiconductors.

In 1985 RCA merged with General Electric. See separate listing for General Electric.

REPUBLIC AIRLINES

Airlines: Republic.

In early 1986, Republic was acquired by Northwest Airlines.

REVLON

Personal care: Revlon cosmetics; Charlie, Jontue, Scoundrel, Ciara, Bill Blass, Ivoire de Balmain, Norell, Cerissa, and Di Borghese fragrances; Flex, Milk Plus, Aquamarine, and Hair's Daily Requirement hair care; Mitchum, Hi & Dri deodorants and antiperspirants.

Nonprescription drugs: Tums antacids; Oxy anti-acne aids; Liquiprin analgesic for children; Orafix and Brace denture adhesives; Esoterica medicated creams; Nature's Remedy laxative.

Eye care: Hydrocurve and Soft Mate contact lenses; Barnes-Hind, Soquette, Comfort Drops, Titan, and Soft Mate contact lens and eye solutions; professional eye-care equipment.

Pharmaceuticals

Diagnostic equipment

In 1985 Revlon was taken over by Pantry Pride. Pantry Pride immediately sold Revlon's Norcliff Thayer division, makers of Tums, Oxy, and other nonprescription drugs, to the British Beecham Group and sold Revlon's pharmaceutical divisions to the Rorer Group drug company.

REYNOLDS METALS

Household: Reynolds aluminum and plastic wraps; Cut-Rite waxed paper.

Food: Eskimo Pie ice cream bars.

Real estate: Reynolds Metals Development Company.

Other: Aluminum mining, production, and recycling; aluminum cans and other products; electrical wire and cable.

RICHARDSON-VICKS

Personal care: Olay skin care products; Vidal Sassoon and Pantene hair care; Mill Creek hair and skin-care products; Clearasil and Topex acne cream; Fixodent dental adhesive; Saxon aftershave lotion.

Nonprescription drugs: Vicks, Nyquil, Sinex, and Creamacoat cold remedies; Tempo antacid; Plus and Lifestage vitamins.

Household: Homer Formby's varnishes and stains; Thompson's waterproofing.

Chemicals and specialty medical instruments

Richardson-Vicks was acquired by Procter & Gamble in 1985.

RJR NABISCO

Tobacco: Camel, Salem, Vantage, Winston, Century, Doral, More, Now, and Century cigarettes.

Liquors: Heublien liquors, including Smirnoff, Popov, and other vodkas; Jose Cuervo tequila; Don Q Rum; Black Velvet whisky; Inglenook and Beaulieu Vineyard wines; Harvey's sherries.

Fast foods: Kentucky Fried Chicken (sold to PepsiCo in July 1986).

Beverages: Hawaiian Punch fruit drink.

Foods: Del Monte canned fruits, vegetables, and juices; Ortega Mexican foods; College Inn broths; My-T-Fine puddings; Vermont Maid and Brer Rabbit syrups; A1 steak sauce; Grey Poupon mustard; Regina vinegar; Davis baking powder; Aylmer prepared foods; Snap-E-Tom cocktail. Nabisco cookies: Almost Home; Barnum's Animal Crackers; Cameo; Chips Ahoy!; Fig Newtons; Lorna Doone; Mallomars; Nilla; Oreo; Social Tea. Nabisco crackers: Cheese Nips; Escort; Honey Maid graham crackers; Oysterettes; Premium saltines; Ritz; Triscuit; Uneeda; Waverly; Wheatsworth; Wheat Thins. Nabisco candies: Baby Ruth; Bubble Yum; Butterfinger; Care*Free gum; Charleston Chew!; Chuckles; Junior mints; Life Savers; Sugar Daddy. Nabisco Shredded Wheat and Cream of Wheat cereals; Fleischmann's and Blue Bonnet margarines; Planters nuts and snacks; Chipsters potato snacks; DooDads snacks; Dromedary dates and mixes; Egg Beaters egg substitutes; Mister Salty pretzels; Royal pudding mixes.
Pet foods: Milk-Bone dog biscuits.

A. H. ROBINS

Nonprescription drugs: Robitussin, Extend 12, and Dimetapp cough and cold medicines; Chap Stick lip balm; Z-BEC vitamins.
Personal care: Caron fragrances.
Pet care: Sergeant's.
Pharmaceuticals and contraceptive devices
Entertainment: Radio stations.

SARA LEE

Foods: Sara Lee, Chef Pierre, Lloyd J. Harriss frozen desserts; Popsicle brand frozen snacks; Hillshire Farms and Rudy's Farm sausages, Kahn's wieners, Jimmy Dean meats, King Cotton, R. B. Rice, MarTenn, Smokey Hollow, and Bryan meats; B&G pickles.

Candies: Hollywood brand: Pay Day, Zero, etc.
Beverages: Capri Sun fruit drinks.
Clothing: Hanes; L'eggs and Sheer Energy pantyhose; Aris and Isotoner gloves; Bali and Canadelle intimate apparel; Wearabouts leisure wear; Coach leatherware.
Household: Electrolux vacuum cleaners, Fuller brushes; Kiwi shoe polish; Preen floor and furniture polishes.
Restaurants: Lyon's restaurants.
Institutional food services

SCHERING-PLOUGH

Personal care: Maybelline cosmetics; Coppertone, Tropical Blend, QT, Solarcaine, and Shade suntan lotions; Muskol insect repellent.
Nonprescription drugs: Di-Gel antacid; Chlor-Trimeton, Afrin, Coricidin, and Drixoral antihistamines and cold remedies; Tinactin antifungal; St. Joseph aspirin; Aspergum; Feenament, and Correctol laxatives; Duration nasal spray.
Other Consumer: Dr. Scholl's foot-care products; Paas Easter Egg kits; Wesley-Jessen contact lenses.
Entertainment: Radio stations.
Pharmaceuticals
Hospital supplies and equipment

SCM

Foods: Durkee snacks.
Office: Smith-Corona typewriters; business forms and paper products.
Household: Glidden paints.
Chemicals: Pigments; aroma and fragrances; chemical finishes and coatings; specialty chemicals.
Metals: Copper powder and specialty products.
Pulp and paper
Commercial food services

SCOTT PAPER

Household: Cottonnelle, Family Scott, ScotTissue, Soft 'n Pretty, and Waldorf bathroom tissues; Job Squad, Viva paper towels; Scott and Viva paper napkins; Scotties facial tissues; Baby Fresh and Wash-a-bye Baby baby wipes.
Commercial sanitary products
Pulp and specialty paper products

SCOVILL

Appliances: Hamilton Beach.
Household: NuTone door chimes, intercoms, and exhaust systems; Gripper snap fasteners; SportSnaps buttons and zippers; Yale locks.
In 1985 Scovill was acquired by the First City Investing Company, owned by the Belzbergs from Canada.

SHELL OIL

Petroleum: Shell gas and oil; petroleum and natural gas.
Chemicals: Agricultural herbicides and pesticides; polymers; detergents; materials manufacturing; plastic packaging.

SMITHKLINE BECKMAN

Nonprescription drugs: Contac, A.R.M., Sine-Off, Teldrin, and Congestac cold medicines; Ecotrin pain reliever.
Pharmaceuticals
Hospital equipment and supplies
Animal health care: Feed additives.
Eye and skin care: Allergan contact lenses; Soflens contact lens cleaner.
Diagnostic equipment

J. M. SMUCKER

Foods: Smucker jams, jellies, syrups, and peanut butter; Knudsen fruit juices.
Commercial food services

SQUIBB

Personal care: Yves Saint Laurent, Charles of the Ritz, and Alexandra de Markoff cosmetics; Jean Naté toiletries; Enjoli, Gianni Versace, and Yves Saint Laurent (Opium, Rive Gauche, Y, Kouros, and Pour Homme) fragrances; Bain de Soleil suntan lotions; Aromance and Aroma Disk environmental fragrances.
Nonprescription drugs: Theragran vitamins; Spec-T cough medicine.
Pharmaceuticals
Animal: Veterinary products; feed additives.
Hospital supplies and equipment

STANDARD OIL

Petroleum: Sohio, Boron, BP, Gibbs, and William Penn gas.
Mining: Kennecott copper mining; Old Ben Coal Company and Kitt Energy company coal mining.
Chemicals
Other: Chase Brass and Copper products; Qit-Fer et Titane titanium processing; industrial ceramics; wastewater treatment systems; synfuels; glass-steel equipment.

STERLING DRUG

Nonprescription drugs: Bayer and Pandol pain relievers; Midol menstrual relief; Campho-Phenique; Bronkaid and Neo-Synephrine decongestants; Vanquish analgesic; Phillips' Milk of Magnesia antacid.
Personal care: Dorothy Gray, Tussy, and Ogilvie toiletries and cosmetics; Diaparene baby powder; Phisoderm skin cleanser; Stri-Dex antiacne treatments; Wet One and Cushies baby wipes.
Household: Lysol cleansers, disinfectants, and deodorizers; Resolve and Love My Carpet carpet care; Mop & Glo, Perk floor care; d-Con, Four/Gone rodenticides and insecticides; Minwax wood finishing products.
Pharmaceuticals
Chemicals

SUN

Petroleum: Sunoco gas; petroleum and natural gas; synthetic petroleum.

Mining: Elk River Resources, Cordero Mining, and Sunedco Coal coal-mining operations.

Real estate: Radnor real estate development company.

Transportation: St. Johnsbury Trucking; Jones Truck Lines; Standard Trucking; Milne Truck Lines; Carrier Systems Motor Freight.

Chemical: Carboline protective coatings.

Financial: Sunoco Credit Corporation; Helios Capital Corporation; Helios Assurance Company.

TENNECO

Petroleum: Tenneco gas; petroleum and natural gas production, refining, and transmission; synthetic fuels production.

Shipbuilding: Military and commercial ships at Newport News Shipbuilding.

Automotive: Monroe and Walker auto parts; Car X repair shops.

Foods: Sun Giant almonds, raisins, dates, and pistachios through Tenneco West; House of Almonds retail outlets.

Farm equipment: J. I. Case and International Harvester farm equipment companies.

Packaging: Packaging Corporation of America.

Household: Ecko aluminum goods and plastic containers.

Real estate: Tenneco Realty.

Chemicals and minerals

Insurance: Philadelphia Life; Southwestern Life; Security Life.

TEXACO

Petroleum: Texaco and Getty gas; petroleum, natural gas, and synthetic fuels.

Chemicals

TEXAS AIR

Airlines: Texas Air; New York Air; Continental Airlines.

In 1986 Texas Air announced that it would acquire Eastern Airlines.

TRANSAMERICA

Transportation: Budget Rent-a-Car car rentals; Transamerica Airlines airlines; Transamerica Interway equipment leasing.

Insurance: Transamerica Occidental Life Insurance; Fred S. James insurance brokerage; Transamerica Insurance property, casualty; Transamerica Title Insurance.

Financial: Transamerica Financial Services for consumer loans.

Manufacturing: Transamerica Delaval generators, pumps, and instruments.

TRANS WORLD AIRLINES

Airlines: Trans World Airline.

UAL

Airlines: United Air Lines.

Hotels: Westin Hotels.

Real estate: Mauna Kea real estate development.

Financial: GAB insurance claims adjustment company.

UNILEVER

Household: All, Surf, Rinso, Wisk, Snuggle, and Final Touch laundry soaps and aids; Lux, Dove, and Sun Light detergents.

Personal care: Pepsodent, Aim, and Close-Up toothpastes; Dove, Shield, Caress, Lux, and Lifebuoy soaps; Dimension shampoo; Impulse body spray; Signal mouthwash.

Foods: Imperial, Promise, Shedd's, and Balance margarines; Mrs. Butterworth's pancake mixes and syrups; Lipton's teas; Lipton's Cup-a-Soup; Sunkist Fruit Roll.

UNITED TECHNOLOGIES

Appliances: Carrier air conditioners.

Aircraft: Sikorsky helicopters for commercial and military purposes; Pratt & Whitney aircraft engines for commercial and military airplanes.

Other industrial: Otis Elevator; Essex wire and cable; Norden computers and chemicals with military applications; Hamilton Standard control systems; automotive parts and accessories.

US AIR GROUP

Airlines: USAir.

WARNER-LAMBERT

Personal care: Schick, Personal Touch, and Ultrex razors and blades; Listerine mouthwash; Efferdent denture products.

Nonprescription drugs: Rolaids, Bromo-Seltzer, Gelusil, and Remegel antacids; Sinutab sinus medicine; Benylin, Halls, and Mediquell cough medicines; Caladryl calamine lotion; Myadec vitamins; Listerex and Lubriderm dermatological products; Anusol hemorrhoid treatments; Agoral laxatives; Lavacol rubbing alcohol; Tucks premoistened pads

Gums: Dentyne, Trident, Freshen-Up, Chewels, Chiclets, Clorets, Bubblicious, and Certs.

Pet foods: Tetra fish food.

Pharmaceuticals

Diagnostic products

Optical and scientific instruments

WENDY'S INTERNATIONAL

Restaurants: Wendy's; Sisters Chicken & Biscuits.

WESTERN AIRLINES

Airlines: Western.

WHIRLPOOL

Appliances: Whirlpool; KitchenAid; Heil heating and air-conditioning equipment; principal supplier to Sears, Roebuck of appliances for resale.

Financial: Whirlpool Acceptance Corporation.

Household: St. Charles kitchen cabinets.

WHITE CONSOLIDATED

Appliances: White-Westinghouse; Kelvinator; Frigidaire; Gibson; Vesta; White, Domestic, Hilton, and Universal sewing machines and accessories.

Industrial: White-Sundstrand, Controls, and Data Systems machine tools and manufacturing systems; Typhoon central air conditioning; Kelvinator commercial refigeration; Richards-Wilcox conveyor systems; Richards-Wilcox, Protective Door steel doors; Aurora storage cabinets; Hupp vehicle heaters.

White was acquired by the Swedish firm Electrolux in early 1986.

WM. WRIGLEY JR.

Chewing gum: Wrigley's Doublemint, Spearmint, Juicy Fruit, Big Red, Freedent, Orbit, Hubba Bubba, Big League Chew, Tidal Wave, and Tubble Gum.

XEROX

Office: Copiers; printers; typewriters; information systems.

Financial: Crum and Forster insurance; Xerox Credit Corporation; Van Kampen Merritt mutual funds.

ZENITH ELECTRONICS

Appliances: Televisions; video equipment.

Office: Computers; printers; software.

Other: Cable television equipment and services; computer and television components.

Chapter Notes

Chapter 2

P. 11: James Burke, "Public Responsibility Is the Basis for a Company's Existence," *Response,* July 1984 (Center for Public Corporate Involvement).

P. 12: Ibid.

Franklin Research and Development, "S&P 500 vs. 100 Best Companies" (unpublished study, 1985).

Michael Useem and Stephen I. Kutner, "Corporate Contributions to the Nonprofit Sector: The Organization of Giving and the Influence of the Chief Executive Officer and Other Firms on Company Contributions in Massachusetts" (Boston: Boston University Center for Applied Social Science, 1985).

Chapter 3

Pp. 18–22: Quotations and much of the discussion of corporate philanthropy were drawn from the collection of essays in *Corporate Philanthropy: Philosophy, Management, Trends, Future, Background* (Washington, D.C.: Council on Foundations, 1982).

P. 30: Alan Paton, "South Africa Is in a Mess," *New York Times,* April 3, 1985.

P. 32: "U.S. Companies No Force for Change in South Africa," *Corporate Examiner,* vol. 13, no. 6 (Interfaith Center on Corporate Responsibility).

P. 41: "FBI Probes Bank's PAC Donations," *Boston Globe,* December 19, 1984.

"Thrift to Plead Guilty in Case Involving a PAC," *Wall Street Journal,* March 11, 1985.

Chapter 5

P. 115: Irwin Ross, "PUSH Collides With Busch," *Fortune,* November 15, 1982.

"In Good Company: 25 Best Places for Blacks to Work," *Black Enterprise,* February 1986.

"Busch Agrees to Pay $750,000 Settlement," *New York Times,* April 1, 1978; "Anheuser-Busch Signs Consent Decree," *Los Angeles Times,* June 23, 1984.

P. 116: "FTC Brings Cheer to Alcohol Marketers," *Advertising Age,* April 22, 1985.

P. 118: Betsy Morris and Robert Johnson, "How Beatrice Adjusts to Latest Takeover, This Time of Itself — Sequence of Mergers Causes Distress Among Workers, Delayed Decision Making," *Wall Street Journal,* December 5, 1985.

P. 119: Evan T. Barr, "Poisoned Well: The New Age of Toxic Tort," *New Republic,* March 17, 1986.

P. 120: David J. Sarokin, Warren R. Muir, Catherine G. Miller, and Sebastian R. Sperber, *Cutting Chemical Waste* (New York: Inform, 1985), pp. 194–195.

P. 123: For details on the Ohio senate subcommittee report, see Investor Responsibility Research Center, "Proxy Issue Report; Analysis R. Supplement No. 2. October 26, 1984: Labor Practices: Campbell Soup."

For a general account of the boycott, see Ward Sinclair, "Saucy Union Battles Tomato Giants," *Washington Post,* July 8, 1982.

P. 125: Kirchhoff quotations from a speech before the New York Financial Writers Association, September 12, 1979, as reported: "Castle & Cooke, Inc., Has Very Dim View of Activist Holders," *Wall Street Journal,* September 13, 1979. See also Larry Rich, "Castle & Cooke, Inc.: An Agribusiness Case Study," *Corporate Examiner,* July 1980 (Interfaith Center on Corporate Responsibility).

P. 126: "In Good Company: 25 Best Places for Blacks to Work," *Black Enterprise,* February 1986.

P. 127: Stephen Kinzer, "Guatemala Unions Watch Plant Feud," *New York Times,* July 10, 1984. See also Anne Manuel, "Coke Battle: Unions and Terror in Guatemala," *The New Republic,* September 17, 1984.

P. 128: ConAgra on its union relations in correspondence with the authors, July 11, 1985.

P. 130: Milton Moskowitz, Michael Katz, and Robert Levering, *Everybody's Business* (New York: Harper & Row, 1980), p. 813.

P. 132: "In Good Company: 25 Best Places for Blacks to Work," *Black Enterprise,* February 1986.

P. 133: Michael Jacobson quotation in correspondence with the authors, July 1985.

William Carlsen, "Justices Allow Suit over Cereal Ads," *San Francisco Chronicle,* December 23, 1983.

P. 136: "The Savvy Sixteen," *Savvy,* May 1982.

P. 137: Moskowitz, et al., p. 36.

P. 149: Thomas W. Lippman, "Out of the Spotlight, Into the Cash Box," *Washington Post,* December 6, 1981.

P. 151: Morton Mintz, "Infant-Formula Maker Battles Boycotters by Painting Them Red," *Washington Post,* January 4, 1981.

P. 153: PepsiCo quotation in correspondence with the authors, August 14, 1985.

P. 155: Peter Taylor, *The Smoke Ring* (New York: Pantheon, 1984), p. 31.

P. 156: Jerry E. Bishop, "Lung Cancer Seen Leading Fatal Form in Women in 1985," *Wall Street Journal*, February 8, 1985.

P. 159: "Vermont's Ice Cream Upstart," *New York Times*, March 29, 1985.

P. 161: "The Savvy Sixteen," *Savvy*, May 1982.

P. 164: "In Good Company: 25 Best Places for Blacks to Work," *Black Enterprise*, February 1986.

P. 165: Steve Mufson, "Cigarette Companies Develop Third World As a Growth Market," *Wall Street Journal*, July 5, 1985.

Steven W. Colford and William F. Gloede, "RJR Lights Antismokers' Fire," *Advertising Age*, April 22, 1985.

P. 169: "Ailments at Hanes Plants Draw Organized Protests," *New York Times*, April 4, 1983.

Sara Lee quotation in correspondence with the authors, July 31, 1985.

Connective Ministry Across the South. "Insofar As Possible and Feasible," June 1985.

Chapter 6

P. 202: "Banned at Home — but Exported," *Business Week*, June 12, 1978.

P. 205: Milton Moskowitz, Michael Katz, and Robert Levering, *Everybody's Business* (New York: Harper & Row, 1980), p. 600.

"Employees Allege Cyanamid Pressured for Sterilization," *Wall Street Journal*, January 3, 1979.

Drew Von Berger, "American Cyanamid Cited for Sterilization Rule," *Washington Post*, October 12, 1979.

"Pigment Plant Wins Fertility Risk Case," *New York Times*, October 1, 1980.

P. 207: Pat Sloan, "Avon ladies to toughen up sales pitch," *Advertising Age*, March 12, 1984.

P. 212: Richard Martin, "Gillette's Giovacchini Rules on the Quality, Safety of 850 Products," *Wall Street Journal*, December 12, 1975.

P. 215: "The Savvy Sixteen," *Savvy*, May 1982.

P. 216: "Multiple charges of union-busting hit Ethicon plant," *AFL-CIO News*, August 23, 1983.

"Producer of Tylenol Is Cleared," *New York Times*, October 23, 1982.

Michael Waldholz and Hank Gilman, "Tylenol's Maker to Stop Selling Some Capsules," *Wall Street Journal*, February 18, 1986.

"Johnson & Johnson's Class Act," editorial in *Business Week*, March 3, 1986.

Pp. 216–217: Robert MacKay, "Firm recalls pain-killer Zomax for new labels after 5 people die," *Oakland Times*, March 5, 1983.

P. 217: Milton Moskowitz, "The Band-Aid People Do It Right," *San Francisco Chronicle*, May 6, 1983.

P. 232: James B. Stewart and Michael Waldholz, "How Richardson-Vicks Fell Prey to Takeover Despite Family's Grip," *Wall Street Journal*, October 30, 1985.

P. 234: Morton Mintz, *At Any Cost: Corporate Greed, Women and the Dalkon Shield* (New York: Pantheon, 1985), p. xiii.

Sonja Steptoe, "Robins Finds Rough Sailing in Chapter 11," *Wall Street Journal*, April 3, 1986.

P. 235: Subrata Chakravarty, "Tunnel Vision," *Forbes*, May 21, 1984.

On Lord quotation in Mintz, *At Any Cost: Corporate Greed, Women and the Dalkon Shield* (New York: Pantheon, 1985), pp. 232–234, 264–269.

P. 239: Richard Koenig, "SmithKline Pleads Guilty to U.S. Charges It Was Slow to Report Drug's Side Effects," *Wall Street Journal*, December 13, 1984.

"SmithKline to Fund Programs as Penalty in Selacryn Drug Case," *Wall Street Journal*, February 26, 1985.

SmithKline quotation in correspondence with authors, July 8, 1985.

P. 242: "FTC Decision Upheld Against Sterling Drug for Misleading Claims," *Wall Street Journal*, August 29, 1984.

On dipyrone: see Sterling Drug's 1984 proxy statement.

P. 243: "FTC Upholds Decision That Warner-Lambert Listerine Ads Are False," *Wall Street Journal*, December 19, 1975.

Richard L. Gordon, "High Court Avoids Listerine Ad Case, FTC Penalty Stands," *Advertising Age,* April 10, 1978.

Chapter 7

P. 249: "American Air, Chief End Antitrust Suit, Agree Not to Discuss Fares with Rivals," *Wall Street Journal*, July 15, 1985.

"Three Airlines to Drop Feature on Flight Listings," *Wall Street Journal*, March 28, 1985.

Jonathan Dahl and Christopher Conte, "American Air Pays FAA Fine of $1.5 Million," *Wall Street Journal*, September 30, 1985.

P. 251: Robert Levering, Milton Moskowitz, and Michel Katz, *The 100 Best Companies to Work for in America* (Reading, MA: Addison-Wesley, 1984), p.74.

P. 253: Gary Cohn, "Eastern Air Says FAA Rejected Bid Related to Fine," *Wall Street Journal*, May 13, 1986.

P. 255: Milton Moskowitz, Michael Katz, and Robert Levering, *Everybody's Business* (New York: Harper & Row, 1980), p. 672.

P. 257: Donald Burr, "People Express Grows Bigger Without Getting Fat," *Wall Street Journal*, January 7, 1985.

Interview with Donald Burr in "Bitter Victories," *Inc.*, August 1985, p. 34.

P. 260: "A Proud Bird Loses Its Wings," *Newsweek*, October 3, 1983.

P. 261: Agis Salpukas, "Gamble Paying Off at Continental Air," *New York Times*, September 11, 1985.

"Continental Air Pays Fine to FAA Totaling $402,000," *Wall Street Journal*, March 28, 1986.

P. 263: Kim Foltz, "The Not-So-Friendly Skies," *Newsweek*, February 13, 1984.

John Koten, "United Air Is Told It Must Offer Jobs to 500 New Pilots," *Wall Street Journal*, August 2, 1986.

P. 273: Dale D. Buss, "AMC's Woes May Give It Bargaining Leverage," *Wall Street Journal*, May 7, 1985.

P. 276: "What's Creating an 'Industrial Miracle' at Ford?," *Business Week*, July 30, 1984.

Mark Green and John Berry, *Challenge of Hidden Profits* (New York: William Morrow, 1985), p. 99.

P. 277: Ernest Holsendolph, "Ford Motor to Spend $23 Million to Settle Bias Case," *New York Times*, November 26, 1980.

P. 278: Reginald Stuart, "Ford Won in Pinto Case, but the Memory Will Linger On," *New York Times*, March 16, 1980.

"Concern Over Ford's Financial Problems Eliminated Recall," *Wall Street Journal*, January 16, 1981.

"Suit Filed to Reopen Probe by U.S. of Some Ford Cars," *Wall Street Journal*, September 10, 1985.

Albert R. Karr, "GAO, Safety Agency Differ on Results of Ford Accord on Possible Auto Defect," *Wall Street Journal*, June 11, 1986.

P. 279: Tim Carrington, "U.S. Cancels Divad Weapon Built by Ford," *Wall Street Journal*, August 28, 1985.

On churches: statement by Dr. Arie Brouwer, General Secretary of National Council of Churches of Christ of the USA (Press conference, May 20, 1985).

P 281: On Poletown: Special issue of *Detroit* magazine. *Detroit Free Press*, September 8, 1985.

On EEOC settlement: see General Motors' *1984 Public Interest Report*, p. 53.

"GM Reaches Pact With U.S. on Hiring Women, Minorities," *Wall Street Journal*, March 29, 1985.

P. 282: Maralyn Edid, "How Power Will Be Balanced on Saturn's Shop Floor," *Business Week*, August 5, 1985.

Reginald Stuart, "U.S. Alters Mileage Rules, Aiding Ford and GM," *New York Times*, June 27, 1985.

P. 283: "The Long and Winding Road of the X-Car Braking Controversy," *Washington Post*, September 5, 1983.

P. 286: Ron Winslow, "Nuclear Industry Faces New Snag Linked to Backup Diesel Engines," *Wall Street Journal*, March 21, 1984.

P. 292: Donald Janson, "Hilton Rejected for License to Operate a Jersey Casino," *New York Times*, March 1, 1985.

"Casino Panel Rejects Hilton License," *Trenton Times*, March 1, 1985.

P. 296: Among the more recent accounts of ITT in the 1970s is Robert J. Schoenberg's *Geneen* (New York: Norton, 1985), pp. 261–299.

Pp. 296–297: Walt Bogdanich, "Irate Borrowers Accuse ITT's Loan Companies of Deceptive Practices," *Wall Street Journal*, February 26, 1985.

"ITT Corp. Settles 'Packing' Charges with Minnesota," *Wall Street Journal*, June 12, 1985.

"ITT Settles with Colorado on Insurance-Policy Sales," *Wall Street Journal*, April 25, 1985.

P. 308: "Big Bill for a Big Spill," *Time*, April 30, 1984.

P. 310: Kirk O. Hanson, "Social Performance of ARCO," *Participation III: Atlantic Richfield and Society*, p. 80 (Atlantic Richfield: no date).

P. 312: Milton Moskowitz, Michael Katz, and Robert Levering, *Everybody's Business* (New York: Harper & Row, 1980), p. 528.

Anthony Sampson, *The Seven Sisters* (New York: Viking, 1975), p. 195.

On churches: statement by Dr. Arie Brouwer, General Secretary of National Council of Churches of Christ of the USA (Press conference, May 20, 1985).

P. 314: Gregg Kerlin and Daniel Rabovsky, *Cleaning Up* (New York: Council on Economic Priorities, 1975), pp. 221–250.

P. 316: "In Good Company: 25 Best Places for Blacks to Work," *Black Enterprise*, February 1986.

P. 317: "Exxon Pays $500,000 to 2 Groups to Avoid Suits on Hudson River," *Wall Street Journal*, April 23, 1984.

Stephen Wermiel, "Supreme Court Refuses to Hear Exxon Appeal," *Wall Street Journal*, January 28, 1986.

"Exxon Says Donations in Italy Exceeded $46 Million, Communists Got $86,000," *Wall Street Journal*, July 14, 1975.

Josh Barbanel, "Exxon to Pay $1.5 Million to Settle Water Dispute," *New York Times*, June 7, 1984.

P. 318: Stephen R. Weisman, "Carter Attacks Mobil Oil," *New York Times*, March 29, 1980.

Jack Anderson, "The Amazing Arrogance of Mobil Oil," *Washington Post*, June 27, 1980.

"Tavoulareas's Libel Suit Against Post to Be Reheard," *Wall Street Journal*, June 12, 1985.

David Sanger, "Tension on the Frontiers of Libel," *New York Times*, December 18, 1983.

"Mobil, Citing 'Problems,' Shuns Wall St. Journal," *New York Times*, December 4, 1984.

Monica Langley, "Mobil Asks Holders to Finance Its PAC via Their Dividends," *Wall Street Journal*, June 19, 1984.

Pp. 318–319: Timothy Smith quotation in correspondence with the authors, July 1985.

Pp. 319–320: Schmertz quotation in correspondence with the authors, July 10, 1985.

Pp. 321–322: "Occidental Petroleum Unit Agrees to Settle Antipollution Lawsuit," *Wall Street Journal*, February 9, 1981.

Georgette Jasen, "Still Reeling from Love Canal's Runoff, Hooker Chemical Tries to Polish Image," *Wall Street Journal*, September 29, 1981.

Richard Severo, "Accord Reached on Cleaning Up Niagara Waste," *New York Times*, January 11, 1984.

P. 324: William E. Blundell, "Phillips Petroleum to Turn Over Control to Outside Directors in Settlement of Suit," *Wall Street Journal*, February 19, 1976.

P. 326: Department of Justice press release, December 9, 1983.

Iver Peterson, "Size of Shell Oil Suit May Be Clue to Other Use of Polluted Arsenal," *New York Times*, December 11, 1983.

Pp. 327–328: Michael Hoffman figures in interview with authors, September 1985.

P. 333: Robert E. Taylor and Bill Richards, "Gasification Plant's Fate Hangs in Balance," *Wall Street Journal*, May 21, 1985.

P. 334: Sampson, *The Seven Sisters*, pp. 196–197.

Chapter 8

P. 351: James O'Toole, *Vanguard Management* (Garden City, NY: Doubleday, 1985), p. 128.

P. 354: Jane Scholl, "Savvy Corporations of the Year," *Savvy*, June 1983.

Grayson Mitchell, "GE Will Pay $32 Million in Jobs Case," *Los Angeles Times*, June 16, 1978.

P. 355: Francine Schwadel, "General Electric Pleads Guilty in Fraud Case," *Wall Street Journal*, May 14, 1985.

"Nuclear Foes' Conviction Thrown Out," *San Francisco Chronicle*, February 20, 1984.

P. 358: O'Toole, *Vanguard Management*, p. 135.

P. 360: Tamar Lewin, "Litton's Angry Labor Conglomerate," *New York Times*, April 24, 1983.

P. 362: "After a Bitter, 7-Month Battle, Magic Chef Appears to Have Soundly Defeated Union," *Wall Street Journal*, August 30, 1983.

P. 372: Scovill quotation in correspondence with the authors, July 1, 1985.

P. 374: "Air Force Plans to Deduct Funds for Engine Work," *Wall Street Journal*, July 13, 1983.

"Otis Unit of United Technologies Set to Settle U.S. Case," *Wall Street Journal*, February 21, 1985.

P. 375: United Technologies quotation in correspondence with the authors, December 18, 1984.

Richard Greene, "Yonkers declares war on United Technologies," *Forbes,* April 11, 1983.

P. 378: "A Strike That White Is Not Rushing to Settle," *Business Week,* May 19, 1980.

P. 411: Jeremy Main, "Dow vs. the Dioxin Monster," *Fortune,* May 30, 1983.

"Dow Cleans Up Its Brine Operations," *Chemical Week,* August 29, 1984.

P. 412: Andy Pasztor, "Dow Chemical and EPA Settle Water Dispute," *Wall Street Journal,* March 29, 1984.

Ralph Nader and William Taylor, *The Big Boys* (New York: Pantheon, 1986), pp. 147, 195.

Jane E. Brody, "Shadow of Doubt Wipes Out Bendectin," *New York Times,* June 19, 1983.

P. 414: Georgia-Pacific quotations in correspondence with the authors, July 11, 1985.

P. 416: Stewart Toy, "Is Greyhound Just Buying Time for Its Buses?," *Business Week,* December 2, 1985.

P. 417: Stephen Engelberg, "GTE Unit Accused of Plot to Gain U.S. Data," *New York Times,* September 11, 1985.

P. 420: Harlan S. Byrne, "'Johnson Wax' Puts Out More Than Wax and It Soon May Diversify Even Further," *Wall Street Journal,* December 26, 1980.

P. 421: "Johnson Wax Chief Says Shift to Nonfluorocarbons in Aerosols Has Worked," *New York Times,* October 10, 1976.

P. 425: "3M Gains by Averting Pollution," *Business Week,* November 22, 1976.

P. 426: Jane Scholl, "Savvy Corporations of the Year," *Savvy,* June 1983.

Index

Roman = text and table references
Italic = company entry in product chart
Bold = company profile

Addendum

Since the first printing of *Rating America's Corporate Conscience* there have been numerous changes in ownership affecting the companies and products listed in the book. Among those particularly relevant to the book are:

Chapter Five:

Anderson Clayton has been acquired by **Quaker Oats. Quaker Oats** intends to sell off all **Anderson Clayton** lines except for **Gaines** dog foods.

Beatrice has sold its dairy product lines (including **Meadow Gold, Viva, Louis Sherry, Mountain High** and **Hotel Bar**) to **Borden.**

Borden has acquired **Pennsylvania Dutch** pastas from **Unilever.**

CPC International has acquired **Arnold** brand baked goods.

General Mills has sold off its furniture group (**Kittinger** and **Pennsylvania House** furnitures).

International Multifoods has sold off all its consumer products lines. Of these Robin Hood flours has been acquired by **General Mills** and **Kretschmer** cereals by **Quaker Oats.**

Kraft has acquired **Knudsen** and **Foremost** lines of dairy products.

Ogden has sold off its food lines (**Progresso, Hain**) to **IC Industries.**

Philip Morris has sold its **7-Up** soft drink line.

Ralston Purina has sold its agricultural feed divisions to **Standard Oil.**

Sara Lee has sold its **Popsicle** frozen dessert line.

Unilever has acquired **Wyler's** drink mixes from **Borden.**

Chapter Six:

Chesebrough-Pond's has been acquired by **Unilever.**

Squibb has sold all its cosmetic lines.

Revlon has acquired **Beatrice's Max Factor** cosmetic lines.

500

Chapter Seven:

Delta Air Lines has acquired **Western Air Lines.**

Texas Air has acquired **Eastern Airlines** and **People Express** (with its **Frontier** and **Britt** subsidiaries). **Texas Air** is now the largest airline in the U.S.

Exxon has sold its **Reliance Electric** subsidiary.

Household International has sold its **National Car Rental** line.

Transamerica has sold off **Budget Rent-a-Car** as well as its Delaval and airline subsidiaries.

TWA has acquired **Ozark Air Lines.**

UAL has acquired **Hilton International** hotels (**Hilton** hotels outside of the U.S. and **Vista** hotels in the U.S.).

Chapter Eight:

Greyhound has sold its bus lines.

Maytag which now owns **Magic Chef** has sold its **Toastmaster** appliance lines.

Scovill has sold its **Hamilton Beach** appliance lines.

ETHICAL INVESTING
How To Make Profitable Investments without Sacrificing Your Principles

Amy L. Domini and Peter D. Kinder

PUT YOUR MONEY WHERE YOUR CONSCIENCE IS . . . PROFITABLY!

Whether you as an investor are concerned about South African apartheid, company-sponsored day-care programs, or hazardous waste disposal, here is an essential guide to making your money work for your beliefs, not against them.

In ETHICAL INVESTING, authors Amy Domini and Peter Kinder provide socially concerned investors with a wealth of hard-to-access information on hundreds of companies and practical tools for spotting companies that are financially attractive and ethically consistent with one's values. ETHICAL INVESTING also includes: a primer on investment principles, strategies for shareholder activism, a directory of resources available to the ethical investor, and ethical and financial self-assessment forms.

As corporations assume greater power domestically and internationally, it is now more important than ever to factor your social concerns into money management. ETHICAL INVESTING is *the* guide to investing in the future.

Amy Domini is an investment counselor at Franklin Research and Development Corporation in Boston. **Peter Kinder** is a lawyer and contributing writer to numerous business publications.

> "*Ethical Investing* is an extremely important and timely book. With incisive analysis and extensive documentation, it fills a real gap in the literature on the social investment movement."
>
> —Timothy Smith, Director
> Interface Center on Corporate
> Responsibility

. . . .

Please send me ＿＿＿＿ copy(ies) of ETHICAL INVESTING at $10.95 each (trade paperback).

＿＿＿＿ I have enclosed my check or money order, including appropriate sales tax, made out to Addison-Wesley Publishing Co. in the amount of $＿＿＿＿. Publisher pays postage.

＿＿＿＿ Please bill my VISA ＿＿＿＿ MASTERCARD ＿＿＿＿ Card # ＿＿＿＿＿＿＿ Expiration Date ＿＿＿＿

SEND TO ＿＿＿＿＿＿＿＿＿＿＿＿＿＿＿＿＿＿＿＿＿＿＿＿＿＿＿

ADDRESS ＿＿＿＿＿＿＿＿＿＿＿＿＿＿＿＿＿＿＿＿＿＿＿＿＿

CITY ＿＿＿＿＿＿＿＿＿＿＿ STATE ＿＿＿＿＿ ZIP ＿＿＿＿＿

(PLEASE SEND ALL ORDERS TO: Addison-Wesley Publishing Company, Inc.; General Books/Special Sales; Reading, MA 01867)